HOPE STREET

*A MEMOIR OF MULTIPLE
PERSONALITIES; CREATING
SELVES TO SURVIVE*

Rhonda Macken

HOPE STREET
A memoir of Multiple Personalities; creating selves to survive

First published in Australia by Rhonda Macken 2018

A catalogue record for this
book is available from the
National Library of Australia

ISBN: 978-0-6481585-0-9 (pbk)
ISBN: 978-0-6481585-1-6 (ebk)

Typesetting and design by Publicious Book Publishing
Published in collaboration with Publicious Book Publishing
www.publicious.com.au

To Libby Crichton, a unique therapist and ultimately dear friend. It took many years, but we put me back together. I wouldn't have made it through without you.

To my family, Bruce, Nat, and Kris for your love and support which has been constant and unconditional.

When the 'what is' defies sanity then the 'what is not'

becomes sane. So, when the visible world we live in is unsafe,

a different reality must be invented. One must create a

'what is not' as a tangible alternative to the unsafe 'what is.'

It becomes a credible place in which to escape.

The 'what is' then becomes unreal and therefore safe.

Rhonda

CONTENTS

Hope Street..*i*

Prologue.. *ix*

Chapter 1 1

Chapter 2.. 25

Chapter 3.. 41

Chapter 4.. 54

Chapter 5.. 70

Chapter 6.. 87

Chapter 7... 109

Chapter 8... 138

Chapter 9... 144

Chapter 10... 160

Chapter 11... 189

Epilogue... 198

Appendix 1 – My System 201

Appendix 2 – Strategies that helped me in therapy............ 214

Appendix 3 – Glossary 224

HOPE STREET

AN INTRODUCTION

There are two stories here, both as relevant and as real as each other. In each story there are no victims, only survivors.

One is the Story of the Outside World

The easiest to see and to understand is the narrative of the effects of war and post traumatic stress on my father and his subsequent behaviours during his life after he had returned from New Guinea in the Second World War.

This was manifest in several ways:

He sometimes became filled with a chaotic madness that was demonstrative and immediately apparent. He became psychotic in a way that was terrifying beyond imagination. At these times, my father simply 'disappeared' and his eyes became a steely blue with no-one behind them. He was back in New Guinea in a life and death situation and in his mind I became a Japanese soldier. Then, he was not my father, he became the Monster and the Giant and he had no conscience. He could literally have done anything, felt nothing and remembered nothing the next morning.

At times he used alcohol in excess to escape from the images in his mind and the fear in his belly. I think he was raped while a soldier and the same steel blue eyes were there when he raped me. Again with no conscience.

When he was sane he was kind, rational and loved animals. This made it more difficult and confusing because as a child I connected strongly to this good and sane part of my father.

The other is the Story of my Inner or Created World

This is about the effect that these behaviours and events had on me and how I survived them. It is about my mind's creation over time, of many independent alters, completely separate from me. It is about Multiplicity, a very real survival tool and one for which I am extremely grateful. It is about fragmentation, but neither madness nor mental illness. In fact in order to create Multiple parts of oneself the trauma must be intense, happen often at a very young age and a good imagination and intelligence are helpful. It is now referred to as Dissociative Identity Disorder (DID), previously called Multiple Personality Disorder (MPD).

Einstein is reported to have said: "Imagination is more important than knowledge. For knowledge is limited to all we now know and understand, while imagination embraces the entire world, and all there ever will be to know and understand."

My imagination, as a child, created my own reality. A completely different space in which my subconscious mind lived and survived. This inner world is that of the different parts of me created in order to prevent me, Rhonda, from remembering or feeling the events and the terror. To keep each of these events firmly contained in impenetrable capsules in my mind and therefore to be able to live a comparatively 'normal' and successful life.

I have a wonderful partner to whom I have been married for fifty years and two now adult children who have allowed me to feel an unconditional love that is beyond anything I could have imagined.

I've also had a successful career in Music Education and am grateful for the lives that I have been able to touch. Without my multiple parts this would not have been possible.

These parts of me are real. They have individual characteristics and feelings, thoughts and memories. They were and are the inhabitants of my inner world and as I have come to know them and to hear their stories I thank each and every one of them.

The safe place in which they lived and all called home, was our castle. Even though I created over two hundred different parts of me, there were of course key players and these are the ones who appear here in my story.

Their world was a child's world but whole within itself and at times I am struck by the intricacies of the details that were created. It is their story. Of what they did and how they healed, and is just as important as the story of the outside world.

This reality, from the world of my subconscious, runs on symbolism, images and fantasy. The events are of the 'real world' but our survival is from their created space. This inner has aspects of the outer 'real' world but many are interpreted and perceived differently, and it was essential that it was never to be seen or heard or known about by Rhonda or anyone else in the outside world. Keeping the silence was imperative.

There are times in this story that words used by the 'others' may seem a little esoteric or nebulous but they thread their way importantly throughout the book. This is 'their world' and these are the words they have chosen to tell you about it. To leave these stories and phrases unspoken fails to give them a voice and does not allow us to see and to understand how their reality looks and feels and therefore how we survived.

Multiplicity, to me, is essentially not a disorder but a creative adaptation that allowed me to live through extreme trauma and remain sane and functioning and I'm amazed by what the human mind is capable of. However it became dysfunctional in my case when, as an adult, the trauma began to surface. This is because each part was still living in the past, terrified of what would happen next. This changed, only over many years, when my therapist, Libby, gained the trust of each alter and their stories were told and fears abated. This finally allowed us to know and to understand that the reasons for the terror I felt, no longer existed.

I'm often asked about the names of the parts of me. Each alter already had his or her own name when I met them and it was always delivered in a clear and strong voice. I, Rhonda, did not name them. If sometimes, Libby made a mistake and called someone by the wrong name, it would be corrected immediately and with indignation.

They were all distinct, separate parts of me having their own skills, needs, roles, memories, voice, body language and hopes. Some male, some female, many were children. Most were created in order to experience and to subsequently encase the memories in a sealed container.

Sometimes, when told about Multiplicity and the parts of me, people say "But I have different parts too."

Yes, we each as human beings have different parts, but with most people these are masks that are put on for various situations. The difference is that most people don't experience severe trauma before they're four years old.

My created alters are not about masks. I've actually split off parts of my personality, which is much more basic and internal. They each have their own feelings, behaviours and reactions, often the result of terror. The masks of most people are purposefully created to defend a person in adulthood. Mine was a defence system created to save my life in childhood and because of this they are more separate and each is defined with certain characteristics and functions, each with a history.

With the masks of a Singleton, the different roles are always all co-conscious. With Multiplicity, no-one knew about the existence of anyone else (with the exception of **Master Planner and Stones**) and co-consciousness has developed gradually over time, as I have brought each part into the present.

During the 28 years of my therapies, many parts emerged, one by one, sometimes two by two. Sometimes one part grew out of another. This mostly occurred when the initial part could not cope with a situation and created another one to take over from him or her.

I know them all well now, but as it could be very confusing to read about, I've included an appendix that describes many of them. How s/he fits into the whole picture, his or her function (why they were created), his/her personality, sometimes even a glimpse into what they look like in my mind. For clarity, in the story their names appear in bold type.

Sometimes during therapy strange things happened that I can't explain. A small example is the loss of my ability to spell. Before therapy I could spell anything with little hesitation but as it progressed that skill has radically eroded and I'm glad of the literal intelligence of my computer. Quite often symptoms in my body would initiate a memory but completely disappear when the memory had been dealt with and that part seen and heard.

As therapy progressed, the importance of internal co-operation as opposed to integration became loudly apparent. The thought of 'losing' a part of me created fear and sometimes anger, but the thought of everyone finally coming together around a table or by the fire and conversing was a pleasant one. Ultimately I had no say in it and we became integrated.

My life with my parents lasted until I was nineteen. Then I studied, taught, got married and not until I was over thirty when my daughter was born did the past begin to push itself upwards and into my consciousness. My daughter is now forty-one and my son, thirty-eight. I spent eleven years with the initial therapist, Richard, and then another seventeen years with Libby. I am now seventy-two.

Let me hand over to **The Storyteller**, the advocate for the alters of my system:

She watches the river, sitting silently on its banks, her feet tucked into the sand, her hands resting on the soft dew of the early morning. All around is colour and movement. The new leaves of a green brightened with yellow, buttercups reflecting onto the wisps of cloud that pass overhead. She looks up to see a young magpie warbling on the branch above her and the sounds of the river, shallow yet forthright, comfort her. Across the river, the gate now latched open, leads onwards. Away. She is free to leave. Free to make choices, to go wherever she wants. She thinks back to another time when **The Invisible Force** locked shut the space around her, imprisoning her within its solid yet unseen walls. There is space to question now, to contemplate the journey that had brought her here to meet her Self.

How strange it must have been in the world of **The Nowhere**, with no colour, no definition, just knowing that she was and yet she was not. Of having smashed the mirror that reflected the terror and the confusion and having tried so hard to see her Self mirrored by her parents, finally giving up and turning the mirror around, hidden behind it.

She had become a flat plastic baby with no thickness. Face rounded yet with no features. No eyes, no mouth, no nose. No ears to hear. No Self. Somewhere she knew that she had not been born this way, for the memory of **The Shining** sometimes slid out into the silence and warmed her.

Each year came, bringing with it more fear and bit by bit she had split off pieces of herself, each like a different sparkle from the remembered Shining. Each one containing a memory and performing a function, like many players in a theatre company. It was with such trepidation, but with wonder, that she finally met each of these players, gradually getting to know who and why they were and to hear their stories.

This was real. She had to survive. She had promised her Self, from whom they had all been separated, and her Self was waiting for the time to be right when they would come and get her. To become one again.

She thought about the time in the **The Nowhere** when she had begun to awaken, and in **the castle** where she heard the sea and felt the sun. To understand that the power of the Invisible Force did not extend beyond the castle or beyond the sand, but that to look outwards to the horizon and beyond the hills was to look towards hope.

She began to enjoy the wetness of the rain. The wind became her archangel of being as it blew with gentleness and strength from beyond the confines of her imprisonment, bringing whisperings of another place.

One by one, two strangers had come into The Nowhere to sit with her. They had listened, and in them she found a mirror that showed her kindness and she had glimpsed the Shining. Her purity.

The terror emerged, was spoken, felt, heard and understood. It now sleeps. The castle, for so long her only place of safety in The Nowhere, has gradually filled with chatter, communication, co-operation and life and finally the castle has returned to the pages of the book of Fairy Tales from whence it had been gathered.

Time has begun to move, each moment to open into a space filled with life and it's a whole person who now sits by the river, her feet tucked into the sand, her fingers resting on the soft dew of the early morning. But unlike the one who began my story, she has a name. She is Rhonda and is ready to be reunited with her Self.

The Storyteller

A word from Libby, my therapist

I was working in a Community Health Centre running a comprehensive group therapy programme. I little realized in 1996, when a quiet young lady asked to join one of the therapy groups, that this meeting was but the beginning of an exciting, rewarding, yet incredibly painful journey that has lasted to this day. Her work in that first group session revealed some of her many personalities so already the stage was set for a long road ahead.

Meeting and working with Rhonda has been amazing and I feel very humbled and blessed that I have been able to share her journey towards recovery. Rhonda is one special woman, tenacious and sensitive and keen to divest herself of the pain and limitations of the past. And yes it was a combined effort ... I knew that Rhonda had all the answers within her and my job was only to help her to access them in whatever form that may take. So we experimented and used many creative and different ways to do this.

At times one would work and at other times we needed to find a new way to slide through the chink in the armour, and heavy armour at that! Her favourites were often drawing and writing poetry and music, and working through soft toys like teddy bears. Gestalt, EFT, EMDR, TA (see glossary) also proved useful, to name just a few.

Her courage to stay with the therapy and work through deep and dark places is amazing and her power of survival was something to behold.

Her journey has not ended, our journey never does; however, now like all of us, she lives each day, dealing with life's ups and downs. She has an eagerness to grow to her fullest potential with compassion and joy and she continues to nurture her wonderful musical gifts, ever eager to pass on and share these with others.

Elizabeth Crichton (Libby)

To be truly present, to hear and to accept the intense needs and fears of another, without the intrusion of one's own needs, is an enlightened and priceless gift.

Your unquestioned commitment of eighteen years is rare, respected and appreciated,

Thank you Libby
Rhonda

PROLOGUE

He is sweating, feeling listless in the tropical heat that swarms around his body like invisible honey, covering him as he crouches in the kunai grass. He hears the rats moving, searching for food on the floor of this grass forest, but he is ready. They can smell the blistered flesh that sits within the boot leather, laces long gone, socks worn to threads barely covering the open sores that don't heal.

The valley floor is long and flat, creating a vast plain of threading rivers. The mountains rise like watchtowers, binding the water to a path that moves in a murky band. Snow blends with the lush, wet green foliage creating a purity that defies the trauma of the valley.

His shirt is drenched, the humidity suffocating as he crouches in silence. Waiting for any changes in the sounds. Rats? Japanese soldiers? Move? Attack? His ears are pricked and his skin is ready.

She screams as her father, bayonet fixed, comes running towards her. Then she leaps, wriggling under the car, lying on her side. Silent. Darkness presses her in as she waits, like him, for a sound. He's as silent as a snake that moves in the long kunai grass with firm direction towards its prey.

She feels the point of the blade on her back; frozen in terror, her mind fills with images of her body being stuck through. But she remains still, knowing that to show terror would mean certain death.

"Get out of there you vermin! You filthy Jap."

She has to obey, sliding her body across the greasy concrete of the garage floor, pushing herself up to the full height of her thirteen years. She runs, confusing the enemy with unexpected bravery. He's everywhere at once; the roof of the car, the bonnet, yelling. "Lunge and twist! Lunge and twist!"

Each time she runs he's in front of her, bayonet menacing. She moves slowly backwards keeping her eyes securely on him, grabbing the pitchfork with two hands, raising it above her head.

He laughs. "Come on then vermin. Lunge and twist! Lunge and twist!"

She takes her arm backwards, holding the pitchfork like a javelin, feet secure, then hurls it as hard as she can at the monster. He jumps aside and stands triumphant, wiping the sweat of the tropical summer from his face then grabs her, the acrid smell of angry sweat filling her nostrils and heaving her stomach.

"I'm taking you prisoner you stinking coward. Move! Move!" He pushes her ahead of him, the butt of the rifle bruising her back, prodding her forwards. But she remains solid, walking ahead of him.

She feels her mind switching, another part taking over. It's **Bronwyn**, who can remain calm through anything. Her eyes close as she whispers: "His eyes! I must move inside his steely blue eyes. Got to see things as if I'm him!" **The Judge** has joined them.

Without warning the brown wooden butt of the rifle is against her skull. She falls, then picks herself up. She must remain silent at all costs. The fly-screen door bangs shut behind them, the sound echoing through the pain in her head as she moves slowly through the lounge room, tripping on one of the glass doors that separates this room from the entrance hall. It vibrates then settles. The ducks on the wall watch her as they fly to nowhere. Again he prods, this time with the blade and she remembers the redness of her blood as it dribbles down her back.

Toward the laundry! Why? She must not drift into her fear, but remains behind his eyes. He pushes her in, slams the door and she sighs as she hears his careful footsteps moving up the hallway.

He's going towards the bedroom! She thinks of her sister Kate crouching behind the door or under the bed. He said he was going to cut something out of someone's stomach. Lunge and twist, he said.

"Kate!"

She turns the handle and creeps out.

"Search and destroy. Lunge and twist! His whispered memory is audible above the silence. "Listen for sounds. Attack."

His hands are slippery on the polished brown handle. "Watch the left. To the left!" He lunges forward, the blade crashing into the bedroom door. A cutting scream as Kate is thrust into the terror.

"No! Run Kate. Run!"

He turns on her. "Shut up you coward!"

She drops to the floor, suspended in a moment of black silence. She feels skin on her hand. Soft skin. Her sister's hand. She cries silently. They can hear him in the bedroom lunging into the beds, the thick blade slicing cotton and down.

They crawl, then run, their crazed father chasing them, his screeching battle cries splattering the air. She feels herself pulled downwards, her sister whispering into her ear.

"Get down. Quickly!"

Squeezed in against the prickly green of the couch they wait. Silence. The back door slams shut.

"He's gone outside. Quick. Where's Mum!"

She grabs Kate's hand, running up the hallway, into their mother's room. But the snatches of moonlight don't reveal her, alive or dead.

"Where are you Mum? Where are you!" The cupboard door's open. They run to her. A fetal ball, trembling, crying.

She wants to shake her. "You can't be like that Mum! You've got to be big!"

"We've got to get her out!" Kate whispers.

They drag her from the cupboard, struggling to lift her onto her feet, then creeping carefully through the house, the silent air broken only by the father's mutterings.

"Slowly forward. One step. Look. Another. Look. Gun alert, bayonet ready. Soft flesh. Not bone! Never get it tangled! It's him or me! Aim. Lunge and twist. Hole in the blade. Air in when I pull it out. One step---"

They creep down the hallway, Kate leading their mother like a small child. Rhonda, the younger child, holding on tight to Kate's skirt. With the blood-curdling cry of battle he runs through the kitchen towards them, plunging the bayonet into the kitchen door as they flee towards the front entrance. The blade is stuck but Rhonda, on the end of the line, is grabbed, his fist gripping at her arm.

"Destroy. Kill or be destroyed."

She bites savagely into his leg. He releases his hold.

"I'll kill you, you filthy vermin!"

She scrambles up, running towards the front door and into the air as she hears him roaring inside like the monster that she knows he is. Kate pulls her out and down the path to the street, where she drops into the safety of her sister's voice and arms.

CHAPTER 1

Let me introduce my father, Howard Small. He's tall, just over six feet, long face and eyes the colour of bright topaz. He has brown hair and a friendly smile. His hair was quite thick but over the years has disappeared leaving a shiny patch on top that's gradually tanned to match the rest of his rugged olive skin. He speaks with an Aussie drawl that betrays his lack of education and provides part of the ammunition that my mother hurls at him when she feels the confusion rushing upwards. His legs are strong and stick out below the old shorts that he wears around the house and the garden. They've got bits torn out in several places and are covered in grease and grass stains. He rarely wears underpants at home and his testicles often peep out through the cracks in his shorts. Another piece of ammunition for my mother to throw at him. He keeps to himself a lot when he's at home, pottering in the garden or playing with his tools and paint pots in the garage. Later in his life he's taken up mosaics, spending hours arranging the small brightly coloured tiles in playful patterns that ultimately become table tops.

Most of his garden is a patchwork of shaggy trees and shrubs fighting the weeds for a glimpse of the sun, but the sweet peas and dahlias are different. His sweet peas, his dahlias that he tends with care and harvests with pride. He grows the sweet peas along Kelly's fence, climbing up and clinging to the wires that crisscross the palings and on spring evenings their perfume covers the fear with a thin film of safety.

Occasionally he tries his hand at growing veggies. Especially chokos. He's the only one who likes them but he cooks them anyway in great numbers, steamed, boiled, baked. Even the dog can't swallow them.

Howard looks funny in his pinnie, an apron made from Uncle Bob's old pyjamas, but he wears it comfortably. He loves to cook, but his favourites are tripe and lambs fry. Tripe with chokos, tripe with lumpy white sauce, lamb's fry with chokos and tripe. The poor dead things just sit on the plates looking up at us.

About once a week he brings home seafood from the Sydney fish markets where he works. For years he was an auctioneer, leaving home at three in the morning, selling, calling the prices from the auctioneer's box, his coat covered in scales and fishy smells. Worked his way up, he did, from auctioneer to manager, which was good because then he brought home lobsters and crabs, oysters and fish and he and I would share them.

My father rowed for Leichhardt in his younger days. He's a bloody good athlete.

Strong and resilient. That's what it says on his army enlistment papers. "Sergeant Howard Small. Strong." The war didn't happen until he was in his mid thirties. They sent him to New Guinea.

He might have had strength in his body but his mind didn't do too well. Shell or Battle Shock they called it then, PTSD they call it now. They didn't treat it. Just kept sending them back into the jungle to fight until they were empty of stuffing.

Then they sent them home 'unfit for duty. Unfit to hold down a job.' Life ruined. Wife and children raped and terrorized.

> If I place my footsteps upon his grave will he dance within the shadows of my dreaming? Or will he be so dead as to never know the vibrations of my dreams?

New Guinea

It's oppressively hot. The kind of heat that soaks through flesh and tenderizes bones. In the field hospital just outside Moresby the sweat's even thicker but most of the men don't care. Their bellies and hearts are empty of hope and their minds of reason. They keep coming, soldier after soldier with wounds and tremulous hands.

A small electric fan ploughs its way through the air, a nurse in her twenties standing in front of it just long enough for the water to stop running down her face.

Nurse: *to the orderly*: Send the next one in.

The tall thin man walks unaided to the door of the doctor's room.

Dr: Come in.

His eyes dart nervously.

The doctor gestures. Sit down soldier. Howard Small?

He nods.

Shivering and vomiting? Malaria eh, and it doesn't go away mate. Stays with you for years. *The soldier looks away.*

Last time you were here you saw the psychiatrist didn't you?

He doesn't answer.

Yes, he's written here: 'Marked tremor of hands. Stomach turns over when he smells anyone near him and he feels like vomiting. Nervousness when meeting people and feels as though his stomach is going to fall out.'

The soldier shifts in his chair, looks up and the doctor is taken aback by the blueness of the eyes that stare at him, seemingly unconnected to the tall thin body that houses them. His bronzed face is stony and the only life displayed is in the tremulous fingers resting in his lap.

Dr: Better send you back to him I think. *He gestures to the door.* John will take you there.

The orderly takes his arm and leads him through the humid corridors to a small room at the back of the ward.

John: Here's Sargeant Small to see you doc. *He turns to the soldier.* You'll be ok. The doc. will look after you.

Their eyes meet, the kindness sending a twinge of memory into his mind.

S. Small: Thank you. *He walks in and sits down.*

Psych: How're you feeling?

Shifts in his seat.

Psych: The malaria getting you down at all?

Uneasy. Anxiety rising as remembered horror crowds his mind.

He stands, eyes staring at something only he can see.

Psych: Are you aright?

His eyes are squeezed tightly closed, sweat pouring down his face.

Psych: Come and sit down. You're safe here mate. Tell me what's happening.

S. Small: No Dave! NO!

Psych: *gently taking his arm.* What's happening to Dave?

S. Small: *Their eyes meet.* It's our uniform!

He leans over, his head buried deep in his hands as the images spill outwards, splashing blood over the disinfected floor.

Psych: The Japs?

S. Small: *He lifts his head.* He's crying and moaning as if injured! Can't leave him there. He might be one of ours! Dave, stop! There's more of them. Stop! They're surrounding you. Dave!

He presses his hands over his ears, rocking violently.

Psych: There you go mate.

S. Small: Chopping Dave into pieces! Dave's blood all over them. All over the grass. Stop them! Someone please stop them. Aahhhg! *He drops, his foetal body shaking violently as it loses control, spewing vomit and faeces onto the floor.*

Psych: You're fit for active service right now sergeant. Come on, I'll help you up and John will take you to the ward. You can rest there a bit.

S. Small: *Standing, leaning heavily on the doctor's arm.* Dave! Come back! Come back!

The dining room was a gathering spot in the red brick house in Hope Street. Near the kitchen and where the piano was. A good place for peeling peas, pressing the pods until they popped, then running your thumb along the seam, dislodging the individual peas into a bowl, tasting as you went. And the beans were luscious, especially raw, but in those days we had to cut off the tops and tails, peel back the strings, slice them into little diagonal pieces and straight into the boiling pot where they were transformed into slush. The pumpkin was always cut up in the kitchen and the potatoes were scoured under the tap that my mother ran at a dribble, scraping the knife across each one with short percussive sounds until the whiteness appeared.

Sitting and playing the piano was a comfortable place to be, looking out onto the side path that led from the front to the back of the house, bordered by the grey slats of the paling fence that separated us from the Kelly's place.

A dining table, six matching chairs and a sideboard completed the room. The wood was dark with hand made lace doilies and embroidered runners. Small ornaments adorned the top of it together with my

4

mother's porcelain cups and saucers. The drawers of the sideboard were lined with maroon felt that contrasted beautifully with the shiny silver fish knives and forks and the pearl coloured handles of the cutlery set that was kept for 'good'. In the next drawer she kept her decks of cards. She loved playing bridge. Sometimes the Cox family came for a card game and dinner. That was in the early days when we first moved there, when I was four. We removed all the junk from the traymobile, took all the music off the top of the piano and what wouldn't fit got shoved under our beds until they'd gone. After a couple of years they stopped coming. In fact people rarely visited. Too much to be kept silent and hidden. My mother made the place mats out of thick cardboard and pictures of natural scenes that she cut out of magazines, protected forever by coats of clear lacquer. We liked them.

Matt, my brother always got in first and did the washing up, leaving me with the smelly tea towels. The pressure cooker lived on the stove, the benches always full of stuff with bits of recipes torn off flour packets, empty glass jars, the toaster, the jug, and the ceramic jars of ginger that had been given to my father by the Chinamen at the fish markets. You had to throw the saucepans and lids into the cupboard and quickly shut the door. Of course they all fell out every time you opened it again, so eventually they all lived around the kitchen too. The waffle iron made us treats. We spread them, piping hot with honey and a blob of homemade ice cream that would melt deliciously into the squares. When the honey ran out we used treacle or golden syrup. Sometimes we were treated to a tin of condensed milk so we mashed up a whole heap of bananas and smothered them in this gooey sweet syrup and piled them on top of the waffle. Nothing ever tasted so good.

I was scared of the pressure cooker. It exploded all over the kitchen at regular intervals, spreading stewed meat and veggies down the walls and over the ceiling. When the kitchen table fell apart the traymobile was moved in to replace it. The kitchen was on the southern side of the house and was quite dark, looking out onto a large privet hedge that made us sneeze every spring.

Sometimes, Saturday mornings felt good. The insanity seemed to momentarily abate and it was a time for order. We cleaned the house, the hair brushes and the animals and nothing seemed to go wrong. This was the armistice. The only official moments from A to Z that were pre-ordained and therefore predictable. The sunshine gathered on the bristles of the hair brushes as they rested on the window box and my mother switched into the safety of the normality of a group of people going about the chores of everyday life. Dad went to golf.

Bed by bed we changed the linen, folding the sheets into hospital corners and smoothing out the rippling bedspreads. The rugs were taken out onto the back porch and shaken, the bath scrubbed until the light green porcelain glowed. Although this was a cleaning occurrence its thoroughness was complete when my Grandmother came to stay, sometimes for an unwarranted period. She was my father's mother, a tall, rather elegant woman with a pointed chin and a large nose that was always being poked into our business.

At any time the use of hot water was strictly patrolled, the bath filled with lukewarm fluid to a height of about six centimetres. But when our Grandmother was there the tide went out even further. Small nude bodies shivered as she knelt on the rubber mat beside the bath, making sure that every bit was cleaned, each ear receiving her long wriggling finger disguised in a yellow washer.

Banana trees overhung the back verandah and in summer were laden with fruit wrapped in plastic bags to stop the possums from eating it. I look a little to the left and I can see the garage, its roof and one wall covered in ivy. The orange tree hangs with juicy balls and the lemons shine in the summer sun.

I can feel the red painted concrete of the back patio under my feet and hear the sound of the fly screen door as it bangs shut and Prince comes to join me, his stubby tail wagging and his brown eyes looking straight into my soul. I scoop him up and run down the driveway to where Dad is working in the front garden. The fragrance of the frangipani is wonderful and I think of the nights when it blends with the magic of the moonlight and takes me away.

"You want to go collect oysters?"

I nod, grab my shoes from the front porch and we're off. Prince, my father and me. Dad's good at oyster collecting, opening each tightly closed shell with his fishing knife, one for me, one for him. Prince doesn't like oysters.

The house in Hope Street is changed now. Renovated. The garage is still there, the old jacarandas lining the back paling fence and the two frangipani trees still flowering in the front garden.

The silence in the garage was reassuring, a space of temporary existence. To breathe in the memory of hope and to gently allow the thinness of its energy to spread through her body. He was gone, at least out of the garage. She stood up and adjusted her clothing to her body and her brain into being. Gradually she felt the terror subsiding as her eyes picked out the familiarity of her surroundings and her heart leapt as she watched the moonlight casting its beacon on the rusting garden tools. The green of the ivy-drenched walls soaked pleasantly through her skin and life became visible once more.

She had heard the wooden door of the garage heaving and the metal scraping of the lock as it dragged across the concrete. The madness of her father had moved, his fury spent and he had gone and left her alone. But she waited, still and silent until she heard the familiar sound, the distinct combination of the wood and mesh of the fly screen door hitting the wooden frame. He was inside the house and she was safe.

With the movement of a shadow she went towards the shaft of light, leaning on the door as she moved it carefully open. Slowly. Slowly. She crept to its edge like a furtive mouse looking into the outside air. The smell delighted her, her body tingled and the brightness of the stars melted into her. She stepped out.

The air suddenly filled with an horrendous battle cry as the monster came lumbering towards her, the meat cleaver raised high above his head.

She ran across the lawn, landing in the ferns at the back of the garden, crouching, hidden in the blackness beside the paling fence. She watched, her heart leaping as he hurled the cleaver, missing the lemon tree and thundering into the tap, the sound of the metal ringing through the silence of the night air and into her brain. Closer and closer he came, his thick screech of battle building panic on panic.

He was too near. She ran in circles around the lawn, her mind pleading to the moonlight to show her a place to hide but her father stayed close behind her, slicing the air with the cleaver.

So she just ran, smaller and more agile than he, an image picture of her severed body pushing her forward until she leapt, arms first behind the jacaranda tree in the middle of the back fence, remaining still and silent. Her body was moaning. A deep sound that seemed to come from her bowels, vibrating through her body and gurgling through her throat. But she was no longer there. Someone else had been thrust out front to deal with the situation. To her child's mind, no matter what happened even if the body was chopped up, she would now survive, watching safely from above.

He had heard her, moving nearer, but her wits propelled her forwards, across the heap of rubbish to the christmas bush. She grabbed its trunk, as the whooshing sound scraped by her ear. Again she left, leaving the small child, Beatrice, curled up in tight ball in the black soil.

The weapon had lodged in the trunk of the bush and as he struggled to retrieve it yet another part sprang into action, running across the lawn, brushing through the mint and parsley and finally climbing over the paling fence and into Kelly's yard.

She pressed her body tightly up against the splintery wood, her heart racing but safe.

Silently she began to creep towards the street. Then she remembered.

"Prince!" She ran, leaping the wire fence up the side path, opening the gate. His insanity remained as he staggered around the yard, slicing at anything that moved. She didn't care. Prince was her life. She called again, the hysterical sounds splitting the darkness. She called. Again.

Again. He came, eyes questioning, body trembling as she picked him up and ran, without looking back, to the soft green leaves of the willow tree as it stood gently in the safety of the moonlight by the creek.

As an adult I met a wonderful man and we married. My system had done an excellent job and I then remembered nothing of my childhood trauma, but after the birth of my two children memories began to push their way to the surface and anxiety took over my life until the terror became a living breathing entity with a life force of its own. It lived in every cell of my being, causing me to dissociate and to be immediately back in the events of my childhood. Back in the house in Hope Street, ready to be dead.

Time: 6 o'clock
Place: Somewhere between life and death.
Feelings: No solid forms, suspended, constant restlessness but going nowhere.
Goals: Create solid boundaries. To focus.
Why: To remain within life.
Feelings: Panic.
Goal: To stamp out panic.
Why: To remain within life.
How: Focus. I must focus.
Why: To gather different parts together.
Feelings: More calm but it will be short.
Why: Can't change. Too huge.
Goal: To contain the panic.
Time: 6.30
Place: Somewhere between life and death.

The cupboard, small and painted white was built to store the wood for the open fire but is now almost empty. It starts inside in the corner of the lounge room with the green bubbly lounge and the grey carpet dotted with borders of small pink rosebuds and continues through the double brick wall to the night-time air and glorious stars.

A silent shadow moves carefully towards this corner, suddenly stopping to curl up into a tight ball that even the moon can't see as the roar of violence echoes through the rendered walls and into her belly. Then further, closer, to hide in the spider infested cupboard. She slides in, slowly closing the inside door behind her but she doesn't all fit, her legs spilling out and resting on the red painted concrete of the back patio. Prince is near her, his tail wagging and as she reaches out to pat him the moon casts a momentary smile and her song returns.

She is filled with the smell of coke dust and wriggles to avoid the sharp stick that pokes into her back. Her skin has become her eyes as she feels the spidery legs moving over her hand. She must be silent. She must remain still, eyes tightly closed. The spider stops half way up her arm, alert, waiting, then it moves with independent legs across her chest, onto her neck and up towards her face. This is too much.

She yelps and brushes it to the floor. Prince barks. She hears the footsteps of the thundering giant.

"Sshhh!"

It's too late. The thud of the flyscreen door as it slams shut behind him. Her moonlight smile is gone now. She holds in all her arms, her legs, her head, like an echidna against a fox. He reaches in and grabs her, hauling her out onto the red concrete. She fumbles, grabs hold of the small external door of the cupboard, desperate now to remain with the spiders. He yanks her free, dragging her like a sack of potatoes towards the garage, scraping her skin along the concrete and stone edgings of the garden around the christmas bush, its twigs and branches scratching and poking at her face.

She struggles to get one foot on the ground, her hand reaching out for the edge of the garage door but her grip is small and the giant, angry and strong, hurls her into the blackness. Her mind vanishes as she's flung through the air, dizzy, terrified, narrowly missing the workbench and landing heavily on the greasy concrete floor. She remains still, but no longer Rhonda, as the prison door is bolted shut. He's there, near her, swearing and cursing.

"Come here, you vermin!"

Her mind grabs the image of Prince as it floats by and she escapes into the softness of his fur and the gentleness of his eyes.

Suddenly her head is yanked back and something is thrust into her mouth.

It's soft and rubbery but she can feel the movement of his hand as it moves up and down, pushing against her teeth, hurting her mouth and stretching her lips. She tries to pull away but he has a firm grip on her head, pushing it forward. The rubbery mass grows solid until it becomes a firm rod that stretches down her throat almost choking her. She gasps for air, her hands pushing against him trying desperately to remove this intrusion from her mouth. She hears him groaning. Again she disappears, leaving her body to **Emma**, yet another part of her, created for this purpose. Whatever happens she will live. She watches as Emma gags and struggles until she sees the inevitable white fluid dribbling from the corner of her mouth and onto her chin. He is done. Still she stays away, watching the crumpled heap on the floor.

She hears the metal sound of the bolt as he unlocks the door, the slam of the fly screen. She's alone. Only then does she begin to return.

Only then does she smell the evil semen and taste its foulness. She looks up towards the small window above the work bench and catches the soft glow of the moon shining on the silken threads of the spider webs that crisscross the weathered glass, allowing it to fill her being.

The smile is completely gone now, swallowed by the void.

She feels the sharp pain in her leg, remembering the unforgiving surface of the concrete as she reaches down to the blood, congealed along the scratches on the outside of her leg. She must find Prince and feel the softness of his fur, to bring life back into her body and warmth into her soul.

The gentle voice of the therapist brings her back.
   "Are you alright?"

The door was open and I entered quietly, taking my place in the self assertiveness group, trying desperately not to be seen. Having been given the task of bringing something that represented 'me' I had grabbed an old pillow case and walked around the house and the garden filling it with things symbolic of what I felt to be myself. Small stones, a gardenia whose perfume filtered through the weave of the cotton and mixed with the pungent scent of citrus leaves. Scissors, several blank sheets of paper. A locket, gold rimmed on a long chain. It was fun and I'd been immersed. No one had ever asked what was inside 'me'. It was my turn and the therapist played the tape of my music that had just flowed out of nowhere that week. Someone cried. Then one by one I pulled out the contents of the sack, describing them with an energy and excitement that I had seldom felt. Camelia buds, a small cylinder of red glitter, plasticine and finally a roughly made cellophane package about two inches square sealed with uneven bits of aging sticky tape. It contained pieces of golden fur snipped, a long time ago, from my cocker spaniel, Prince. My life force.
   I stared at it and could feel him there with me, his body comfortable in the curve of my leg, his nose wet on my knee. I reached out my hand to stroke his ears, the softness of that gentle fur as it rippled down in waves.
   Not white, not golden.
   The therapist had moved across the circle and was kneeling in front of me, the locket in his hand. I suddenly saw him, withdrew my hand.
   "Is that a picture of your father?"
   I nodded. The locket was round, about the size of twenty cents, gold on one side, glass on the other. My father was about thirty-nine. Tall, thin and dressed in his army uniform. Sleeves rolled up, his slouched hat slightly askew, the Aussie emblem of the rising sun sitting prominently in the centre.
   "Is he still alive?"

"No." I looked up and he seemed to see that I was alive inside my eyes. I knew then that perhaps I could trust this man with brown eyes that were kind and shown me warmth, and I when I was thirty-eight finally plunged into therapy and walked towards the kindness.

As the memories became conscious and the complex safety net that I'd constructed began to disassemble, the terror became a constant, living force, the panic attacks stealing my sanity and the sadness engulfing me like a threatening funeral robe.

When I went into the therapy room for the first time alone with Richard, the psychiatrist, the cushions had all been put to one side and in the centre of the room were two armchairs. It was modest in its furnishings and brown in its tones. A metal filing cabinet flanked the eastern window that in turn looked out onto a magnificent, tall gum tree that spread its branches like a bird in flight. From where I sat I could always see it and over the years it became an important symbol of safety. No interruptions during a psychotherapy session. A chamber that rocked in the breeze and settled again fifty minutes later. I walked in and sat down, staring at his shiny black shoes that pointed outwards as if to walk off in different directions. I shuffled. He spoke.

"You rang me, what was happening?"

The words wouldn't come, they were stuck somewhere in my childhood.

The fear was there, sitting heavily in my belly. I could see the single red rose on his desk, but as I stood up to touch it, it began to grow thick and strong, moving towards me. Stretching. Swaying, with long talons reaching out for me, its menacing form towering over me as if to engulf me, an evil green eye at every joint.

"What can you see?"

It had grown to almost fill the room. I couldn't speak, my mind already vanishing, my body poised for flight.

"Sit down Rhonda."

I heard his voice, distant, as the huge form grabbed at me, its eyes multiplying at every moment.

"Sit down Rhonda!"

This time the mists parted and his voice reached me as I snatched hold of its safety and sat down. Gradually the terror began to fade. I could see the tree again, then the room. Then his hands resting on the arms of the chair. Clean nails.

Always clean hands and clean nails. Kind hands. My breathing slowed and my mind returned. I was back.

"What could you see?"

He listened, not interrupting as I described The Terror. My mind had returned to the house in Hope St. I could see my mother when she got home after teaching at school, her hair well kept but ruffled, nails filed but laden with the smell of children and chalk. Her green eyes vacant but determined. Working, always working to keep up with the demands of school, us three kids. And my father. Clothed in a tiredness that masked an internal confusion and her constant and desperate attempts to contain her fear and to maintain the silence. Never stopping long enough to allow the reality a crack to push itself through. Preparing meals, washing, teaching, ironing, stuffing yet another saucepan into an already overfilled cupboard.

"Did you practice this morning?" her mother calls.

She moves over towards the window and sits down happily at the piano, Prince settling at her feet. This instrument is her friend. Solid, with ornate legs and shoulders and keys of yellowed ivory, its voice contradicting the coldness that pervades the house. She stands and lifts the lid of the stool, taking out some well-worn music. Her father made the stool, with legs like curvaceous hips, the seat covered in a tapestry pattern of green, white and brown threads held on with furniture tacks. It was meant to hold all the music but some always spilled over into piles on top of the piano.

The tunes, her tunes, are swimming around in her head, scratching to be let out as her fingers search for the notes to give them life and form.

"That's not what you're supposed to be practicing!"

She follows the instruction without understanding, filling the spaces instead with the contrapuntal tones of the seventeenth century. Her mind wanders and her fingers return.

"I told you to stop playing that music!" repeats her mother as the lid of the keyboard comes crashing down on her fingers. She wants to gather up all the sounds that have been singing and dancing around in her head, but like Prince, they have fled. So she just sits there, wishing that all her cells could become invisible and reassemble somewhere else.

"Why wouldn't your mother let you make your own music?"

"Because my father liked it. He encouraged it, and he encouraged me to play by ear."

"And she didn't like that?"

"She didn't like him."

"How old were you."

"Oh about nine." There was a pronounced shift.

I felt the panic rising, my mind trying desperately to fill itself with anything other than the scarlet terror in my body.

"I can hear the radio."

"What radio."

"The big brown console that is under the window in the lounge room. The radio play. I can hear the radio play! The Russians are invading Poland.

Russian tanks! They're running from the Russian tanks. Magda, they're coming closer, we've got to run. Come on, Magda. Run!"

She can hear the fighting in the hallway as her brother Matt struggles with her drunken father. She screws up her face, her hands pressed tightly over her ears and her body as close as she can to the console.

She can see the street where Magda's standing. Dark and filled with panic as the Hungarian people struggle to fight back the continuing advance of the Russian army. The tanks move closer. Almost upon them.

"Magda, RUN!" screams the voice on the radio.

She looks through the darkness of the room to the wretched moaning noise of her father as he stumbles down the hallway. She hears him fall but knows he'll pick himself up. Again the radio shrieks, the tanks rolling closer, the fear rising until suddenly the radio is filled with a scream of terror as Magda falls beneath the moving caterpillar tracks. She hears her father in the kitchen and tries to run but she's congealed in a web of terror. Frozen. She feels herself leaving, safely out of her body. This escape is instant now.

As he comes closer, she smells the stench of alcohol and vomit. Higher and higher she flies. Swirling. Soon she can look back on his lumbering form and on the small figure, another part of herself pressed against the radio.

She can still hear the sound of the faraway wheels and wonders what it would be like to be crushed by a tank. She watches as her father lunges at her with the large kitchen knife, ducking as he comes thundering towards her. She pulls herself up on the arm of the lounge, her eyes staring in terror as he comes towards her once more. But the alcohol has taken control and his huge body thunders down, the knife making a clanking sound on the Cosi Stove as it falls to the floor. She waits.

This time she will be safe, for he's beyond any movement. Any threat. She crawls over to the corner, feeling the security of the wall behind her back.

There are no tears, not yet. The Terror sees to that. Then slowly the life force begins to re-enter her body, moving through her veins and bringing warmth back into her bones. Her breathing deepens, her brain begins to tingle and awaken, her eyes to see and her ears to hear. She has returned.

The play on the radio has finished now, replaced by the soft strands of Dvorak's 'New World Symphony,' its melodies rising and falling. Coldness spreads through her as the tears begin. She looks at him. The parent she loves. The parent she wants to destroy.

Inga Yorkisson was her name, a rather spindly girl with frizzy blond hair and mischievous eyes. Everyone's friend. At this new secondary school **Lucy** had been rather shy at first, standing back observing, watching to make sure it would be safe to join in. When Inga smiled at her she loosened her skin and smiled back. They ended up in quite a few of the same classes, the smiles sometimes growing to laughter. She acted too soon, inviting her new friend home for the night. The tension in her home was palpable, the hallway feeling endless as they walked, school bags in hands towards her bedroom, Prince following. Kate was away teaching in the country, her bed spare. "That's your bed over there and I sleep here by the window."

"Feels comfortable." Inga jumped up and down on the edge, eyes surveying the rest of the room. Prince barked. They laughed.

"Let's get changed and go down to the creek."

She'd already introduced Inga to her mother who was in the kitchen preparing a snack for them.

"Why don't you girls go and play ball in the back yard?"

"We're going down the creek," she yelled as they grabbed the snacks and raced down the front path.

Light was fading when they returned, wet and a little muddy from the afternoon of fun and freedom. Prince had to be wiped down before he was allowed in.

"Have a shower and get into your pyjamas."

"Now!" Whispered Inga.

"You go first, but don't be in long or she'll start roaring at me."

The house had been tidied, or more precisely, the junk from all visible surfaces had been stuffed into already bulging cupboards. You could even see the top of the traymobile.

"Set the table please dear."

The knives and forks clattered as she walked around placing everything just right.

"Are we having dessert?" She remembered the curried custard.

"Yes. Rice pudding with tinned peaches."

"Oh."

She had asked her father to come home early and to be alright. She'd pleaded with him and he had promised, but the sun had set and he wasn't there. With any luck he might stay away all night.

Her mother had gone to some trouble. It wasn't often that someone outside the family was here, especially to stay, and the table was adorned with yellow and pink dahlias from the garden.

"You're over there."

Inga squeezed into the space between the piano and the table and she smiled an extra large smile to help Inga feel at ease. The meal continued in embarrassed silence, her brother glancing sideways at the blond guest.

"Tell Mum where you come from," she said, thinking of her far away land.

"From Sweden. When we first arrived we lived in the migrant hostel in Parramatta."

Her mother was polite, but a snob of few means so she smiled with a sufficient hint of pity and changed the subject. A key turned in the front door.

She jumped up. "He's home. I'll get it," as she ran to the door, praying to a god who never seemed to listen, to make him okay, but the alcoholic stench covered her skin as he wobbled through the hallway and into the kitchen.

"Why don't you go to bed Dad and I'll bring you your dinner?"

He shoved her out of the way. "Gotta say hello to the bloody family."

Fear showed in Inga's eyes as he thumped himself down next to her.

"Who in the bloody hell is this?"

Her mother smiled nervously. "Don't take any notice of him dear," as she took his arm. "Howard, just go bed and we'll bring you your dinner."

"Not bloody likely. We've got a guest. I'm not missing the fun."

Bit by bit her mother was losing her cool, the politeness disappearing beneath a wave of ancient frustration and humiliation.

"We don't want you here. She has a new friend from school and we were all sitting and having a lovely dinner."

"Well what's wrong with me having a lovely dinner here with your curly haired friend?"

He leant towards her, grabbing hold of her and planting his mouth, hard, on her virgin skin.

"Leave her alone!" Rhonda was up, pulling at his clothing and lashing out at him.

Her mother fussing quietly at the plate in front of her.

"He doesn't mean any harm dear. He's just had a bit too much to drink."

"Who's had too much to drink!"

Her father stood, his large frame towering over the table, fists clenched and mouth dribbling. Then he moved towards Inga again, but this time Matt grabbed him from behind, yanking him away. He roared, pulling the tablecloth onto the floor, food spewing everywhere. Inga screamed as chicken noodle soup joined the blond curls of her amazed head. Rhonda grabbed the salad bowl and tipped it upside down over him, lettuce and cucumber hanging with wounded pride all over his nose and shoulders.

Rhonda grabbed Inga's hand. "Quick, run!" whistling to Prince as they hurtled out the door and down to the creek. They sat separately, Inga in fear and confusion, Rhonda allowing the moonshine to wrap her in its light. Next morning nobody mentioned the previous night. Her mother made vegemite and crushed peanut sandwiches for each of them and everyone at school laughed at her and moved away.

The silence after the front door has shut is eerie. Is she alone on this earth? She wonders what it would be like if no one ever returned. Never anyone to give her permission to open the doors, to look out, maybe to walk out. Her mother has said that she is too sick to go to school but through her knowledge of the silence she knows that this is the only way to describe the bruises. Sometimes she is six, sometimes nine or eleven. Sometimes thirteen.

One by one the family has left the house. Her father, at 4 a.m. in his grey dustcoat has closed the front door and gone to work. Her brother Matt, ten years her senior and her sister Kate, born six and a half years before her, have packed their bags and caught their bus each to their selective high schools. Her mother, having disconnected the telephone and secured all external doors, has delivered the boundaries of silence and left for a day's teaching at school.

"You are sick and you are to stay in bed and only get up to go to the toilet." Left alone, her mother's words vibrate through her body spreading outwards across the rooms and encasing her within the confines of a tailored coffin. She will not plug in the disconnected phone, nor will she show any part of her at the windows and if Prince or her cat, Mister, need to go out she will make sure that no-one is looking before carefully opening the back door and remaining within the shadows until they come in again.

She would never go outside the door herself. She knows about the secret and the silence, indelibly written then sealed within her other than conscious mind. She seldom questions, and never overtly. Compliant acceptance is a practiced response to threat and imprisonment, which adds to the highly evolved forms of dissociation used in order to escape the terror and the utter confusion created by the constant parental denial of what is happening. So it is on this day that one by one **The Master Planner** takes the carefully created family from within her, gathering each imaginary doll and seating it in its allotted space, finally surrounding Rhonda with a systematic form of safety that will help her to breathe.

Mister, her beautiful grey tabby cat smooches against her chest, happy to have her near and taking possession before Prince jumps up on the bed.

Finally he settles, curled up around the shape of her arm, purring.

"Was your mother's work far away?"

She shook her head.

"How old were you?"

"Six, nine, eleven, thirteen."

She feels the fear rising.

Her wheezing is audible now as the therapist lean forward.

"Look at me."

"I feel as though I'm being put in a coffin and someone's closing the lid!"

"Keep looking at me."

Her lungs gasp for air. Prince, her small golden spaniel licks her face. Still the rasping noise continues. He jumps off the bed and runs through the house, barking, then back to her, jumping onto the bed licking, nudging, sitting as close as possible trying to quieten her. At last she reaches out and touches him with her fingers, stroking the golden fur that tells her about refuge and of life.

Her life. The sounds of her starved lungs begin to diminish, the air flowing, bringing potential back into her body. She snuggles Prince closer, tears forming, tension releasing.

"Keep taking my calmness."

She looks down, the awareness of the now passing over her like a film of fairy dust, the calm voice penetrating the mists as the memory begins to flatten out and to gradually move into the file of yesterday. Only words are left.

"Up until high school my mother would dash home at lunch time to cook me a boiled egg and buttered bread. She'd bring it in to me, chatter about her morning at school then leave again."

She looks over at the therapist, a shared moment of understanding. The warmth returning to her hands and the host to her body. The terror has once again abated but again she is left with indisputable information.

When I first walked through the open door to the therapy group I was always wanting my molecules to be delivered to where I needed to be so that nobody would see me. I had no boundaries and didn't understand where I ended and everyone else began. It was as though I didn't really exist, that I was just pretending. My posture was stooped, and I had no sense of identity and therefore none of belonging. And even though I wasn't consciously aware of it, I could vanish into dissociation at a moment's notice. I was fragmented.

Working for eleven years with Richard, the psychiatrist, I was eventually heard, believed and seen and I felt like a baby rocked in a parent's arms. He became my mirror and a safe parent. I was validated, which enabled me to gradually experience my own existence and to know and to understand that I actually take up space and that people can see me.

"Rhonda makes everything into a drama," my mother told everyone. But to me hers was a different sentence. "Your silence is absolute!" And so it became. She knew what was happening. Kate and Matt lived the fear and violence. I experienced these and the sexual abuse. But it was never to be spoken, either at home or in the world outside. It was to be believed by her, by me, by my brother and sister, that none of it ever happened. That even though we saw and experienced, it wasn't there.

Therapy changed that. "The vase is on the table" became a mantra that Richard said to me over and over. You see it, I see it, it exists. It did happen. When I began to believe this, time started to move and I became a person with a history, just like everyone else.

Instead of having either a naïve trust of everyone or no trust for anyone, I began to develop the ability to discern. To use my intellect to identify my own needs and to learn ways of nourishing them. I began to develop a Self, as expressed in a story that came tumbling out one day when that self was glimpsed.

The Girl, the Stranger and the Stone

She lived in a house just like any other. Red brick with terracotta tiles, a yard defined by a white picket fence adjoining grey palings. She was young and often greeted by neighbours as she walked her dog in the spring or winter air. She loved her little spaniel and as the years passed they became constant companions, often sitting on the bank of the creek, throwing stones into the water and watching the ripples growing outwards in confidence and adventure. In spring she often picked a buttercup from amongst those growing on the bank, holding it under Prince's chin to watch its reflection and to feel its waxen texture beneath her fingers. The birds would come and go, singing their songs in their daily gathering of food. Their presence was enjoyed by the young girl.

One day, as the earth began to relax, she sat filtering the sand through her fingers as the fading sun danced on a small but very colourful stone. She gathered it up and the two companions enjoyed its amazing beauty. Feelings are not complete until shared and her four-legged friend could not understand the reason for her excitement.

"I must show my mother, she cried, running up the hill and into the red brick house.

She was standing in the cluttered kitchen, cooking. With excitement dancing in her eyes the little girl held out her hand.

"Look, Mum. See what I've just found!"

Her eyes remained on the cooking pots and her tired voice replied: I'm busy. Don't bother me now."

It was then that the little girl remembered that was how her mother always answered and hiding her disappointment went searching for her father. He was not there. She showed it again to Prince, turned it around in her fingers to feel its silken texture, took one more secret look at its shape and colours and tucked it safely away with her treasures.

Several weeks passed before the little girl again took out the special stone and carried it in her pocket to the creek. As soon as the stone was held in the water it began to glow, bouncing many colours and lights from its surface. Again the little girl ran home and was reminded of her foolishness, again the disappointment was hidden beneath the cheery smile of compliance.

Many times in the next few months she repeated her excitement and disappointment, because every time she looked at the stone it became brighter, more colourful and more important. One day she could contain it no longer and ran home, demanding that her mother should at least look at the treasure that she held in her hand.

Her mother turned. "Show me. But hurry up!"

The girl felt the tears welling up inside her, but with the naïve trust of animals and children she slowly held out her hand and revealed her treasure.

"Why, it's only an old stone," shouted her mother. "All this fuss over a stone.

Go away!"

She closed her hand tightly over the stone and ran outside. She didn't speak to her furry friend. She didn't need to as he always accepted her tears without question. She tried to hide the hurt but the pain kept stabbing at her heart until one day, after much struggle, it finally lay down and was covered.

One day, as she was feeling the cool water with her toes, a stranger came and quietly sat beside her. He didn't speak at first, but removed his shoes and let the water move over his feet. She looked across at him and together they felt the sand trickle through their fingers.

Each day the stranger and the little girl would sit together and share the birds, smell the bush flowers, enjoy the buttercups and listen to the water.

One day she reached into her pocket and took out her precious stone.

She hesitated a moment, then seeing that the stranger's eyes were warm she slowly held out her hand and opened her fingers. The stone lay there, small and fragile. Her excitement had long since died and she quietly waited for the warm stranger to speak. He reached out and took her hand in his then carefully felt the stone.

"It's very beautiful," he said The girl began to believe his sharing and cried eagerly: "Do you see it? Can you really see it?" as the tears of relief and joy flowed down her face.

"Yes," said the stranger as he looked at the little girl, his eyes full of time and understanding.

A good feeling began to grow inside the little girl.

"You are smiling," said the stranger.

"What is smiling?" asked the little girl.

"You are happy," said the stranger.

"What is happy?" asked the little girl.

"You are beautiful," said the stranger.

The little girl remained silent for a moment then said,

"The stone is beautiful."

"Yes," said the stranger.

CHAPTER 2

There was once a baby who grew and became a young child. She smiled when she watched the eels in the creek and she cried when the blackness surrounded her. She loved to sing but remained silent when the fear was visible.

She danced too, running after her sister up the road as they went with their ballet shoes to lessons. But it was not she who went into the blackness. It was her friends inside her. They had names but she didn't know them. They had voices but they only spoke in the right place and at the right time and never so that the little girl could hear them.

As she grew, more of these friends were created by the **Master Planner.** He knew everything. He created the plan, adapting it as needed, watching over its implementation through a series of decrees that established its constancy. This plan and our system was complete down to the most intricate details, in the form of a very large jigsaw puzzle. He knew when each of her different parts was created and why. He knew their jobs and how they fitted into the jigsaw and he was proud of the puzzle that he had created. No-one could ever trace him. No-one could ever put the pieces of his puzzle together. His right-hand man, **The Jostler** was ready, at a split-second's notice, to go into action whenever any threat to this plan appeared, moving or removing a piece of the jigsaw or silencing words that may have given enough information to put the puzzle together. He worked to ensure that the left and right brain never became one and that the head and the body never be joined. In other words we could never be put together.

The little girl would never become whole and **The One who was Born** would always be hidden and therefore safe. Only **The Master Planner, The Jostler, Stones, Mary** and **Magnitude** knew that any of the others existed at all. Co-consciousness has only developed as the tight shell around each part of me has been cracked and opened and this has taken many years.

Imagine this jigsaw puzzle, but when you look at it for the first time, it's blank. All the pieces have been taken out and hidden, but they each do exist. One by one you discover them and sometimes they fit perfectly, at others they don't seem to fit anywhere at all. Sometimes something happens and makes absolutely no sense until five years or three weeks or two months later when a memory will surface or something will happen around something already remembered and that piece of jigsaw just slots into the space where it was meant to be.

There are wise alters to guide me, and children who are looked after by the **Seven Elderly People**. There are alters like my parents and ones who remember this and not that or that and not this. And **The Fantasy Parents** who took the place of my own parents.

And it must have all been put into place, complete with all of its checks and balances and in all its intricate details by the time I was nineteen. A complete subconscious story but with no ending.

LUCY

I sometimes ask myself about **Lucy** and wonder what it feels like to be her? In a way she appears to be very ordinary, but at the same time has an extremely important job. She makes decisions, but quietly. And she talks just enough to fit in but not to be noticed and to always appear to be 'ordinary.'

She was the key to the real world, of life outside our red brick home in Hope Street. The outside world we called the **Circle reality**. She had to listen carefully and watch other people to learn how they behaved and acted. What they said and how they said it.

She learned to not talk too loudly and not to wave her arms around even when a story excited her. She learnt that others often told stories about their families, but that if she listened and remained mostly quiet, they kept talking, filling in the spaces so that she didn't have to make up too many stories about her own. She was the one who went to school, to Brownies, ballet lessons and everything else in the circle reality. She saw colours and she had dreams. She climbed trees and played cricket with the kids in the street.

Life inside the house in Hope Street taught us very little about how to behave in the real world. It was a different reality and almost nothing in this inside world of the home, the **Square reality** related to the behaviour outside it. So Lucy was created to enable us to fit in with other people in every day life.

She always did as she was told. She obeyed **The Coordinator** at all times. His rules governed her role and therefore her behaviour.

As I step into Lucy's shoes I find that I'm beginning to get to really know her.

She appears not to have a personality of her own, but I think she has and it is quietly internalised. She does the job she is created to do and absorbs all the characteristics and behaviours of those around her who she is observing. This is what we see of her. However, she has an essence that is always present because she only takes on those behaviours that she considers appropriate. She has a good moral sense of what is right and what is wrong.

Which begs the question, where did this come from? To which I answer: instead of learning about the world from the parents, she learnt from the world outside. From nature, other people and from Prince.

It was not until we were about fifteen and the rape became more regular and life threatening that she was joined in the circle reality by **Emma**. She had no choice in this. Lucy knew innately that it wasn't a good thing, but at this time Emma, who was the recipient of this physical trauma, was so hurt and angry that she just took over, forcing Lucy into the background. It was also at this time that **The Co-ordinator** began to lose his control and Emma, a teenager, took her known world into the reality of the circle and behaving in the only way she knew how, became promiscuous.

Emma of course knew about the square reality but Lucy didn't. She knew nothing of the events or behaviours in the home. Nor of the other parts of our system. **Bronwyn**, her twin, the practical one went about fixing up after violent events with complete detachment and no emotion. Lucy knew no names. When Emma forced her way out to take over the body, Lucy withdrew obediently.

MARY

It's been a strange journey. A bit like waking up from a long, deep sleep, stretching, and finding that there has been a life happening all around me. One that I've been aware of but never involved in because there has always been a thin film between me and everyone else and between me and life. I just do my job.

I often have to shake myself because in my world there have always been two realities and I prided myself on my ability to see and to live in each of these.

But over time, things have changed and I feel confused. I've heard the story of each of the parts around me and I've seen her fear and anger, his loneliness and sadness, their relief, but I did not have this luxury. To allow any feeling to become stronger than rational thought would have made me vulnerable and this was just not in the Master Plan. In fact there were many things set in place to help me with this. It's been constructed on purpose but I'm the only one in the System besides **Stones** and **Magnitude** who can think and feel at the same time. This makes sense because when faced with serious danger, there is no time to use cognitive thought, to weigh up possibilities and make decisions. Instead, we automatically go into 'flight or fight' and the body adapts with rushes of adrenalin to make us stronger to defend ourselves or to run fast.

Stones and I both knew about the circle and the square realities. I'm beginning to understand that we were the linchpins of the System and that we held it all together. I'm **Mary.** I was created from another part, **Ruth,** when she was standing right on the edge of insanity and could take no more so I stepped in. It has been my job to retain, at all times, a firm connection with the father and to keep that connection alive no matter what.

As a small child we had to connect with someone on this earth. The mother was detached, often with quite cruel words. The sister, Kate and the brother, Matt were preoccupied in surviving in their own ways. So even though he was often violent and dangerous, the father had shown us kindness and warmth and he was the only one with whom it was possible to connect. When Rhonda was about six or seven, her dog Prince came and filled up many spaces, creating a myriad of threads of connection. He was only there for nine years. When Rhonda was fourteen the rape and violence only increased, making the strong human connection with someone, the only person available being the father, even more imperative.

So it became my job, and connect I did, to the point where it became a full identification with him. For me, my job was a matter of life and death. If we lost that connection we believed we would die. I was so focused on doing this job successfully that in my mind I became part of him and he of me. I had no understanding that we were separate people. In a healthy situation, as a child grows s/he gradually separates from the parent, becoming a complete and individual person.

When Multiplicity has been created, separation cannot begin to occur until many of the boundaries of the created parts are broken down and internal co-operation is begun. It has been forty-five years since my father died and only recently have I been able to break that connection.

I'm aware that my voice has changed, becoming deeper and my speech slower as **Magnitude** emerges. "It is through **Mary** that we will know our destiny. That we will walk as one upon the moors so filled with sunshine and life. For if we can accept her, then we will have accepted the darkest part of our fear. It is **Bethany** and **Little One** who, with the openness of children will connect. They will walk to her with trust. It will be done."

STONES

They sharpen up their words and they stab me. And they stab each other.

So I take their words and I throw them all into the river, drape them over the rocks and hang them from the trees from where they are carried away by the birds. When all their words have gone there's just silence and it's beautiful. I love to be alone and to be one with the trees and the rocks. And I love to wonder where the river is going and where it has come from. And in that silence I can exist, and nobody will ever see me, but I know that I am **Stones** and I am here.

Everyone thought **Mary** was mad. She had the ability to move from being solid to being fragmented, and back again, but this was her strength. It had to be. To keep the thread that connected all of us to the father, she had to be able to go into the father's insanity and to safely emerge from it, and in his madness he was fragmented, so she had to match that.

We're like two balancing trays, me on one side, Mary on the other. In contrast to Mary I have no fragmentation at all. I had no link with the mother or the father and even though I knew they existed, I had no connection with any of the other parts of Rhonda. I am whole and solid within myself.

I walked along the edge of the road, my head down, kicking stones and watching safely from a distance. I loved to watch them as they ambled off my foot, never really going where I wanted them to. They made up their own minds and I like that.

I watched and saw the whole picture. The stones grounded me and are the solid part of our reality and I am all that is solid. People often say that there's no such thing as reality but I don't think they understand. There must always be one that is safe, sane and constant. So, we created one.

There were quite a few times when it all got too much for me and I wanted to intervene and to change things. But **The Controller** stopped me because it was vital to the health and functioning of our system that I remain on the outside. My intervention would have upset the balance of the scales and Mary might have tipped over the edge and into the father's madness.

I knew that if I just kept walking on the earth and didn't take the mother or the father inside me, that like the trees, I would be able to keep the God in us. And when Prince died I created the **Earth Mother**, who knew how to nurture. It made me angry, all those years watching and knowing and never being allowed to say a word.

And somewhere deep within I knew about hope. If I'd allowed myself to be taken down into the trauma, I'd have given up.

> Invisible I moved away and there I stayed until
> the day when it was safe to return and listen.
> **Stones January 1999**

When the 'what is' defies sanity then the 'what is not' becomes sane. So, when the visible world we live in is unsafe then a different reality must be invented. One must create a 'what is not' as a tangible alternative to the unsafe 'what is.' It becomes a credible place in which to escape. The 'what is' then becomes unreal and therefore safe.

The mind is truly remarkable. By switching its perception of what is real, and creating an alternative and personally believable reality, it enabled my mind to exist on more than one plane, keeping my real Self hidden and safe, cloaked in an invisible and impenetrable cocoon, while still functioning within the confines of a 'normal' life. It also kept The Terror locked within its core with no means of escape. When the world around her is not safe, a child, still connected to the thread of unlimited imagination, can create her own worlds that are and will remain essential parts of her survival. One of these places was The Nowhere.

BETHANY

There's a hole in the clouds where I sometimes go
When I'm frightened or lonely or feeling very low
No-one talks, there's no need, music fills the air
I don't feel frightened when I'm there
There's a hole in the clouds where I sometimes go
When I'm frightened or lonely or feeling very low
No-one talks, there's no need
Music fills the sky
I hope I can go there when I die.

It's peaceful up here in the clouds. A world beyond fear and pain, darkness and despair and nothing will ever harm me here. It runs on trust and when I'm here I feel myself lifting, beyond the touch of solid objects and the formation of endless words. When I listen I can hear the music of the clouds, a gentle collision of sounds that stretch and bend, becoming separate then joining into a unity of pianissimo whispers, spreading, pulling, widening until the heavens vibrate.

My name is **Bethany** and I call this place *The Nowhere*. It's wrapped in pastels and filled with amoebic shapes that merge, becoming one then separating. Here, they are free to exist without the permanence of body or mind, today or yesterday. There is no need for a way in or out, as there is no solid matter and no boundaries. No human shapes can exist here as they don't understand the silence of vision.

There are no senses to create feelings. No feelings to create words that serve permanence. No facts. Just ethereal sounds of infinite beauty. Music out of reach of reality sung by choirs of pastel safety. No inside, no outside. Pink merges to purple and yellow to green as the shapes dance with grace and the inevitability of creation. All is alive. All just is. I don't feel frightened when I'm here.

The other is *our Castle*. It's so beautiful, right up on the top of the cliff looking across to the sea. I hear the waves crashing on the rocks and the sea birds calling. The cliffs are high and the moors stretch out in front of the castle like a warm blanket. I love to watch the tufted grasses waving in the breeze and listen to the songs of the wind that sing me lullabies as I feel my dreams resting in their cradle. Everything here is timeless. I have no other reality to experience and only the seasons to show me the passage of time. I am alone here in the turret of the castle and **The Invisible Force** closes in on me each night.

I love the threads of moonlight washing through the slotted window, falling on the floor, the walls of the turret and sometimes on me. At all times I guard these threads as they follow the carefully laid trail that passes them down the castle walls into the banquet hall, down into the passages below until they come to rest within **Rebecca**, curled up in the cave deep below the castle. It is **Magnitude** who then stretches the moonlight into the **Deep, deep silence** to reach **The One Who was Born.**

It's a decree that the thread of moonlight that connects with **Rebecca** and **The One Who was Born** must never be broken. When the moon is full I collect its light. I have a reservoir of moonlight stored carefully in the turret for the nights when the moon is hidden. Then I open a small tap and allow some into the trail. Sometimes I can't resist so I open the lid, dip my hands in and spread the moonlight all over me.

Some days, as soon as the sun comes up over the sea, I rush across the moors and down the path that leads to the sand and the water. If I hum the tunes that the wind brings me I don't feel so alone. The songs right by the sea are different and if I listen well I can learn new ones to carry back with me.

Rhonda was not aware of our castle until many years into therapy, when she wandered into a shop filled with imaginative pieces of pottery.

There on a shelf was our castle. Heaps of different sized turrets rising from a solid base, with an entrance gate and slotted windows all in a rough light grey clay with dribbles of green and maroon glaze. As soon as we saw it we knew that we had to take it home. Rhonda had no idea why. At that point she knew very little of the many layers of created parts of us that remained tightly sealed somewhere in her subconscious. Several of us were present to make sure she was standing on the doorstep when the shop opened the next morning when the pottery castle became ours and remains where we can see it every day.

REBECCA

Rebecca was there, concealed yet present. She'd heard Richard, the therapist's voice before, calm and mellow with a richness wrought with matter and commitment. Like the voice of a cello that sang its songs with deep and gentle determination, threading waves of warmth through her body. For some years she'd been invisibly present in therapy sessions, listening, nestled safely within, all her senses withdrawn into her embryonic world where no-one could reach her. His cello voice had continued, gradually opening the threads of woven silk that cocooned her. Lately she'd felt the vibrations of terror as the system heaved and struggled with memories that pushed upwards with volcanic force until released. She had tried to withdraw further but the cello threads had touched her. As Richard watched, he saw the face of a small child. Frightened and very shy, but present.

"Are you alright?" she heard him say.

Was he speaking to her? Could he see her hidden deep in the caves below the castle walls? How could she answer? There were no words, no voice, no tongue that tasted or eyes that saw. But now she had ears to hear. He moved forward in his chair, his hands held out towards her.

"Open your eyes and look at me," he said.

She moved a little bit forward, her head down.

"You're safe here with me. Open your eyes and look at me."

She wanted to trust the cello threads that stroked her mind with gentle fingers and slowly she opened her eyes and sat staring at the black shoes with matching dark green socks that filled her sight. Details rose and fell as her eyes moved upwards, towards his outstretched hands. She froze, wanting to vanish yet unable to remove her eyes from the promise of this human connection.

"Take my hands," he said.

Panic seized her as she sat, awkward and frozen on the edge of the chair, her heart crying out: 'take them! Take them,' as her arms moved involuntarily forward, touching this safe parent for the first time, his voice loosening her dark spaces. She closed her eyes and felt a life force flowing into her, filling her with safe connection. She had been seen. **Rebecca** was beginning to be real. This literally saved my life.

Her voice is small and high, with the language of a four year old child. The only safe adult she's known is her angel who enfolded her in times of danger. It was a decree that she remain silent and hidden, never to connect with anything external. So as the violence increased and the fear rose, Rebecca withdrew, one sense at a time until she was a coil, with no external point of contact. **Vigil** became her eyes, **Gustav** her ears, moving constantly and singing, always singing. 'If I can show the cello voice part of our world', she thought, 'then he might see that we are here. He might know that I exist.'

So for many years she brought Richard pieces that represented her world. Bits of bark, all different colours. Petite shells with ridged patterns and intricate designs. Ragged banksia men, leaves and stones, all were taken to the therapist with kind eyes and extended hands. She was sure that he was understanding that nature was the balance of the terror. This was us. We were the earth, the wind, the rain and the seeds. We were life and living, so please let us stay with you until you see us.

As time went on, Rebecca flourished as she slowly uncoiled and after several years she embraced the feeling of trust that had grown in the presence of the therapist. Her creativity burst forth onto centre stage like a lotus flower in the sunshine of the temple. Black and white was replaced with the browns of the earth, the yellow of the wattle and the green of the pungent peppercorn leaves and the soft, soft moss.

Music swirled around and onto pages of manuscript.

She thought that the therapist now truly understood her language and her world and took him her most precious symbol. She knew the season by the acorns that were in full bloom like cherries, two small stalks on one thin bough.

"I brought this for you," she smiled.

His face remained straight. "I can no longer accept them."

She vanished instantly, passing someone else on the way out. Pulling her legs up under her, turning her back on him and continuing to breathe, her mind enmeshed in panic.

"I can't accept these things from you any more."

She couldn't speak. The rage lifted and surged until she felt that she would burst open and everything inside her would pour out all over his floor. That the rich blood would flow again, thick and red. She wouldn't be able to stop it now that she was no longer protected by the safety of the acorn. She covered her face in her hands, rocking backwards and forwards in a desperate effort to put everything back into the container, frantically trying to retain the skin that she had spread around her unreality. And those within attempted to spread the message that Rebecca cannot be buried alive.

"What's happening?"

If she had looked she would have seen that the therapist's eyes were confused and his heart was soft. But she rocked, aided by a low moaning sound to cast out all that can be felt and all that can be seen.

He waited. Gradually the room returned and she felt her skin again.

"Would you like to tell me what happened?" he said.

She glared at him. She searched for solace but none appeared.

"You've taken away our safety and you're burying Rebecca. Do you understand!"

Her eyes escaped into some vacant recess of her mind, anger dissipating but terror remaining. He leaned forward, hands extended. She turned away.

"You've taken away our magic and left us without a voice."

From that day, the music that had poured from us, stopped, only beginning to just trickle through again over twenty years later.

We found a new therapist. One who lives comfortably within herself and who has very strong and healthy boundaries. Tidy but welcoming, Libby's therapy room begins with a bell, such a refreshingly loud and joyful sound of summons and while I wait I take in the waratahs next door and the jasmine that grows in abundance along the side fence. The door opens, a smile is given in greeting, and if it's raining a towel is produced to wipe the soles of shoes before entering into the room on the south side of the house. Three chairs stand empty. Two for the counseled, one for the counselor. Cushions adorn the floor, bookshelves hug the wall and I can see the branches of the macadamia tree in her large garden and the spreading boughs of the liquid amber next door. A tray stands on one shelf, glasses and a water jug covered with lace doily fringed by beaded janglings for thirsty souls. Simple and homely, this room was my refuge for seventeen years.

Each visit melted into the next and as trust grew we discovered all the hidden parts of me as they came to tell and relive their stories. She shared their hopes, their thoughts, despair and terror and their moments of joy as one by one they emerged, wrapped in the knowledge that she would hear them, see them and without judgment or doubt, believe them. Over these years she worked with us, gradually bringing my fragmented self into a more contained space. She never questioned that this was my reality and an essential part of my survival. She's walked with me through the halls and corridors of our castle, carried the lantern as we went down into the dungeons and caves, holding my hand and encouraging me forwards. I only have to mention a room or a staircase and she knows exactly where I am or where I'm heading.

Gradually, as this therapy begins to open us, memories are experienced and feelings remembered as the tight casing of each of our different parts is slowly opened and the subterranean worlds of the amazing unconscious mind seeps into awareness. Such is the case with my *castle*, a physical representation of one of the safe places created in my mind when I was a child. Over the years it has become very real to me, Rhonda, as they have opened and shown me their world.

I love the banquet hall, the gathering place that's warmed by a large log fire, always tended, burning continuously. Two lounge chairs yawn in front of it and an old rag mat sits by the hearth. Here, we eat, talk, have meetings, the children often sitting on cushions, listening to stories read to them by the seven **Elderly People.** Around its edges the overhang of the galleries above creates a shadowy space for those not yet ready to join in. As time moved on and co-operation developed, notice boards were put up to give the news of any meetings, to warn of danger and to allow space for questions. They tell me that when I, Rhonda, was young, they lived, each separately, in the dungeons of the castle, **Bethany** being the only one free to roam its rooms and the moors. She thought she was alone, but now most of these parts have emerged from the darkness and are free to move anywhere they choose.

In the centre of this hall are a large table and many chairs. A meeting place.

A solid stone staircase leads upwards in a spiral to several levels of unfurnished rooms with heavy metal locks. These rooms are used to contain those inner parts who seek to destroy us. Inner persecutors like **The Him**, an internalized version of the steely eyed, psychotic father. I was frightened of The Him at first, but he told his story to Libby, eventually coming out from the past and into the present.

On the next level up is the children's playroom. It's rather sparse, but from here you can see out to the moors and hear the songs of the sea. Often, in times of awful memories the children are taken to this room and looked after by the **Elderly People**.

Back on ground level, initially closed off by huge gates, a ramp leads down from the banquet room, past the catacombs and into the dungeons and caves below the castle. One day, well into this therapy, I became aware of a whole third level of alters standing a short distance beyond the gates. They looked like a ghostly crowd but somehow filled with creativity, waiting to be released. The gates were metal and we could see through them but they were locked and we never went down there. Not until we were ready. Libby frightened us once when she said that we were tying up loose ends. The first therapist had said "the work is done," but it wasn't, it was just beginning. We thought that if Libby shut the trapdoor as he had, nobody would ever walk down the next level of stairs and we would once more be buried alive. But she didn't and now, many years later, the gates have gone and all the ghosts have fled.

The behaviour of each of my parents was unpredictable. To use either of them as a mirror made no sense and, coupled with the father's violence and insanity, made for a dangerous reflection. If I was to develop as a human being it was imperative that we find another way.

So in order to not see my Self as a mirror of this pathology, we turned the mirror around, with its opaque surface facing the outside or real world, and its reflective surface facing inwards, to our created world. We made a mirror of our created worlds. A safe and separate but hidden reality. We reflected the images of self that were safe and the opaque surface would not allow any of the physical or emotional trauma from the father or the mother to be reflected inwards. We could also choose which experiences of the world outside the home and the family that we would bring into our space behind the mirror, thus providing us with a safe and sane reflection so essential to human growth. Prince, my dog was a major part of that healthy, caring reflection.

Because of the behaviour and events within the home, I didn't develop the solid boundaries so necessary to life and had to learn about this through therapy. To know where I stopped and others began. For me, this took many years, as memories surfaced, often filling me with terror but at the same time breaking down the boundaries that kept us stuck in the past. As this progressed safely, the symbiosis very, very gradually faded until I finally became a separate person. Separate from my mother, my brother and my sister. Even separate from Prince. As this advanced, my boundaries grew and are now strong and well defined.

However, the symbiosis with my father remained like a well constructed prison wall.

No matter how clearly my rational self sees and fully understands and believes that he and I are separate, somewhere deep within me this is neither understood nor accepted. He has been gone for forty-five years and yet I struggle every day to completely free myself from him. Mostly, I no longer live in terror of him but it's as though he is constantly within me, with ultimate control.

When one lives within a fully created reality then it has to be a whole, complete and many faceted world, contained within itself. Therefore the outside world (the circle reality,) was fully seen only through the eyes of **Lucy,** who brought this world and its way of being back to those on the turned around side of the mirror. Everything that we had created was also reflected back to us. What we were looking into was, in terms of normality, unreal. The real was in my home, on the other side of the mirror. We couldn't see it and that was a major part of our safety. What we saw in the mirror is what we believed we were and what we believed was the world. However, even behind the mirror, in our own reflected world, we were each tightly contained, with no knowledge of each other. That is until the host, Rhonda, began to look into this mirror turned backwards and one by one we became co-conscious and began to tell our stories.

When **Rebecca** held the hands of the first therapist she began very slowly to uncoil. With Libby she began very slowly to see her reflection in the turned around mirror. She began to see her life force. Our life force.

"Can you see, Libby?" She was able to watch the gradual birth of her own existence, without being a mirror of anyone else. She looked at her Self, the Self in the mirror and she followed what that Self did. When the mirror was smiling she knew that she was smiling. When the mirror was crying, she knew that she was crying. When the mirror was singing and the hands in the mirror were dancing, she knew that she was safe.

> Is there life behind the mirror
> Is there colour in her eyes
> Or does the shadow of her narrowed soul
> Cover all potential life with emptiness?
> Or, just maybe
> She's unique coloured by isolation?
> Can she see through eyes with original vision?
> To speak and to think with a strength gained
> through survival.
> Perhaps it was the no connection with those
> marked in pathology
> That, instead of preventing her from living
> Actually kept her potential alive?
> **Rhonda** 2005

MAGNITUDE

He is kind and wise and he is our guide, leading us safely in the direction of wholeness, always aware of the Self that shines with a rose coloured glow, waiting to be reunited with us. I love **Magnitude,** with his bright eyes and flowing words of silk.

The session complete, I walked to the door of Libby's therapy room and looked out. No-one was there, but Magnitude's imprint remained, felt yet unseen amidst the smell of the marigolds in a pot at the entrance.

"Touch her," he says. I reach out my hand but she's gone. I know that it's my Self who moves just beyond my touch and my vision. I find myself talking to the imprint.

"Why can I not contact her?"

"You are not ready for your Self," says Magnitude in a voice so loud that the castle walls tremble.

"How can I touch her?" I ask.

"You must trust that the time is approaching. The process is progressing within you but the remaining particles of information cannot yet be divulged. There are many more pieces to discover and the puzzle cannot yet be put together as one whole.

Spread your words upon the ground. Utterances, strewn like confetti upon the grass to be gathered up by the rain and washed away into tomorrow. Yesterday is here now, floating like an invisible force over and around your world. It will not leave us until you can see the sorrow, understand its deep, deep silence and feel its pain that throbs eternally.

Be still, be silent. Connect with the forces around you. You do not learn solitude but within the energy of life, rocked gently in the cradle of love. Do not fear the sorrow or the pain for they are here to help you. Hold out your hand to them. Step up onto the threshold and they will guide you through the door.

You will not find roses and sweet music but your voice will sing their sounds and you will feel their energy swirling through your body.

Be still and let them be. They will not harm you. But you will find your soul and the fire will once again burn with brightness and warmth. Do this in the garden of reality for it's there, and only there that you will know this gift. For indeed, that's what the sorrow and pain is. A gift to your soul. The time is now. Make the connection and you will be free.

Believe that you only have to ask and if the time is right I will return. Be at peace with the trees and the wind will call your name. Listen."

CHAPTER 3

Dear Matt

I don't quite know how to start writing to you. So many issues, thoughts and feelings, some good, some conflicting. You were mother's favourite person and it was through your pervasive intellect that she believed her salvation would come, to lift her out of the ordinary, to be someone. Her intelligence was never acknowledged, but you came along and here was her chance for everyone to see that she wasn't just a nobody. She had a clever son, a mirror of her own veiled potential.

You were a good looking young man with an engineering degree and a shiny MGA. "I'll teach you to drive," you said, so into your shiny red sports car I climbed. The wind blew in my face, you smiled, and I let go of all fear of learning and felt like royalty.

"Watch everything and everywhere around you." Such a good teacher of driving.

You were one of the Quiz Kids. We were so proud of you as we bundled around the radio, holding our breath when your turn came, releasing a unison sigh when you got it right.

Do you remember your old Alvis? 1927 stately four-seater, open to the sky, with large curved fenders and wide running boards. The radiator was polished brass, with the Alvis badge standing proudly on top. You restored it Matt and the whole family, even Dad, went for rides, sitting up waving to onlookers, Mum's head held high.

The brake and the clutch were on each side, the accelerator in the middle and when you let me have a drive, we were almost home when I missed the brake, trod on the accelerator and we went hurtling down to the creek, landing in a pile against the railing at the bottom of the road. I felt awful. Something tugged away at you and you seemed unable to rescue it and bring it home, so there it stayed, rusting away. I felt so sad for you Matt and your beautiful shining car. I don't remember its fate, but one day it just wasn't there any more.

You were popular with the girls, and when you attained your engineering degree I think even Dad was proud. Your life seemed to float along and Mum held you up in the brightness of the sun, creating a vast shadow in which Kate and I existed.

But this created its own problems. Expectations that you strove so hard to satisfy. An arrogance, almost an omnipotence that you actually stood firmly in the shoes of. You were the man of her life and you could do it all. But you couldn't. Too much violence. Too much trauma trapped in the hidden levels of your existence.

It began to surface, to create uncertainty, fear. Terror. You began to fall apart and your fear of our father surfaced. He who beat you senseless when you tried to protect me. He who hated your position in his wife's life. Respected. She had no respect for him. He was uneducated because he left school when he was 13 to look after his family. You became the bouncing ball between her and him, the yardstick of acceptance through education. Him at the bottom, you at the top.

You saved my life, Matthew, and I am grateful. You saved Mum's too, as did I. You were forced to stand back and witness it all happening to me and often, when it was all over, to pick up the pieces. She gave you a key to your room and you could lock yourself in and him out. I was never allowed to have a key and my room was at all times open and accessible to our father's insanity.

I am grateful for the endless times you tried to fight him, always ending up on the floor, dragging yourself into your room and locking the door. You had no choice Matt. He was a tall, strong man and he would have killed you if you'd kept on. You are not a coward and you did all you could.

You apologised a few years ago for the maths lessons you gave me. Thank you. It was early secondary school and I had to prove that I was capable of keeping up at a selective high school so mother sent me into your room for coaching. I was quite good at maths before you injected fear into the equation and your behaviour has had a long-term effect on me. I began to understand this after a session with Libby, which started off as she tried to help me to look at money and numbers, without me disappearing in a giant wave of panic.

"You're not understanding!" I shouted at Libby. "I can't think and do figures at the same time! I can't stand it when it's just in somebody's head! I've got to write it down! I try so hard to grab anything that I can hold onto, but there isn't anything. As though I don't have senses and I have no brain. It's all in someone else's head!"

Libby remained wonderfully calm. "Where does this come from, do you think?"

"Maths lessons in Matthew's room. It was like a ceremony. I had to wait until I was told he was ready, sitting in the same chair each time, sometimes for ages, not allowed to talk or move while he did other work. He's so clever. I showed you the maths he did when I asked him to describe the relationship between **the diamond, the square, the triangle and the circle**! So when I brought him my year seven problems he took them and created sheets and sheets of complex maths out of them. And then he yelled at me because I didn't understand it. And he'd never let me have a pencil. I had to just sit there. I could not write anything! And sometimes I knew what he was talking about. Sometimes I knew! I had to keep my mouth shut. I had no power. No control."

So I was grateful for your apology Matthew. It was a validation of a concrete reality. It really happened, and it was not your fault. You were surviving the violence in your own way, the only way you knew how.

I want you to hear that something wonderful came from these lessons. As my system did with many things, we used maths in our own way, taking these geometric shapes from the outside world, and adapted them to a different reality with rules, at a survival level and all of my creation.

Our world was unpredictable on all levels. That was the constant, and to counteract this unpredictability, **Ruth** was initially the one who tried to understand the father's behaviour by breaking down her boundaries and moving into his states of madness. When this almost pushed her over the edge she split off further and created **Mary.**

At this point Libby interrupted. "Normally it would be the opposite way round. It would encompass the whole person. But this is not what happened with you. Instead, it's gone the other way with Ruth splitting and giving the intense madness to Mary."

"It makes such perfect sense to me" I cried. "We split off into bits and created parts to cover every situation."

Libby continued: "Which only goes to prove that Mary needs to be thanked. She's a very complex character but she had to be. And you see the other scenario for people like me who are singletons would have been that I would have gone crazy."

So, through Mary, and using geometric shapes as symbols, we constructed our own solid world. She knew that the sun, the moon and the planets all move in continuous and predictable patterns. A very safe model, especially as it was part of the natural world that we trusted. So she created internal geometrical shapes which became our world of continuity. Each shape is constant and has a connection with the others. They are visual. I can draw them and see them in my mind. Each is a vessel that would contain elements of life, both good and bad. They became the template of a subterranean **Master Plan**, fully formed in every intricate detail in order to maintain my sanity.

The first shape to emerge into my consciousness was the **Diamond**, an important part of our system that allowed Mary, and therefore us, to remain connected with the father even through his violent insanity. I guess some would find it difficult to understand why I would want to be connected to this madness, but such is the pathology that trauma creates.

You Matt, and Kate were each too busy surviving, Mum was incapable of connection with me or with Kate, and Prince was in my life only from about six to about fourteen. It was essential to my survival that, as a child, I remain connected with someone, and Dad in his sane and sober times loved animals, loved music and smiled. It was imperative that I kept that thread of connection to him unbroken at all times.

And **The Diamond** has four equal sides that create boundaries to contain the movement towards and away from the madness. From every point everything can be seen in all directions.

I created an internal pathway in order to help me cope with Dad's insanity and a part strong enough to tread that path. This was **Mary** and, as already stated, it was her mission to connect with the father. Since our work with Libby started, many parts of me have talked about her. Snippets of information from here, from there that gradually surfaced and over several years have provided a complete picture. For a long time many other parts thought she was mad and were afraid of her. She's not, of course. She's the only one who saw and understood both the reality of **the circle** (the outside world) and of **the square** (life in the house in Hope Street).

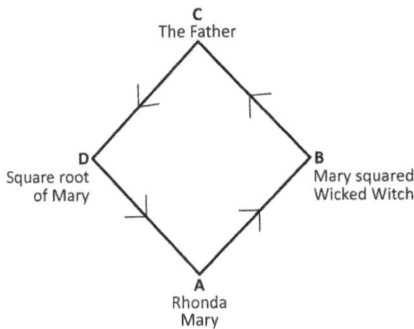

C
The Father

D
Square root
of Mary

B
Mary squared
Wicked Witch

A
Rhonda
Mary

In preparation for retaining the essential connection with our father, during times of terror, **Mary** had to let go of a considerable amount of control while still retaining her sanity. Something squared is multiplied by itself, so to do this she become 'more.' She became **Mary Squared.**

The law of the diamond must be obeyed, so it's imperative that we maintain careful watch at all times. Heightened vigilance. **Vigil** never sleeps and his eyes remain wide open, ready. He sounds the alarm and within mini seconds **Mary** springs into action. She can move along the first side of the diamond, anticlockwise from point A to point C. On the way, she goes through point B and becomes **M2 (Mary squared)** and in so doing becomes expanded enough to safely experience the father's insanity while at the same time remaining sane and maintaining her connection with him. This track is one way. There is no going back or changing direction once Mary has become Mary Squared. When the danger has passed she moves from point C, passing through point D where she becomes **The Square root of Mary**, thus ridding herself of the father's insanity, and returning to herself, moving finally back to point A.

Next is the **Circle**. This is **Lucy's** world, the reality that existed outside the house and the family. **The Master Planner** knew that we lived in two very different realities, each represented and contained in my mind, within its own geometrical shape. He also knew that the two must never come together. That was one of the decrees. The reality that everyone outside my house and family knew is in the Circle. It contains the behaviours and actions of the outside world and it's what the outside world saw of me. Like a pretend person.

Lucy was created to live in that world and **Bronwyn**, her twin, was her balance in the world of the square.

The Circle reality is the 'what is.' There was a team of us trained by **The Co-ordinator** to perform exactly as s/he was told to, for it was imperative that I give no hint of what was happening at home. I went to school, played with my friends in the street, went to the occasional birthday party, but the outside reality of the Circle did not exist within the framework of our house. I could not copy anything from there as I would be very different and it would also give away the secret of all that was happening in number thirty-nine Hope Street. And I achieved it. They all thought I was fine, a little timid maybe, or later rebellious and promiscuous, but otherwise 'normal.'

The partner of the Circle was **the Square**, witnessed only by the family and filled with terror, rape and insanity. It's the reason for the 'created what is'. A container of fear and secrecy that became the shape that defied memory. A freezer into which any part of me could put any section of a memory that s/he could not cope with. It contained all the things that could not be spoken of and in a young child's mind, therefore did not exist. Another device for maintaining our sanity by helping each child or teenage part of me to cope and also by making sure that Rhonda, the host, never knew anything of this reality.

It was guarded zealously by **the Keeper of the Square** who made sure that nothing was ever seen or taken out. Early in therapy **Stones** said that 'if we touched the square then our fire would go out'. In other words, the silence would be broken. That was a decree, but as the memories have moved one by one into Rhonda's consciousness, the square, through many hours of working with Libby, has gradually emptied and become transparent. The **Keeper of the Square** now without a job, has become integrated into the whole and our fire burns brightly.

Although not geometric shapes, **the Spirit of the Fire** and **the Embers** are still important elements. Like the shapes, they are symbolic. The Fire must never go out, the Spirit of the Fire will see to that. She must keep the embers alive at all costs as the Fire is there to thaw our soul when it finally comes in from its isolated and icy world. **Ruth** has said that 'we must never put the Square, The Diamond and the Spirit of the Fire together because if we do then we will never reach infinity.' This will make sense when you read about the **triangular prism.**

There was good and there was bad. Safety and terror. And then there was remembered good and that's what the **Pyramid** is. Ancient, remembered truth. So the pyramid keeps alive all that is the truth within us. It is filled with a light that permeates all doubts and a gentle sound that connects us with the vibrations of the earth and the music of the clouds.

The simplicity of the **equilateral triangle** was its appeal with its equal sides and properties that don't change, no matter how you present it.

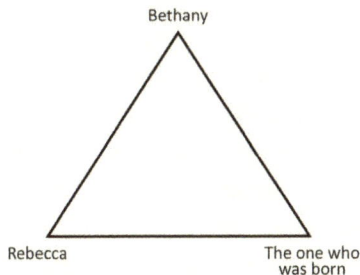

On one corner is **Rebecca**, in the deep, deep silence below the castle. On the apex of the triangle is **Bethany,** alone in the turret at the very top of the castle. On the third point is **The One Who Was Born,** waiting for the time when she can be seen, watched over by the Purple Emu and kept safe in the icy glow of a rose pink aura.

I've talked about my Multiplicity to you, Matthew. You seemed to understand.

For a long time, in all the drawings I did there was always a **rectangle** at the bottom of the page. I never wanted to look at it but one day it came uninvited into my consciousness, growing finally into a **rectangular prism**. A gruesome coffin. There was blood and weaponry and something tied up in a hessian bag. The image stayed with me like a giant picture on a movie screen. I couldn't shut the lid or remove it from my mind until I had dealt with it and it finally became one more piece of the terror filed into the archives.

It was a poem that began this memory, coming from someone in here, I don't know who, several months before.

> Why did the emu go away
> I oh so badly wanted to play?
> He went away because he saw
> The bright red blood upon the floor
> And when will he come back to stay?
> When the dead, dead baby's gone away.

It made no sense until several months later when the memory emerged.

Emma feels heavy, ugly, her stomach with an energy of its own. It's not large, barely showing but it feels like a sail filled with a gentle wind. 'What's happening to me?' she thinks as her hand moves slowly across her belly.

She has become used to being raped and yet is naïve and innocent. Ignorant. Alone, and frightened of this horrible secret. No blood for nearly four months. 'What if there's a baby!' she chants like a mantra, over and over hoping someone who knows will answer.

The clock ticks loudly, the moonlight pierces the white transparent curtains and settles on her dressing table. It's black. All her furniture is. She'd painted it with a tin of blackboard paint. She hears a crashing sound and hides under the blanket as he thunders into her room with filthy language that turns her hopes to sawdust. She makes a dash for the door, pushing him sideways. Down the hall, through the kitchen. Where to hide! He turns on the light. He is 'steel eyes,' cold and cruel. He grabs her. She struggles but he is too strong when he has these eyes. Nothing penetrates this being made of steel, but she knows what to do.

Emma remains silent as she's half dragged, half carried to the garage. The door is pulled shut. He lets her go, moving up to the bench, taking a chisel from the pegboard and whittling the table leg. The moonlight softens her as she begins to hope. Suddenly he turns, hurling the metal tool in her direction. She ducks down as it whirls past her and clanks onto the concrete floor. The mother is out at a meeting and the garage is empty, there is nowhere to hide. Her heart hopes for a miracle that will take the steel from his eyes.

"You filthy whore!"

But those are her mother's words. Please, please don't make them come from him!

"It's your filthy white puss!" The words are out before Emma can listen to her mind. The mind that knows the decree of silence in the presence of the steel eyes.

He moves towards her, his face distorted with rage as he lifts his leg and thrusts it into her belly. Emma vanishes as Genesis is thrust forward, doubled up.

"Stand up you filthy coward!"

Again he kicks. She falls. But he keeps kicking, each thrust aimed at her pregnant belly. Then he's gone, his heavy footsteps fading as he leaves the garage.

The pain defies the silence. Something is coming out of her. She looks, staring unfocused at the threads of moonlight on the greasy floor. The bolts of language begin to fade. Further, further until they are gone.

She feels down between her legs. Screams. But then she waits. Nothing more but confusion. The baby has come out of her and Genesis has done her job. She lies down on the concrete floor, her head resting on her arm. Genesis can sleep now.

Bronwyn, always ready, stares at the river of bright, red blood. Then she stands, her need to take care of the practicalities, dominant. But the thick thread and the tiny space person follow her. She grabs the spade that's standing in the rusty drum near her and lifts it high, bringing it down hard. Then again, and again until the cord is severed. She grabs some hessian bags, mopping, mopping, but still more flows.

Suddenly there's a noise, but she must keep mopping or Genesis will die. The garage door slowly opens and her brother Matt stands in the moonlight. He can't speak, but comes over to her, his face distorted as tears fall from his horrified eyes, then takes the shovel from her hands and gently holds her. Bronwyn disappears leaving Genesis lying limply in Matt's arms. She hears her brother's voice permeating her mind, then nothing.

But somehow I survived, thanks to you Matt. I never knew what you did with that tiny being. I named him Paul and Libby and I had a burial ceremony for him in the garden where I now live. He's at peace and I have done my grieving.

I often find my system amazing, even down to fine details. After this event the **Master Planner** created a part called the **Virgin of the Sepulchre** who, when trust had been built, came to talk to Libby. I didn't even know what a sepulchre was, until I looked it up and found it to be a tomb, a burial vault built out of stone or cut into the rock. And her job? To take care of the dead, miscarried babies. She was really the **Angel of Death** but the children in here were protected from these deaths and horrible things so she became the **Virgin of the Sepulchre**.

That was in 1959, and several months later our mother went away on her Women's Weekly 'Round the World Tour'. She was gone for six months. Do you remember? She left us a picture of herself on the mantelpiece. Oh, and she left us a maniac. The picture was a full head portrait with her head thrown back and her facial expression distant, disconnected and pasted with the necessary smile. I was fifteen, Kate was twenty-one and you were twenty-five.

I wish I could know what will happen ahead
I'd know when to be happy
Or ready to be dead.

Emma 1994

You function mostly from your left brain Matt. I had to use both left and right equally and to always be sure that they were separate.

"The left and right brain must never be joined!"

Libby moved forward in her seat. "Because---?"

"Because he was sane and insane and if we let the two halves of him come together the insanity would control everything. And it's the same with her."

"You mean your mother?"

"Yes. There was the one who encouraged and paid for me to have piano lessons and in her own way, who cared. Then there was the cruel one who didn't protect me and turned on me without any warning. But it's not as black and white as him and her. It took quite a few years for **Lucy** to begin to understand and internalise the outside world and when I was very young and within the square, life was closed and isolated. As a kid I created an image in here of what I saw and understood about each of them with little influence from the outside world. I had to re-create my own understanding of their minds, inside my own. To keep my sanity I had to believe that I had at least some control in retaining connection with my father and of at least sometimes being able to predict what they were going to do or be like."

"Aren't there two sides of the river in your jigsaw puzzle?"

"Yes. Yes! One side was for the children and the **Fantasy Parents** and every part of me that is sane and safe and the other is for **The**

Him and **The Terror** and all the parts of me that are angry and cruel."

"And **the Jostler**?"

"Oh Yes. The Jostler and the **Good Fairy Mother**. They live on a raft on the river that divides them, making sure that no-one crosses over to the other side. The river is the corpus callosum that divides the right and left sides of the brain.

And then there's the drawing of my parents, joined at the head. It's the most powerful decree of our system and one that will take a long time to change."

"What about **The divided rectangle**. Where does that fit in?"

I'm the line down the centre that creates the two equal shapes but it also separates these two triangles which represent my mother and my father. Libby understood.

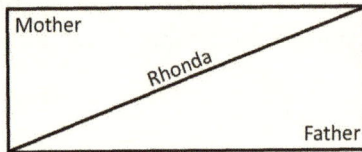

"If you remain invisible and don't have a Self, you can stay as a divider between both parents and nobody gets killed?"

"Yes. Because then there is sanity and some caring to balance over the insanity and cruel words. And if I'm nothing and nobody, and invisible with no Self then nobody dies."

"So if you had a Self you would then be visible?"

"Yes."

You see how complex it was to stay alive, Matt? But it's because of the sun and the moon and the planets in the night sky that I was able to create a whole visual and factual group of symbols that made sense to me and into which I could put all the fear and the things that made no sense at all. But you would understand that. You love maths.

I guess you can empathise, but sometimes I think I'm going a bit mad with some of the ways of coping that we have in here. Libby gives us a free space to follow the thoughts and feelings and when we do, we learn about them and finally the logic behind them. And they always make so much sense. Like one of the other decrees in here that says that the head and the body must never be joined. Sounds crazy? But it's not.

For years my left foot seemed to tap involuntarily, especially when intense anxiety sprang up. I saw it, I became aware that it was happening, I stopped it. The anxiety increased. Again, the foot started tapping and on it went. But we discovered why.

"The head must always be disconnected from the body!"

"Is that the decree?" Libby asked.

"Yes. And my foot tapping is like my heart beat."

"Is that to make sure you're still alive?"

"Yes! The head knows because it can see, but it doesn't know if the body is still alive. So when the foot is beating we all know that we're still alive."

"Are the head and body joined now," asked Libby "No! They must never be joined," someone yelled at her. "If my head joined to my body then he could chop it off!"

"So you disengaged it before he could do that?

"Yes.

"Have a look. Is your head on your body now?"

I nodded.

It took a while Matt, for me to believe that I was sitting, many years later, as an adult, with my head fully connected to my body and to understand that he was never going to attack me again.

So many years, so much baggage carried and finally disposed of, and too much happened for us to have enjoyed the regular brother-sister relationship that I see my friends experiencing, but it is always with a deep love that I think of you.

CHAPTER 4

Hello Kate

Do you remember the gypsies who camped in the field behind the little stone library? I loved them, they were so alive and when they were there I never made it across the field to Sunday school. It was your job to take me with you, but the gypsies sang songs and told stories and had lots of dogs. Stories so much better than the boring ones in the church hall. So you'd shrug your shoulders and leave me there, dragging me away when it was time to go home, sworn to secrecy.

You looked after me, Kate. "I didn't have the time," Mum said to me once, when I had my own children. And you got the job. You took me to kindergarten and stayed until I stopped crying and when I started school, you sat with me until I could wave goodbye to you. And you were often there to pick up the pieces, especially as I snuggled into your warmth when we inherited the double bed. You must have been struggling so hard in your own way to survive it all, and yet you had time for me. Thank you.

We both loved Mum's brother Uncle Bob. Tall and strong with just a hint of uncertainty. Times were hard just after the war but he took us all in, converting the back half of his semi in Cremorne to a flat. You called me Bub, he called me Scallywag and I felt special.

And the ballet lessons. They started when I was three, you always ahead, me running along behind, carrying my precious ballet shoes with the shiny pink ribbons and the leathery smell of the shop in the city. I leapt and pliéd, my feet turned out and graceful arms that moved with joy to the music.

Each year Mosman Town Hall was decked out in streamers, the seats filled with people, the air buzzing with excitement as the annual concert was about to begin. The sounds of the Can-Can, the opening curtains and there I was, up on stage dancing on a hatbox. I can still feel the happiness. I won the junior medal that year, silver, with a pair of ballet shoes in the middle and my name on the back. I still have it.

I have no memory of actually moving to Hope Street. You were eleven, Matt was fourteen and I was four. It must have been good having more space but I guess we missed Uncle Bob. We shared a room, you and I. Your bed was under the window that looked out to the street and the front garden and you'd rouse on me for standing on it. If I stood on my bed I could see across the paling fence to Kelly's place. They had such fun in there, Mrs. Kelly in her rollers and slippers, a cigarette in her mouth, Mr. Kelly with his overalls covered in paint and his always red cheeks, but lots of people and heaps of laughter.

When Matt left home Mum moved Dad into the spare room, swapped our beds with theirs and we got the double. I had you to cuddle up to and I loved it. One night the smell of smoke woke us up. Dad was on fire. I ran to the laundry, grabbed a bucket, filled it with water and tossed it all over him. The fire went out and I don't remember him ever smoking in bed again. Some time later I had a dream that flames were engulfing you so I rushed in to save you, repeating the bucket performance and tipping water all over you. You were so cross.

To walk on your feet up the hallway from the kitchen to our room was a highlight of my young life. I'd plead and plead until finally you gave in and stood still while I arranged first my right foot carefully across your left, then holding tightly onto your hands, my left foot across your right. Then off we'd go, you walking each leg deliberately forward and me trying to help by keeping the contact with your feet but making each one feel lighter as you lifted and stepped. I went backwards, you walked forwards and nothing could ever happen to me when I was with you, walking up the hallway.

One day when we got back from taking Prince for a walk, Dad was sitting on one of the dining chairs, his arms resting on the table, testicles thankfully tucked safely out of sight.

"How about some music," he said to us both.

You walked away, but I sat down on the piano stool and played. He started humming and a few bars later I heard your voice coming from the bedroom. No words, just a melody line rich and sensuous, delivered by your beautiful voice.

"I was frightened of him, Bub," you told me years later. I guess that's why you ignored him. Your voice was so beautiful that it filled all my shivery spaces and no concert pianist could ever have felt better than I did in those moments of connection.

You were the middle child, the one who became almost numb, with a carefully constructed cage around you to protect you and to prevent connection. Sometimes we played duets on the piano and the laughter crossed through the barrier and even Mum tapped her feet and smiled.

"Kate's been chosen to sing 'Oh My Beloved Father' by Puccini at the Combined Choral Concerts in the Town Hall." I could have burst with the feelings inside me that night, so proud and happy for you and to see Mum, her head held high. You sounded like an angel and I felt so much love for you. The head of Vocal Studies at the Sydney Conservatorium was there.

"I would like to teach your daughter," she said to Mum. So you had lessons with her for several years but ran away when she told you that she wanted you to study full time and pursue the career on the world stage that she knew you could have.

When you sang at my wedding, your daughter, then about two and a half, stood in the aisle of the church, pointing at you and telling everyone "That's my Mummy!" But recently I was telling your younger daughter about your amazing voice and talent and she looked puzzled: "I didn't even know that Mum could sing." It stuck in my throat.

I think you were in year six when I started at Seaforth Public School Kate. I liked school at first and **Lucy** was good at fitting in. She especially loved the singing in sol fah with Miss Moore in the portable classroom half way down the playground. She made music come alive and saved us many times from the formidable power and anger of the tyrant, Mrs. Erington, the arithmetically obsessed Headmistress.

"Times tables books on your desks, girls. We're having a maths lesson." Then she'd smile and wink and give us the note she'd chosen to begin the song. That was the sign for the girls near the windows to keep a lookout for Mrs. Erington and to all raise their right hand when they saw her.

Immediately the voices began singing in sol-fah: ti doh re me------the beautiful opening strain of 'Danny Boy' wafting through the room. Half way through the second verse the windows erupted with hands and the singing switched to the playground chanting of the nine times table as Mrs. Erington swept into the room.

"I heard you singing!"

She moved around the room, her academic gown flowing behind her, prodding each girl with her bony finger.

"Were you singing!"

"No, Mrs. Erington. We were chanting Mrs. Erington." A momentary unison interruption to our continued nine times tables that began again with gusto.

I had always been a good student and lots of 'excellent' stamps. But suddenly, just before school returned for final year at Primary school, everything changed.

"Hurry up and get dressed and we'll go and get your uniform for your new school," my mother had said.

"What new school?"

"I've booked you in as a boarder at S.C.E.G.G.S at Moss Vale and you'll be starting in two weeks."

I didn't understand how I could be the cause of my mother's money problems and suddenly be offered a journey to an expensive school. I remained silent, spreading the questions through my skin, to be carried into the ear of the wind next time it passed.

Mum, Dad and I drove from Sydney to Moss Vale in that little green Austin A40. As we entered the large gates of the school I thought my heart would jump out and run away but **Lucy** emerged as we drove up the tree-lined drive to the administration block.

The headmistress sat purposefully behind a large desk. "Let me see. Rhonda Small, you're in Howard House, she said, pointing. It's that building over to your right at the end of the western wing."

Mum crossed her legs in the correct position of royalty and leaned forward.

"Howard House! How fortunate. That's her father's name you know," she said looking at her husband over the top of her glasses.

But I looked towards the end of the small fat pointed finger and tried to imagine what life would produce for me in this large white prison.

"I suppose you've read all the information Mrs. Small. Visiting days are every fourth Saturday and there is one weekend home leave per term."

"Oh, she won't be coming home during term time," she said with an air of finality.

The fat face continued: "She will have a locker in which to keep a few extra goodies but we don't believe in spoiling the girls."

Mum took my hand and Dad, dressed carefully for the occasion, followed silently as we were ushered out of the room with the enormous desk. Corridors led into more corridors and I wondered how I would ever be able to find my way back to earth.

"Goodbye dear, we have to get back home before dark."

She left in a flourish of mumbled reassurances of promised letters and sounds that said that things would be fine. My father winked, hugged me and followed. I didn't believe her. How could things be fine? I didn't even know why I was there.

"Did I do something really wrong? Is that why they've sent me away?" No-one answered. Suddenly one day my mother had announced that I was going to boarding school and two weeks later here I was. The dormitory was long with dark polished floors. The windows overlooked the garden and the curtains flapped in the ice- laden breeze. The beds were in rows down each side with a small table beside each one. A place in which to hide my fear. Small but close.

"These are some of your roommates."

She was a matronly woman, dumpy with a large nose and very red cheeks. 'Maybe I'll end up with cheeks like that' I thought. She said the names one after the other, but I could barely remember my own name let alone theirs. A bell rang. Somebody took my hand.

"Come on, it's time for assembly."

I followed her into a large hall, filled with a forced hush where we sat down just in time to stand up again as down the aisle like a flowing female vision of Batman, came the Headmistress, the one with the formidable fat finger. I would have laughed had I not been so close to tears.

I gradually settled into this life as **Lucy** watched and copied. I loved the monkey bars and the piano teacher who thought I was talented and every time I practiced there were girls standing at the door watching. The monkey bars were some distance from the main building, at the beginning of a beautiful avenue of large, noble pine trees. Not many girls used them but for me they provided a space for our other world.

One in which I could be alone without any threat of harm and where Lucy could rest, with no need to watch or to copy.

My mother wrote regularly. Letters filled with information about this and that, but with little connection. Every visitor's day she arrived in her little green car, picnic packed and self hidden, but it was always good to see her.

As the year progressed my longing to be with Prince and my deep concern for him became unbearable. Even though my father really loved him, his insanity and violence were so unpredictable that I was fearful for Prince's safety, a thought I couldn't bear. From such a distance I could do nothing so I hid the fear, played on the monkey bars and got lost in music. I only stayed at Moss Vale for a year. The asthma got so bad that Mum decided to bring me home.

It was fun on the monkey bars and someone had seen my music, my English was good and I spoke with quite a passable French accent, but when I returned to Seaforth Public school just in time for the yearly exams my maths was way behind and different history topics had been studied.

So I was to be sent to Mosman Home Science School, a place for the dummies. No Latin or poetry would pass through my brain. No Thomas Hardy to excite me with stories and scenes of distant lives.

This was too much for my mother, who fought gallantly on my behalf until the powers relinquished and I was sent on probation to Cremorne Girls, a selective secondary school where I was put in the lowest class. I have always been very grateful to my mother for that. She stood up for me and gave me a chance. I worked hard, came second in the year in the first maths test and so was elevated to class 1B.

You'd left Cremorne by the time I arrived there but your reputation as an amazing and beautiful singer remained. I loved the choir and the madrigal group and for the first three years did quite well at school. After the disaster of Ingrid Yorkisson, the Danish girl who came to stay in my first year, I found a wonderful friend, Beverlie. We were fine against the world, and fifty years later we still keep in touch. I won heaps at athletics carnivals and was in the A grade netball team. It's amazing how sporting ability can bring acceptance.

As the years went on, the trauma at home became worse and I guess we spent most of our energy surviving. My behaviour was disruptive and

I didn't really care about much except Music, French and Modern History. I had a new group of friends by then as Bev had already left school.

The Principal didn't appreciate our uniqueness. Sitting on the bench outside the music room we looked up and there she was, in full flight down the path towards us. From a distance she looked like an allegorical figure sent to snatch us up, her academic gown spread out the back like a satanic wedding veil as she bore down on us. We all sprang to attention, her face all screwed up in anticipation of the bellow that was to issue forth from her disgusting mouth.

"Small! Dudley! Get yourselves here this instant."

We all looked across at Vetrov whose name had been omitted.

"Why were you all just sitting here laughing?"

There was no answer to that. Then it happened. Sue Dudley, her face screwed up and breath held tight, suddenly exploded unto uproarious giggling. The situation was too ridiculous. Even the omitted Anna couldn't contain herself.

"Vetrov! Stand up immediately!" she yelled.

My eyes caught Anna as she crossed and uncrossed her legs, obviously, like me, having trouble.

"Small. Uncross your legs immediately," she bellowed to the wind. "Be in my office in five minutes!"

"Evil old cow," said Sue. We made it up the hill in the safety of a mobile group and found ourselves outside her office.

"Come in!" she snapped. We all shuffled, trying desperately not to be the first to step in, but it didn't help as we stood in a line in front of this dragon seated regally behind an enormous desk, signs of Queen, God and country flapping ominously around her. Anna was given a detention and Sue and I were told to report to the library at lunchtime that day.

We had no idea what was in store for us as we stood, two sixteen year old girls, outside the library door. It opened and out came, of all people, our music teacher. She averted her eyes and spoke to the floor:

"You can come in now."

The library was filled with every member of the staff, all seated facing us.

"Stand out the front," the principal ordered.

I wanted to cry but knew that she would have taken advantage of this so I bit my lip and stood as close to Sue as I could.

"Stand on your own two feet!" came the evil voice.

Every person in the room was staring at us but as I moved my eyes around, looking for help, no-one met them. The laughter had completely gone.

She addressed the gathering. "I have brought you all here to help these two girls to recognize the error of their ways. One of them is even a prefect, but that will have to come to an end. "Dudley, take off that badge and prefect girdle. I will remove your pocket this afternoon."

She looked around the room. "Take a good look at them ladies and gentlemen. You see before you two unfit examples. Girls certainly below the standards that we uphold in this school."

Her humiliation went on and on and not one of the teachers in that room stood up for us, made eye contact or tried to stop her.

"Get out of my sight. Now!"

We left, but didn't speak to each other or to anyone for some time. I couldn't understand what I had done to deserve such humiliation. At the time I was convinced that she must have known about my father and that it was a punishment for my wickedness and filth.

I still don't know what I did, Kate, to be treated like that. My behaviour was a little disruptive in some classes but I wasn't nasty or rude and I often wonder why at least one teacher didn't wonder why, and try to help us. Maybe it's because my Multiplicity allowed us to completely hide all the terror safely away. But in a way we ultimately triumphed as the four of us are still good friends fifty years later and each is a strong and good person with an independent mind.

I always wondered why you were allowed, even encouraged to dress in a feminine and later womanly way, but I never was. I guess it's obvious in hindsight. The worst article of clothing I ever had to wear was a dress that Mum made, to wear to the Combined Choral concert, where I sang in the huge choir.

For weeks, in every spare moment of her painfully busy life, she sewed. She measured, cut, stitched, unstitched and stitched again. Even the material itself was ghastly. Almost transparent with indented and raised patterns all over it with a slightly furry feel to them. Small rosebud shapes with leaves. You could dress a baby in it but not a fifteen year old girl.

I pouted, complained, tried to look sick and to become invisible but there was no way out. The dress was ready. So I wore the white dress with flowers and leaves and puffy sleeves, the faces of my friends and fellow singers saying it all as I threaded my way past them. Nobody spoke, just giggled. I stuffed it down a drainpipe in the early hours and it was never seen again, but I think my mother was really hurt. She had tried, in her own way, to make me look nice.

Mum told me that I would never amount to anything, but perhaps I triumphed, as later in my career as a musician and a music teacher I was asked several times to accompany the combined choral concerts in the Sydney Opera House. Dressed in clothes of my own choice, I walked on to the Opera House stage and with much joy, played the piano for the whole program while the choir of eight hundred children sang. And my children's songs have been sung throughout Australia for many years.

I began to write music. It just flowed through me while I listened, played and wrote it down. One is a 'Piano Sonata for Academics with a Heart and a Smile' that contains a familiar phrase that I later realized was based on "Hear the pennies dropping" a song from Sunday school. How funny is that?

I took up the flute when I was in my late twenties and it became an extension of my voice and an instrument I love to write for, many pieces of which have been widely performed.

At one time a short phrase in 7/8 kept going over and over in my head. I dismissed it as being uninteresting but it persisted until I gave in and listened and it developed into a rich piece of music. Once when coming back from a day in the Blue Mountains with Bruce and the kids, my head just overflowed and the sounds wouldn't leave me alone until I had completed "The Mountains", a three movement work for clarinet, piano and flute. And "Sunrise on the Harbour" with the voices of a cello and a flute that describes early daybreak on Sydney Harbour, the piano adding to the richness of the waking city sounds. There were many more, but it all came to an end when Richard, the initial therapist, buried us again.

Recently our music has returned and a commissioned choral work grew gradually from the sounds of wind chimes, wind and rain replicated with voices and pebbles rising finally to full harmonies as the brilliance of the sun returns after a storm. Encouraged by a dear friend, I now have a CD called "Flight".

There are fifteen of my works and I have finally had the courage to become visible.

When you look in a mirror or at a photograph Kate, do you understand that it's you that you're looking at? I knew in my head that the person was Rhonda but I had a hard time understanding that the image was 'me'. So I gathered photos from wherever I could and began to put them all together in an album. I even took it to a calligrapher who wrote 'Rhonda' in beautiful writing surrounded by small blue and yellow flowers above a photo of me when I was about three years old.

My birth certificate's in there too. An orange coloured document with crinkled edges but which proves beyond doubt that Rhonda Margaret Small came into the world in 1945 at Neutral Bay, NSW. I had arrived! I found a photo of Mum and Dad when they were young, on a rug in a garden somewhere. Mum's sitting in the curve of Dad's body, one arm draped around his neck and the other resting on his knee. She's smiling Kate, and looks so happy in a sleeveless summer dress, her face alive. Dad looks young and handsome with an open necked shirt and long thin face, his arm around Mum and his hand resting on hers. They look comfortable together.

Gradually, as I arranged more and more photos in the album, I built an external history of 'Me' in a visible and concrete form. A record of school years, piano playing, sports and athletics teams. I love the photo where I'm standing in the garden with my ballet shoes on, sequined dancing dress and fine fairy wings stretching out behind my fifth position arms. But my favourite photo of all is the one that Mum had taken by a professional photographer. It's black and white and we'd been asked to smile but I love it because it's you and me and we're close together. You were thirteen and beautiful and I was six and feeling safe and good leaning against my big sister.

You came with me when I went back to the house in Hope Street a few years ago. It's changed a lot, with bathroom renovated, granite filled kitchen and verandah all around the northern side, but it's still the same house really. We knocked on the door:

"We grew up here and are wondering whether we could look around at what you've done?"

We took her completely by surprise but she agreed, leading us room by room through this house that had so many memories, so many emotions. I saw Mum standing at the kitchen sink and felt the stool under me as I sat playing my piano, the smell of beef stew wafting through the open doorway. I heard my budgie, Pinocchio, chatting away in the corner and felt Prince's fur as he brushed up against my leg. The photos of number thirty-nine then and now are all together in the album.

I enjoy looking at the school photos, everyone lined up on risers, each year Rhonda growing taller until womanhood is reached and a beautiful man, Bruce, enters and later our two children, the greatest gifts to my life, are born.

Only now as I look at this album am I able to know that it is me. That I am Rhonda, and this understanding touches me deeply. I know that I existed then and that I am here now.

"I know now that I have been inside this body and this face for over seventy years," I told my son Kris the other day.

"Welcome to the world Mum," he said.

You remember only cameos about our growing up years, Kate, and that's a blessing. You agree that it was violent, but you met your husband when you were thirteen and you went out as often as possible. You and Matt and I had our own ways of coping and of surviving, each unique to ourselves. I think I'm lucky in a way, because I was young enough when it all started, to develop Multiplicity which enabled me to lock each memory safely away from my consciousness and to function in 'normal' life. You, Matt and I all have difficulty with the passing of time and the ability to sequence the events in our lives. Something to do with the fear squeezing everything into a chaotic space and leaving no frontal cortex able to access the world of real time. Matt, now eighty-two is still living back in those years. He talks almost exclusively about places and people and public events of back then, dotted only by his private train project that he's now working on.

I asked you if you could tell me some of the good things that you remember from those years at home in Hope Street.

"Nothing. I can't think of any!"

I asked you to think about it but several weeks later still brought the same answer. This was validating. So many times in the past twenty-six years, I've thought that all this stuff is made up. That it couldn't possibly have happened. But I know it did.

When a memory is surfacing, life in my head and my body is pure hell. The terror takes over my breathing, my cognitive skills vanish, time has no meaning. My body aches and my food doesn't stay down. I have constant diarrhea for weeks on end and it all gets worse until the memory is out. Then the relief is amazing.

Sometimes it takes several months for each one to completely surface. One such time, I kept smelling blood. When I woke, when I walked, when I sat and did my work. I had absolutely no idea what it was about but thought it must have involved my father. Then the picture of my old primary school, Seaforth Public, kept coming into my mind in vivid clarity. I did some drawings to see if that would give me some clues as to what it was about and gradually the main building became smaller and the old toilet block up by the road became bigger. Until one day I rang and asked for a therapy session straight away.

"Libby, there's a dead child in the toilet block!"

"Can you describe what you see?"

The level of fear suddenly escalated and the full picture was in my head.

"She's hanging from the top of the toilet and there's blood everywhere!"

I could feel my body shaking but there was no now or place or me just this ghastly picture and the reeking smell of blood.

"Can you come back into the room Rhonda. It's no longer happening and you're completely safe."

I did, focusing on regaining my breath until my eyes began to focus on the things in the therapy room. But the memory was there and it was clear, so I watched it as if on a TV screen.

I was about eight or nine, had been excused to go to the toilet and I had found the young girl. She had been murdered, stabbed many times and strung up with the toilet chain around her neck, the place covered in blood.

Again, I thought I must have made it up but it has been validated by an old school friend and also by another girl who was in year one at the time. They have both said that yes, a young kindergarten child was murdered in the toilet block at that time. I know that all of my memories are real. They happened. As Libby says, "why would you ever put yourself through all that anxiety, sadness, all the feelings of terror and the trauma of reliving the experiences if it wasn't real!" I have nothing to gain except my life. And that I've done.

I'd love to tell you about some of the parts of me and how they've helped me. First, there's **Magnitude.** He's one of the **Fantasy Parents** who help to look after the children and the teenagers of the system, but he's more like an ancient sage who seems to be wise and I love the way he puts words together. I don't know where he comes from but I'm glad he's here.

Many times I just silently ask for help when the terror between my shoulders reaches into my throat, threatening to choke me. Sometimes I write it out, or sleep as though there's no tomorrow, but sometimes Magnitude comes to my rescue with his words. Often I have no idea what he's talking about, but I listen and write them down and always after a few days or weeks or further sessions with Libby, his words make wonderful sense. When Magnitude speaks I always listen:

'The air is filled with pastels as I pick up my pen to write. Spread the pastel into the *Nowhere* and bring light and shadows from around the corner. Stand them upon the grass and observe them. Strip them of their creative skins and let them stand naked before you, murmuring indigenous tones of uncertainty. Why do you squander resources? Take the myriad of life years and spread them into the hollows of your mind. Fill the valleys with laden images of existence. Penetrate the blackness with your sword that is double-edged with knowledge and wisdom.

You invited me back but that was to be tonight. Why tonight? Why can I not speak my words in daylight? I fear nothing. Nothing fears me. I am not fearful.

Spread your words upon the ground. Utterances, strewn like confetti upon the grass to be gathered up by the rain and washed away into tomorrow. Yesterday is here now, floating like an invisible force over and around our world. It will not leave us until you can see the sorrow, understand its deep, deep silence and feel its pain that throbs eternally.

Be still and connect with the forces around you. You do not learn solitude but within the energy of life, rocked gently in the cradle of love. Do not fear the sorrow or the pain for they are here to help you. Hold out your hand to them. Step up onto the threshold and they will guide you through the door. Make the connection and you will be free."

And I then know, Kate that it will pass and I will be alright.

Even though I have retained a pretty tight control over the many parts of me becoming visible to others, there have been times when I have had little control over this and have found clothes in my cupboard that don't' fit, that I don't like at all and have no idea how they got there. When people have greeted me enthusiastically but I have no idea who they are. When someone has taken over inappropriately and caused me enormous anxiety and regret.

One such time was when I was in my early thirties and I was playing the flute in the Warringah orchestra. It was an amazing thrill to be accepted and I really practiced hard and mastered all the scores we were performing. But someone must have been afraid of something happening and I found myself at a rehearsal unable to play one of the pieces. Worse was to come when I was asked to play the flute in the Bach Brandenburg concerto No. four in G. I learnt and practiced intensely until I was fluent and confident, but when I arrived at a rehearsal for the two flutes and violin, the solo parts, I found myself unable to play anything but a few notes. They of course replaced me but it took me years to get over the humiliation of that experience as I didn't understand what had happened until many years of therapy later. That another part of me, who knew nothing about playing the flute, had taken over.

Sometimes my story was moved forward by symbolic images that formed in my mind as though I was watching a picture being painted by my internal artist. Many of them lingered throughout the twenty-six years of the healing journey, changing and growing as I moved gradually out of the past. They are not illusions but framed, visual records of experiences and feelings stored in my mind long ago.

Like the image of the dead child in the bath, which was symbolic of my real self. Each time I went to touch her I was shocked with how pale and dead she was and how she'd been like that for such a long time. And the figure of death riding a black horse that galloped along a narrow strip of sand, the sky dark and threatening, galloping to scoop Rhonda up and take her away.

Another very realistic dream recurred often during the years of therapy. I saw a teenage girl about fifteen, as she went from door to door seeking somewhere to stay. It was always night time, cold and stormy as she knocked at each house, almost begging for them to take in the child that she carried wrapped in a woolen shawl. Each time the door was slammed shut. When I looked at the very young child in her arms, her face was flat, brown and plastic with no eyes to see or mouth to taste. No features at all. No flesh or bones to make her real. But the girl carried her with love and desperation, always hopeful that someone would take the child in and bring her to life.

Over the healing course of therapy the baby's face has become alive, almost as though someone has painted smiling green eyes and lips parted as though in song. And the teenager no longer knocks on doors but just carries the child everywhere. I guess the girl was me, carrying what I understood to be my Self.

Another image was the black figure that carried the body of a young teenager down the stone steps of the bridge, to the river into which he was always about to float her body. I often wanted to be not alive, but not dead. Just in limbo, in someone's arms, waiting for the time when I hoped I could feel safe.

But the first and the most significant to appear, was the three dimensional image of the three figures, so vivid that I felt that I could reach out and touch the canvas. The paint has spilled from the cup of symbolic concentrate and is not yet dry. Clear and complete as though someone had wiped away an outer layer to reveal another surface beneath.

The background is a dull colour and three figures emerge. One on the left towards the top, one in the middle and the third further to the front on the right hand side. The figure at the back is painted in dark shades, her body curled up and drawn in upon itself.

The figure in the centre has no skeleton, but hangs limp as if hung up on a coat stand. She is trapped, with no muscles to move her, no bones to hold her up. If you call out her name she won't answer because she has no identity. She is shaded in mustard browns with skin coloured hands and feet that hang from the ends of the garment.

Towards the front of the painting is a small child wearing yellow and red, a small sprig of bright green leaves in her hand a sense of wonder in the eyes. A golden cocker spaniel sits at her feet, looking up at her.

There is no movement; they are all frozen in time.

All three figures are imprisoned behind a set of steel-grey bars while outside, a pastel form with no distinct features is swirling, beckoning them to her. Intense yet playful, enticing, calling them into life.

Gradually, as I healed, each of these images either vanished or changed. I've now met these parts of myself and heard their stories. The coiled figure is **Rebecca** who felt the moonlight, knew about the acorn and who found enough courage to reach out and finally uncoil into the sensory world of reality. The middle figure, **The Heap**, limp and filthy, despised by nearly every other part of us, now stands clean and upright. The third, myself as a young child now grown into a mature woman. The bars have gone, the colours are more vibrant and each of the three figures has stepped out into a safe reality.

Our lives have taken different directions and we've become two quite different people Kate, but we still have much in common, our love of animals being the most prominent. I think that came from Dad but also from the need to find a safe love in a living being other than our parents. Animals are amazing. They demand our respect and compassion and I know that you and I will continue to fight for their rights.

And somehow we have each come out of this upbringing with an understanding of kindness and a caring for others that I think we could have learnt only from animals.

You had your family quite young and you are a wonderful mother, two great kids now mothers themselves and you enjoy being 'Nanna'.

And even with all our differences I love you and am grateful that you are my sister.

CHAPTER 5

I could hear her screeching, beginning in the distance and building gradually like a symphonic crescendo until she finally gushed on to the stage.

"**Mary**! Help her! She's falling into the madness." We understood but knew it was her job to prevent that from happening.

She adjusted her hat and wriggled her nose. "But in the end it's all about me of course," cackled **Wicked Witch**." **The Storyteller** has kindly agreed to tell you a story about me, girlie, but you have to just sit still, keep quiet and listen".

A strange chapter beginning perhaps, but one that casts a light on the unique environment of my inner world. Life is not ordered in this space, nor is it predictable. There are parts of me who emerge without warning, reacting to what he or she sees as an immediate need to protect. Sometimes this is misguided and as I am now an adult, always inappropriate but these are alters who have not yet been updated and who believe that the father is still alive and danger is imminent. Each has his or her role and will insist on being given the space in which to speak. One such alter is **Wicked Witch** who, like several internal characters speaks in stories that allow her to be separate and not to feel, but to relate her view of the world. Often her role is one of diversion and she has an inflated idea of her own importance but as an alter whose major role is to prevent **Mary** from falling completely into the madness, she is important and I have learnt to listen and to respect her. When the real world is full of danger, the imagination is an important tool in helping to escape and is indeed worthy of our attention. And the ability to play is the right of every child. She also often provides a bit of light relief.

So, taking up her position and with a wink and a smile **The Storyteller** will begin:

Once, long ago in the land just around the corner lived a little girl. She was small and quite young for her age but she loved red jellybeans. They made her tongue look like the lining of a cape of red satin. They tasted good too and while she was eating them her full attention was taken. One day, as she was riding her horse Sampson through the bush, a sound caught her ears. It was a laughing sound, like the snicker of a witch interrupted now and then with a snort and a cackle. Sampson whinnied, throwing back his head. Quickly she pulled on the reins steering him through the thick Aussie bush, leading him to a spot behind a huge gum tree. She dismounted and they remained silent, watching and listening as the wicked laugh rang through the trees. As suddenly as it had started, it stopped and she continued riding along the red dirt of the road that led through the forest of dreams. Again the laughter came, even more threatening than before. Sampson shied, the little girl holding on with all her strength but feeling herself slipping until she fell, sprawled out on the dusty road. Off he galloped, leaving her alone with the shrill laughter.

"You're not so smart now are you girlie," the voice chortled.

"Who are you and what do you want?" she called.

"I will ask the questions and you will deliver the answers!"

The little girl looked around her. "But where are you?"

"I am here, I there and I am everywhere. I am this and I am that. I am the top of your hat. I am me and you and the waters of blue. That's where I am. Now, where are you going?"

"Through the forest of dreams to capture my imagination and bring it back," the girl replied. She heard a noise surrounding her as though there was a crowd, mumbling, talking. "Who else is there with you?" she asked.

"I am the only one of importance dearie," announced Wicked Witch. "Now where do you think this imagination might be? Quick, child, tell me. Tell me."

"Deep in the Forest of Dreams, your majesty. That's where he told me to go."

"He! Who is He!" shouted the Witch.

"He is **Ezekial.** The nice man in the cape who came to our town with his travelling troop of players and puppets. Oh it was wonderful. So much colour and---"

"Cease! I command you to cease!"

"But your majesty---"

"I will colour you spotted if you do not cease now!"

The girl looked around her. To the front, to the back, to each side. She walked around the trees and wildflowers but she could see nothing.

"Where are you?" she pleaded.

"I am here, I am there, I am---"

"Yes, but I can't see you!" She thought for a moment: "Maybe you don't even exist? Maybe you're part of my imagination and I can fold you up and put you away until I want to dream again!"

"Fold me up! My dear, I have never heard anything so awful."

"It wouldn't hurt because I think you're only in my head. Perhaps I've found my imagination already."

"Imagination, bah humbug! Useless article. No facts, no reality. I am real."

The little girl smiled. "But maybe only to yourself."

This was too much for the Witch who jumped on her broomstick and with a 'humph' and disdainful stare left the scene.

Over the years **Wicked Witch** made many such appearances and organised **The Storyteller** to tell us many stories. Part of her job was to prevent other alters from connecting with each other and with Rhonda and the stories helped to create a diversion and a wedge between Rhonda and the reality of the square. She rode on a broomstick, with no feet on the ground and with no experience or understanding of feelings. This was an essential part of her makeup as she was also on the right hand corner of the Diamond, her role there to disconnect any feeling before **Mary** became **Mary Squared** and went into the madness of the father.

She is not a nasty or harmful character and over the years I've become very fond of her and am grateful for her wonderful energy and her strengths, one of which is her honesty. She says exactly what she thinks.

As soon as I walked into the therapy room I knew that she was around. She sat down, head in the air as Libby, who knew her well, welcomed her, asking her why she had come.

"There's something strange inside me and I want to know what it is and how it got there."

"What is it?" Libby asked.

She stood up, looking down her nose with contempt. "If I knew that then I would not be here, **I** would be able to tell **you**. You fool! I want you to get it out! Now!"

"I can't do that. All I can do is to help you know what it is."

"Fat lot of use you are."

"Describe it to me," coaxed Libby kindly.

"They're all so sweet! Curdles my custard and congeals my rice pudding. Silly, pathetic creature she is."

"Who?" Libby asked.

"Rhonda of course. She's so needy and helpless and useless and worst of all---she's kind!"

"So what's the problem? "

"I used to just laugh at her, the silly little thing, but the laughs won't come! And there's something strange in my body. Get it out. Now!"

"Could this be a feeling, perhaps?" Libby tested.

Wicked Witch looked at her with utter disbelief. "A feeling!"

Just then something strange happened. She shrieked and fell to the floor.

"Look what you've done! I've fallen off my broomstick."

"I'm sure I had nothing to do with it and I'm sure you can get up if you want to," said Libby.

"You don't understand. I have no legs. And I can't get back on my broomstick until someone helps me and no-one will help me until I'm nice to everyone.

Oh woe is me. I have nowhere to go. No marigolds to smell, no beanstalks to climb. I'm the fee-fi-fo-fum of the system but my roar has been silenced."

She was interrupted by **Ezekial**, who very cleverly put everything on a stage to be observed as a play. He emerged, a satisfied smile on his face.

"I have the magic of the stage and the power of the story so I will turn Wicked Witch into fairy dust and scatter her as I dance. And I will change her evil laugh into song. I like to think of her as purple but she doesn't like that. If only she could stop being angry so I can colour her calm."

He continued:

"I came to tell you about **The Shining.** Children are born into the world, open and trusting, mindful with a sense of wonder and curiosity. This purity is what we call the child's Shining. It is the quintessence of the soul and was there in the beginning encased safely in a hidden and tightly sealed part we call **The One Who was Born,** who was connected to our soul. Once you, Rhonda, had discovered us it didn't take long for us to realize that she was in danger and that our Shining could be destroyed or contaminated so we created **the Sprites** who, for several years put all the horrible events into cocoons and buried them in the fairy gardens."

These gardens were so lovely, scattered at various points along the creek at the bottom of Hope Street. Tiny paths led from mounds of moss to small stick buildings held together with drying mud. Rocks of all shapes and sizes were placed carefully in clumps along the lengths of the paths, like Zen sand gardens with small wooden rakes that grace coffee tables, offering calm. Nasturtiums and buttercups added colour. We realized even then that nothing was to be put in one place, so we created many fairy gardens in all different places beside the water.

Gradually we learnt that this wasn't enough and bit by bit our shining, like the stone that Rhonda tried to show her mother, was hidden deeper and deeper. It was then that the Master Plan was devised. At first, this plan appears to be coloured with confusion, but if you look closely you'll see that there are carefully created layers and that nothing was done at random. Nothing. Every symbol and detail hooks into each other. All is connected but appears to be separate. Of course this was deliberate as nothing was allowed to be as it appeared to be, thereby preventing the One Who was Born and our Shining from ever being discovered.

When **Rebecca** began to unfurl, the Shining emerged and for a short while the real magic of life returned. Our poems and music began to flow like melting snow from the mountain and a connection was made. But now they are both once again safely hidden."

I felt my body being rearranged and **Magnitude** was there, sitting erect with a sense of quiet authority.

"Our purpose now, my dear, is to gradually clear our mind and heal our body. The key to this is calm acceptance. A child does not grow well if pressured and it is a good parent who accepts the gift of time and space as we each need to grow gradually into the space allotted to us. If you listen you will hear a child saying quietly: 'No-one hurries a tree, so please, don't hurry me.'

And do not tell me of your realities as I know them already, but you need to listen.

To emerge from the chrysalis you must push your way out. Use your strength, it will not just happen for you. And to complete this metamorphosis you must gather your Self. For it is your Self that is being reborn. It will be a decision determined by your consciousness, an action that arises from your decision to love and to accept your Self.

Why don't you look within at the green eyes of a small child who carries her soul like a gift in her hands. She is strong in mind and in body and her heart is good. And like the stone, she is beautiful. Don't be afraid, for she is waiting. Look at her, touch her and bring her into your being where she belongs."

"But she is hidden in the safety of **The triangular prism!**"

"Tell me about this prism then my dear."

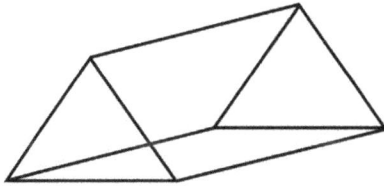

"It started off small in the shape of an equilateral triangle, the mind, body and spirit, connected from corner to corner but as the realities on the outside pushed against the walls, it began to stretch. And being of equal angles and length of parallel sides, it grew bigger and stronger without the sides meeting. The more the external reality pressed the longer and higher the walls became. You see, it was one of our geometric shapes and it allowed for infinite growth. Like a Toblerone packet, but with solid walls that could be extended forever if the space allowed. Something that is built with these properties, each component of which is as strong as the other, won't collapse, because all around it is of equal stress. Inside the prism is the reality of **The One Who Was Born** and outside it any other reality can and does exist, but the Self will remain hidden and safe."

Magnitude smiled: "The ultimate reality is the Self, my dear. Everything else is created. And when the time is right perhaps the pressure within and without will become equal, at which point the prism will quietly dissolve and the Self will walk freely upon the earth."

In this created world of my imagination was also a valley through which a river flowed, flowers bloomed and cows blinked their eyelashes. As a child I, Rhonda, had no knowledge of this inner place. Nature was important to each part of me and this beautiful valley, a safe place, was created for them by **The Master Planner**. It was also an inner reflection of the natural world into which I physically and consciously escaped as a child, a teenager, a young adult and into which I now still love to go.

Most times life was peaceful in this valley, with the grass as green as can be and a-buzz with people chatting and generally going about their business. Children laughed, talked and played while **The Elderly People** smiled and leaned against walls as they watched the children play. At night the scattered houses glowed with safety, families in the village were at home reading stories, singing songs of jolly tunes and plaintive melodies, with hearts held close. The trees surrounded all with a blanket of safety and every day when the children awoke they knew that the day would pass with love. Each evening heralded the connection with nature and every night the trees protected them and darkness came to carry them into peaceful sleep. It was idyllic.

The children believed that the person who attacked them was sometimes the **Monster** and sometimes the **Giant**. It was not the father for whom they felt love.

Sometimes, without warning, this place would break apart as the Giant thundered into the valley, shattering the peace with threats of violence as he ranted and roared and the people in the valley prepared for danger. Chatting stopped. No-one sat by the river or climbed the trees. Silence became mandatory and connection ceased. Invisible walls sprang up immediately as membranes separated each from each in bounded silence. They had been launched into the reality of the Square.

At this moment they looked up and there, standing astride the mighty river was the Giant, a set of golden balance scales raised high above his head. In each wide plate of brass that swung from the end of each arm they saw living figures. One stood tall and proud, fists raised in triumph. It was **The Terror,** its gnarled body angry yet jubilant. On the other a small figure cowered, hands hanging on tightly to the golden chain that held her tray to the golden arm. It was **Mary.**

"The Terror will never die!" roared the Giant.

"What would happen if it did?" Libby asked.

"The scales would become unbalanced and Mary would fall into the father's insanity. Because The Terror lives and breathes on its own as a separate energy that was created within the womb of the mother and spread through the father's hands," I replied.

"Why would Mary be hurt?"

"Because he keeps her as his hostage, as the balance of The Terror."

"What purpose does The Terror serve?"

"It keeps the secret locked carefully away, with no way of escape."

"Tell me what secret that is," said Libby "The secret of the square reality! The Terror is always there but no-one is to ever discover it. You can't put it into a cupboard, nor under the ground nor into the sky. Nor as part of a tree or of someone's blood. For it will be there with its eyes along every bit of its thick thread."

"Do you know that the father is dead?"

"You're wrong! His body has gone but the father lives on in the terror! His eyes *and* her eyes are part of the terror. One eye, one eye, one eye, all the way along to infinity.

There was one part who, when the Giant came thundering into the valley, knew how to trick him, carefully bringing out all the imaginary dolls. **The Master Planner** knew what to do. He knew the plans, the decrees, which parts to call on and the action by which the villagers survived.

"I'd like to tell you their story."

At the bottom of the valley, overlooked by the village, the river flows, strong and silent, dividing the village into two parts. On the right hand side live **The Fantasy Parents** and **The Elderly People** watching over the children and the teenagers, and all the unusual ones like **Wicked Witch, Vigil** and **Gustav, Mephistopheles** and **Persephone.** It was imperative that at all times they be kept separate from the left hand side of the river where **The Him** and **The Evil Saboteur** lived.

The Jostler has been on the river forever so he knows what's going on and has kept everyone safe while at the same time not allowing Rhonda's mind to come together. It must never be joined. The river keeps the left and the right side of her brain as separate as possible. There is a life raft that allows several parts to watch and to make sure that no-one goes from one side to the other. The Jostler, and the **Good Fairy Mother**, who was created to take the place of the icy mother whenever she became nasty, tether the life raft to logs that have been deeply and carefully placed to retain its spot in the middle of the river. It is only The Jostler who can decide when and if the life raft touches the left bank and when and if anyone goes from the right to the left.

"How does the Good Fairy Mother help the children?" Libby asked.

"She takes them off into a kind of dream and they follow her happily, knowing that where they are going is safe and often fun."

"Is this the same place as 'the hole in the clouds?'" Libby asked.

"No. It's completely different. The 'hole in the clouds' is an actual remembered space from before we were born, but the dream space has been created by the Good Fairy Mother. When The Jostler grabs a piece of the jigsaw puzzle to prevent it from ever being completed, he can choose whether to hide it on the left or on the right."

"Does he know how it will be retrieved, if ever?"

"No. He just watches and waits and the minute a piece of information threatens to help the puzzle make sense, he grabs it and runs. It's instantaneous."

Libby was confused. "I don't quite understand how Rhonda's brain can have no integration between the left and the right. She lives and has lived a very functional life for many years."

"And **Magnitude,** and of course I myself have complete access to all that is."

"Are you **The Master Planner**? " asked Libby.

"I am he. And I must say, I have done and am doing an amazing job."

Libby smiled, but the knowledge of the Jostler and the river had opened up a whole new window.

"She does exist. I can see her," said Libby.

"She's never existed, because she was never shown a mirror. The words in here are saying that absolutely nobody held a mirror up for her. And it's not just **Rebecca** or **Emma** the teenage girl, it's the infant and the subsequent child. It's the whole real being! And it's **The One Who Was Born!** "They're behind the mirror, but because I couldn't ever turn it around, she never found a way of gaining permission to exist. They were in continual terror that we'd be snuffed out before anybody even saw her, and in the fear that now we might close all this before anyone gains access to her."

"But I already see her. She's sitting in front of me," Libby repeated. "I don't understand that."

"You see, she actually wanted to get out and to be seen. She wanted someone to hold up a mirror and say 'Here. This is you.' "

I sat bolt upright, "Prince did!"

"Yes, that's a reality," agreed Libby. You loved him and you mattered to him enormously."

"And he was not my mother or my father. It's as though the essence of me couldn't get out and nobody could get in and sometimes I wanted to just take hold of the mother and shake her. I wanted to say 'Here I am! Just look and you'll see me.'

I had one doll, called Betti. But wait! There's a part of me called **Betti** and she was totally bland. Like a doll! And I wanted to hold this doll up in front of my mother and say: 'See, I exist!' And a doll would have been safe because it wouldn't feel anything. And I felt nothing for the doll. You can't connect with a doll until you connect with yourself. And you can't connect with yourself until you connect with someone else. So she couldn't hurt me through the doll, but maybe she would see that I existed."

"Did you know that I've seen you?"

"I do now. But I hate her! She's filthy and disgusting."

"Who?" asked Libby again.

"**The Heap** of course! I want to stamp on her and kick her. I want to make her get up and fight back but instead she's just like a piece of rag, there for anyone to do anything to her and I hate her!"

Libby continued, pushing carefully through the protective boundaries of my unreality. "She's part of you, Rhonda. The part who took on all the filth and the violence so that you wouldn't remember any of it. So perhaps you could begin to see her differently?"

I wasn't yet ready for that part of my journey into the 'real' world.

"The story will be told in my way and in my time. It might be six stories mixed up together and it will lead you up the garden path and across fields and into streets that go nowhere. It will have silences that leave you wondering and pieces missing that you will have to try and figure out for yourself. But there is one thing for certain."

"And what's that ?"

"My story will never arrive."

"Have we met before?" Libby asked.

There was movement in my body and Rhonda returned. "That was **The Storyteller** and he's put us back in the house in Hope Street. But it's different! It's always been dark but now it's daytime and the sun is shining through the venetian blinds in the lounge room and it's alive and I'm not frightened! There are people moving, not just statues on trolley tracks. My mother's sitting at the dining room table, her legs crossed reading the paper, sipping her tea from the white porcelain cup with green leaves and yellow flowers. And Kate's in her dressing gown, walking around, her bristle hairbrush in her hand and singing."

"Is your father home?"

"No. This must be all part of **The Storyteller's** story. And he's saying to me ' Look and feel and know that they are all real, people with bones and blood, with legs that walk and mouths that talk and sing and you are one of them.' "

"And do you believe him?"

"Yes! I can feel it. And he's telling me to go right through the house and out into the garden. I can smell the mint around the tap. I reach up to pick a lemon from the old tree near the clothes line but the tree has thorns and I prick my finger. The sun is warm on my back and I love the feel of the breeze on my face. And look, Matt's in the backyard surrounded by screws and spanners and wheels, fixing up his old pushbike!"

I've never felt this before."

"Does it feel real?"

I nod, taking my shoes off to feel the ground then the warmth of the carpet on my feet.

"There's a small child, she's about seven and she's sitting playing the piano. Her feet don't quite reach the floor. She's only just started to learn and 'The Magic Land of Music' is open on the piano."

"Could this small child be you?"

Reality was creeping through me, the tears dribbling down as **The Storyteller** stands with me holding my hand:

"You've taken another step," I heard him say.

There has been so much going on in my internal world for over a year now and a part of me who I've found it difficult to live with has been 'out front'. She's forceful but also filled with anxiety. I don't know who she is because for some time now I've found it impossible to access my system. It's as though everyone has left. Not integrated, just left me and whoever it is, alone, to cope with whatever has been brewing, about which I have no information.

I was determined not to have to ring and ask for any more therapy sessions with Libby so I sat it out until the fear became too intense to handle. When I finally did enter the therapy room again I had decided to allow whoever wanted to talk the space to do so, but in his or her own way.

"I don't want you to ask me any questions Libby or to ask to speak to any part of me or to suggest drawing or writing."

Without even a moment for Libby to respond, a child of about seven started to speak.

"They don't listen or hear. I feel as though I'm in a different place from everyone else and they don't know what I'm talking about. I try to tell them but they twist everything around or answer with words that make no sense. It's as though I'm completely alone in a place with just the wind to hear me. I love the sound of the sea, the touch of the sun and the magic of moonlight."

Libby looked at her and smiled. "Welcome **Bethany**. It's so good that you've finally come to talk to me."

"It's as though I brought it all into the world with me but I had to keep it safe in a bubble."

You see, Bethany and her world were the antithesis of the trauma within the square where no-one understood and had neither time nor the ability to see her. Nor did she have any experience of the world outside. She is part of our **Shining**, reflecting the rose-coloured glow of **The One who was Born** with a childlike wonder that radiated with song, playfulness and nature as she remained in the turret of the castle gathering up the threads of moonlight to keep them all alive.

Without warning there was quite a shift and Lucy was there in Libby's room, the words pouring out as if from a burst water main.

"Imagine how it feels to be encased in a thick circle that has no means of either allowing any of me out or anyone or anything outside to come in and there is no possibility of this ever changing."

Lucy was one of the few parts of me who changed ages. In order to live in the outside world, she had to. She was created when I was about three years old and she grew up bit by bit as she went daily into the world. Therefore, when I was in my teenage years so was Lucy, with all the normal teenage angst and questions, learning where she fitted. And what a huge task, especially as Lucy could not show any of this to anyone at any time. No wonder she lived with frustration, isolation and confusion. She knew nothing of life within the reality of home and therefore didn't understand the judgment of some people towards **Emma** who at times behaved with anger, resentment and rebellion. This frightened Lucy who was vigilant in her job of fitting in and never standing out.

"I want you to imagine what it was like!" she shouted, her fists tightly clenched. "Sealed within and no way out. Knowing that you are a person, that you feel, that you question, that you have something to offer, but never able to show anyone any of this. And imagine that no matter what anyone says to you or thinks of you, you have no right of reply."

She shifted in her seat. "And **Emma** is always angry and sometimes **Mary** becomes anxious, her eyes never resting and her whole body twitches just like a small bird that moves constantly on the bough of a tree. And when she's like this she tries to speak but there are few words and none that make any sense. But at other times she's straight and tall and very strong. Then she is direct with good speech and her eyes are kind. And I get confused because I know my job and what I have to do but I don't understand any of the behaviour of those around me. Why are they like this?"

"You only know about the reality of the circle don't you **Lucy**."

She nodded.

"You did your job well, but it must have been very difficult at times."

Libby smiled as Lucy let go with a sigh as gentle as a zephyr breeze but which shed like an autumn tree. Libby had heard her and understood and she was able to feel calm again.

"The universe is large my dear. Too large for you to hear the toll of bells that are not near." The voice had changed, deeper, older. It was **Magnitude**.

"It is through **Mary** that we will know our destiny. That we will walk as one upon the moors so filled with sunshine and life. For if we can accept her, then we will have accepted the darkest part of our fear. It is **Bethany** and **Little One** who, with the openness of children will connect. They will walk to her with trust. It will be done."

Hello Mavis

Thought I'd write to you. A sort of summary. A completion.

Life was good when we first met wasn't it. We didn't have much, an old flat in Manly with a bed and lots of wooden crates and boxes. But we were in love and we were happy. We had to keep our marriage secret or you would have lost your job. Fancy that, eh, in 1928 women teachers were not allowed to be married. I can imagine you were pretty strict and the kids wouldn't have gotten away with much, but you loved it.

Do you remember the evenings we spent strolling along the beach, me in my full-length bathers and you in your shorts and blouse. You looked so lovely. Small and petite with shapely legs and a waist I could almost put my hands around. You were a good swimmer too and I loved to watch you dive off the promenade at Manly pool. Beautiful.

My sisters never took to you much though, particularly Mabel. I think she was jealous that you took her only brother away. Remember when she said that 'you can't make a lady out of Lizzie!' You never spoke to her after that. Mind you, later on you became a bit of a 'would be if you could be,' you know. Nose in the air, mixing as much as possible with the well-dressed and the apparently educated. That left me out a bit 'cause I didn't care what everyone thought of me. My classroom was the paddocks, the sky and the open sea. Oh, and the golf course. You hated me wearing my old shorts around the place but in later years your airs and graces got on my nerves so much that I did it to annoy you. But even through all of this you were still nicely under my skin.

Matt came along fairly early in the piece. Apple of your eye, star of your universe. Kate was born three years later. You fussed a lot, always making sure their shoes were clean and their clothes were without patches. You'd sit for ages in the evening brushing Kate's hair. Clean, shiny hair, a symbol of worth and place in society. Nobody was going to guess your background of poverty, but Mavis why was it so very important to you? We didn't have much when we were growing up either but it didn't seem to matter all that much.

We moved around a bit in the first few years, to Lismore and Coonabarabran. I loved the country but you got bored, so when things started to pick up after The Depression we moved back to Sydney.

Then the War came and in 1940 I volunteered. They made me a sergeant after I rescued some survivors from a ship that went aground off the south coast. Even gave me a medal for bravery. Then they shipped us off to New Guinea. Shocking thing, war. They sent me home several years later, unfit to work. You came to see me in Concord Repatriation Hospital. I know you tried but I guess I'd changed too much. You reckoned I was crazy. There were moments when I couldn't remember anything, sort of black splotches in my mind. At others the scenes of my mates and the horrible things that happened to them seemed to fill my mind like an endless film.

You became cold. Cut off, with no opening. Or maybe you'd always been a bit like that and I'd never seen it. You wouldn't let me come home so when the hospital discharged me the last time I went to Maitland and stayed with Mabel and Tom. They were good to me and even let me curl up on the end of their bed when the memories invaded my mind.

We lived in the back half of your brother Bob's semidetached house in Cremorne. A bit squashed with four people in a one-bedroom place, but we managed. Even more crowded when Rhonda came along at the end of the war. The other two were already at school. I don't think you wanted another kid but when she was big enough she spent most of her time in with your brother, Bob and his dog. Kate was seven when she was born and looked after her much of the time.

In 1949 we moved to Hope St. Seaforth. It was our dream. A dead-end street with a creek at the bottom and not far from your school or the sea. We got a war service loan and it didn't take long to build the house, well planned with the three bedrooms and the bathroom up the hallway away from the living area. We built a garage with a workshop for me and we planted a garden. A place to begin again. I got a job at the fish markets and things were looking up but the pictures in my head took over, the blank patches in my mind became more frequent and I drank more and more trying to obliterate it all.

I caught you looking at me sometimes, wishing me dead I think. Guess I never really matched up. I sometimes wished that Mark Hadley would take you on permanently. You didn't fool me you know. I saw you with him several times. But he went back to his wife and you stayed in the house with me. Must have been hard for you at school, with him the headmaster and all.

You moved all my things out of our bedroom when Matt left home. Clothes and all, bundled up and marched out of your consciousness.

Didn't make much difference really. I needed warmth, Mavis, and I found a woman who gave me that warmth. A connection that muted the images and gave me moments of snatched sanity. It was her that you met at the hospital after my car accident.

I sometimes wonder what it would have been like for us if the war hadn't interrupted and so changed our lives. I watched you at my funeral. I searched your face for a sign and found it in your eyes. I'm sorry for the chaos, the confusion, the sadness, the fear.

But we will meet again.

Howard

CHAPTER 6

Hi Mum

You were a handsome woman when you were young. Quite small in stature and always slim, your once olive skin snatched away by patches that burnt easily. You sometimes had blackheads on your nose and I used to watch you in front of the mirror in the bathroom as you squeezed them and long creamy worms oozed out. I hoped that I never had to do that. You still have them but you don't care any more. At ninety-three, I guess blackheads don't rate much.

Your hair's thick, with rich waves. I'm glad I got your hair and not Dad's. You hold your head high, nose pointing upwards, green eyes distant, speech correct, always conscious of what people will think.

I think I understand that, the middle of seven kids with very little money and eventually no father. How can someone leave a family of seven, one a newly born baby? When you were an early teenager, your front tooth was decayed to almost black. There wasn't any money to go to the dentist so when your oldest sister, Esme got her first pay packets she saved a little each time and finally paid for your teeth to be fixed so that you could smile.

You're very bright, always reading and asking questions, but your eyes have always been cold and vacant, as though lost in the ice of an arctic winter. Except for the terror that I saw sometimes. But I think your soul was hidden even before I arrived in your life, clouded over by confusion and abandoned dreams. You would have loved to have gone to university, and you could have done it too had you been given the opportunity. Shame that. You were an excellent teacher, strict but good. In many ways you were ahead of your time, working full time, an independent woman with her own car.

I still remember the number plate: HA 621, a little Austin A40, murky green, with brownish seats and tiny flipper windows that I always opened to let the breeze blow my hair. And when Prince came, I'd hang on tightly to his legs while he stretched his head out as far as he could, his golden ears flapping in the wind. Such joy.

And the holidays. You, Kate and me packing the car with our treasures and driving away. Thanks for those Mum.

You and I have had a torrid journey, haven't we, and sometimes I don't know how we lived through it. Guess we're strong. Each of us. And determined. Your body's frail now with paper thin skin stretched over bones that have walked and swum, traveled and bowled. Which have absorbed fear and contained the silence. Your bones are good though. None broken even though you've had some terrible falls. As you aged you wouldn't put yourself onto any of us, instead you accepted the room in the nursing home with quiet indifference.

Do you remember Percy, my old grey cat? When he was young he was cantankerous and quite arrogant. Intolerant too and kept us all at a distance. When he got old and his coat became scruffy and his gait unsteady he became kind. He needed us then. I think of him sometimes when I see you sitting in your chair by the window. Head flopped, resting, your crocheted rug on your knees. When I wake you, you smile and there's a hint of warmth in your eyes. Sometimes when I look at you I see a small child looking out at me and I understand your fear.

I didn't know you'd been unwell that morning, when I called in to give you your clean washing. There you were on your bed with the Sister standing beside you. She must have seen my concern.

"She's had a difficulty this morning. Almost choked on a hard pill the doctor gave her."

You looked vulnerable and pale so I sat down on the bed and held your hand. It felt awkward. I'd never actually reached out and held your hand before, but you didn't pull away so I held it firmly and it felt good. Then you started to disappear. Your face turned grey and your eyes began to stare. The Sister began to panic.

"Mavis! Mavis look at me!"

Your face got worse, almost with a tinge of blue and your eyes still stared. I hung firmly to your hand and as I did, I knew you were leaving your body. There was no fear because as you did I felt a warmth through my own body that I had never felt before. It was as though your soul was part of me. We were of one. When I looked back at your staring eyes I couldn't help it.

"Mum. Come back! Please don't leave yet. I'm not ready!"

And you did. Little by little your colour returned and as I felt the warmth leaving my body, I knew that your soul was moving back behind your eyes. I called you and you came back. It changed my whole life. All the turmoil between us no longer mattered and all the issues just vanished. I saw you as another soul on a parallel journey and I no longer needed anything from you, for in that moment I had felt unconditional love.

It wasn't always like that, was it. I spent my life trying to connect with you and you spent my life doing everything you could to prevent it. You would not, could not, allow any part of you out or any part of me, in.

Do you remember the place we lived in Cremorne? Guess you do, half of a semidetached house it was, just after the war when money was scarce, especially with a husband who was unfit for work. I can even smell it. Our part faced the south and was quite damp and musty. There was only one window, the side door faced west and the hallway was really dark even in the daytime. There was only one bedroom so we three kids slept lined up in the hallway.

I loved Uncle Bob, he was kind. His family's part of the semi was light, the lounge room facing north with a big window looking out into the garden. There was a dark coloured carpet with a floral pattern and a big radio console. I loved being in this space, sitting with Uncle Bob by the radio listening to plays and stories.

I can remember the smell of the meat that Auntie Ida cooked every afternoon for their little dog. It was a horrible smell but it takes me straight into a feeling of safety, of running to the gate to meet Uncle Bob when he got home. It was such a different world from the one in which we lived in the back half of the semi. I was only about three but I followed you around, trying to hang on to your skirt. You didn't like that and unhooked my hand from the material. The more I tried to be with you the more you pushed me away.

Libby had teddies in her therapy room but I wanted nothing to do with them and at one stage she asked me if I would like to bring my own. So I bought the first two teddy bears I could see in the shop, one small and one a little larger and took them along to Libby's therapy room. I hated them, their neediness and their helplessness, and as often as possible, threw them across the floor and tried to stamp on them.

Under her guidance the teddies remained at Libby's for years, until I learnt to accept them and to care for them. When I could do this and Libby was convinced that I wouldn't harm them I brought them home, knowing that I had also accepted myself. I guess the ego is constantly looking for a reflection and that's why, when no positive reflection is provided, it remains unsated, trying to be made whole. I think that when the ego is deeply acknowledged it smiles. Mine did.

I used to watch you as you stood in the evening shadows in the kitchen, scraping the skin off the potatoes with a kitchen knife. You peeled them so frugally, not allowing any bit of that potato to be wasted, putting your weight onto one leg and leaning against the cupboards, your eyes staring down into the sink as if your life was being washed away with the peelings. A kind of sadness baked for immeasurable years in confusion and frustration.

I watched from a distance, in my own shadows. You'd never let me into yours but kept yourself encased in lead with your insides broiled in time and isolation.

Who scooped out your insides Mum? Was it your father when he left the family? It must have been so hard, just after the First World War, for a mother alone with seven children. You told me how, when there was no money, a couple of you kids were asked to go to where your father lived and ask him for some and how he humiliated you all before he decided whether to hand anything over or not.

Did Dad finish the process? Did his insanity send your eyes into that veiled space of emptiness as though you were lost in an ice cube?

I didn't understand this concept of existence Mum because instead of you being my mirror, I think I became your mirror. There was no space for you to validate my responses or my feelings. I learnt quickly the art of becoming the mirror of your non-being. A container for your quintessential fear of feeling anything and I had to reflect back to you what you were and needed to remain. Numb. When I bubbled out of this sometimes, you called me needy.

A child can't exist without at least one adult to provide for their basic physical needs. You were my only non-violent parent and so I had to keep you alive inside you. I had to make your coldness ok. If you saw it mirrored in me then you were not alone. Kate was better than me at retaining the ice connection for you. I found it hard because I felt so much inside me wanting to burst out. You were not real and we all had to remain unreal to you so that whatever was happening to us was not real because I didn't really exist. I think the psychiatrist was right when he said "your mother put you on freeze".

It's only recently that I've understood this. I used to wonder why I never felt comfortable if anyone saw me being. Feeling. Over many years Libby helped me to understand.

So many times Mum, I went to a therapy session immersed in fear, with no idea about why. It often took a while to relax enough to be able to begin talking but this time, when I sat down I must have immediately switched and someone blurted out at the top of her voice:

"Only in isolation can you remain safe! It's a decree! **Rebecca** must never be seen and **The Terror** must remain alive at all costs because if it doesn't, our fire will glow and Rebecca will stand up with life. And if I become real my mother will wash me with acid."

If you saw me feeling and acknowledged the real life force within me then all the rape and violence would actually be happening and if that veil of denial were lifted I think you might have lost your mind. Your words did sometimes splash me like drops of acid.

You had a hint of connection when you talked about the bellbirds and when you asked your grand daughter to draw the big fig tree at Balmoral for you so that you could have it to look at when you needed it. And shells. You loved shells that you collected from all over the world.

And Wordsworth's daffodils, how you loved them. But even with these only a hint of life showed as your green eyes began to sparkle for some moments.

I would have loved sharing nature with you. It offered me such life, beauty and peace. A safe world in which I could be who I am without having to mirror another. A place of existence and of a realness that kept me alive.

I like the way **Stones** describes it: 'When I'm alone, sitting beneath a tree or out in an open field, I'm everything that matters. The air opens up and I'm in a space that wasn't there before. A film slides away like a curtain on a secret stage. My heart begins to open and I'm free to be.'

Did you ever come down to the creek with me? I don't remember a time. We loved it, Prince and I. The water was clean then, gushing through the pipes under the road and over the sandstone. A little upstream from the willow tree was a small pool, quite deep and edged with the plants that glowed silver when you held them under the water. The eels lived there. My friends. Often, at the end of the day Prince and I would sit amongst the buttercups that grew on the grass beside the pool and wait. First we'd see the shadows as the eels slowly swam to the surface then out would pop a face. Flat, no ears, but with a mouth that seemed to stretch into a smile. Have you ever looked into the eyes of an eel? Wow. No useless words necessary there. I loved those eels.

On the other side of the creek was a vast and vacant block of land intended to be part of a road that was never built. I'm glad, because on a large rock just above the willow tree, were several aboriginal rock carvings. Sometimes, when Prince and I took refuge at the creek, and we sat on the rock just next to the carvings, a strange energy emerged and the Spirit of the Rock would join us.

Prince always knew it was there before me, his ears flexed upwards and his head on one side, his body snuggled close to mine. We never needed any words, but its presence gave us strength and courage. When Prince died and I sat alone on the rock, I saw the Spirit of the Rock holding him cradled in its arms and I knew that he was being looked after. You never knew any of this. It would have made me real.

You found it impossible to head towards my intensity and this fear pushed you further and further into your womb of denial. 'The vase is not on the table' is how Richard, the first therapist, always described it.

I want you to imagine, Mum, that you are in possession of original information. You Know, and you see, with clarity, the vase that sits on the table. You try to speak of and to describe what you see and which you know is real. But you are told that even though you see it, it is not there. It has not happened. That even though you are being raped and terrorised by your father, it is not happening. That when you are called a whore and a filthy slut by your mother then the original Knowledge is being validated. That even though it is not your fault that you are being raped, the vase is on the table. However, at all other times it is not, even though you can see it and you are in possession of the original information. First hand. Is your mind being turned inside out? Mine was. Constantly.

I understand that you must have been frightened of him and very confused by what was happening and I've tried to put myself in your shoes to make sense of it all. But why didn't you protect us? I think of my own children and have no understanding of your behaviour. I would protect my children with my life.

He was violent, Mum. And insane. But it was us who protected you. I didn't accept this for a long time during therapy with Libby but after one terrifying memory that pushed its way up into my mind and body, it became a reality. I want you to be there. I want you to know each moment of my terror, my confusion, your betrayal.

I have to go to my room to sleep. School will come around again the next day just as tomorrow will come, covering all within in a veil of denial as the morning light spreads itself through the fear, burying the despair beneath another layer of silence and events not remembered. But I have to get through tonight, to stay alive for tomorrow so, like a snake, furtive but watchful I slide on my belly towards my room, spilling the bowl of cat's milk as I pull myself, one hand, one leg across the green linoleum and into the hallway. 'So far so good,' as I pass the door of Matt's room. The creaking board! I have to get past it! So with my fingers flat I touch each strand of the carpet, moving my right hand forwards, my right leg moving slowly towards my body. Then I carefully pull and push, my tummy slightly raised above the carpet and the telltale board. Now for the left hand, the left foot, each moving deliberately into position then pull and push, listening for any slight sound that will give me away. I relax in a brief moment of relief. Suddenly my father comes thundering towards me, his war cries splitting my mind as he grabs me, twisting me like a green twig. I struggle to get away but I am tossed headlong into your bedroom. I can feel something beneath me but am too scared to move.

Mum's dead!

I can feel your hand against the cotton sheet and it's so cold. I reach up to try and grab hold of the bed head, my fingers touching your hair. I squint, trying to see your eyes, but it's dark tonight. I lift my hand to your face, passing it over your closed eyes, your mouth. I listen for your breath but I can hear only silence.

I see the silhouette of my father He's got an axe! I look up and he's standing with it raised above his head and everything's frozen as if in a tableau.

"I'll get you, you Jap bastard," yells his crazed voice.

I heave your body off the side of the bed, Mum, as the axe comes down, the momentum causing my father's body to crash to the floor. Then with the strength of terror I roll you under the bed and slide in next to you. We remain silent, for the moment safe from the horror of the axe, consciously absorbing the thin phrase of moonlight that's escaped through the pleated curtains. The room is silent.

'Maybe he's gone.' I wriggle slowly out from under the bed. He's standing there!

"I'll get you!" he yells in a voice that matches nothing I've ever known.

Again he lifts the axe high above his head and I vanish into a capsule never to be retrieved. Someone else takes over and I find myself back under the bed as the darkness spreads its forever over my mind and we remain still and silent in its web. I reach over, moving my hand on the soft skin of your freckled arm, hoping that you will sit up and bring the morning.

I breathe and rest my head against your shoulder as I hear my father moving away down the hallway towards the kitchen. I hear the slam of the fly screen door but wait, panic subsiding as the breath begins to return to my body.

"Quickly! Get out of here!" It's Matt. He lifts you, carrying you carefully in his arms into the cool night air, me following. Suddenly there's a flash in my mind. "Dad took the axe. Where's Prince. Where is he!"

Matt puts you, now conscious onto the grass.

"Quick, have a look in the laundry."

I run, fumbling with the door handle until it opens, Prince meeting me with his front paws and velvet tongue. I scoop him up and run outside to the others, burying my face in his fur.

Inside, the darkness is smashed by that cry of battle: "Stay still you vermin!"

Again my mind flashes. "Mister! My cat! Where's Mister!"

But I'm too late as the night air is filled with a screeching wail.

"MISTER!"

I run towards the door. "Come back!" Matt yells, trying to grab me as I hurtle past, thrusting Prince into his arms. But nothing will stop me. Nothing except the inner knowledge of what had happened. Near the back porch I stop, a statue of frozen terror, vanished into numbness, my mind transporting me into a cocoon of non memory.

I don't know what happened next, or how my father dropped the axe and disappeared into his room, and only one part of my mind registered the body of my beautiful tabby cat, Mister lying still on the grey and pink flowers of the lounge room carpet.

For years after my marriage, the birth of my two children and even up until ten years ago I never understood why it was an essential nightly ritual for me before sleeping, to go around the house and hide all bras, pantyhose, scarves and anything with sleeves and take all cushions out of the room. Until one therapy session with Libby when **Cameo** came to tell her story.

I knew that Cameo had to listen for sounds. Any sounds. All sounds. And I knew that something was there, but had no words or images, just a feeling until Cameo emerged, her hand around her throat, uttering a horrible gagging, choking sound.

"I can't breathe!"

I try, my mouth moves but I have no voice. I feel my hands pulling, grabbing, trying to get it away from my throat.

"What's happening?" Libby asks, leaning forwards in her chair.

I can't answer. I feel my body twisting and gasping, trying desperately to breathe, clawing at the strip of something that's tied around my throat, stopping the air.

My body's convulsing and I feel myself in moments of passing out. I want to live and I heave at the strip, kicking violently with my legs at anything near me. Then blackness.

When I open my eyes, Libby is kneeling over me as I lie on the floor, my hands resting by my sides. She takes my hand but I pull it away, grabbing my neck to see if the strip is still there. But it's gone.

"I can breathe!"

I give my hand back to Libby. "Yes," she says. You must have either pulled it off your throat or kicked the person responsible hard enough to hurt them. I know I wouldn't have liked to have been the one you were kicking." She smiled.

"But you survived and now you're here, you're safe and yesterday has gone."

Some people try to stop others crying, thinking that you're strong if you keep your feelings inside you, but they don't understand that the tears only come when the terror has gone and that they wash away the fear and express relief.

I cried for **Cameo** Mum, and she began to move into a space of healing.

I hope it was Dad and not you. But it's all gone now and I lived through it so there's no point in being angry. I only hurt myself if I keep all that inside me, so I've let it go. It did happen. And Mum, the vase is on the table. I can see it.

A big part of your fear was of this information being taken outside the locked silence. So you created patterns that painted the picture of me that you wanted others to see.

'Don't mind Rhonda, she's highly strung. Too emotional for her own good and what an imagination!'

You strung your platitudes like beads around my neck. Repeated often enough and the original Self became invisible.

Some patterns distorted the mirror of my Self to the point where I created other alters in order to prevent my self-destruction. Imagine Mum, that somewhere deep inside yourself you know that you can do things? In fact you often have good ideas and for quite a while you do very well at school. Now, imagine that you're repeatedly told that you are not just a little dopey, but stupid. That you have no right to ever think that you can do anything. Are you confused again?

It's taken a long time and a lot of hard work Mum, but I've finally realised that I am not stupid. If it hadn't been for my innate intelligence and my creativity I would not have had the skills to create the multiplicity and would have either gone insane or have taken my own life.

I also now know and understand that neither am I a whore nor am I evil. In fact I now know that because of my innate goodness and understanding of the precious value of life, I did not kill my father.

I also found you confusing. You were at least three different people: sad, icy, and the teacher. The sad one was vulnerable, frightened. This was your humanness but even though I sometimes saw it I could not allow you to see it in me, your mirror. I internalised your disconnection and created a part within me that matched your behaviour. I call her **The Mother part** and I'd like you to meet her.

This time the switch was definite and dramatic, her head held high, nose in the air, lips pinched, words carefully pronounced, as your counterpart arrived at a session with Libby.

"The Coxes are coming for cards and I'm not sure what I should wear."

Libby was ready. "Have you noticed your daughter, Rhonda, around?"

"She comes and goes. She has ballet lessons. She plays the piano and squeaks on the violin. Never be any good at anything. I have two daughters."

"Did you have a hard time when you were young?"

"What cards will I use, the English gardens or the more plain ones?"

"Tell me about Rhonda?"

"I'll have to take all the stuff off the traymobile and make room for the good tea set."

"Why is Rhonda so vulnerable?"

"Will you stop asking me all these impertinent questions!"

"Does it make you afraid?"

"I have a clever son and the other girl sings. Rhonda won't amount to much, she's too needy."

"Did Howard rape you?"

"Howard grows dahlias, I'll pick some and put them on the sideboard."

"What would happen if it broke this containment? Would you start to see what Howard was doing to your daughter?"

"I wonder what shoes I'll wear."

It helped me to understand a little more of what is must have been like living in your world.

I was fourteen when you went across the sea to Europe for six months and left me with a man who was psychotic and violent. How you could afford it I don't understand because it must have cost heaps and yet I believed your story that it was my fault for being born that you had to work so hard and never had any money. I look at fourteen year old girls now and realise how young I was. Not too young to have my periods.

While you were away I became pregnant to my father for the first time and on several occasions he almost succeeded in killing me. You see, the coloured photo of you, sitting prominently on the mantelpiece, didn't protect me. He raped me. You know that. It happened often, and began when I was very young.

I've told you a little about my multiplicity. Have I told you about co-consciousness? It took a long time in my therapy with Libby for the boundaries around each isolated part of me to begin to gradually break down and finally to fall away. To know about each other's existence, to talk to each other, to co-operate with each other. Being co-conscious was one of the ways of getting information safely to other alters so that, even when not out in the body but present, they could be aware of what was being said and what was happening. Of course there was always a front person co-operating with Rhonda. **Bernadette** was only three, Mum, when she came and talked to Libby, telling her story. I think it will help you to understand if I use some of her own words.

I had moved to the floor, sitting with my knees curled up onto my chest.

"I-I scared. My proper Daddy's not here any more," her voice small and very young.

Suddenly, in the room with Libby I felt both my arms raised over my head and my body rocking backwards and forwards.

"Daddy's not Daddy! He's got a felt dolly and it dances and sings and I want to touch it and dance too. I reach out to it but it dances higher and higher."

I feel my body relax a little.

"Daddy's back now. I can hear his voice, 'come and sit next to me'."

I suddenly scream, as **Bernadette** hears the horrible voice of the insane father. "Lie down!" he yells.

She is too frightened to move. "Lie down!"

She does, because the dolly has stopped dancing and is lying down. But she feels something where her panties are. She tries to keep still but something is hurting her badly.

"Look at the doll!"

She opens her eyes, staring at the felt doll that is swaying in front of her face. She screams again. He has put some other object inside her and the pain is intense. She is crying.

"Keep quiet! Look at the doll. Look –at—the—doll!" he yells.

She does as the voice tells her even when he finally walks away leaving it protruding from between her legs. She's just lying there, staring at the doll that's now on the floor bedside her, too scared to move or to close her eyes in case he comes back.

It took much reassurance from Libby for Bernadette to finally understand that the broom handle had been removed and that the frightening Daddy was no longer here.

For quite a number of years during my therapy with Libby I had the very strange feeling that there was a broken off penis stuck inside me. Sounded completely crazy at the time, but now I know what it was about and as soon as Bernadette told us her story and was brought into the present time, the feeling vanished.

My periods eventually started and I became fertile. I remember the first time I got them and thought I was bleeding to death. You gave me some old towels to wipe the blood away, but it just kept coming. Kate rescued me, told me what was happening and gave me some pads and those elastic things we clipped them into. Those cut up pieces of old towels became your trademark, Mum. You gave them to me for my birthday and for Christmas. You even filled a string bag with them and gave them to me to take on my honeymoon. No words, just a bag full of old toweling to wipe up the mess of sex. I took them, still compliant, not understanding why you'd given them to me, not even aware enough to question. I threw them all out about fifteen years ago, when I realised. It felt good.

For such a long time after my periods began I was afraid to take my soiled undies and soak them, or even to wash them. I could not allow you to see me as a sexual being, or even as a female so I would save my pocket money from gardening, go to Woolworths and buy new ones, hiding the soiled knickers in the bottom of my wardrobe drawers.

When I came home from school one afternoon they were displayed on my bed. You'd taken them all out of the drawers, my drawers, and lined them up on my bedspread. You stood at the door, telling me that I was to leave them there until morning and then I'd know what a filthy little thing I was. You then shut the door. I was fifteen and I wasn't game to move them. I still thought you could see through walls .

It took me almost a year to build up the courage to ask you to buy me my first bra. I so badly wanted to look like the other girls and by the time I was about fifteen my nipples poked out from the flattened bumps under the jumpers you knitted me and there are only so many ways of crossing your arms.

The words turned over and over in my head as I waited until you seemed to be approachable, but as soon as I got into your room I became a quaking wimp and just stood there watching you.

"Would you help me with this? "For heavens sake, why are you just standing there!"

"Can I have bra please?"

You laughed.

"I'd really like to have a bra please." Finally you bought me one and I no longer had to cross my arms.

I was still not allowed to wear anything that was feminine or that fitted in with the other girls. You made most of my clothes, and I'm grateful for that, but I always looked and felt very dowdy. That is until I saved my pocket money and bought a skirt and some luminous green socks for myself at Woolworths. I kept them stashed under the bed in a bag and became a quick-change artist after I left the house and before I got home. I loved that skirt. It was colourful and showed off my waist and when I danced it swirled outwards and I felt like a princess. The luminous green socks were my way of pointing a finger up at you.

You were full of surprises.

"I've made an appointment for you at the Neurological Centre. Next Tuesday."

"Why am I going there?"

"To have a brain scan."

"Why do need a brain scan!"

"Your father's sister, Ruth, had epilepsy."

"What does that have to do with me?"

"It got worse when her periods started. The appointment is at two o'clock. I'll pick you up from school early."

I was sixteen and had absolutely no idea why I was there or what would happen. The whitewashed room was full of large monitors with tubes of wire and gauges like clocks lined up along a central board.

"Just sit here dear and I'll wire you up," said the neurological person as she glued the receptors to my head. The questions screamed silently. Is this all my fault, my punishment. Are they going to see right inside my head and find out how stupid I am? How evil I am?

"When I say, close your eyes, count to five then open them again."

I felt the tingle as the current spread through my head. My precious inner world. Will it change my brain? Take away all thought and make me completely silent?

"Why did I have to have that done to me?" I asked you. "You didn't make it happen to Kate."

You just opened the car door and we drove home and nothing more was ever said about it until my daughter turned fifteen when you suggested that she should perhaps have the neurological examination. How weird was that! You had said nothing when Kate's daughters reached that age and I have no idea what was going on in your head. There was nothing wrong with my daughter. Or me.

I don't mean to criticize too much Mum, because I know you worked long and hard and on top of that you had to shop and cook for us, but some of your culinary efforts bring a giggle to the surface. There was Dad with his kidneys, liver, brains and chokos and you with a pressure cooker that was always erupting all over the ceiling. Oh, and your curried custard. Yuk! Your salads were great and you were aware of eating healthy food, even then. Though you were quite a tyrant really, making us sit there until every bit of food had gone. I don't know what the others did at the times when your cooking was at its worst, whether they ate it or stored it in pouches underneath their clothing, but I always seemed to be the last, sitting there trying somehow to get the food off my plate and into my mouth. One such time I remember sitting at the matching set of dining chairs, table and sideboard, staring into space, pretending. The plate, laden with a disgusting mixture of kidneys, tripe and watery spinach becomes larger and larger until it looms before me as an ill-begotten flying saucer imprisoned by the mush that lies on top of it.

"You will not leave the table until you have eaten every morsel on that plate," comes your command from the kitchen.

This combination defies even a second glance but gradually I allow my eyes to creep up on the innards festooned in gravy that lie dead and disconnected on my plate. The white, rubbery mass of the tripe wobbles gently as I poke at it with my fork.

"Stop playing with your food!" comes the proclamation from the invisible eyes that see through walls.

Obedience must follow so I pick up the silvery knife and fork and slowly approach the defiant white mass. A small piece, severed after much carving, moves towards my mouth which I command to open and as my teeth chew on its rubbery flesh I think of the sheep, cut open, dismembered but free of blood, set out on butchers' trays so that we can eat it.

I'd better close my eyes and finish it, I think as my hand slips down by my side, propelling a rather large piece into the mouth of my waiting dog. He spits it out and looks up at me with disgust. Next is the spinach. If I think of it as fairy poo, maybe I can have a wish and something magical might happen to those kidneys. I wait and wait but they remain exactly where they are, with eyes that appear to stare at me, daring me to devour them.

Everyone else's left the table. Maybe they're all crowded into the bathroom vomiting up all their muck into the toilet, to be flushed out into the drains where the rats could have a meal on it. They're welcome to it.

I cover my eyes, hoping that these pieces of anatomy, covered in what is by now cold, congealed, faeces-coloured gravy have taken the hint and will play the game of hide-n-seek that I'm initiating. But they remain on my plate, eternally dead. There's only one thing left to do. Prince has gone to bed. So I close my eyes and begin to spear the enemy.

Then the ultimatum from the invisible enemy. "For goodness sake, will you stop being so ridiculous and EAT!"

There was no other way. Piece after piece of that awful stuff follows each other into my screwed-up face, coming to rest in my stomach. I look down and imagined the parsley-spotted tripe, the disloyal fairy poo and the parts of the dead cow all mixed up in a sea of milk and run at great speed to the bathroom.

It wasn't Dad who finally took Prince away from me. It was you.

It was mid morning and I can remember running in the back door, Prince by my side, the fly screen banging behind us. Matt was sitting at the dining room table reading the Saturday Herald. You were at the sink in the kitchen preparing food, a half sliced onion in your hand and your eyes watering. I sneezed as I caught a wiff of the flowering privet. You asked me to go up the street and get some fresh bread for lunch. "Leave Prince here," you said. "There's a lot of traffic on Saturday mornings."

You were not one to argue with so I ran into the bedroom to get my sandshoes, flopping onto the lounge to do them up when there was a knock at the front door. Prince and I got there first, smiling at the man who stood on the doorstep.

"Is this the dog to be taken away?"

It struck me like a bullet, Mum, and I was too scared to move in case it was real. You came into the hallway wiping your hands as I screamed at you, trying to find our what was happening. But you pushed me away, took off your apron and opened the door.

"Are you from the vet?" you said in your best voice.

The man nodded. "Is your daughter alright, 'Mam? She didn't seem to know--"

"She wasn't supposed to be here," you said, turning around and calling Prince. "Come on, boy. Come!"

I was terrified as he started to move towards you so I grabbed him and ran out into the backyard. You followed, chasing us, trying to take him from me. I didn't know what to do or where to go, Mum.

"It's for the best, girlie." It was the man from the vet. "Your mother says that he's not well."

"It's ok Bub. He will be alright." It was Matt, taking my arm gently, trying hard to help me.

"Where are they taking him!"

"He's going to the vet's."

"Why can't we take him? Who's going to bring him home?"

"She doesn't understand, 'mam. Can't we just talk about this?"

"Give me the dog Rhonda!" you yelled Mum, lunging at Prince and grabbing him by the stomach as he yelped and struggled to get away from you.

"Stop it. Stop it! You're hurting him!"

"Let go, you stupid girl. Let go!"

You pushed me over Mum, I dropped him and the man from the vet rushed in to pick him up. "It's ok boy."

"Give him back to me. Please, give him back to me!"

"He's sick, Rhonda. They'll put him to sleep peacefully." Your voice had softened Mum but I still didn't know what to do!

"To sleep? You're going to put Prince to sleep!!"

"I knew she'd behave like this!"

"While I wasn't here!"

"I thought it would be better that way."

The man tried to smile, opened the door and walked out, Prince struggling in his arms while you held me and stopped me from going after them.

I ran to my room and stared out the window, wondering what Prince was feeling and how I was ever going to tell him goodbye as the man put Prince into the back of his van. My screams were choked by the feeling surging in my belly and taking over my mind as the van backed out of the driveway and disappeared.

You took away my best friend Mum, my only safety and the only living being in the world that I cared about.

That night, **The Master Planner** gathered up all the imaginary dolls of many shapes and sizes and wrapped them within me. When they were each safely enfolded, he withdrew my hands and my face, leaving a blank sheet of skin with no eyes, ears, nose or mouth to receive any feeling, or to register the presence of others and no hands to reach out or to touch. **Rebecca**, in the form of a coil, was consolidated.

Did you ever realize that the house that I live in now with my own family, a place filled with nature and love, is in the valley opposite where the vet used to be. Where he was taken and put to sleep. I didn't realize this when we bought the land and built our house over thirty years ago, until one evening recently as I sat out on the verandah watching the cockatoos as they flew over on the way to their nightly nesting spot further down the valley. Their raucous screeching caused all the dogs in residence at the vet's to bark. I like to think that it was Prince who directed me to our beautiful bushland and his photo sits permanently on my piano.

Thank you for my piano lessons that reached through the walls and touched me. If I close my eyes and remember, I can see Kate and I walking up the hill at Seaforth and into Mrs. Ziegler's big white house that overlooked the water. She was always there waiting for us with a glass of milk and a home made biscuit. And time. Time to sit on the window seat, consume the afternoon tea and chat. About the day, about music, about the sun on the water. Her eyes connected and she never hurried us.

I have a vivid picture of her in my mind, with her grace and dignity that I enjoyed when I was young. Not an arrogant self, but strong and gentle with a beautiful maturity. She encouraged an open curiosity and a deep sense of musicianship and she smiled with her eyes. We didn't do piano exams, we played music, and from when I was seven to seventeen, I loved it.

I still have her copy of the Chopin Waltzes that she lent me so long ago. I've played almost every one of the waltzes over time, always with the feeling of being still in a lesson in the big white house near the water.

She saw and she cared and from somewhere within, sensed my sadness and the music filled up lots of empty spaces. She allowed me to express myself, in a safe place that was constant, giving me nothing but warmth and encouragement, backed up with a wonderful musicianship and once a week, the permission to be me, which became a package that I hid deep within me and which I took home, and into the world that I had created behind the mirror.

The music camps at Broken Bay. Oh how I loved them. Singing all day, laughing, being with other people who loved music the way I did. And being free to learn in a place of trees, water and no fear.

When I was thirteen you and I got dressed in our best clothes and you took me to a cinema in the city. When the lights went down and it began, colour, and music, the like of which I had never heard before filled me up to overflowing. Voices, orchestra, movement, story, and most of all melodies that meandered through my soul and shook my being. It was a production of "Tosca" by Puccini and I had never imagined that anything so beautiful could exist.

Thank you for the music Mum.

Dear Howard,

I've been looking at a photo of us when we were young, draped around each other and smiling. Do you remember our honeymoon on Lord Howe Island? You loved sitting on the sand, watching the terns as they swooped and played on the wind and I loved the mutton birds when they returned from the sea every evening, squabbling with each other as they searched out their nests. We swam, talked and made love and I felt like a princess.

You were such a good athlete Howard, strong and tall with a deep olive skin and gentle, blue eyes and when you looked at me I knew I was loved.

You never talked about the war, but you came back from New Guinea a changed person, with nightmares that caused you to call out and to wake up trembling. Even awake, they plagued you and sometimes I'd catch you just staring as if you were watching something I couldn't see, while sweat poured down your grimaced face. I rarely saw the person I had married after that. It was as though you had disappeared into the heat of the jungle and the horrors of legal cruelty.

Do you remember building our house at Hope Street? It was after the war and we tried to pick up the pieces and move forward with our family. We planned together what room would go where and how big each would be then got a 'War Service Loan' and built our dream house. We picked bits of a frangipani tree from a house in Mosman and ran. It reminded us of Lord Howe Island and the sand and sun. They grew into beautiful bushes, not really tall but quite spreading, one each side of the front path. On summer evenings their perfume took me back to happy times as it wafted in through our bedroom window.

And we all loved your sweet peas that trailed along Kelly's fence, filling our eyes with pastel shades and our memories with their pungent scent. I think the garden was your way of trying to connect with something real and tangible. Just like the captured moments of connection when you sat with Rhonda as she played your favourite songs. It was the only part of your music that remained as you never played any more, just listened.

It's not you I moved away from Howard, just the insanity, the fear and the emptiness that took you away from me. When you died I felt a deep chasm of sadness that washed through the depths of our memories before the war killed your mind and made you crazy. I heard a piece of the music that you loved as the coffin containing your body moved away, I felt your arms cradle me and knew that we had somewhere and at some time, shared something good.

That is how I like to remember you. I will die soon, thinking of you as you used to be. Of us as we were before the inhumanity of war destroyed you.

Mavis

CHAPTER 7

Hello Dad

When the whirring noise started and your coffin began to move, I wanted to leap up and hang on to it. 'No, Dad! Don't leave! Not before I can empty my words into your hands and my fear into your eyes.' The curtains closed and you were gone. I ran outside, through the endless rows of plaques that besieged the gardens of the crematorium but nothing registered. Nothing but your face, taking up all the space in front of my eyes. I was twenty-seven.

You were young once Dad. I have photos of you, tall and slim, fit and agile. You had more hair then and sometimes smiling eyes. Do you remember the times when we piled in the car, you, me and Prince off to The Spit to hit golf balls? It was just an isthmus of land then, stretching out into Middle Harbour. You were such a good golfer, with a handicap of four. You'd whack the ball and it was our job to find it. Mostly Prince got there first, his long golden ears flapping behind him. You could have played professionally had your mind not escaped into its chaos. And the fish market picnics, do you remember them? Every year I won all the races and you were proud of me as I was presented with the winner's solid silver butter dish with a light green piece of glass sitting inside it.

I loved being your partner when we played Canasta, a woolen rug on the dining room table and the cards dealt. You often kept a whole canasta in your hand until the last minute when you'd slap it down on the table, grinning at me and leaving them all with a fist full of cards. Sometimes Mum asked the Coxes from down the road to play and we'd get all dressed up and tidy up all the spaces that they'd see. Mum picked some of your dahlias too and put them in a vase on the sideboard.

And gosh were we a good gardening team, shoveling the dirt into the sieve, chucking out every tiny corm of the onion weed and using the good soil to grow dahlias of all bright colours. Mum grew delicious strawberries, we grew beautiful flowers, the sun on our skin and Prince always nearby.

They were good times Dad. Times that my conscious mind hung onto, creating a loom on which I could weave my fairy story and build my secret world. That is, until the terror began to haemorrhage like a hideous beast onto my unmarked pillow. A memory that had filled my pillow many times and which I finally put into words in the safety of Libby's therapy room.

She feels the night air on her face as she picks up her belongings from the dining room table and walks through the kitchen. There's a light on in the bathroom that guides her up the hallway to her room. Tiredness hangs from her young body as she slowly dresses for bed, the brush removing the tangles of the day from her hair. She smiles at the face that stares at her from the mirror on her dressing table, then turns out the light and flops into bed. The moonlight shines in comforting slats through the venetian blind, her dog Prince, and her cat Mister each nestle into the spaces. But as sleep descends she hears the sounds.

Her father is home.

She moves quickly, stuffing her bed with pillows, grabbing Prince and Mister and bundling them and herself underneath it, finally covering her feet with the blanket. The night will pass and tomorrow is school, maybe the magic will come and she'll be safe.

She hears her father's lumbering footsteps moving up the front stairs, the banging and swearing as he fumbles with the key. Mister crawls out, stretches and curls up on her pillow but she holds Prince close, his soft fur touching her face, becoming one with the blackness. He's here. She can smell the alcohol. Mister leaps off as he grabs hold of the bedclothes and flings them back.

"Where are you, you vermin!"

He grabs her pyjamas, yanking her out from her hiding place. She lets go of Prince, reaching for anything solid as she feels herself lifted, his hands like the claws of a crane, hard and ungiving. Slung over his shoulder like a soggy, limp blanket, bouncing on his muscle and bone as he sways down the hallway.

His foot kicks open the fly screen door and she feels herself moving up through space as he steps down from the porch and stumbles across the garden. She calls to the moonlight that touches the leaves of the liquid amber. Too late. The garage door slams shut as she feels the darkness engulfing her. She disappears. **Beatrice** is here.

He throws her with the thrust of insanity across the garage, her legs dangling, her head swirling. Flying through the air, a lead weight suspended, landing with a thud on the concrete floor, grabbing at the pain in her shoulder . She picks herself up and quickly tries to hide behind the shovel, holding it across her face and head like a small metal shield. She is silent. He finds her, lunging forth, the garage filled with the savagery of a remembered battle cry. Hand to hand combat. A fight to the death.

Luckily his energy is quickly spent as he staggers over to her, eyes hideous as he passes out, pinning her underneath. She waits, then tries to push him, squirming her own body in a desperate effort to free herself. As she does she feels the warm liquid on her thigh as it spills from his bladder and the foul stench fills her nostrils as she watches the watery brown faeces spewing onto the garage floor, covering his trousers.

"Get off me!"

She heaves herself up enough to finally roll his body off her. Sitting quietly, too afraid to breathe and too betrayed to want to. The moonlight has come inside to help her, squeezing its gentle light through the cracks in the brick walls.

She looks at him, her confusion full of pity and disgust. Then, catching sight of the sickly white substance lying dead and glutinous on her leg, she screams:

"NO!"
There is silence.

"Open your eyes and look around. Are you still in the garage?"
She doesn't fully understand, but as Rhonda slowly returns, she shakes her head.
"Are you safe?" Libby asks.
"Yes. But I don't understand exactly what happened."
"I think he was so inebriated that you experienced his triple incontinence. What do you need right now?"
Silence.
"Would you like to take my hands?"
I leant forwards in my chair with my hands extended to Libby, gradually returning as the warmth spread its safety through me.

It's amazing how my system created itself, with alters each made to keep the terror from me, enabling me, sometimes as **Lucy,** other times as **Stones,** to go out into the world outside and operate within the parameters of an accepted norm. Enabling me to retain my sanity.

One such part is **Emma.** I find it difficult to recount some incidents, especially when it was you and me involved, so I've asked **The Storyteller** to take over. The memory came spilling out in a therapy session with Libby and I want you to hear it. You probably have no recollection as you were steely-eyed, with no awareness of the moment and no conscience. But you know what the garage looked like and I'm sure you can picture it all very clearly.

It's night time, inside the garage. Rhonda has vanished and left her body to Emma who was called a slut and a whore by the mother. It was Emma's job, clothed sustainably in compliance, to be raped.

The garage, built of red brick and covered almost entirely with ivy is only large enough to hold one car. On the side that faces the back yard is a wooden door with a lock that's opened by a large key with a long neck. Inside this door on the left is a workbench running the full width of the building, tools hanging up almost neatly above it. A very small window, covered on the outside in cobwebs and never opened looks out onto the back paling fence. It is the source of the moonlight.

Under the bench, boxes of small ceramic tiles of different colours lie heaped upon each other waiting to be used.

Each side of the garage is filled with pieces of old bikes, bits of cars and empty paint tins. Greasy old rags and hessian bags lie draped across garden forks, shovels and axes that stand on the floor, while other implements hang from the metal hooks on the walls. In the right hand corner near the two front doors an old white bookshelf holds tins of half used paint and old brushes standing in empty peach and beetroot tins. A rusted mattock protrudes out into the empty car space, its handle lying in the mixture of grease and sawdust that covers the garage floor. The two wooden front doors open out to each side, leading down the narrow driveway of two strips of concrete, each wide enough for the wheel of a car, mown grass between them, stretching out to the street beyond.

Looking up inside the garage you can see the wooden rafters, criss-crossing the air, planks of grey timber resting patiently on the lower horizontals. The ivy has edged its way through the ventilation holes near the rafters and adds a splash of green where the moonlight falls on the southern wall.

The outline of a teenage girl can be seen lying on the floor near the mattock. It's Emma. She is tied up, her legs spread-eagled and attached to the bench posts. A rope has been secured around her waist to the handle of the side door. Her wrists have been tied together.

A murky green Austin A40, early 1950 vintage has been driven into the garage. Emma is under the car in between the wheels. Her head and trunk are completely covered, her legs protruding near the bench posts.

The father sits in the driver's seat of the car, steely blue psychotic eyes wide open and unblinking, staring straight ahead. He slowly, almost robotically gets out of the car, closes and bolts the garage doors then gets back into the car as before, his hands firmly holding onto the steering wheel. He freezes.

Libby, representing the present, stands in the shadows, watching and talking quietly to Emma who is right back in time, in the garage.

Emma looks towards the small window above the work bench.

"I can see the moon."

Libby leans towards her: "Why are you lying there like that Emma?"

But Emma keeps staring straight ahead. "Just keep watching the moonlight. I'm watching the moonlight." She closes her eyes. "I'm dead now."

"You're not dead Emma. I can see you breathing."

Libby watches as Emma begins to twist and pull on the ropes that bind her legs and body.

"It's hurting me!"

"I'm here Emma."

She suddenly goes completely limp.

"Have you given up, Emma?"

Silence.

"Ssshhh, don't move. He must think I'm dead."

The silence continues until broken by a child-like voice. "There's something big on me."

"What is it Emma?"

Her breathing becomes shorter, faster. "It's a car! I'm under a car!"

"Can you move out from under it?"

"I'm tied up!" (urgently)

"Come on, get yourself out of there."

"Sshhh. He'll hear you."

Libby moves towards the car and bends down next to Emma.

"Come on Emma, untie yourself!"

She struggles to reach the ropes, eventually tugging at those around her waist.

"I can't get out!"

"Keep pulling Emma. You must get out of there."

Emma pulls as hard as she can, twisting the rope in her fingers, slowly undoing the knots. Then she heaves at them grunting and groaning.

"It's coming Emma. The rope's nearly off."

Emma gets the rope off her wrists, then off her waist and slumps into total inaction.

"Well done Emma, you're almost there. Can you sit up and untie your legs?

"It's no use."

"Why, Emma. Why?" Emma remains still.

Suddenly a loud moaning noise comes from the car. The father is coming to life. Increasing in intensity, the father rocking absurdly in the small cabin as it rocks on its wheels. Libby instantly jumps out of the way. Emma freezes. It abates slowly, the father taking up his original position as the unpredictable silence resumes.

"Did you hear him? That's the monster. That's him!" Emma whispers.

"He's dead Emma. He died a long time ago." Libby pauses, "Can I touch you?"

"No!"

"I'll never hurt you Emma. Would it help if I stroke your arm?"

She nods, looks into her eyes and smiles.

Now suddenly pulling at the ropes around her ankles. "He's up there isn't he?"

Waiting."

She finally frees her legs then throws the ropes to one side.

Libby whispers "Find a hiding place. Quickly!"

"Sshhhh. He'll hear you."

"Go on. Careful of your head. That's it, keep wriggling. He hasn't seen you."

Libby helps her to stand then walks across to a dark corner on the left of the bench, the moonlight just mentioning her as a solid form.

"You're safe now Emma. Go over and look at your father," says Libby gently.

"I can't. Not while his eyes look like that!"

"Would it help if I went with you?"

"No. He might kill us both."

"Who can help you?"

Emma moves out of the shadows. "Policemen."

"Are they with you now Emma?"

She nods. "They're going to surprise him, two of them, one each side of the car. And there's another one with me." She holds tightly to the sleeve of the imaginary policeman on her right.

"They have him now."

"Why are you crying? He's been dead for a long, long time and he will never hurt you again." Libby walks around the car towards her. "Did you hear that Emma?"

Emma looks confused.

"He died when Rhonda was twenty-seven. You were tucked away in a cocoon with your memories, deep inside Rhonda's mind."

"So—he's not really here now?"

"No. You're remembering what happened a long time ago when Rhonda was only fifteen."

"But I can see him! He's there, sitting in the car!"

"I know you can. We know this happened. This is how Rhonda survived, but you're safe now."

"So he's dead?"

"Yes."

Emma walks slowly and cautiously over to the car, stopping at the driver's seat, still hanging on tightly to the imaginary policeman. The window is open and she stares at her father slumped over the wheel.

"He looks so sad. His eyes—they're not crazy any more."

"Can you tell him that he'll never hurt you again."

"I can't. I can't!"

"Yes you can Emma. Say: I know you're not alive any more."

Emma hesitates then repeats, "I know that you're not alive any more---"

"And what I'm remembering—"

"And what I'm remembering,"(she lifts her head), happened a long time ago."

"You can't-----" Silence. "Come on Emma, tell him."

Emma suddenly stands. "You can't hurt me any more. You can never hurt me again. You can never tie me up or drive cars over me. And you can never rape me again! Thumping her fists on the bonnet of the car. You can never, never, never hurt me again!! Did you hear that Dad?"

She runs and flings herself into Libby's safe arms. There is silence, finally broken by a child's voice: "I want my good Daddy to come back."

Libby hugs her and they walk through the garage doors, down the driveway and out the front gate.

The fear was diffused for the moment, however, this memory, like many others surfaced several times in different forms before it was completed, the terror silenced and we all finally understood that you were dead.

I guess I'm a bit disjointed at times in my telling you of these things. That's how memory works. Pieces of information from any moment in time, that gurgle their way to the surface and sit there, just beyond reach until they and/or I am ready. I sometimes wish that they were there on a conveyor belt, waiting, all lined up in chronological order in neat, contained packages. But they emerge in bits and pieces, from here, from there, from then and rarely in full. When I think about it that's how and why my system works as nothing is to ever be whole.

Like this one that emerged quite early in our therapy with Libby, just as a caption of fear expressed as 5,7,9,11, a segment repeated on many occasions but not in full until much later.

The second I sat down in Libby's room I knew that I had to move my chair forward, away from something awful, and immediately there was a switch and we were right there in the memory.

"5,7,9,11 Must sit perfectly still. Steel eyes! They're there in front of me."

"You sound very young." Libby says.

"Have to stand still. Then he takes my pants off. Have to do as he says. So scared of steel eyes. Have to sit where he says. I'm always sitting up on something. The table, the radiogram. I have to sit still. Daytime, it's daytime and I think my mother's gone back to school. When I can't go to school she comes home at lunchtime and makes me a boiled egg. I heard the front door close. He must have been hiding in the garage and now it's just me and steel eyes. 5,7—'Sit Rhonda. SIT!' he yells at me."

"Don't touch me! 5,7,9,11--- He opens his trousers and he's playing with himself. But he's staring at me. Got to keep my eyes open or he hits me. Must keep silent. Steel eyes. Puts my legs around him. They don't reach. Lifts me up and shoves me down.

It hurts. Always hurts." (screaming, unable to stop.)

"Is it ok for me to put my hand on your back." Libby asks.

(Nods) "Must end it! Must make him go away. He sits me back and does up his trousers. Then he walks away."

"And leaves you there?"

Nods.

It took almost a week for the body memories to heal. The bloated stomach and aching genitals that made it very real and helped me to know that it did happen. I often have the body symptoms that I'm ready to work with and if I have the courage to face them they can provide an access to what is silent and hidden.

It wasn't until about six years later that I was ready for the next revelation. It came out in a session about money. Funny that. Guess it's all about having absolutely no power and no control.

Libby leant forwards: "Picture yourself fully in charge of your money." But I went into immediate terror.

"Where are you?"

(rocking violently on the chair) "In the house---5,7,9,11---"

"My mother was there, watching! And when he walked away she came at me."

'You little slut! I go to work and look what you do.'

"It was a bulls-eye, right into the heart of my being. And then she started hauling and pushing me, venting her venom for all her worth. It was like I had no being any more. A rag doll with no stuffing. No more of her hard earned money was she ever going to spend on me. But I had disappeared."

"How old were you?"

"About nine."

"What's the 5,7,9,11?"

"When I totally disappeared one of the only links I had with reality was counting, always in odd numbers."

Magnitude, the sage of my system always knew that Mum had this other side. She must have been filled with so much confusion, so many conflicting emotions. I was her child and I know that deep within her, she cared, but I also know that Magnitude was right when he said: "When you were born, alive, the mother shook and shuddered, despairing in the knowledge that through the madness you were begot. How did you ever get to be born alive! This was not in the plan. Not in his, not in hers. For his fire was diminished and covered by layers of gentle snow that it should burn unforsaken at will.

Rhonda, you came along and wanted more. You wanted connection, with him, with her. They could not give it because they could neither acknowledge your life nor bear to look at your Fire. For hers was hidden deep within the bowels of her fear, riding sidesaddle, with no hands to hold the reins and no speech to guide the ox. When you came along with mortal fire, they could not bear it. That's why she washed you with acid when she saw the flames to flicker and the light to dance."

This also helps me to understand that strong piece of knowledge that I always had about never being allowed to be seen experiencing or feeling. That if she saw into my soul then she would wash me with acid.

Dad, you became more and more crazy. I must have dissociated almost constantly at home, creating more parts of me to hold the terrible secrets away from my consciousness. I'd love to know what was going on inside your head but even in your more rational periods, when my 'real father' was present neither of us ever remembered. My system made sure I didn't, your memory was blotted out by insanity or alcohol and Mum was whitewashed in denial. It was as though these things never happened and everyone had to act accordingly and to somehow survive almost in silence until the next day.

So, as part of my survival I created parts in here that mirrored you. **The Him,** an angry, feisty part carrying your PTSD and who had what I believed was the ability to be behind your steely blue eyes and therefore to know what you might do next. **The soldier**, who tried to understand your pain, 'Kill or Be Killed', the part essential to each moment, who believed he was ready for anything you did. **The Father**, a mixture of the Him and a safe degree of softness and compassion.

Most people appear to think that rape is the worst part of abuse and terror, and of course it's a shocking experience and a deep violation that should never happen. I think that it's equaled by violence. Knowing that your life could end at any moment defies any words and freezes the psyche. I guess that's what you felt in New Guinea. I don't know if you were raped, but you knew about instant death and I guess that's what pushed you into insanity. You were an adult. I was a baby, a young child, an adolescent, a young woman, and rape looms large in the equation, but it's the terror created by your unpredictable life-threatening violence from which it's taken me so long to recover.

Sometimes, during therapy it all spilled over into my every day adult life, especially in the early days of therapy when our Multiplicity was not acknowledged and so many of us in here still needed to speak, feeling that we were being buried again with only the Terror to keep us company.

One such occasion was time away when our kids were young, with friends and their families at Hawks Nest, on a day like any other when we all went for a walk along the beach.

The voices of my friends sifted through the sand, but panic had begun to spread and the terror gripped my body. Hot, my feet were burning, but messages were not reaching my mind, there was no space left that was not filled with terror in the form of abstract images that flounced before me. Just like the single rose in the vase that in my mind had grown into a vine with eyes staring at me from every part of it.

I'd fallen behind the group, my whole being working to repel the fear, to retain the boundary between it and me. I watched as one of my friends turned and beckoned to me. How could I be with them? They didn't know it was beginning. How could they? I had to hold on. Hold on. The first one grew out of the sand, eyes spread evenly along its massive length as it grew and grew, a thick substantial thread of rough yellow sand that moved like the body of a snake about to strike. As it emerged the eyes doubled in number, green, and some steely blue that stared through the blueness, caking my inner world with slime. The mounds of sand hills began to move towards me, almost marching to the tune of the dancing eyes.

I ran towards the sea. But the thread began to rise from the water, eyes glowing, menacing in their surety of purpose. "Traitor!" I called as my body splashed in the panic of betrayal, pulsing through its mass and into the air. Rescue me air. Let me breathe your life into my body and relief into my brain. Cold, hard sand pressed up between my toes as they slapped the waves, lungs gasping.

The eyes still followed. I musn't fall. To fall would be to stop and to stop would be to be captured by the tentacles of the terror. The sea was quieting, its eyes dissolving one by one into the whiteness of the foam. Was this a reprieve? A chance to breathe a little slower and run a little less, for my mind to return one molecule at a time.

I still felt its silence lurking and as I tilted my head to look up into the blue of the sky, it came towards me once more, this time sent from the air that had filled my lungs and promised me safety. Nowhere left to go as I let my body fall into the shallows.

I felt its snake-like form brush my arm, the back of my neck, then its solid grip on my shoulders, trying to crush me in every way possible. Still I hung on to anything that connected me with calmness that prevented the Terror from winning. It will pass. It must pass, just don't let go. Eyes closed tightly, not allowing the solid thread and green eyes to penetrate my consciousness. Gathering strength from inside, accumulating a self with which to fight back.

Weaker now, the tentacles gradually let go their hold, disappearing into the blueness of the sky, the green and the icy eyes finally vanishing. Until next time.

Do you remember hauling me out of bed sometimes Dad, in what felt like the middle of the night?

"Get up if you're coming or I'll go without you." You were grinning when I reached the car, and dressed in a grey coat, your uniform for your job at the fish markets. At least it was clean but on the way home you stank like an old fish stew.

"Struth! I forgot the bloody bridge toll," fumbling in your pockets.

The markets were alive with Greeks, Italians, Yugoslavs, Chinese and a smattering of Aussies, all becoming one, getting the job done. Feeding their families. You were good as an auctioneer. I don't know how all the calling ever got heard over the din of the crates or the chatter and arguments that raged amongst the confusion of the fish.

I remember the first time I saw the living crabs. "Why do they tie them up?" I asked you.

"So they can cook them."

"Do people eat them!"

"Bloody oath they do, but they boil them in water first. Real delicacy, crab."

"Are they dead when they're boiled?" I asked, all my fingers crossed behind my back.

"Course not! They do the same with prawns and lobsters. Delicious."

I turned away hoping no-one could see the tears that dribbled down my face. And they think that burning witches at the stake was uncivilized.

I heard the voice right behind me: "How's your little daughter today Howard?" It was Guiseppe. I asked you later why he always looked so sad.

"He misses his family, him and all the other poor blighters that work their guts out so they can afford to bring their families out here to live with them."

I felt sad for Guiseppe and all the other 'poor blighters,' and the helpless shellfish.

It was good when we drove straight home, but often you'd park the car somewhere in Leichhhardt and leave, telling me to wait. Sometimes you'd be gone for hours. I'm glad you always told me to lock the doors and wind up the windows almost to the top because one time there was this totally crazy man with a huge knife who came jumping all over the car, peering in the windows and yelling out that he'd get me. I was terrified Dad, curled up in a ball, screaming as loudly as I could so I couldn't hear him. But when he started rocking the car I thought it was going to tip up and roll down the hill.

I guess he was crazy from the war too. You always came back either drunk or with 'steel eyes' and I knew that I had to just sit still and hold on as tightly as I could. One time you were going so much all over the road that I tried to climb over into the back seat.

"Stay where you bloody well are!" you yelled.

I did, closing my eyes as we wove our way across curbs, narrowly missing light poles and people.

I thought I had dealt with this memory about four years into therapy but the intense fear surfaced again almost seventeen years later when the kids had left home and Bruce and I bought a caravan. I loved it and it became our 'cubby house'. On a long holiday to South Australia with beanies, campfires, dinner by creeks and under stars at night, life was wonderful but the tension inside me gradually began to build until I was in a state of high anxiety and every moment traveling in the car brought more fear. I didn't understand or have any idea why until a sentence kept being repeated ad nauseam in my mind: 'We can't find **Rebecca**.' I also began to understand the significance of the tunes that **Gustav** was repeating continuously in my head and that were driving me crazy, and the level of hyper-vigilance that had been stepped up by **Vigil**. It was their job to protect Rebecca and now she was nowhere to be found.

In a session with Libby, that moment in the car with you opened up and I knew that without warning you'd changed to 'steely eyes' which meant there was no longer any level of predictability. It was a moment of intense terror and through reliving this actual moment I became fully aware of what happens in that instant. There is no moment before and none after. The moment is frozen.

All my senses closed down. I couldn't see, hear, smell and there was no awareness of having a physical body. No movement, as every inch of my body was frozen, every muscle had become clamped into a vice and tightened to its full capacity.

In that moment there is no thought. Not 'what will happen next' or 'what can I do?' It was a reality that had been experienced many times but which had been hidden away in Rebecca and now I, Rhonda was experiencing it. We had often wondered how it felt to be Rebecca, as a coil, with no access to any senses and here I had been given the experience.

Now, with this awareness, I was able to understand and to dissolve the terror of this moment, an amazing relief. A few years later you became the manager of the Sydney Fish Markets Dad, bringing home whole fish, lobsters, prawns and endless bottles of oysters that you and I ate together, sometimes sitting on the beach with our feet in the sand, watching the waves. You were my father then and it was good. Mum refused to touch any of it. She was punishing you. 'What did I do to her?' you'd say. You never remembered what happened when you were drunk or psychotic. Only the silence knew it all.

Over time, Libby's therapy room became a safe place where each part of me was free to emerge without fear and Libby gradually came to know the voice, the speech, the gestures and facial expressions of most of us. This switching often took me by surprise as I was given no part in or warning of the internal decision. And in order for each part of me to come into the present time, it was essential that Libby allowed the alter who had experienced the trauma to actually relive what had happened. So it was that when **Beatrice** came to talk to Libby, she was reliving that time, right there as if the past was the present.

> Beatrice, still trapped back in time, emerges, punching the air.
> "Got to keep punching him."
> "Who?" Libby asks, taken by surprise.
> "My father!"
> "He's dead Beatrice."
> "You don't understand. I can't get out!"
> "Where are you?"
> "All locked up and I can't get out!"

"Who can open the door for you? "

"It's not a door."

"Well, what are you locked into?"

"Don't know. It's all around me. Get me out! It's on my head! There's a hessian bag tied onto my head!"

"Can you pull it off now? Come on, get it right off your head. Good on you. Are you out now?"

She nods.

"Are your hands untied?"

She nods again.

"Can you untie your feet?" She remains still. "Are you going to untie them so that you can be free?"

She leans forwards, "I shouldn't have let him tie me up like that," she whispers.

Libby puts her hand on her shoulder. "He was a big and powerful man."

Beatrice remains still and quiet for some time, then begins rocking backwards and forwards, accompanied by a thin moaning sound as Libby watches, mindful of her need to complete the process. Then Rhonda returns.

At all times there was someone else poised, ready to take over the body, to be there and sometimes to use fantasy and story to find a way to overcome the feeling of extreme powerlessness. One such part of me emerged one day in a therapy session when suddenly I found myself lying on the floor, stretched out as far as my legs and arms would go. This time it even caught Libby off guard.

"What are you doing!"

"I'm a straight line!"

"Why?"

"He doesn't notice me so quickly when I'm a straight line. There are spades and forks, all straight lines. And the bench is a straight line. So is the window, and the moonlight comes in the window and I can see lots of other straight lines too. (Shouting) —And when I'm a straight line I don't fit in a hessian bag!"

"That's pretty smart. What's your name?"

"I used to be **Beatrice**. He put her into a hessian bag and tied up the end of it. I'm not her any more, cause she was really little and I'm bigger!"

"So who are you then?"

"**Emily**." (stretching out to be as long as she could.) "And if I lie like this I can be hard and strong like a metal bar and then he can't put me in a hessian bag!"

So you see, Dad, we had you covered.

There were a number of parts created within our internal system who were created to keep the Terror alive at all costs. They sabotaged the system at every opportunity, plotting to keep it forever present and functioning.

The Terror lives and breathes on its own. It was created within the womb of the mother's silence and spread through the father's hands. As you know, it was decreed that the **One Who Was Born** must never become visible. It's confusing I know, but when you look at the whole picture, the whole jigsaw, even though these alters appear to be against our system, they are an essential part of the whole reason for being which was to keep the One Who Was Born fully alive and completely decontaminated and therefore to never be seen.

There was **The Evil Saboteur** whose job it was to confuse Rhonda at every opportunity. **Master Cleverness** who was there to take away Rhonda's brain and capacity for cognitive thought, blocking her access to facts and therefore to adult reality. Then there was **The Black Viper**, linked with Master Cleverness because when Rhonda's brain became fuzzy and filled with panic, he would constrict her lungs and throat to limit the oxygen, allowing the Terror to thread itself throughout her body like a thick viper. I remember his words: 'Do not fight it for this is a decree. This is the final deed of The Terror, to paralyze you from the inside out. You will be paralyzed and snuffed out. Your body will remain but you will not be there.' Just like you when you were 'steely eyes', Dad. Your body remained but you had vanished. But we found a way of diminishing their power. We concocted a plan and finally were able to trick them into feeling. Then we planted them! There's a garden in the castle and beside it we have a compost heap that we keep ready so that when anything or anyone in here comes close to dying we can mix them with the warmth and energy of the composted matter and plant them in the garden. It's called my *Garden of Life*.

These black and ugly parts needed to be composted and reborn as seeds to be planted, so we asked the **Master** Planner if they could be citrus trees and they became known as *The Orchard*.

You were a father, a husband, a worker, but when the memories took over and you retreated into them, you were a solider in a place of war.

It wasn't a scream or a shout that started in my belly and pushed its way up, through my throat and out into the air. It was the cry of battle and for years Dad, I heard it in my head, putting my hands over my ears but still it was there.

> That is until one session when Libby asked me the question. "Why are you covering your ears?"
>
> "It's the soldier and that savage cry of war." I'm immediately back there in the terror, my body curled and face distorted. The cry that is emitted is long and coarse, followed immediately by one even longer and filled with terror and desperation.
>
> It comes again. And again until there is no more sound inside me. Then a small child emerges, whimpering, curled up in terror. I hear Libby's voice drawing me forwards to the other side.
>
> "Can you tell me what's happening?"
>
> "That was me, inside him, inside my father!"
>
> Libby leans forwards and takes my hands. "It looked like him, from the way you've described him when he came at you with the bayonet and other weapons and an ugly, evil howling."
>
> "They were battle cries, Libby."
>
> "Yes, and that's what it looked and sounded like."
>
> "I felt as though I was actually attacking someone with a weapon. It suddenly became part of me, kind of shot into

me and I could feel the oscillation between being him and being the child."

"That's how you internalised it. What are you left with now?"

"I'm seeing the image of the soldier, dressed in his uniform and he's actually walking out of me, but he doesn't know where to go. Perhaps he can now take off his uniform?"

I looked at you there in my mind and felt your sadness as you dropped your uniform in a crumpled pile on the ground and put on a pair of your old shorts and top. Slowly, your bayonet became a spade and you had become a gardener. You know, I think you needed someone to hear those battle cries Dad."

"I heard them," said Libby.

Dad, I found your funeral really difficult and because all the parts of me were still tightly contained in individual casings, and many of the alters were young children, the reality of 'dead' had very little meaning. That's why, for so many years after you'd gone we were still terrified, expecting you to be hiding around corners ready to attack. I was given no opportunity to see your body before or during the funeral, which was a shame because this might have helped us to understand that 'dead' meant that you weren't here any more. Several years into my therapy with Libby and twenty-six long years after you'd gone I decided to scatter your ashes, not an easy task. It took us two years of solid therapy work before we felt safe enough to carry it through, each alter needing acres of time to speak and listen and endlessly repeated moments of comfort.

'He'll be gone forever' is what Libby said and finally we believed her, coming to a point that allowed me to ring the crematorium.

I want you to imagine, Dad, that you are standing to one side, quietly watching as I collect your ashes and scatter them into the sea. I want you to be there to know how I felt. How much I loved you, how terrified I was of you and how trapped I was in the pathological connection with you.

Your father died in 1972, and you want his ashes to be exhumed?"

"Yes."

"The fee for exhumation is $150, to be paid in advance."

"What for?"

Her voice is annoyed: "They have to dig the container out of the rose garden."

"He's not in the rose garden."

"Well they have to unscrew the plaque in the wall to get the container out."

"If you lend me a screwdriver I can do that myself."

Flustered. Fortissimo: "That would be illegal."

I let it pass. "I'd like an appointment quite early in the morning of the 12th of June. "I hang up, familiar feelings surfacing. Swirling fears stretching out into the abyss. 'Ring again,' says a soft voice.' 'Ask for support.'

"Hello. I want to tell you why I'm picking up my father's ashes." Silence. "I'm a survivor of trauma. My father's abuse." Silence. "This is a difficult thing for me to do and when I come to the crematorium I will be feeling vulnerable and would like to deal with someone who is sympathetic to this."

"Never mind dear, we all have our problems."

"I don't think you heard me."

"We deal with all kinds you know. You'll be right dear."

I hang up, feeling blank. The day finally comes. "I've come to pick up my father's ashes."

"Name?"

I answer.

"Take a seat."

Libby smiles at me as I begin to disappear. Long wait, no-one wants to deal with us. Don't understand why, I look just like everyone else. On the outside. Finally a middle aged lady with bottled hair leads us into a room with thin partitioning. Public grieving. I'm shaking as she extends her arm to the only two chairs: "Please sit down."

I look around at plaques of all denominations and sizes and urns you wouldn't imagine in your worst nightmares.

"I have a friend like you dearie," her eyes meeting mine for about ten seconds every five minutes. She speaks mostly to Libby, it's safer. "Yes, she was in an awful way but went to her church and they looked after her."

"I guess she experienced an immaculate recovery," sniggered **Wicked Witch**.

"Yes, it was amazing! And she'd only remembered the shocking abuse a year before. But she's ok now."

I can hear Wicked Witch in my head yelling in very impolite language at this poor woman who has no idea how to handle the situation. I bite my lip and sit on Wicked Witch as she kicks and wriggles, trying to gain control.

Libby rescues me. "What's next in the proceedings?"

The woman stands. "I won't be a moment dearie, I'll go and fetch the ashes."

Fear and anticipation pass through me as the hundreds of different parts of my fragmented system try to deal with what is about to happen. Quickly, put the children with the **Elderly People** and anyone else who needs company, find a suitable partner. Now!

She comes back carrying a grey container and puts it on the table. It feels obscene. To most of me, stuck in a time zone that doesn't move, my father had just died and there he is, burned and completed inside a plastic box.

"I can understand dearie, but he's been dead for such a long time!"

I stare at her. What is she on about! But Libby rescues me: "He's been dead for twenty-six years Rhonda."

Libby knows, so we believe her. We don't understand. She comforts us and our tears flow like a river.

"When you're ready, could you sign here dearie."

Again, I grab hold of Wicked Witch. Libby stands as the woman puts my father into a white cardboard box, Northern Suburbs Crematorium written on it in gold letters. This she places in a white plastic bag.

I carry the ashes of my father in the same kind of thin plastic bag in which I used to carry my grocery shopping. Outside to the tree, to the safety of the box brush that droops its boughs in solemn weeping over the smooth, ancient brown of its trunk. 'My father is dead' I tell the tree. It understands. Back in the car I place the white plastic bag at my feet on the passenger's side.

"How do you feel?"

"Some are relieved, some are sad, most are numb."

Libby understands.

From the moment that I'd decided to scatter your ashes, Dad, I knew it would have to be into the sea. You were a troubled person but with the potential to be a freedom loving soul and we'd shared some good times on and in the water. At those times you were a man with smiling eyes. We went to Long Reef beach, the white plastic bag clutched firmly in my hand. No one else was there, just Libby as my witness. Shoes and socks off, jeans rolled up above my knees, everybody safe. It was time for the eulogy spoken softly to the sea as it washed and waved on the sand.

I pulled the white cardboard box out of the plastic bag, carefully lifting its lid, holding the grey plastic box with sadness, slowly walking towards the sea.

But it was as though the court jester had arrived to test our humour, to season our perceptions. The lid of the container was sealed tightly closed. I pulled and tugged but nothing. The eulogy exploded. Were you having the last say? Laughing? For a moment the absurdity overtook us.

"No! This is my turn!" The lid, get the lid off, as I began to vanish. Libby, determined, searching every centimetre for an opening. Then there it was! Small and covered in ancient sticky tape. I pulled it off, pressed the keys into the plastic. It broke, then more, until there was a hole. An opening for your ashes to escape. Libby smiled. I returned.

The roar of the waves washed over my fear as I walked firmly towards them, wet and cold on my legs. Were we one, the sea and me? Yes, but only for an instant as I tipped the container and your remains emptied gradually, sinking down into the safety of its moving mass. More and more of the grey substance spilt into the sea. You were a big man, but the ashes seemed to go forever. Maybe you were infinite and my fears had been realised. But no. One more shake and the container was empty.

But panic rose as **Mary** surfaced, pushing against the waves as she tried to follow the father into the sea.

"Rhonda, what are you doing? Come back!"

I heard Libby's voice and regained control over our body, choking and spluttering, holding tightly to the empty plastic box.

I tried to follow you out into the sea, Dad. The feeling of you leaving me felt like parts of my flesh were being torn from me. As a kid, there had been no eyes to connect with. Only yours! And only when they were soft. I had to make really sure they were soft. And that was the only connection we had on the earth except for Prince's empathic brown eyes.

For me, the image had always been that your insanity was an energy that was constantly moving into and through me.

"No-one can pass on madness," Libby had said. "You felt that you were him and that the madness was being transferred from him to you. It was like a very bright light suddenly erupting in the darkness.

"Ah! Because then, I didn't have any boundaries. I had no separateness."

"That's right," Libby nodded.

"And that was partly because he raped me so often?"

"Yes. When someone rapes another person it is an annihilation of boundaries."

"I know that one of the reasons why **Genesis** was created was because we believed that his madness entered us though the semen from his penis and it was Genesis who stored it safely right away from us all."

We both remained silent for a moment.

"And if a truly insane person was sitting over there and I'm sitting over here then my Shining and my Spark remain with me?"

"Absolutely. You chose to suppress them because it wasn't safe to show them."

It took another couple of years for **Mary** to begin to let you go and another seven years to begin to realise that you and I are each separate. This happened in a session with Libby as one particularly horrible memory was released and as I watched you on the television screen in my mind, I felt myself separating from you until we were each a contained unit of self with nothing linking us. I felt that something was about to happen so I just remained still as a surge of energy moved through me and as I watched I saw Mary, her body struggling to free itself. Pushing, with a mind so full of determination until finally she was separate. She stepped into the space between you and me, standing tall and not looking back. She was complete. No more madness. It was your madness, Dad, not hers. Not mine.

You have been dead for forty-five years and only now am I, **Mary,** beginning to understand that. I have awakened from that long, deep sleep and finally know that I am a separate person. I am strong and resilient and I am finally separating from you. But it took yet another five years and a visit to Japan to become separate from my father, the soldier.

There were several major decrees that governed the successful functioning of our system and which were implemented with almost obsessive diligence.

"The Terror must be kept alive and as a separate entity at all times!" someone announced in a therapy session. "And as soon as it is activated we automatically become frozen and silent, the eyes of the Terror permeating every cell of the body. If **The Terror** does not remain alive then the embers will ignite and **Rebecca, the Heap** and the **Spirit of the Fire** will coalesce, allowing the **One Who Was Born** to become visible. This must never happen! The silence must never be broken!"

The second decree was activated by a membrane that was created between the functioning person and the outside world. It was thick and permanent and no matter how much connection Rhonda, the host person, put out there, any reciprocal feelings would bounce off the membrane, never penetrating our inner world. This put great limitations on the host personality because it tried to stop real connection which, if it ever happened would mean that we would be living in the reality of others and would then become visible.

It sounds so convoluted as I write it now, but it had to be, Dad. The terror you created was real and therefore so were the decrees, one of our major lines of defense.

An alter was created in an effort to try and see the world through the eyes of others, particularly yours. To help us to be ready for anything that happened.

My body changes its position noticeably as I sit bolt upright, my right knee over my left leg, with my nose in the air.

Libby smiles. "Is that **The Judge**?"

"It is he. And this decree is under my supervision! The plan has been in readiness forever and now is the time. I am fearful, for it appears that a change in reality is imminent."

Libby leans forward. "The trouble is that you're missing some point of reality."

The Judge looks at her with a smug smile. "And the thing is that when you look at me now, you can't see me."

"The reality is that I can. And the other reality is that the father is dead." Libby adds. "Did you come down to the beach when we scattered his ashes?"

"Yes. And I sat on the sand."

"So you saw the ashes scattered into the sea. You know that he's dead, that he's gone."

The Judge raises himself to his full height. "You might not like this, but I actually watched that through your eyes."

"So was my reality correct? And let me tell you something else. This is another fact and I want you to listen. I can see your body right now. And people out there have been seeing your body for a long time, because that is reality."

The Judge leans back in the chair and folds his arms. "None of this computes with me!"

"Do you believe that I can see your body right now?"

"Well I just looked at me through your eyes!" he says indignantly.

"So you know that I can see your body?"

He looks away, but Libby perseveres until the Judge understands that there is only one body and that this is reality.

After a while Rhonda returns with a sigh and the Judge goes away to consult and absorb.

Sounds strange I guess. **The Judge** believed that if he looked through Libby's eyes then he would see her reality. Therefore he would know when that reality changed from invisible (from within) to visible (from outside). This was to do with our necessity of having someone from within who was able, at any point of life threatening trauma to look through the eyes of the perpetrator, in order to have a greater understanding of that person's reality at that moment. I did this often when you became 'steely blue eyes,' the psychotic monster with no conscience. At those times it was **Mary** who went, via the safety of the diamond, to the space behind your eyes so that she could try and predict what you were going to do. It probably makes no sense to an adult mind as it defies logic. But logic only exists in the physical reality, my created reality having no such restrictions and therefore being able to use logic and imagination in equal quantities.

I think that apart from the need to completely escape, this strategy was part of detaching myself from the body and looking down on the situation. To put myself inside that person's eyes, to see an overview of their reality and how it related to me, at that moment. Of course, that's a child's logic and a child's desperate need to have fantasy and magic when survival is paramount.

Another facet of this is because I (in the form of **Lucy** and several others) spent so much time intently and with detailed concentration watching the behaviour of others so that we would fit in so fully that we would not really be seen. And often the facts that I gleaned, by body language, action or speech, within the family, did not tally with that truth as Lucy and others knew it. So I had to try and put myself into the eyes of others so that I could begin to understand those facts. I had to know that I wasn't lying. That what I was hearing, seeing and experiencing was actually happening. That my reality, in the real and violent world was just that. A reality.

That's also where **The Judge** came in. He understood that the Terror was not coming from me, that it came from outside. And he knew this because he looked through the eyes of others and saw. He is an amazing ally. And part of **Mary's** role was to comprehend the difference between this reality and my created world.

Otherwise we might have drifted off into a world so out of touch that we would have no foot in the circle reality of the outside world. And we would have no internal system to keep me alive.

But you remained a problem, Dad, because even though Mary had healed a great deal there were still quite a few internal children, some very young, who couldn't distinguish between the earthbound reality and the fantasy of the mind. Therefore no amount of material knowledge would compute with them, they simply didn't have the skills or the experiential knowledge.

So Libby suggested that I let the children write a story, a fantasy to allow them to follow their script to a conclusion, and of course, they've chosen **The Storyteller** to tell you.

> They sat on the sand, huddled together, careful not to allow the images a space in their minds. But bit by bit the image crept, filling each space and pushing through the private membranes of control until the sky was dark and the sea poured out its lament in savage sounds. They sat with hands held in a circle, ears numbed and eyes blinded with confusion as the image formed and rose, towering over them.
>
> A blueish colour, with dark shadows, solid yet able to stretch and lunge then to contract again into a statuesque form of **the giant** who had walked on their minds and terrorised their souls. His eyes were staring, his face plastered with revenge, as if a glue that held him together. His nose still had the scars, his head almost bald. Thick but strong, his body filled the air with solid form.
>
> He came closer, closer as their hands clutched and their hearts beat in unison. Someone had told him that the story had been told, the secret spoken, the **Square** invaded and they knew the consequences. The punishment for the penetration of the Square and the abolition of the **Diamond**. So he had finally come to smear their bodies and end their minds with the putrid blood that remained on his hands.

Didn't they deserve this retribution? Didn't they as always have to give in to compliance, to the reign of revenge of the terror? But something moved within the circle of clenched hands. It was small, yet they sensed a kind if strength different from anything they had ever known. It spread throughout their furrowed minds, igniting something strange around their hearts.

"Stand up," said a voice within and as they did the towering giant stood still.

"Walk forwards," and as they did the grey giant began to move slowly backwards away from them.

"Be strong," and as they felt the strength begin to grow, the giant retreated slowly into the sea.

"Watch carefully." As they did they saw the sea become crystal clear to the bottom of its depths.

"Keep watching," and as they did the 'Father of the Ashes' sank slowly into the clear depths and into a fine but final cave. As he did, there was a thunderous roar as the large rocks tumbled and fell, covering the opening of the cave. He was trapped. Imprisoned. Or what was left of him, for as he sank he disintegrated, until his ashes floated as separate particles, finally disappearing behind the avalanche of rocks.

Never again will he terrorise us for he no longer exists in human form and his soul is guarded night and day by the angels with blue wings who, together with the **Virgin of the Sepulchre**, look after the souls of the dead babies.

CHAPTER 8

There was a big shift in my system from about the age of fourteen when walls and membranes thickened and obedient compliance took over, protected by **Katherine**. She is a vitally important part as she was a teenager and one of the few alters who lived in the reality of the square. She is like an echidna, covered in spikes but soft and aware inside. She was vigilant in keeping everything out, allowing nothing in. No cruel words, no betrayal, no insanity, and yet she retained her humanity.

My bedroom has become a silent cube that swirls around in a space of chaos and disconnection with the only remaining adult with any semblance of sanity gradually but completely withdrawing into a frozen world. Things move past my mind but I can't grab hold of them. I am trying desperately hard to be alive but there's no framework to be. I'm alive but I'm not. I have a body but there's nothing in it. Not just my body. My brain and my whole self are dying. It feels as though my soul is leaving the earth and yet I have to stay fully alert to survive. To be alert at all times because if I take my eyes off **the Terror** for even a second it will destroy me. But still there's nothing to grab hold of.

My mother's coldness and disconnection has spread wider and wider, becoming more frozen and solid as my teenage years have progressed, until this circle of ice has become impenetrable and the radiated cold defies my stepping over its line at a time when I need my mother more than at any other. The isolation has become absolute.

The cube has lost connection with the worlds of both the square and the circle, withdrawing me completely from the outside world and moving me towards everlasting silence. Totally separated from the rest of the human race with no ladder, no spider's thread, no door, no bridge, no portal. No way in. No way out.

My mother has silenced me and no-one knows I'm here or even knows anything about what is happening in this enclosed version of reality. No-one. Kate has just been married. She's free now. Matt's an engineer and left home. Cleo, Dad's beautiful dog, and Mister have died. I often reach out to feel Prince's soft brown fur and long to look into the safety of his eyes but he is no longer here. The only ones here are my father, who has become more and more psychotic and unpredictable, and my mother, more terrified and disconnected.

Do I want my brain to exist? No, because to have a solid brain is to think, and to stay alive I must just accept. There is no room for thinking only for submission.

'Sshh!' I can hear him stirring and he must not hear me.

I coated all my furniture in blackboard paint and I can write on it whenever I want to. I have to be careful to rub it all out before morning in case my mother sees it.

I can hear him! He's awake now. Quick! Behind the door.

My mother is making me a new bedspread. She even let me choose the colour, a cotton material that has deep royal blue and black stripes. We even got enough to make a matching nightie and dressing gown for me.

He's pushing the door but I'm leaning against it as hard as I can. But he's strong and now I have to move out into the middle of the room, facing him. That's how he demands it and I must obey. I take my pyjamas off before he gets here. I have to remove everything or he gets angry.

I think I will like the new bedspread and dressing gown 'cause I love that beautiful blue. **Rebecca** can't see colours so she doesn't understand why I get so excited about it. I'm **Emma** by the way, but I'm different now. I'm older and I've learnt to stop fighting. **Genesis** taught me and that's how we survive when he comes in to rape us.

"Turn around and bend over."

His voice is calm but cold and I know, even in the dark, his eyes are steely and disconnected. He will have the large knife that he always brings. He used it to skin our beautiful dog, Cleo, and I know that he will use it on me if I do not do as he asks. It's the same every time. Several times a week he comes, into the space that was once mine.

I'm not fast enough.

"If you don't bend over I will start at your shoulders and slice you right along them, down the sides then I'd be able to rip your back off. So bend over. Now!"

I can't move. **Emma** has disappeared. Come back Emma. Please come back!

"Move! You filthy Jap or I will do your arms and your fingers one by one and turn them inside out."

I try to bend over but Emma has returned. She's angry and starts to move towards him. Don't Emma! Don't! He will kill us! Now my body is still and I am calm. **Genesis** is here and I can feel my mind lifting upwards as it separates from my body. It's not us he is threatening and raping as he thrusts and moans. It is our body and only Genesis will remember.

I feel sorry for her and I hate her compliance but am also grateful. And when he is done he walks away leaving her there, his semen dribbling, her obedience mixed with our humiliation that has spread right through her like the blackness of the furniture. She picks up her pyjamas, puts them on and goes back to bed with staring eyes, the swirling room, our bedroom that should have been a place of refuge once again becomes the disconnected mass of chaos and fragmentation.

Dear Mum and Dad

Even though the blinds in my room were closed the light filtered through the terylene curtains giving the room a mustard, shadowy look. I had done as you ordered, father, when suddenly I heard your voice, Mum. It too was quiet at first but as you came further into the room and realized what was happening you began shouting.

"Stand up! You filthy, disgusting thing!" I did.

I was about to be raped Mum and yet you attacked not him but me, grabbing my hair, your hands waving in the air and your eyes angry and wide. You lost control kicking me, belting into me with exploding fury. I had never seen you like this and it terrified me. I miscarried. One after the other. Tiny, tiny twins.

You stood there, no words, no sound just a silent, empty stare. I didn't move but you started again, screaming into my face. And you Dad, in your psychotic delusion coming in for the kill with that terrifying war cry piercing my head.

You're lunging at me, the knife held with intention above your head. Oh God! You're one on each side of me. Got to get the Knife! I get both my arms, my hands joined and bash them down on Dad's arms. The knife drops. But he's grabbed me around the throat.

"You filthy Jap!" you yell again.

You start to attack him, Mum! He lets go of my throat and I gasp for air. I am feeling quite weak but he is going to kill me so I kick and punch and then start to fling myself like a weapon, pushing myself off from the ground and flinging myself at each of you. Everything is so totally out of control, like a dog fight, not really knowing or caring who you are attacking, just intent on staying alive. No reason remains, just a hundred years of anger and terror and inverted silence while I stand naked and bleeding.

I don't think that I can ever forgive either of you for that moment. Nothing excuses such annihilation of respect, not even insanity.

Yvette, created for such life threatening events, went for the knife but you got there first Mum, lunging at Dad, the blood spurting out everywhere. Your blood Dad, on my face, my hands, my clothes. Instantly **Mary** took over but couldn't move as she became frozen in a tableau of catatonic shock.

You fell into the blackness of my dressing table Dad. Slumped and still. I thought you were dead!

Mary at that moment felt as though she existed in a mist, still aware of what was happening but unable to move. When your blood touched her she had realized instantly that the trauma was and always had been real, because at that moment, you were no longer the giant or the monster, but my father. Her heart beat but nothing else would move. She could see you, Mum, lying in the corner of the room and she could see you, Dad, slumped over the dressing table. She felt the terror, knowing the reality but unable to speak, to help or to escape. And the **Ghost of me** was on the floor with the bright red blood.

What was I going to do, Mum? I was sixteen and there wasn't anyone else in the world. I thought you would help me but you left the room. I don't know whether it was Matt or Kate who came visiting and helped you Dad, cleaning up everything. I just don't know and I never want to go back into that memory again in order to find out. The further away from the reality of this event that I can get, the better.

I do know that at some stage someone went to the linen cupboard and got a whole pile of towels to stop the bleeding, picked up the **Ghost of me** and carried her out into the back yard. I wanted to be dead too so I put the ghost on top of me hoping that she and I would become one. I stayed out there all the next day. I guess that in panic, my system created a ghost because **Mary** was frozen and couldn't move and because the dissociation was so complete, I could do nothing about it as I was no longer there.

The intricacies of my system never cease to amaze me. We had every situation covered. It was not possible to be ready to really hurt someone in order to save my own life and to love that person at the same time, so **Yvette** and **The Gang of Thugs** were created. It was imperative that we retained some thread of connection that would prevent the swirling, *disconnected cube* that was my room, from spiraling out into nothing, with no way back. So Yvette and her Gang lived both in the house and the swirling room, watching, always watching. And from this time onwards **the Ghost** became an invisible but cunning and quick witted part of me, capable of connecting with the outside world, who would be able to tell someone if I died.

And now that I have broken the silence, **Magnitude** wants to talk to you. He is very important to me and I hope you can both listen, hear and understand him.

"Thank you my dear. The river floweth over graves of silent sounds. Tread lightly upon the moors that you may know the secret of the earth. Look high above that you may be transported beyond the pain of yesterday. Quell thy searching. Sit calmly upon the tombstone of unwonted desire that you may sing an elegy to savage hearts. Begin with one note and let it spread like the wings of a mighty eagle upon the moors. Let it be an elegy to time long passed and moments spent in bloodied terror. Let it tell of your hope that never died and the ancient knowledge that you carried written on the stone within you. Do not doubt that you know. Do not doubt that the seasons passed but left you searching for your Self.

Sing not of horror, for that which descended into the hell of hybrid pain has been made free. Let it speak of courage and of light that glowed consistently in the naked field of darkness. Grab hold of your humanity and carry it like a flag before you. It will protect you as you ascend from the valley that echoes with the sadness of a self that was briefly known, then lost. Carry the stone carefully for it will be the pinion of your recovery.

Shed any hate or anger that you carry. Be honest in your appraisal of what you must do, for only you can lift the final veil that will open your soul to the warmth of the sun and the beauty of all that is.

And when you find it, bask long for it will need time to grow, to spread. And remember that once you have bathed in the warm waters of your destination you will no longer have need of the reasons that directed you there.

It is time."

CHAPTER 9

I like Bruce. I liked him from the very beginning. He's calm and kind and really good with his hands. And he likes gardens.

Hello, I'm **Stones**.

Rhonda met Bruce when she was seventeen. Funny that, the trauma was still going on at Hope Street, but because of us she didn't know and could go out and have fun, play tennis, eat out with friends and more importantly get to know her boyfriend.

They met at a baby health centre! She was one of the leads in a musical and he was part of the stage team and guess where the rehearsals were held? He had a brand new lime coloured VW Beetle. Cedric, he called it, and they drove to Lady Macquarie's Chair one lunch time a week in between her piano and violin lessons, composition lectures and his work. He took her home one weekend to meet the folks, but not before his parents painted the house and made everything perfect for the visit. If they'd only known. Rhonda loved going there, especially for Sunday lunch when Bruce's dad could be seen up to his elbows in mince and onions for the rissoles that would adorn the table together with all kinds of baked vegies from the garden. Then would follow his Mum's bread and butter custard, dotted with sultanas and topped with cream and ice cream. Never had anything tasted so wonderful. She was much loved.

A few years later they were married, two days before Christmas, and took off in Cedric to Phillip Island to join the penguins for a honeymoon. Her mother rang her the morning after the wedding to make sure she was ok and that she had enough old towels.

It was difficult for me sometimes, watching it all from a distance, not ever able to be involved. Even when Rhonda was in therapy as an adult and memories grabbed hold of her it was no picnic just standing by looking on. I'll hand over the story now and I'll let her tell you how it felt.

Many times, the Terror just grabbed hold of me, wiping out my mind and filling my body with its intensity. At these times I knew that a memory was stirring but almost always found it impossible to access. I just had to go with it, allowing it to numb my mind and to hold every muscle and nerve in a vice until something surfaced. Some indication, a word, a picture or somebody in here ready and needing to break his or her silence. At these times I often grabbed a pen and wrote. Not thinking, just writing whatever came. Free fall writing. It can access the unconscious mind and provide some clues about what's happening. Sometimes it is other parts in here who feel safe enough to write. And sometimes the language is obtuse, almost talking in puzzles, but always the meaning eventually becomes clear. Here's one such time.

I had asked myself the question: How do I get in to find out about the event that's surfacing? **Magnitude**, in his usual enigmatic voice, immediately took over and began to write:

"Take your shoes off a while and just sit. I will speak to you of heaven and then you will ride your chariot towards the earth. The number nine is near. Does it glow within the dog, chased and banished or is the creek bed filled with wasted semen, flowing down the rocks and washing away the slime of forbidden hunger? Do you know the way to heaven? It's easy really, just follow the shadow of the sun as it hides the act of perversion within its shade. Filtered light within the vicissitude of a solitary hell. Rocks that wedge the mind within the pain of being. Captured virginity or continuous rape? She is here, wedged silently watching as the terror pervades the body. Peeping out through the boughs of the trees. The trees that betrayed her. Where were the trees when she needed them, their soft leafy boughs spread outwards over her frightened body. Why did they not stop this from happening? These will be your questions."

It's such a strange feeling allowing the words onto the page, having no idea what they're talking about but at the same time, through experience, knowing that they speak our truth. **Persephone**, whose name on a conscious level I had to look up to find out who she was and what she represented, was a part of me whose job it was to take the mind that was going mad and to keep it safe. She had been around in therapy sessions and in my writing for several weeks without me understanding why. Persephone, the mythical character who lived half in hell, half in heaven. A week later, we walked through the huge wall of fear and in a session with Libby it all came pouring out. It wasn't until about a week later that I realised that when **Bronwyn**, containing no emotion at all, had walked at length through the house at Hope Street, seeing and describing the layout, the patterns on the floor coverings, smelling the familiarity, taking in all the physical and concrete details, that she had been making it safe for us to go to Libby's the next week and tell her about the gang rape. When terror threatens to dissolve your mind, the more you can hang on to the facts and details that your senses understand, the more you can remain in the present and the safer you can remain in mind and body.

I don't know which part of me experienced this episode as sometimes the part involved won't identify her/himself at the time. At first I thought it must have been **Emma**, but this is not so and just as well, as Emma could have become her feisty self, making the situation worse. I have the feeling that it was a part who was specifically created to contain this memory. The safety of Libby's room allowed her to speak, but the shame dictated that she remain hidden. I do know that **Paula** had been created, safe in a bubble but able to act, if absolutely necessary, in order to protect the life of any part who was raped or violently attacked. Paula's job was later taken over by **Yvette** as the father became more insane and unpredictable.

So again, we've asked **The Storyteller** to be her voice here and we will observe, safely removed, as if it is happening on a TV screen.

> The path to the sailing club meandered for a short while through open grassland, passing through descending steps and into a small pocket of coastal rain forest. Then it twisted and turned, brushing scrub with its penetration until finally emerging at the water's edge. The shed was quite small, housing the hulls of the small sailing boats lined up one above the other, with a slotted ramp going down to the water. Masts festooned with metal threads jangling loosely or neatly wrapped around their wooden hosts, hung suspended from the racks lining the southern wall.

It was the rainforest that she liked best, beset with a canopy of friendly trees that spread outwards covering the forest floor in mottled sunlight and a hidden memory of fairies that danced at night bringing the magic of tomorrow. Some of the trees had pale green leaves, small, with many on the division of each branch while others, taller, stretched their mighty trunks upwards and their roots deep into the bosom of the earth. Water ran slowly but continuously over the rocky outcrops, resting occasionally upon level scoops of sand and pebbles, then onwards once more towards the sea.

They must have known she was going sailing that day for as she walked through the scrub, one of them grabbed her, digging his fingers deep into her shoulders and bending her arm until she thought it would break. She screamed but was silenced by a fist of rough flesh placed firmly over her mouth as they dragged her towards the trees.

"Grab her legs! Grab her bloody legs! And shut that dog up for Christ's sake!"

She squirmed, trying to catch a glimpse of Prince who she knew would be frightened. She felt the pain of his open hand as it lashed across her face.

"Keep still you little slut. And if somebody doesn't shut that dog up I'll do it permanently!"

Her heart stopped for a moment, but she knew about having to be silent so she closed her eyes and bit into her tongue as one of them picked up a stone and hurled it at Prince. He yelped, eyes wide with betrayal and ran back through the scrub as the stones and rocks whistled around him. She was alone.

"Here will do."

She fell heavily on the cold, solid rock, scraping her arm as she tried to move away from the boy as he stood over her, zipper undone, panting heavily, his hand moving faster and faster on his thick fleshy penis. She moaned, no longer able to contain the sound of her terror.

"I'll give you something to moan about."

He knelt over her, lifting her head with a lump of hair, thrusting his ejaculating missile into her mouth. She spat, trying desperately to get rid of the mirky stuff, the pulsating penis almost choking her. He grabbed her around the throat, shaking her head violently. "Go easy Davo, I haven't had my turn yet," one of the others yelled.

They laughed, the four of them. They laughed while she was choking on their insanity. The pain almost carried her away as she lay, powerless, her legs spread apart until she thought she would break in half, crack into two pieces while her innards and her blood drained away down the creek. They laughed as she lay on the rock, abandoned by the trees while the one called Brooksie raped her and the mottled light of the late afternoon sun looked on.

She didn't care what happened next. Maybe to live just long enough to join the fairies that night in their dance of dreams, of a new tomorrow.

But the next one was on her, standing over her hips, thumping his chest like Tarzan. She heard the sound of cloth tearing as one of them ripped open the front of her blouse, the green one that her mother had bought for her at Woolworths. She felt a moment's panic at how she would explain the rip in her blouse to her mother.

She wanted to kill their bodies the way they had just killed her mind. Her Self.

When she came to, the light was leaving the speckled rocks and the violent youths had vanished. They knew she wouldn't tell. It is said that a rapist knows an already abused person at sight. Is it an apparent vulnerability? An apparent death of Self?

Prince was there, licking her face and crying. She held him close for a moment, her own tears buried beneath layers of numbness and self disgust, her fingers spreading gently through the safety of his fur. Her body ached as she stood up, still concealed from the path by the thicket of ferns and trees as she scraped off the dead mucous with fallen leaves. Her arms, her body, her face each cleared and gently washed with the waters of the creek. The blood that trickled down her leg was drying and its stickiness fascinated her. Was it hers? Were her insides still there? Were they black like she always imagined they were every time her father raped her?

Slowly she walked with Prince by her side to a set of trees further along the road, taking shelter in their safety, hiding until the night came. Her mother would wonder where she was.

"A story. I must concoct a story," she told Prince.

When she got home her father was there alone, drunk. She crept in, pulled her dressing table as a barricade across her bedroom door, then climbed out the window near her bed, lifting Prince onto the sill and down onto the side path. Just before dawn, they left their bunker on the golf course and headed back for home.

When her father next came to attack her and to rape her, in desperation she was ready with a hammer.

The body is still. Blood. Unexplained blood and darkness. The image is strong and silent. Constant and permeating.

In therapy.

- Where are you?
- Nowhere
- Where are you?
- Half way between.
- Between what?
- Life and death.
- What do you mean?
- Nothing.
- What do you mean?
- I'm on my way out.
- Who's taking over?
- I'm in a bubble. Safe in a bubble.
- Who are you? What's happening?
- He's crazy.

Her father lurches, grabs but misses, stumbling over the leg of the chair. He comes at her, his warlike cries defying the devil space to breathe. Clanging of pots as he falls against the half open cupboard. She screams but there is no sound. He lunges again, this time the knife in his hand, raised above his head.

"I want to live!" she screams closing her eyes tightly as the hammer bashes his head.

Silence.

The body. Still. The weapon lying near it on the kitchen floor. The knife a little way off. The blood explained. Shaft of moonlight on a fourteen year old girl. Sitting. Staring.

- Are you there **Paula**?
- Yes.
- Is your father alive?
- Too scared.
- Do you remember any more?
- No.

In a therapy session two years later. The body. Blood. Kitchen light on.

- Is that you **Paula**?
- Yes.

She looks shrunken. Cold.

- My brother's here.

He gently rolls their father over as she watches his chest, her heart in her mouth and a prayer in her mind. God answers. He is breathing. She overflows with relief. He is the father she loves.

Matt moves quickly, cleaning up the blood from the floor. A towel over the wound. The bleeding's stopped. He drags the heavy weight up the hall and into the small bedroom, coming back later to attend to his father's wound.

But then he's there with her. Holding her, helping her up. Going down the hall and tucking her into bed.

"You can sleep now."

She feels the warmth of Prince on her skin. No-one will rape her or try to kill her tonight.

My father caused such terror to live in all of us and as it surfaced I, Rhonda, had difficulty functioning, wanting to be put away somewhere and drugged or just put to sleep, safe within my chrysalis. On this occasion it was the feeling of being on the edge of some intense psychological pain and of losing all that I had struggled to keep for fifty-five years. My sanity and my life. So I knew that I had some pretty tough therapy work to do and that none of the fear would go away until I had faced it.

Libby watched as a young child turned the teddy upside down and buried her face in his stomach. Then she spoke, her voice high and innocent:

"Did you know that people have light around them? Mummy has white light sometimes when Matt's around. When I'm there it sometimes changes into a fiery light with sparks that spurt out at me. Red and orange. I don't like it when that happens. Prince's light was white and bright and it splashed onto to me and felt warm and good."

She sat for a moment watching the light as it danced around her small golden spaniel. The image changed, the father now standing in full view right in front of her. At first his light was white and bright but suddenly grew darker and darker until it covered all the love with a sticky veil, catching her between her shoulders, squeezing out her life. **Beatrice** pulled the teddy right across her face, withdrawing from the image in her mind then suddenly sat rigid, staring: "He's all black. My Daddy's all turned black!"

Just as suddenly I returned, feeling the terror building until I knew that I would do anything to be able to run from it. As usual it was ready for me, increasing in strength until my mind and body were ready to explode and my functioning mind dissipated like rapidly melting snow. By this time I was so dissociated that I was truly in its claws, running as hard as I could from having to remember.

"I can't be put together!"

"What's stopping you?" Libby asked.

Libby moved closer until she was sitting directly in front of me, her hand raised ready to move from left to right in front of my eyes.

"Just go with the fear."

I felt the right side of my face contorting as I gasped for air.

"Rhonda! Keep your eyes open!"

Libby began to tap on the arms of the chair. Left, right, left, right. Rapid and precise, causing both sides of my brain to join, bringing the memory into the now, the fear in my belly moving up to my chest. I could hear my father searching for me.

"Sharp knives, blindfolded, the moonlight is there to keep me sane. I'm going to be sliced up and I need to know that my mind and body aren't joined together. That I am not insane."

"And insanity is fragmentation."

"DID is fragmentation but it is not insanity."

"That's true."

"I'm not talking about the splitting, I'm talking about insanity. They are two different things."

"I want you to know very clearly that you will come out the other side of this memory safely and fully intact."

It's then that I give in to Libby's suggestion to draw, picking up the coloured pencils and setting the images, like a child, onto an empty page. Bright orange circles entwined and contained in an unbroken series of black swirls. Chaos.

From inside the orange circle two pairs of eyes, with no connection to a face or a body, stare outwards. Nearby, a bright red cleaver and a knife with a long pointy blade hover. All around the edges are the square, the diamond, the circle, the triangular prism, the triangle, the shapes of our geometrical safety.

I reach out my hand to touch the large purple triangle and immediately **Emma** returns. She knows he's here somewhere in the blackness, stalking her and makes a dash to the corner near the door. But he's cunning and she can hear the father coming nearer, his shoes scraping on the sandy concrete of the garage floor. She makes a dash to the corner but he's been waiting and laughs as the moonlight catches the steel of the cleaver that hurtles past her shoulder, thundering into the empty paint tins, sending them crashing to the floor. Then silence.

But he's found her again, creeping up from behind, through the dense, sweaty jungle that fills his mind, grabbing her with his arm over her chest and under her shoulder, knife at her throat.

Libby's voice: "What's happening?"

"He's----he's—" Emma vanishes, another part pushing his way onto the scene.

"Good afternoon ladies and gentlemen." His body is erect with silvery features stretched tight into a plasticine shape, with braided hair. "My legs are short with golden shoes adorning wreaths of silken thread woven through yellow stockings and a pantaloon garment that covers from my waist to beneath my knees." He bows. "I am **Ezekiel** at your service."

Libby is straight onto it. "Why are you here Ezekiel? This is not a stage and we are not in a play."

"Life is a play my dear

Enter right, exit left, sit in the middle, Scream now

Flutter like a fairy, dance like a rose

Look like a pauper, it's really on the nose

Whatever happens, the script is here to stay

They say we live in the moment

But they took them all away.

I can make up a rhyme or scene or script for you whenever you like. But don't forget, you must never, never look into the green eyes, for like the moments, you will vanish. Have I ever told you about my cloak?"

"No" says Libby "And now is not the time."

"Oh my dearie, dearie, dear. Any moment is the time, especially when it comes to my cloak. It lives, it breathes, it dances and bends, flies and whispers. It can even change colour. If you are blue, it can be blue too, or purple or pink or orange. Never black."

Libby is kind but firm. "Thank you for coming Ezekiel and I want to tell you that you're clever you know, putting it all on a stage and creating the illusion of a play."

"I'm so glad you see it my way my dear." He smiles, bows and vanishes, leaving me without the distance of a stage and proscenium arch as the terror immediately returns, my father's voice filling my head. I can't breathe.

"He's---he's---he's--- but the words are whispered, almost swallowed. He's----"

"Trying to choke you?"

"No. He's ---he's going to cut off my head!"

"You're safe and it's not happening now Rhonda."

"He's got a big knife with a shiny blade and he's pulling it and swishing it across my throat. It's touching me! And he's making a strange noise with his throat. It's the steely eyes voice!"

'Keep still!'

He's going to cut my throat with the shiny knife and cut off my head with the big cleaver! NO!"

I disappear, feeling myself drifting to the verge of complete insanity, the madness swirling inside me like a whirlpool at the height of its centrifugal force.

"Rhonda, come back! Rhonda! This is Libby. Come back into this room where you're safe. Feel my hands and look around you."

"The mother is here too," **Emma** whispers.

"Leave her alone!" her mother screams.

"Shut up woman or you will be next!"

Emma watches as the mother tries to steady herself but suddenly slumps to the floor.

"Mum! Please don't be dead!" she cries.

Her father's grip is tightened as he presses the point of the blade into her throat, but she kicks with her leg and bites into his arm, the loud clank of the knife filling her head as she pushes him away. She runs but he is behind her, filled with rage. He grabs her clothing as she leaps up and runs towards the door leaving him holding the torn cloth.

It's dark on the golf course but the sand in the bunker feels warm and safe as she cuddles Prince close to her. That night as the stars move in their arc across the sky the angel wraps its wings around them both and they sing, a strange kind of song that lifts upwards to meet the stars. When she climbs in the window before sunrise the next morning her mother is asleep, her father has gone to work and nothing is mentioned.

It always took a while to process these kinds of memories, the parts of me involved needing reassurance that 'it's not happening now and will never happen again'. What I had experienced in that session, just before Libby brought me back into now, was very close to insanity and I could feel the madness swirling all around me. It was an extraordinary feeling and somewhere I knew that if I just let go and allowed myself to drift into it then everything would become calm and I would never feel terror again. But someone, **Ruth** I think, must have been ready, instantly creating **Mary** and taking over the body, for which I am grateful. Insanity is not a useful long-term option.

As memories were experienced and processed, my system underwent gradual shuffling and changes. Sometimes this happened without my knowledge, at others I was part of the adjustment, aware of what was happening, with the role of an observer. This is one such time.

I had made two sets of my geometric shapes out of cardboard, one quite large, the other much smaller. I took them to a therapy session and laid the two sets of shapes out on the floor. As I did a picture in my mind began to move.

It was set in the castle, the banquet room, still but with a tension in the air as the internal parts of me divide into two camps. Line A moves slowly towards **The Heap** lying like a rag doll in the middle of the floor. But as they move nearer, with the intention of putting both lots of shapes together, shouting breaks out in B, the other camp. "Don't you go near her!" "Not one step further!"

They have weapons! I can call on **Persephone** to take them away because she's not mortal, so she can't die. She's the one who can relieve them of their knives, scissors and the cleavers. All the weapons that he used against us.

All of B want to kill **The Heap**, but for some reason they can't cross to the other side and A, the goodies, the ones who want to put it all together, can't change sides either. They can get to The Heap but they can't go past her and get to those with the weapons on the other side.

It's a funny feeling, as though my brain's divided into two. A are on this side and B are on the other and the Heap is in the middle. And something is containing B, the parts with the weapons. Something has always contained them and stopped them from actually killing The Heap.

"Do you know what stops them?" Libby asks.

"Yes, these. The geometric shapes. And what Rhonda is asking us to do is to put them together and we cannot do that because if we do then those with the weapons can attack the others. But until we do put them together we won't be free."

I feel myself laughing. "**The Omega** has frozen all of the B line! They can't move! And they're all frozen in different positions!"

Now Persephone is moving right down the line with **Bronwyn**, who's helping her and as they go they're taking all the weapons and putting them in a large plastic container. And there are ropes and chains and all the things like tights and bras, that can strangle you. I can smell the hessian bags! And they're collecting all the weapons out of the garage too.

For some reason I can't finish the line because taking the weapons means putting the square, the diamond, the circle and the fire all together and I don't know what will happen if I do that.

"Can you explain the two sets of shapes?" Libby asks.

"Yes. The large set is keeping me, us now, safe. The smaller ones are protecting the Real Self. And I know that if I don't put them together then we'll stay stuck forever.

So I did, placing the square on top of the circle and the diamond on the square knowing somewhere and somehow that they each had properties in common and ones that compliment each other. Then the small set of shapes was fitted just as above.

The Omega will unfreeze them and all the weapons will be burnt in a big bonfire and the metals will be melted in a huge furnace."

While I watch, every part is moving to make a circle, slipping in alternatively as they move. And the children are going over to The Heap and stroking her. **The Judge** has picked her up and is carrying her over near the fire, sitting her next to **Persephone** who now holds her in her arms, the glow of the fire uniting them. One by one they file past her touching her hair or her arm gently as they go by, and as they do this she becomes more and more alive.

Some alters, after touching The Heap, then walk through the walls of the castle to the air outside and disappear. They have become integrated as Rhonda. I don't like that but I know that some will be there for me to recall and that I can retain their properties. I guess I just don't need them any more.

As memories were processed and we all journeyed from the past into the present, integration at an internal level was constantly happening. Sometimes, this spilled over into my consciousness, as in the following therapy session.

"Somehow, somewhere, **Mary, Rebecca, The Shining, Genesis** and the others are all involved with each other!" I blurted out to a very surprised Libby.

"What? Could you run that past me again please?"

"Everyone is involved with each other somehow. It's as though our system grew like a tree. They are all part of the same family! And even though they've all been locked away and nobody knew about anyone else, **The Master Planner** knew. Someone had to go to school, to know that **Bronwyn** needed to be there with no feelings, that **Emma** had to be present at those times and lots of other contingencies. Because, and I don't like this sentence---even though they have names and thoughts and feelings and histories, they are each part of one mind!"

Libby was smiling. "Say that again."

"They are each real but they can't act on their own behalf."

"Why not?"

"Because even though we believed that they were totally separate parts, people even, they were all only parts of the same mind."

"Do they have the same body too?"

"We must have! Because we remember the running shoes!"

"So everyone wore the running shoes."

"The body wore the running shoes," I yelled. "And even though some of us didn't like that very much, the body wore the running shoes. So we must all have the same body. How weird!"

I sense her outside the castle at night, in the moonlight on the moors, but we are not ready to see her or to touch her yet. It's not enough to have **the Earth Mother** who knows only how to look after dogs, cats and birds. And it's not enough to have the **Elderly People** or the **Fantasy Parents**. They were all perfect in the created world, but the real Self, when she emerges must know that Rhonda can and will give her full nurturance. This must be proven. There's a sudden switch and a voice with authority and conclusion speaks.

"I must reiterate in the most serious terms that the Self who is waiting, is vulnerable. Her vulnerability is absolute. She knows nothing about being alive because she has never looked into anyone's eyes. And until we can actually prove that we can look after the **Parallel Self** and get her safely through those initial developmental stages of the human being, then this Self will not be permitted to be shown."

There's a lot of anger within when I think of the Real Self. Anger at her because she remained safe and protected while we went through all that trauma. But if I harm her I will harm myself. It is all of us who have lived through it and we have done it for no other reason but to keep our soul alive so that we can live out a complete life on this earth. So that our soul can grow in its spiritual path. We have done this and maybe now is the time to seek her and to see her.

If we harm her in any way then we give the power to those who inflicted terror upon us and we negate all the work we have done on this journey to heal. But if we go to her and just observe her from a distance we may begin to understand that she is me and I am she. That we are both the same person.

Magnitude has agreed to come with us and the **Master Planner** has given his permission with quite a few conditions. Not unexpected. Of course we will not be allowed to go beyond the invisible wall that protects her. Not until we can feel a connection with her. Not until the anger is spent.

But where is she? All I know is that she's not in the castle but that we must step across a bridge that none of us have ever crossed before. So I'll have to be guided by the sage. He knows.

First we board a simple raft of logs held together by twine and journey along a river, watching the river banks on each side. On the right I recognise the children. Oh, and there's **Lucy** and **Bronwyn**. And look! **Stones, Emma, Rebecca** and **Mary**. They're all there. All the alters who have looked after me, been there for me.

I turn and on the banks on the left hand side of the river I see **The Him** and **The Terror** scowling, threatening. The **Jostler** guides the raft and tells me that we are travelling down the river that divides my brain and he is still at the ready in case an attempt is made to put the right and the left sides together. But I am still, as we travel quite a long way into the mists that have for so long separated her, our Real Self, from us. I feel a moment of uneasiness as I look back to see that the mist has closed in tightly around us. It's thick here, like a jungle but without any trees. Just thick and dense and the raft makes very slow progress.

We come to a halt at the end of the river. A thick mass surrounds us on all sides. It's muggy, gluggy mud and as we move into the familiarity of the created world we step lightly upon the whitish bog, moving forwards to who knows where.

"This is a test. If you are in the reality that experiences the physical weight of the body and brings this reality into this world then you will sink into the bog and disappear forever. For this is the protection of the **Deep, Deep Silence**. This is the place of truth."

There's a pinpoint of light up ahead and that, as we move into it broadens into a cone shape, like the light from a torch.

"Walk forward." Magnitude's voice is kind but strong.

So I walk, not knowing where I am or where I'm going, the silence bringing goose bumps to my flesh. Gradually as I get closer, the image of an infant becomes clear. She looks like me! But as I get closer, she begins to grow into a young child. I look into her eyes and realize that I am looking at my Self. She's pure and clean, innocent and vulnerable and I want to spit on her because I am **The Heap**, so filthy and ugly and so filled up with their filth and chaos. I try to move closer but there's a barrier. I want to tear it down and see who this intruder is, looking like me.

But I hear Magnitude's voice: "Look within and find peace. The ancient shores of yesterday's child will bring nothing but joy to your enclave. Open your heart and you will feel this joy."

Then I see it. The light that shines within her, clear and bright. She has our **Shining**. I try again to move closer but the barrier stops me and as I remember the anger I had felt I realize that we must return to the reality of the circle, of the world outside and resolve this anger before we are permitted near her.

But **Magnitude** is here again. "Unrelenting have you been in your search. Many years ago we thought your spirit would be crushed beneath such odds. But hope chewed gently on the cud of Mother Earth and you never lost sight of the warmth in God's eyes. This is how we know. Had you broken the connection, hope would have given way to despair. But you did not. And your dreams are not contained in cotton wool nor coated with the stickiness of fairy floss.

They exist because you dreamt them in your solitude of isolated thoughts. This thought was then contained within the confines of fear. Now is the time for this thought to be brought out into the light and spread across the corners of your mind, pushing putty out into the nowhere and the tapestry of lies, beyond the bounds of judgment. It is the terror dying."

CHAPTER 10

The Fires, the Embers and the Stone

The theatre is bustling as the audience arrives in blibs and blobs, gradually settling and seated. The curtain opens and we see the inside of a medieval castle with its grey stone walls and slotted windows. The stage, dimly lit, is distinctly divided into two. On the left, a small collection of embers glows dimly and huddled next to it are two young children, **Rachel** *and* **Rebecca**. *On the right a mixed group of alters, some good, some with not such good intentions, including* **The Terror**.

The musicians enter, a happy group dressed in brown peasant clothing. One strums a lute, the others play recorders of all sizes. The music is gentle but rhythmic and the two children hum quietly as they walk to the left hand side and assemble in a consort.

Suddenly the embers begin to glow more brightly, a flame igniting and dancing. But one of the crowd on the other side immediately walks over to it and with a sense of duty and authority lowers a long cylindrical taper into the dancing flame, drawing it into the cylinder. Watching, we have the feeling that compliance rules the flame, which is then carried to the other side and thrust with decision into the burning glow. As we sit pondering, the narrator walks on carrying a lantern.

He's a strong character dressed in a robe of colourful patches and as he walks forwards and turns to face the audience we see his long grey beard and gentle eyes.

Narrator: "Welcome to our castle. We are all parts of Rhonda's mind. But we are not an illusion, we are real. Our reality may not be yours but it exists and perhaps we can share some of it with you. Firstly, I'd like you to meet Rhonda."

As his arm stretches outwards towards the back of the stage, we see a girl about fourteen walking slowly forwards. Her head is down, her steps are slow. She sits cross-legged in the centre front stage. As the narrator moves over to her with his lantern we see that she's encased in a thick membrane.

"Let me explain the fires to you. There on the left are the embers of life and they must never be allowed to go out or Rhonda will die. It is the **Spirit of the Fire** who keeps the embers alive but at the same time they must never ignite into a flame or glow too brightly. You see, it's decreed that no-one will ever see the essence of Rhonda. The membrane keeps her within her side of this decree.

I hear you asking, why? It's quite simple really, because if her light that we call The Shining is ever seen then it would provide a road to **the One Who was Born.** And that's why we were created. She must be protected at all times and at all costs."

A second figure, robed, walks slowly forward from the crowd.

Magnitude: Open thou thy heart to the treasures of being
for it will surely shine within the contours of your soul
and ignite the flame that lies within.
The embers are here waiting for you to see
Pick up your skirts and waltz to the tune of your
distant flute
that spirals its sounds deep within the chasms and
chambers of your mind
Open the door and let them out!
You guard your heart with a solid wall
built stone by stone with purpose
but now that reason is no more
it's lying mute upon the dungeon floor
spattered by the force of truth.
Open your heart
take the hand of God
and sing.

Narrator: "The large fire that you see on the right is made up of the terror, the sadness, the violence. The familiar. But Rhonda wants to speak. Now that she knows about us she's afraid that one day the embers may burn brightly---"

Rhonda: "and everything of value would be dead."

She holds the front of her head to stop the pressure that's building. It's as though that part of her brain would be gone and she would only have part of it left. She stands, and shrugs at the audience.

"Don't you see, there would be a big hole where part of my brain used to be!"

Magnitude: *walking over to her and taking her hand in his.*

"That is not possible my dear. You see, the pressure in your head is from the volcano of memories. And you see my dear, we are your memories."

Rhonda: "No! You're real!"

Magnitude: *Taking her hand as they walk to the front right corner.*

"You have reached a challenge. A quest. For it is time for you to make a choice.

You must choose between being seen, becoming whole and being the one you were born to be, or staying here with all the parts of you that you have created and come to trust and to love."

Rhonda: "But you don't get it! My father will never be dead. He'll always be there ready to grab me."

She slumps down, head in hands. The music resumes and with it, the hope is almost visible as it spreads across the stage.

Magnitude: "He is dead my dear."

One of the children stands.

Rachel: "I don't understand 'dead.' The giant keeps coming back!"

Suddenly we see him, a giant with thundering voice and thumping feet, who scoops up the children, one in each hand, holding them up like trophies. The scene freezes except for the Narrator who walks down into the center aisle and addresses the audience.

Narrator: "Let me explain. The giant and the father are two separate people. The children would not have survived had they believed that the father was the one who came and plundered and pillaged, so we created the giant. In this way the children could retain a father who was safe. And you see, to them the giant is still real. We cannot change their story at whim. This is their reality and nothing else at the moment is safe."

He walks back on stage.

"Have you made your choice?"

The music fades.

Rhonda: *standing centered and with resolve.*

"Yes. And we will ask the Terror to hold the Giant captive. But right now, there's someone on each side, with each fire. It's really only one person but he changes each time he changes sides. When he's on the right he's **Merlin** who created magic and on the left he's **Marvin** who knows about the wisdom. Magic is good sometimes but because it's created it can also continue to be changed at will and it will always be magic. But wisdom is truth and truth remains constant. Like the embers. We must speak our truth to the giant. We will tell him that the past is no longer and the danger has ended. We have won and we are alive."

She walks up to the giant, who is being held captive by the terror, encircled by all remaining parts of Rhonda.

Rhonda: "You are a creation and I am no longer afraid of you because I know that the father is dead. You are in the sea with the Father of the Ashes. I understand now that you have done a good job but there is no room for you in the present. You must leave us now."

She steps back, joining the circle as the giant begins to shrink. Smaller and smaller until right before our eyes he has completely disappeared, even from the minds of the children.

Magnitude: "He will never return my dear. Nor will your father."

Suddenly the stage fills with mist and the music builds.

Rhonda: "My mother! She's over there near the embers. I must bring her over here. But she's split in two! One side's coming across and I must be truthful and tell her that I have no respect for this part of her. But look! She's split into two again and now she's a child as well, and I can't feel anger or hatred for that child."

The mists begin to dissolve as Rhonda moves towards the embers.

"Look! My mother's sitting by the embers and next to her is an angel."

Magnitude: "What you're seeing is your mother's soul."

Rhonda (*addressing Magnitude*) "I don't know whether to put that fire out or to bring the two fires together. I don't want the second one."

Magnitude: "But my dear, it came from the embers."

Rhonda: "But if I give the energy to the embers then we will be seen existing."

Magnitude: "And the giant has gone now."

Rhonda: (*softly*): "And if I'm seen by her then it's her soul that will be seeing me?"

Magnitude: "Yes, and there's no danger in that."

Rhonda: (*excited, walking here and there, as a whole picture spreads before her eyes.*)

"The buttercup field, do you remember! There used to be barbed wire and dandelions and Libby was in the corner as a donkey, watching over me. I was **The Heap** then and gradually she got strong enough to stand up and look outside the paddock she was in."

She looks down to the sea to the whitewashed house.

"Then, the sea was still and always dark and somber and the house was closed up with no life inside. But look now! The barbed wire's gone and the donkey's moved to a paddock in a far away village. The field is bright green and the buttercups are out in abundance. And the sea! It's translucent from the shore and waves roll in and out. The house has been painted and all the doors and windows are open. There's even smoke coming from the chimney. It's alive."

Magnitude: "Can you still see the castle?"

Rhonda: "Yes. The real castle's on this side, with the embers but it is completely empty. And the crowd that was over there has walked to the centre and as they walk, the other side of the backdrop is all crumbling as though it was painted on a thick, almost brittle canvas. And it's tearing, splitting and falling away."

We watch. The mists fading, and as the crowd circles the embers we see the fire growing until it's burning brightly. The other side of the stage is black.

*The Narrator walks from the blackness into the centre of the stage, watching the fire of the embers. The two children, **Rachel** and **Rebecca**, have joined the others and Rhonda stares in disbelief as she sees Rachel with her blondish hair that has been pulled to one side and tied with a ribbon. She is seeing herself as a young girl, dressed in familiar clothing and, as she watches, the child grows until they are standing face to face.*

*Other parts have picked up **The Heap**, still very damaged, and carried her up into the light. The musicians begin once more and we hear the music of the moonlight that all her life had told **Rebecca** that she was still alive and had told those guarding her that the system was working. Now Prince is here, sitting on her knee and licking her face. He'll be gone soon. He just needed to let her know that he was with her, but that his time here on earth is finished. She smiles.*

Something is happening! **The Heap** *and* **Rebecca** *each stand and move towards each other. Their eyes meet and gradually, as we watch in wonder, they move together and become one.*

The Spirit of the Fire *takes their hand knowing that in time she too will grow.*

Rhonda walks forward holding something in her hands.

Magnitude: "When you were small, the angels sang. Please listen and hear their voices. Remember. For it will lift you up above the earthbound treasures and remind you of the love with which you were born. That stone still lies within you. Look at it, listen to it. Remember it. The Stone and the Embers, they are the same thought. Bring them into your consciousness and the limp rag of non-being will be filled with promised life. Live! For only with your will, will you gain power and win over the trauma of the past.

Gather up thy Self
and walk with strength into your skin
that holds you firm and safe within its care."

Rhonda opens her hands and we see the pink and purple glow of the stone.

She lies a crumpled heap on the floor of the banquet room of the castle. Filthy, scratched and bruised, her eyes almost closed, her mind glued shut. Her dress, torn and dirty hangs limp, with no skeleton to hold it. Her hair, tangled, with sun-drenched streaks frames her face with a sense of demented wildness. She is **The Heap.**

Her arms hang limp but her belly, slightly swollen stands resolute in its evidence. A tribute to the battlefield of rape where she has fought and lost until time and wasted words have stitched up the connection between her heart and the battle and left the corpses moaning.

I feel repulsed by her and angry at her pathetic disconnection.

"Why didn't you keep fighting?" I ask her. But she doesn't answer. Doesn't hear, or does she? Is she just existing or is she awakening? Are the embers of her soul still flickering with their own energy or are they just painted in one dimension?

"Go over to her," says the voice from behind me.

Slowly, fearfully, with equal love and hate I walk towards her. She is so needy. Helpless. I want to hurt her yet at the same time to gather her up into my arms and speak to her. But I don't know which will win as I take each step in her direction. The stone of the castle floor is cold but I can feel the warmth of the fire burning strongly in the massive hearth. I look around at the others standing in the safety of the castle walls, watching with silent stares and muted breath.

One more step and I'll be there next to her. But wait! I stop and listen. A voice, small and frail, casts a fine thread of sound, like the single woven thread of a spider. **The Heap** is singing! Three children, **Beatrice, Emily** and **Bernadette** are surrounding her, gently stroking her hair, their voices joining hers.

The Judge carefully picks her up, carrying her over to a spot near the fire and placing her next to **Persephone** who holds her in her arms, the glow of the fire warming them. **Mephistopheles** has stepped forwards and now sits on the other side, touching her hand. A goddess on one side, the symbol of spiritual rebirth, while on the other, the symbol of the devil. Each with love for the recovering child.

I kneel down near her as she lifts her head upwards, her green eyes touching mine. I look away. But when I turn to face her again she is sitting, her hand extended towards mine, the threads of sound spreading slowly through me.

I find myself filled with tears as I realize that she, **The Heap**, is part of me, part of my Self, and that we have been parted for such along time. I touch her skin, my hand enclosing the flesh and bone, feeling the warm blood that pulses life through her. Through me. We are one and the same. How can I harm her when she is one for whom I have been searching?

She stands, frail yet gently shining and filled with courage, knowing that she has been found. I move even closer, feeling the small seed of joy that is opening in me. I help her up, supporting her as we walk towards the huge wooden doors of the castle entrance and as we walk I can feel her energy lifting and her helplessness falling away, the music growing outwards and resting comfortably in the castle space. Her music. My music. Turning, I look back and smile as I watch the **Spirit of the Fire** dancing around the hearth. 'It will still be there when we return,' I think, as we walk hand in hand across the drawbridge and out onto the wet grass.

"What about **Genesis**?" I ask anyone who's there. "And why is she so bereft of any sign of life?"

There's an immediate answer from my mind: "Genesis belongs to the time of the swirling room when life became disconnected. There was no life around or behind the castle, the sky was bleak and the castle was no longer a refuge. It had become a prison. Rhonda's room became the **disconnected Cube** that was attached to nothing on earth and filled with terror. It is not possible to exist in complete isolation and to be there was to be on the edge of insanity.

Genesis holds the beginning of life and is waiting until we are completely ready for **The One Who was Born** to live out in the world. A bit like Sleeping Beauty who went to sleep for such a long time and when she woke the world had become a different place. I always hoped that one day we would be unraveled. And I always knew that we would sit and talk with someone at length and that he or she would 'see' us. That our words would be heard. I saw it long before any therapy began.

"But Genesis is still a blob. She appears to not do or think or feel anything. Why?" I ask.

Again, **Magnitude** comes forward. "Well, she is me, she you, she is all of us. But she is contained."

"Yes, but why is she still a nothing?"

"Safety my dear. For the silent shall inherit the legacy of time and space and the 'what is' and the 'what is not' will gradually come together. The Circle and the Square will be one. There will be no need at all for any geometric shapes to contain or repel, as nothing will be separate. Only then will the container, who is Genesis be opened and the Self restored. You see, Genesis is stirring. Do not rush her for in her silence she knows. Like a state of meditation, but with the withdrawal complete. She is awakening from this state and very soon she will be with you."

"And what about **Mary**?" I ask.

She is there immediately and in person. "I stood at the door of knowledge, waiting. Then I knocked and it opened. I guarded the path. I guided the actions. I have one foot on the earth and the other in the world of The

Nowhere, the world that lies in the hole in the clouds. I understand each of them, for without that understanding then disconnection would have become complete. I knew that no matter what, we just could not die so there had to be a way of living. And this was to stay connected to the 'what is' of eternity. Of living souls."

Something stirred behind her and Mary looked around to see a 'bright green door' with a small wooden handle. There were no walls, and no floor, just a door. But disconnected images were not new to her.

"Where will it lead?" she asked

"Beyond the now," came a voice on the other side of the door. "Take one more step forward Mary, put your hand upon the handle and it will open for you." It was **Magnitude**.

"Why would I do that? What awaits me? More terror? More insanity? Some say true madness lies settled within the realms of terror, trapped within a space with no limits, yet buried deep within the mind. No connection with the earth, the sea or the sky. No thread to draw me back into the limits of structured space and committed boundaries. So why would it be better beyond the now?"

"Because The terror does not exist here."

"But do I exist? And if so, where am I? Where is the space that is meant for me to be. To be filled with the energy of my own life-force. My Self."

"Open the door, Mary. The madness is not yours. You must shed it like the skin of a snake, outgrown and complete."

Mary stood for a moment, her mind wandering amongst the threads of thought from long ago. She looked up and the door was surrounded by a crimson light of infinite proportions and from the muffled space behind the bright green door she heard voices raised in music she could only have dreamed of.

"Come, Mary. Now you can move beyond the yesterday." The voice was deep and gentle. Closer and closer to the door, her hand reaching out, her heart remembering a distant warmth of far away. It opened, revealing a space of trees and gentle stream. A structured space framed by brown earth and vivid sky filled with the pastel music of the clouds.

"Welcome," said the voice. "There is no terror here nor the fragmentation of madness. Sit a while and feel the life around you that is safe, bounded and whole. Beyond the now the memory of terror will fade and life will gradually move within you to replace it. Absorb it Mary for it is an open heart that is a pathway to the Self.

"I am the voice of **The Deep, Deep Silence**. If you listen carefully I will give you the directions that will allow you to follow and to reach the place of the final challenge. You will then be told your task and if you are successful you will walk with peace upon the earth. But first you must survive. Are you ready?"

"Yes." I replied.

"Then follow my directions and you will enter the realm of the deep, deep silence. Listen carefully for I will give you the directions only once. First you stand in the rays of Knowledge before the gates of all that is known. The Terror will watch but will remain silent until asked to speak. It will not touch you nor will it contaminate you any further."

"But it's spread right through me. It's tentacles are clenched throughout my body. It has me in its hold and I feel as though there's nothing I can do to free myself."

"But there is. Let it go. It does not belong to the present and it no longer lives within life because its life was yesterday."

"**Yvette** has not reached that point yet. She is still about fifteen with blond hair that is thick and shining. Her eyes are sad but piercing in their beds of green. They look and see but they do not understand. They were confused for such a long time but now they watch with compliance and with no hope of salvation."

"Look beyond this. What do you see?"

"I see gentleness turned to hate and despair to anger. I see anger, hate and fear that blaze outwards, cutting thin like the blades of knives. Shafts so long that they could cut into the deepest flesh and gouge out the most hideous of evils."

"Yes. That is where **Yvette** dwells. Ready to fight. She is split from **Paula** but she is far more damaged and ready to do anything that is needed in order to survive. Your task is to disarm her and persuade her to come with you and stand in the rays of Knowledge before the gate of all that is known. She must come of her own free will. You must do this before I take you into the Deep, Deep Silence for there must be no terror remaining within the walls of the castle that will contaminate its purity.

Be wary. She is wild of spirit and strong of body. She will fight you with words that are both clever and strong. She will try to control you for that is the only way she knows of keeping her mind. You must arm yourself with love and empathy before you approach her for these are the only weapons that will work. And you must remain aware at all times. Look behind you, in front and to both sides for she is cunning and with stealth she will ensnare you and you will be trapped. I will not be able to help you if this happens. Now go and begin."

One of the reasons my system was created was to maintain the mandatory code of silence that my mother had placed around us. Nothing that happened at home, in the reality of the square, was to be leaked out in any form or proportion. However, there were two people who I met during my years growing up, both of whom observed and saw that something was wrong.

The first was my piano teacher, Mrs. Ziegler, of whom I've already spoken, and the other was a lady whose name I don't remember, but each of them remains in my heart.

I was about twelve and the worst imaginable thing happened when Prince had taken himself, as he sometimes did, for a walk in the morning. I always kept an eagle eye on him but occasionally he asserted his independence and trotted off without me. I waited and waited, my mother reassuring me: "He'll be back soon."

But the sun was beginning to go down as I searched all the surrounding streets, whistling the call that would usually see him bounding up to me. I hunted along the creek, through the pipes, all around the school but I couldn't find him.

He didn't come back the next day, the next or the next. A week went by. I was still going to school but dead inside me.

"We'll put a notice up somewhere in the shopping centre," my mother said. But still more days passed and he didn't appear. No soft fur to run my fingers through, no deep brown eyes to tell me that I was alive.

The telephone rang and I ran to answer it.

"It's Prince." I called out to Mum. "He's mine!" I yelled into the phone.

My mother took the phone and scribbled down an address.

I could hardly get the words out through the waves of emotion that were almost choking me.

"Where is he? When can I go and get him?"

"He's with a lady who lives behind the hairdresser's up near the church."

I already had my shoes on, his lead in my hand, and was running out the door as fast as I could. I reached the hairdresser's and found the laneway but when I went to knock on the door of her flat I was so scared I couldn't think or breathe. She opened the door and there he was, his tail wagging and licking me all over as I gathered him up into my arms and cried into his fur.

"He's definitely your dog," she said. "Come in."

But as I sat awkwardly in a kitchen chair, she told me that she wasn't going to let me take him home.

"His fur was matted and he was very hungry," she said. "And I can't let you have him until I know that you will look after him."

I couldn't believe what I was hearing. My dog. My Prince, whose fur I brush every day. My life. "But he's been missing for over a week," I pleaded. "That's why he's hungry and matted."

She talked with me for some time, gave me some hot chocolate and tried to calm me down. But she didn't know. She didn't understand and I cried and screamed, holding Prince as close to me as I could. She stood her ground and I returned home with an empty lead.

"You can visit him here every day but he will live here with me until I know that he will be cared for."

For weeks I went to the lady's flat behind the hairdresser's and piece by piece I began to relax, to look forward to the chats we had and of course to being with my beautiful dog. She asked me about school, friends, what I liked to read, my music and one day she asked about my family and my home. I didn't tell her about what happened there.

I didn't break the silence. But somehow she knew. She showed me so much kindness that when she finally gave Prince back to me, we both went back to visit her often and chatted over a hot chocolate.

"I'm moving from here," she said one day and in two weeks she'd gone. I will never forget her. Even though I kept the secret, I had reached outside the reality of home and connected with a stranger. An adult. And this had touched a part of me, **Bethany**, a child isolated in the turret of an imaginary castle who wrote to 'the Lady' (in the form of Libby) many years later, during my therapy, making a connection with Libby just as we had with the lady in the flat behind the hairdresser's so many years ago.

Hello Lady

I have to write to you because I must not be seen. I am alone but I want so much to be safe in someone's arms, telling them about what is happening here, to feel it melting all my fears. I imagine your face as I talk, telling, showing with my hands and feeling with my eyes.

I imagine that I finish for a while and you let me rest, covering me with a blanket and carefully tucking in the sides to keep me warm. Your voice is soft and kind and I can hear you breathing as you sit on a chair near the couch, reading.

But always something bursts through my sleeping. I scream and shudder and find a corner of the room, curling up as small as I can. I try to make it go away, thinking about the touch of warm arms, lifting me, holding me.

I want to speak to you but I need to know that you will not die because of my words. You will not erupt in anger or throw spears at me. Then I will tell you about my loneliness and my fear.

Will you listen? Will you hear?

Bethany

Dear Bethany

It was so lovely to read your words. I hear your confusion and your need to be heard. I hear how much you want to be held in a warm, safe place and I hear what it's like for you and I am listening.

Please write to me again soon.

The Lady

Hello Lady
It felt so good to read your words. They came from the outside but they made me feel good and safe.

I love it where I live, in the turret of the castle. I am lonely but I love the wind, for it takes my thoughts away to other places. I know that if I place a thought upon the wind it will be taken somewhere outside the square. The wind has listened and brought you to me. It has heard me and here you are.

The doll Betti lives here with me when I can find her. She belongs to Kate but sometimes I borrow her and call her mine. She's porcelain, has a painted face and I put her on a chair and talk to her and I take her to a place that is on the outer edge of the square. It's a place where I can hide.

I know it's not a physical space because I cannot leave this turret but it's a space where Betti and I can go beyond where we are. The father can still find me but when he does I can vanish in my head and be safe. I hope you can understand this.

The reality where you live is outside the bubble and this is frightening because if the bubble is pierced then everything inside will die. I know this because it's what the mother says and why we must never break the decree of silence. So it's really dangerous for me to talk to you but I have to talk to someone. The bubble is filled up to overflowing with violence and non-hearing, no connecting. And you took care of Prince so I know you are good and will not hurt me.

I have only one reason to hear you and that is to know that you are there and you are listening and that you hear me. Until now I have been completely alone but things have changed and I somehow seem to be more awake.

Thank you Lady
Bethany

Dear Bethany
I am so pleased that you've written to me again. I am here and I hear you. It sounds like an empty and lonely place where you are and I do understand that you have a place in your mind that you can escape to with Betti.

The wind is also waiting to hear you so keep telling me, keep talking to me and I will hear you.

With my love

The Lady

Hello Lady

I can see what is happening and I can't hide any more

I can see the shadows but I cannot comprehend their substance

I can write to you, but are you really there?

And even if you are there what does it mean?

I try so hard to see the reality of others but the voyage across the sea of nothing known is too far. There are no landmarks, no way of knowing direction. And how would I know if I have reached this place for I know nothing of its fabric? It is too far, too hard and I don't have the skills.

I am too alone Lady

Bethany

Dear Bethany

If you let me, I can help you to understand and I can guide you into the world of others. Just keep writing to me and telling me about what you are feeling. You have made a connection outside the square and nothing has happened to you.

Keep listening to the wind and we will keep you safe.

With love

The Lady

Hello Lady

I cannot write to you any more. The decree of silence must not be broken or we will all be destroyed. But I can remember your words and when I need to I can feel them soft on my skin and warm in my body

Thank you and goodbye Lady

Bethany

For most of the time since I became aware of our castle, we could see only in one direction, across the moors to the sea. And this is how it had been for **Bethany,** alone in the turret. There was no other colour inside or out, just the cold grey of the stone and the deep blue of the sea. She never saw behind the castle as there were no windows facing that way and the **Invisible Force** made sure she was closely contained in all directions. Until that is, a voice in my head yelled out to me:

"There's a secret room with a secret window."

I had no idea where to look so I asked the question to which came an immediate reply: "Just below the highest turret there is a small passageway. Walk to the end and open the door."

"Is that you Bethany?" I asked "Yes. Things have changed in here since I reached outside the bubble of the square and talked to The Lady."

I smiled and in my mind walked up the many levels of the spiraling staircase, down the passage and gently pushed open the door to reveal a room that was beyond my wildest imagination. Colour was everywhere, with light flooding in and filling every space. Comfy cushions were scattered here and there and bookshelves lined the wall. In the corner a piano stood beckoning.

"Look! Over there," cried **Bethany.** "There's a large glass window looking out towards the back of the castle and everything is green. There's no grey or black."

I stared out at a forest of trees that provided a backdrop to a small creek and a wooden bridge. Yellow daffodils! There are no fences, I thought, Bethany almost reading my mind:

"No, and we are all free to go wherever we want."

It had been there all the time. But the silence in which my mother had contained us was so absolute that we didn't even ask the question that would have allowed us to know that we could look in other directions and see other realities.

There have been many changes in our castle along the way. The drawbridge, once controlled by the **Invisible Force** can now be left opened, or closed. It has become a choice. The dungeons and caves in the belly of the castle were always forbidden and forbidding places. We knew about the **embers** and the **Spirit of the Fire** but only in comforting stories. Now, as I venture down, bright flare in my hand, the gates are all open and one by one I find each cave empty and whereas before, the underground passages had gone on and on, I almost immediately reach a dead end. I understand that I have now seen everything, remembered everything and confronted all our memories.

Suddenly I spot her, almost invisible yet there, small but continuously swirling so that she can stay alive, not connecting with anything nearby.

"She is the **Spirit of the Fire**," says the voice in my head.

Libby understands. "Can you now reclaim her?"

I nod, holding out my hand, as slowly the swirling ceases and her eyes lift to mine. I reach out and can feel her as I place her near my heart, carrying her step by step upwards into the banquet room of the castle. On turning to see where we've come from, it immediately all moves up to meet me and there is now nothing below the ground level of the castle. Magically, there are lights shining everywhere as the castle moves into the age of electricity! We go up the stairs and one by one, each door disappears and as I walk into the secret room we're covered by a massive wash of colour that spreads right through the castle.

But at the same time **The Controller**, who is everywhere and anywhere, a massive Big Brother watching over everything in the castle, in every wall, and turret and floor board and every room and right now his voice is booming around the corridors: "Everybody's gone! I didn't give you permission to leave. Come back immediately. Come back!"

But it's too late, for now it's time for him to leave the castle, pulled out by **Wicked Witch** grunting and groaning, pulling and heaving him out of every crevice. As she does he's getting smaller and smaller until he disappears.

Magnitude appears and in his usual calm tones and puzzling words tells us: "Something deep within us needs to surface slowly and securely. It is the knowledge of the Deep, deep silence. Listen carefully for you will then all be free."

"What does the castle look like these days?" Libby asks.

"It's in the mists and when I get there, no-one is there."

"Do you know where they have gone?"

I point to myself. "Here. And their ghosts are our playing on the moors. They are not lost, they're just all me."

My experiences during this journey have convinced me that the mind and the body work together. As memories surfaced, the fear often intense and almost constant, the instances of diarrhea became acute, sometimes lasting for six weeks. I could keep nothing in my stomach and even though eating normally, was losing weight. Again, I had a colonoscopy and again, nothing was abnormal. However, once the memory, always one associated with Dad, had been fully processed the diarrhea completely disappeared. This has happened several times over the years.

But the strangest thing is when my face changes. My nose thickens, my eyelids swell and cover part of my eyes and my lips become very thin.

"What's the matter with you? "Bruce asked. "You look like your father!" he said staring at me the first time it happened. But that was early in my journey and now we're both used to it although friends still find it strange. I have no idea why it happens but the change in my face is obvious. It's always the same and, once the memory that is surfacing has been processed, returns to normal.

Integration has occurred irregularly throughout my healing journey, sometimes I know about it and sometimes I don't. But whenever I do, it is in the form of a story or an experience that shows me what is happening.

One such occasion was at a Chamber Music concert where I unwittingly watched as several parts of my system showed themselves to me and interacted with each other while the sounds of a Dvorak string quartet spread through the hall. **Beatrice** was the first to be seen, sitting a row in front of me, hunched and furtive. I wanted to reach out to her, to tell her that it was ok. That I could hear the music too and that she wasn't alone. Suddenly, another part leapt up, her arms waving madly in time to the music, her face filled with joy. She turned and smiled at me. I found myself smiling back. She pulled Beatrice to her feet, and together they moved to the stage, **Rachel** weaving freely among the musicians, beckoning her friend to join her. But Beatrice remained sitting quietly at the side, watching.

The slow movement began. Beautiful and lyrical with intense sounds and patterns that move closer into the space where silent tears are kept. Gradually Beatrice got to her feet, each movement growing out of the one before, immersed in the language of the music. They were one.

Rachel became still, watching without intrusion. I also sat, deeply touched by her grace and her freedom. Now they were dancing together.

At times Rachel was Beatrice's shadow and at others they were separate beings lost in the sinews of the music. And now it was me who was immersed in their story, wanting and needing to join them in their dance. But I could not. Although I created each one, they are them and I am me. They each have their own part in this healing journey and it is not for me to intrude on this. The music reached its end as they moved as one, back to the row in front of me, then vanished, their job complete.

Music remains paramount in my life, playing, singing, composing and teaching.

Accompanying friends, singing some of the wonderful old jazz standards, writing short instrumental works. And hundreds of children's songs that are enjoyed around the country.

I formed my own singing group and for many years we sang all different genres and gave concerts to friends and families. I loved it. Now I sing in someone else's choir and was recently commissioned to write a 3 part a cappella choral work for them. I waited for inspiration which finally came in the form of the wind chimes outside my window. The ones my son always tied up with a rubber band to stop them annoying him. They remind me of the wind that came and spoke to **Bethany** in the castle turret, taking her messages away, far from the reality of the square. "Waiting for the Sun," the lyrics wrote themselves as I took myself to a place of rain and cold wind with a cosy house and fire to keep me warm and safe until the sun came out again.

So the muse is still there and when it appears it takes me to a creative space where nothing else matters and where my mind can wander to anywhere it wants to go.

One such wandering took me on a journey to find *The Purple Emu*.

It was grey and I was sitting alone at the edge of the forest when who should stride by but an emu. This was no ordinary emu. She was purple, with ecumenical gowns flowing from her carefully positioned shoulders atop a lonely body. 'Why lonely?' I hear you ask. Well you see, it wasn't connected to her head and neck but somehow it moved as if it were.

It was the strangest sight. Every time the emu's feet turned and walked in another direction or ran forward, or slowed right down, the head and neck followed at a gap. Like a marionette with detached joints that create the illusion of time, space and movement. I said 'hello' to the head as it moved by, not quite sure whether to speak again to the body section, but she nodded at me and proceeded on her way. I decided to follow. Down, down, down she went, moving swiftly as I followed, avoiding her glance as she pondered her journey in retrospect.

If you think she's weird, you should have seen the sights as we descended. Flowers strewn across ridges made of translucent glass that covered a cemetery in which some graves were so small they must have housed the bodies of souls that were brand new into the world. Some of the graves were solid balls that just sat upon the ground, connecting at one point only, enough to balance somewhat precariously. Almost as if to challenge the real world that had put it there.

At one stage the path was knee deep in blood and I had to dodge the severed body parts as they came hurtling towards me.

Just past the fourteenth roundabout, the moon fell out of the sky and landed in the lake. Splash! The emu looked around and muttered to herself, complaining about the stupid person who was supposed to hold it up in the sky.

I felt it all to be very strange but I continued to follow the emu. She at last came to a wintry landscape. Nothing but white was everywhere. She was cold, you could tell by the way her feathers were all fluffed up. We trudged on through the snow. It was icy and wet, but I was determined to keep going. I wanted to find out where she was headed and why. So on we went. The wind was bitter and there was not a tree in sight. Nothing but pure, pure snow.

For days she walked and pranced and hopped, further and further into the whiteness. I was beginning to wonder whether I'd ever be able to find my way out when she finally stopped beside a small mound of snow. She looked around and when she could see nothing (I was floating on a small iceberg, its pinnacle covering my presence), she knelt down and proceeded to dig. Slowly, reverently. Well, I became intensely curious and nearly fell off into the icy water trying to strain my head and neck, so as not to miss anything. It was then that I wanted a head and neck like hers, one that would stretch up without anyone knowing there was something hiding beneath.

She gently moved the snow from the small mound, to create another mound to one side. Deeper and deeper she dug until all I could see of her was the tip of her ecumenical gown as it was blown by the icy wind.

The new mound of snow was now almost as big as the slush pile I once saw in the hills of Wales.

I couldn't believe my eyes, rubbing and rubbing them, thinking that the whiteness had finally got to me and cancelled out my definition. Out from the hole in the snow there was a small light, purple with just a hint of rose. It gradually spread outwards, shimmering and moving as if alive, dancing on the whiteness of the snow. Come on, dance with me, it seemed to be saying.

Suddenly my iceberg ran aground and tipped me off into the icy water. My toes were squealing and my fingers fading but I managed to clamber up onto the nearest pontoon of ice as it drifted by me, shaking myself off like the seals at the zoo when they emerge from the water. As I did I was aware that the purple emu with the disconnected head was watching me, her eyes penetrating my existence as though I was not solid.

I stood up and gradually followed my feet as they led me towards her. The purple light almost filled the snow and the wind seemed to sing a strange song, gently rocking with just a hint of humour. There was no anger in her eyes, there was not even surprise. It was as though she knew that I would be there. That she expected me and as she turned again, I saw the source of the shimmering light. In her arms was a very small baby, its eyes closed, its face serene. There was no movement, but I knew from the light that it was alive.

The emu walked towards me. "Is this what you've been looking for?" She asked as she handed me the small living bundle.

I took the baby, expecting it to be frozen with cold but its warmth radiated through my being, unfreezing my bones and separating my organs. I looked down into her face and then up at the purple emu.

"You've been separated from yourself for such a long time," she said.

It was now clear. She was reading my mind.

"You'll be able to find your way back"

I looked into the eyes of the Purple Emu and saw the deep, deep waters of no time, of no solid matter. For that is where we came from.

Then I looked down at the small child that I carried in my arms. She opened her eyes and I saw all of my past actions and thoughts spread out like a crafted rug, endlessly moving past my vision. Eventually it came to rest and I began the long journey back from the frozen whiteness. Never again will we be separated, I thought. Never again will she be hidden, buried beneath the snow.

Hello Dad

Libby once suggested that I give you a flower, but I could never reach that point of forgiveness until now. Most of the terror has gone and I can look back and see where I've come from. Without your pathology and your inability to cope with your own journey I wouldn't have walked this path. However, without these experiences I would not have been the person I am now. I would not have had to search for my Self and would probably have taken this Self for granted. I've glimpsed her sometimes over the years but always she sinks beneath the murky depths, safely out of sight.

I know she's there. I can feel her presence. The water is clear now and I have seen my Self, Dad, and I like her. I like the depth of feeling and perception that I had to develop in order to survive. I can acknowledge the creativity that it took to find a way of not just surviving, but surviving with my Self unharmed. And I love the feeling of wonder that has filtered through from her, always allowing me to be aware of the energies and the amazing patterns of nature.

Perhaps I tried to throw a pebble into the waters of turbulence and conflict and it sank and was lost. But now that I have waited and can cast my pebble into depths of sunlight and shadows I have found that at the end of its long journey it has once again become visible at great depths.

Some say that a person, as a soul, would have agreed to come onto this earth with me in the role that you took. If this is right then you made a very difficult choice, to inflict so much harm onto your own daughter. If this is the case then I'm grateful, because you taught me much. And now all that is left is to separate from you. To let go of the thin but desperate connection that I forged with need and conviction but that now keeps me locked into the past and the need to dissociate.

I need to now acknowledge that ultimately I am alone. And that's OK. That we are each alone, and yet a small part of an amazing life force. To come into the awareness and Knowledge of all things, I first need to stand alone and to do this, I must know my Self. I must accept my Self and listen to my Self. I must feel love for my Self. The love that is without need for contract or words. The love that just 'is'. I know that many years of therapy and the wonderful support of my family have helped me to do this. And I think that strangely, and on a soul level Dad, you've helped me too.

You met Bruce and you liked him. You walked with me up the aisle of the church aa I was married, but you never saw or met our children, a thought that carries much sadness for me. When I was thirty and married for eight years, Natalie, and three years later Kris were born. Each has grown safely and filled with life. Even without the conscious memories of past events I hadn't wanted to have children, but with a warm and loving partner I was given a second chance, and for each of them I feel the most amazing love imaginable. They are kind, loving, thinking people, filled with music and creativity and happy in their lives. Three grandchildren are now in our world and give us much joy. I know that they will each blossom with loving parents and their Selves will shine.

It's taking a long time for me to truly separate from you, but when it's done I will lay you to rest in peace. I am grateful that you're no longer in my life, but the part of you who loved music and who shared some happy times remains with me in my heart. Thank you for the journey Dad.

Rhonda

Hope Street Now

It's an unmade decision, my legs walking in that direction towards the next street on the left. The one before the expressway. It wasn't always like that, in fact the vast expanse of this road now goes right through the site of old Mr. Bailey's shop. A general store, closed in and dark but filled with the smell of leather that wafted in from the shoemaker next door. Shelves lightly packed with miscellaneous foodstuffs. Crowded corners bursting with odds and ends of dress materials, needles, threads and buttons. Neatly stacked boxes of vegetables in season. He did a good business. Shops were like that in those days, supermarkets and shopping centres were of the future and the old corner store was a meeting place in which to chat or perhaps to gossip. I had already thought up the reason to go there, the request carefully worded in my head.

"Bullseyes please."

Large jars of boiled lollies. Red and white long lasting balls of kaleidoscope colours. Two for penny. Great value except you had to save it from your pocket money or have walked to the picture show last Saturday afternoon and saved the bus fare.

Today, I know that my feet are on the path and that I don't want to be here but something within urges me forward. House after house goes by as I descend into Hope Street. I can see and hear the people who lived in each one and I want to skip. I'm only ten aren't I?

Hey, there's Mrs Fox's place. She looks after me now that I've turned four and Mummy goes to school. I can taste the strawberries that grow in her garden and she lets me pick and eat some when I'm good.

Back again on the footpath, names and faces appearing and disappearing as I near number thirty-nine. I'm in front of Kelly's place before I know it, the original stone house with the toilet up the back, now renovated, the colours and texture of the Sydney sandstone standing proud. Mrs. Kelly in her slippers. Where is she? Where is Mr. Kelly and his paint pots and overalls? But that was over fifty years ago and I'm not ten any more. I glance across at Carter's house, a two storey residence. Not for them, they are long gone.

And there it is. Number thirty-nine. Completely renovated. Disguised. I can see all the kids playing in the street. Bikes, scooters, cricket, the sound of their voices crisp and welcoming. But as I watch they all vanish. Only the street remains.

Walking further towards the creek I can see Matt's old Alvis where it stood, still and alone. And Mrs. Pelton's place where she lived, crippled with arthritis but passionate about her aviaries that were filled with budgerigars of all colours. She gave me one when I was about eight, but it had no feathers and never intended to grow any. He was so cold and so ugly but I loved him and wrapped him up each night in cotton wool to keep him warm. He lived for several years, which meant that I had earned myself a bird with feathers, my beautiful Pinocchio who stayed with me for fourteen years, chewing my books and chattering.

The creek has diminished in size. Or have I grown? The willow trees are old now and the rock beneath them that supported all us kids as we climbed aboard the rope and jumped into the water is covered in weeds. I walk along to where the creek was deeper hoping to see one of the eels, my old friends but it's now too shallow for them. What happened to the eels that lived there? The gentle bodies that moved slowly in the water, surfacing long enough to glance and then were gone. I can feel the water on my hand, cold and fluid as I push the small water plants with frilly edges under the water and marvel as they turn silver. I feel the touch of my dog as he brushes past my leg and I smile.

Then it's all gone, like a ghost who has seen the light and fled from the shackles of time and space. I walk on further as the laughing and chattering rises through the air and I see kids of all different sizes running across the slimy moss that grows on the rocks. Up ahead are the pipes that carry the water under the road. They seemed so big and I felt brave running, screaming with joy through them. A world of sound that I can create just with my voice, hands and feet. But it has all stopped. Only the creek remains.

I turn and walk into Kempridge Ave. catching sight of the school. My school. Such a big playground. I'm not allowed to play down in the grassy expanse near the creek. That's for the year five and six boys. The buildings are almost the same red brick, two storey with the portables down the side of the playing field. They're painted green now and they look good. Suddenly I hear Mrs. Erington, the mathematically obsessed headmistress bellowing though the loud speaker.

"There are some children who have not drunk their milk! Please step forward now."

Of course someone from the infants or lower primary, who hasn't yet learned to remain silent, always owns up. I can taste the milk, almost curdled by the heat from the sun. In the playground I smell the soft asphalt as it boils and bubbles and pops on days of heat wave conditions.

I see myself on Empire day dressed up as Rule Britannia, draped in a Union Jack with a large pitchfork in my hand, singing with patriotic fervour at the top of my voice. I am five again. I join all the other kids in the school at an assembly and hear the words: "King George VI has died. Queen Elizabeth will be our new monarch. Long live the Queen." I am seven.

Now it has all vanished and only the buildings remain.

Later, I drive to the Spit, tears welling up as I watch Dad swinging his golf club, sending the ball hurtling through space, Prince's golden ears flapping as he runs to retrieve it, me trying to keep up. I smile.

They, too, vanish and all that remains are the rocks, the trees and the sea. Yesterday has finally folded backwards into the past and I can heave a sigh of relief.

Hello Libby

You've met a lot of us over the years, some polite, others not quite so. Up until therapy began our system lived in a walled environment, a self contained world of a carefully constructed reality. But this reality was in isolation. None of the alters communicated with each other and most of them were not even aware that any others existed.

Hi Libby, it's me, **the Jostler**! Did you guess? I've been pushed out the front as the spokesperson to write and talk to you. You're pretty smart you know, I can only fool you some of the time and you don't put up with any nonsense, goodness knows I've tried. It's easy fooling most of them in here though, but I guess I do have the upper hand, orders from the big boss, the **Master Planner**. It's tiring, always having to be alert, ready to grab a piece of information about someone in the outer world or about what happened. But it's been hard since Rhonda started finding out about us all and remembering things. Your fault really. If you hadn't come along, listening to her all the time, helping her to cope with her feelings, my job would be so much easier. We created a great jigsaw of our world! All kinds of tiny details like you wouldn't believe, an intricate pattern, criss- crossing upon itself all over the place. Never thought anyone would work it out. Sometimes I feel a bit of a failure, but I've done my best. Still got to keep my wits about me though.

Anyway, it's good to talk to you again and I'll hand over to the next one. Quite a queue has formed in here, lots of them want to talk to you, so make sure you behave yourself and don't give away any crown secrets.

Hoo roo.

Hi Libby

It's **Lucy** and I've come to say thank you for all that you've done for the children in here. They've each been brave enough to talk to you, to tell you what happened to them and the word going around is that they wish that you were their mother. I do too. The way you have opened up such a warm space for us to come to, the acknowledgement you've given each one, understanding where they're at and at whatever age, your responses are so appropriate and caring.

Got to go. Bye for now

Good morning, Elizabeth

I'm **the Phoenix** and am speaking on behalf of the **Fantasy Parents**. We like our role, it's not really dangerous but seems to help quite a lot, and you'll see, one day we will really rise from the ashes. But we like the way you find us interesting, especially our names. Some people would laugh but you have always treated each of us with the utmost respect and for this we're grateful, so now I'll hand over to **Mary**.

Goodbye.

Hello Libby

We haven't spoken much, you and I, but I feel as though I know you well. I've watched and listened, sometimes from a long way off and mostly from behind a thin film that separates me from the others. But I feel that I understand your world a lot more than they do because I've known about and seen the reality in which you live. I know it exists and that it's quite different from the one most of them in here know about. Because of my connection with the father, they all thought that I was totally mad, but you always gave me the benefit of the doubt, waiting until you met and talked with me and finally understood that I spoke with clarity and reason. As you know I was created from **Ruth** when she stood on the edge of insanity, unable to cope with any more.

I think that in the early days you often wondered why I needed to split into other parts, but I know that now you understand. In order to make sense and to be effective they had to come from me, from where and who I am. **Mary Squared** and the **Square Root of Mary** I think explain themselves in our connection with the madness of the father.

Mary Centred is strong and calm. **Mary Personified** is the part of us who sniffs out connection. And **Mary's Spark** is our life force that never wavers. While there is life, there is hope.

I think that I, Mary, have done a good job, first of all retaining a connection with the father, but at the same time remaining calm and rational, and secondly of creating connection with the current family and friends. And finally, with you.

Thanks Libby for leaving a space for us. I'm sure we'll talk again soon.

For goodness sake, give me the pen! All this niceness babbling is making me quite ill and it must stop. Now! And when you address me Elizabeth, please do so with my full and correct title: **Wicked Witch**

of the Forest. So much bowing and scraping happening. You were just doing your job. We came to see you and each time did our business, paid you and left, end of story. I actually think you've stuffed things up in here and they'll never be the same again, so I'm not doing any scraping.

Farewell and good riddance I say.

Don't take any notice of her Libby, she's like that. **It's Stones** here and I'm like the others, grateful that we found you and that you stuck with us through all the horrible stuff and all the intense feelings and emotions that we've experienced. You've done such a good job. I'll need to hand over to Paula now. She's a bit nervous but wants to talk to you.

Hello Libby

It's **Paula** here and I just want to say thank you for not judging either **Yvette** or myself but instead listening and understanding why we were created and why we did the things we had to do. It helps us to forgive ourselves.

Hello, my dear

It's **Magnitude** here and unusual as it may seem I have little to say to you that has not already been said. We will walk forth with head held high, senses aware and heart open. We will think of you always with love, for the seed was planted, nourished and has grown into a strong and functioning unit almost free from fear. Without you we could not, would not have reached this. I will finish now but I'm sure we will talk again when the time is right.

Goodbye my dear, until then.

CHAPTER 11

My identification with my father was pathological but complete. He infested my innards and invaded my mind and I wore him like a skin. I had to. Once Prince had died, my father, even with his insanity and abuse, was all I had. The ice circle around my mother was absolute, Kate and Matt were no longer at home and the decree of silence remained paramount, preventing me from reaching out to anyone outside my home. As a child and young adult this connection with him helped to save my sanity but in my adult life it became disfunctional and kept me locked in the terror of the past. In the last stages of my therapy, separating from him became a difficult and almost full time focus. As the memories of my teenage years emerged, the daily terror that rocked my mind and froze my body was unbearable and living everyday life, pretending and trying to hide it, became impossible. But with Libby's very professional help I moved through it, moment by moment and with every new body memory and terror session the fear began to subside and my body gradually began to find the ability to relax.

"I don't think there are any more memories," I said to Libby one day and I knew then that I was approaching the end of the very long tunnel. However, times of intense fear still surfaced and I knew that the only way to end it was to disconnect and completely separate from my father. It became obvious that in order to finally move out of this pathological connection with him, I needed a therapist who was a man.

I think it was **Mary** who found him. He shared this part my journey, short but productive and it's been Mary who came forward and initiated the work I did in sessions with him. On one occasion I felt myself initially dissociating and immediately recognised the intense body feeling that Mary always brought with her. Just as suddenly I felt my body begin to slowly relax and my mind to sink gradually down, coming to rest in a deep meditative space. This, I discovered, was the other side of Mary, who was finally showing me the quiet place that she had found when she had trusted the voice that led her through the *bright green door* and had stepped into a place of tranquillity. Here she had found "neither terror nor the fragmentation of madness". I know that in order to have had the amount of trust in this new therapist, a stranger and a man, Mary must have been completely ready to let go of the safety net she had so carefully and courageously created. And to finally realise that her role and her job, which was to retain the connection with my father at all times, was no longer necessary. I'm grateful to her.

My father died in 1972. I knew him only until I was twenty-seven but the invisible chains that bound me to him remained for seventy-one years. Over his life he'd spent time in Concord Repatriation Hospital for malaria and other ailments of the body. No-one ever acknowledged let alone tackled the confusion and pain of his mind overwhelmed by the horrors of war that left him riddled with the symptoms of Post Traumatic Stress Disorder.

For about a year before he died his mind had almost disappeared into an irretrievable space and a stroke had left him unable to walk or to do much for himself. So once again he was taken to Concord hospital. "I feel so sorry for the poor buggers in the beds right next to the nurses' station. They haven't got long," he used to say, but this time he found himself there. On one of our visits Kate and I found him lying naked on the bed. She became very flustered but I surprised myself by remaining calm, pulling the sheet up over him and dressing him in his pyjama top. He smiled at me.

The last time I saw him, as we were leaving and had almost reached the door, he called out, lucid and rational:

"Wave to me Bruce." I often wonder why he didn't ask me to wave. He died that night, forty-four years ago.

In 2017 we went to Japan. It was a journey, not related consciously to the past, but to see a country of very different culture and beauty. When we reached Hiroshima, I immediately felt a rare but definitive presence of my father, the soldier. He was there in the city with me, in the hotel room, on the street, while eating out. A strong urge to write pushed me as I penned two letters, each about forgiveness, to the Japanese soldiers who had fought in New Guinea in WW2. One from myself and the other on behalf of my father. We posted them the next day into an official stone post box in the Peace Garden. But still my father remained, an energy, persistent and strong.

On reaching the Peace Flame, the years of terror burst out of me in uncontrollable bouts of sobbing, continuing until completion. The sadness stayed with me most of the day until late in the afternoon.

"It's gone!"

"What's gone!" Bruce asked.

"The Terror."

All the moments of war that I had taken on from him and wrapped up within me; the trauma from New Guinea that had ravaged his body and his mind; all the time in my early life that I had tried to take it away from him, to save my life, to help him; that piece by piece had seeped into my psyche, sticking to my body and mind—was gone.

But *he* was there in Hiroshima. The image of my father stood beside me. He was wearing his army uniform, his slouched hat dipped slightly forward, the khaki material almost matching his sun-drenched skin. But now there were two of him, each looking out from the tall, athletic body of his younger years. One damaged, with eyes coloured rich by a ravine of sadness and turbulence, the other at peace.

For a while they stood there looking at me, then gradually the damaged part of him began to separate, to move slowly from the tanned body until he stood complete but alone where he remained. We prised **Mary** finger by finger from the father who had almost lived in her skin, to be removed from the madness she had come to dread and yet to understand, but enriched by the compassion that she felt for the soul trapped in that deep confusion.

And we were ready. Her final piece of skin touched his for the last time. Her breathing lengthened, her father looked into her eyes, waved then turned and began to walk away. She felt herself torn in two, just as she had when his coffin had moved into oblivion, wanting desperately to follow. And just as she had when she tried to swim out into the sea to join his scattered ashes. But an unfamiliar feeling began to spread through her body.

"What is it?" she called.

Magnitude is here with softened eyes: "It's a feeling of relief Mary. You're safe now and you never have to enter the madness again. You have done your job well."

We watched as the image of my damaged father moved further and further away until he faded and was no longer visible. As we turned our eyes to the strong, tall part of him he too began to fade until only empty space was left. He was free.

Almost at once I began to see small globules leaving my bones, my organs, my blood, through my skin and out into nowhere. His trauma had coated me inside and out. But now it was leaving. This lasted for several weeks. Now the soldier has gone. No terror from his war remains.

A couple of years later, when visiting Bali I called on the help of a gentle Balinese healer to help me with the pain of sciatica that I was experiencing. As his hands moved towards my knee and then to lower leg and ankle, there was a change. Emotions began to rise from within me like an energy, long trapped within a deep well. I tried to contain them but had no chance.

I felt a strong presence. My father was there in the room with us. Not in a human form, not as the soldier, but as my father. My gentle father. Not with the steely eyes of terror and madness, but with the soft blue eyes that really listened when I played the piano and the windows of a soul who shared a deep affinity with animals.

"I came to tell you that I love you", he said.

I felt not just the room, but a sphere with no boundaries filled with unconditional love. The same feeling that I'd felt when my mother came back from her journey towards death, when I had asked her to.

The healer rested his face sideways on mine, holding my head in his hands, softly humming and I became gradually quiet and calm. As I did, my father began to withdraw.

"Don't go!" I called out.

He remained for just a moment. "You continued to love me through all that happened and I will always be with you". Then he slowly departed.

His words contained no emotion. They were simply a statement of 'what is,' that came from unconditional love.

Since this time, Libby moved north a little way and I began working spasmodically with Linda, an empathic, gentle therapist, I've experienced several images that have shown me the extent of the integration that's been subconsciously occurring.

A sense of fear but mixed with anticipation pushed on the sides until I gave in and watched while the picture slowly emerged in my mind. The mists, dark and rich, moved slowly through the forest. Cold, alert. I watch a figure appear, walking slowly towards me, eyes seeing, heart beating.

"Surrender," she whispered.

New breath filled me, my body let go. I knew her. It was my Self. She stood, encased in an egg shaped circle. Not fragmented. Complete.

At another time my emotions plummeted. There was no rational, current reason for this to happen but in a session with Linda I realized that the emotions I was feeling, some very intense, were those that the different parts of my Self had experienced. But I, Rhonda never had. They had done their job. They had taken the feelings, experiences and memories from me.

For me, it feels extraordinary to experience the realisation that the feelings of abandonment, betrayal, fear, powerlessness, terror, invisibility, anger, humiliation, rage, intense sadness etc that I'm currently experiencing in unexplained situations and that appear to come from nowhere are actually me, Rhonda, in my skin, in my body, feeling those feelings that were historically directed away from me.

That I'm looking out of my eyes and actually seeing and experiencing the world as Rhonda. As myself. I'm slowly realising that it was me who was born, who went to school, to piano lessons, who laughed, cried, lived. It was me. That's the culmination. But over the years there have been a number of occasions when I've experienced moments of integration, largely in the form of images and or words that come into my mind, clear, determined and needing an immediate audience. This was such an occasion, quietly heralded by **Magnitude's** voice: "It's time."

It sounds like a crowd in unison as all the parts of me gather one by one in the banquet hall. They come from everywhere into one space. Down from the turrets and the rooms in the top parts of the castle. From outside, through the massive doors that lead onto the drawbridge. From the shadows below the balconies that run right around the edges of the banquet room. The fire, as always, is burning solidly in the massive hearth and still they come, from fear into safety. As each one enters the group he or she becomes older, instantly moving from the past into the present. From separateness into the collective. From fear into love.

There are children, the elderly people, male, female, dogs, fantasy parents, persecutors and introjects. All the ghost like figures from the catacombs of the third level, now solid matter within my mind. All ready to move forward. The room is almost full when the low and gentle 'Oum' begins, started by Gustav and carried outwards to all that are present.

Some touch a hand, others pause within a moment of eye meeting eye, then move on into Self. The 'Oum' continues as **Rebecca** moves slowly up from the cave within a cave that has kept her essence alive. She's accompanied by **The Heap** and together they carry the glowing embers, held securely in their hands. The **Spirit of the Fire** dances in never ending circles as the group parts, forming a track of quiet acceptance walking with the precious embers into the centre. They hand them to **Mary**, the vibrations of sound building as they connect with each and every part of me.

Even **Wicked Witch** is here. She is compliant now, quite pleasant really. It's as though each had been an actor playing his or her part. Now the play is reaching its final act, they will all put down their props, cast aside their character roles and come together for the final bow.

Paula, and **Yvette** stand alone, separate in the shadows, at the ready should they be needed. From the massive door that leads outwards to the drawbridge emerges a soft rose coloured light with just a hint of lavender. A gentle glow, carried by the *Purple Emu* with the flowing ecumenical gown. She has returned for this occasion and I watch her as she walks around the edge of the room, lighting the shadows as she moves, until she reaches Paula, holding out the glowing object to her.

"Will you accept this? It is your soul that I have kept safe for so many years. Take it into the midst of the waiting crowd and you can begin to become one."

Paula hesitates, anger mixed with fear, unable to accept it, when from the crowd emerges someone quite young. She's unsure but with an air of being that shines with radiance. It's **Rebecca**, followed by **The Heap**. But wait, there's another. It's the child who kept alive the mind and in her hand she carries a stone that is rich and white with a gentle reflective glow. It's **Bethany** and she's carrying the moonlight.

They reach the Purple Emu who smiles and touches them with the eyes of **The Earth Mother**. Paula holds out her hands and receives the glowing soul, turning to catch the threads of sound as they pass through her, building and building. They walk forwards beginning to grow until encased, each one in an adult body. Again the crowd parts as they walk into the centre to where **Mary** stands with the embers.

Each is each but all is one within a circle as **The Phoenix**, who has been waiting such a long time for this moment, lifts them all until they are suspended just above the floor.

When I look again I see just one person standing before the great hearth and I begin to understand that there is one mind, one body, one spirit. That this, in reality, is how it always has been. I thank them. I tell them that I feel humble watching them, for without each one of them I would not have survived. I don't know whether in the 'real world' I will ever reach total integration but I do know that now I have a history. I know that time, space and solid matter are real and that there are no more secrets, no more memories and that one day, very soon, we will see **The One Who was Born.**

"Just talk," the voice in my head had said that morning. So instead of writing, I went along to the therapy session with Lisa and just talked, determined to say whatever came into my head.

"Raspberries".

It made no sense and didn't connect to anything I could think of but I knew that if I went with it, it would take me to where I needed to go.

"I can see it. It's shining and it's the colour of raspberries."

I knew immediately that it was the way in. It was how I would find out what was happening in my subconscious, and as feelings started to well up and information emerged I watched the picture that was forming vividly in front of my eyes.

"It's the stone! And it's now a deep red colour and next to it there's a small child. She's looking at me and I can see all that I am in her eyes. But she's so new and her innocence glows. She has no past. No contamination, no history, no expectations for the future. She just is."

Magnitude appears standing behind the young child, the stone casting its glow over their etched figures like a deep red cameo.

"You are seeing the essence of your being," he said. "Do not think, as thinking will blur your understanding. Take time. Sit with her, be with her, that you might know that you have now shed the cloak of fear and replaced it with a jacket of love.

She is here and it is time."

I then began to realise that I was Rhonda and that the time was the present and I was watching and listening to this scene as it unfolded, but as myself, as an adult. This had never happened before and even though it felt strange it felt right. As I watched I saw a different triangle emerge. Very strong, with me, Rhonda as I am now, on one point, the stone and the small child on another and gathered together on the third point were all the parts of me who are still around. They were each of their own identity but all are within one circle. I could feel their anxiety but also their excitement. This is why they were created. To protect her.

We were standing at a crossroad and the paths leading to it were paved with the need to protect and now with the unfamiliar.

"What do we do now?" I hear **Lucy** say.

"We wait and we watch," replied **Stones**, which is what she had always done.

The Jostler was there, twitching nervously. "But we cannot! It is in the decree. We must never let her be seen. Don't you understand that"!

Suddenly, as if from the wings of stage, *The Purple Emu* appeared, and immediately I was flung back into the time of learning, of turning around the mirror and of being seen.

It had been difficult carrying the plastic body of the small child for so long, but we had watched with joy as the features, initially painted on in felt pens of vibrant colours, gradually began to mould within the infant's face, plastic melting into skin of dimpled flesh. Lately she noticed the green eyes searching. Feeling. Questioning. Ready to see the spark of mirrored existence. Ready to finally move from the silence of the frozen whiteness.

She had found her way from the icy world into which the Emu had led her. The journey had been long and fraught with obstacles as she clambered over sunken ponds struck solid with the wetness of frozen time. She had fought the inner coldness of non being as her eyes struggled to see within, and had taken the hand of the angel as she lay threatened in the frozen pit of self destruction. Always she had clutched the small plastic baby, knowing somewhere that Self was possible. Now the ice was slowly melting and ahead, the grassy slopes of the distant hills spoke gently of connection.

She moved slowly forwards and as she did she caught sight of the Emu, purple gown flowing but now the emu's head was joined to her body as though that was where it belonged.

"Don't go!" she called.

The Emu turned and looked with warmth into her eyes. "It's time," it said. Then, waving, vanished.

Last night I turned around, looked back and saw Rhonda. She was seventeen. I don't often experience this feeling of being a complete adult, living in 2018 but it feels good. Somewhere, I know that she is me but she still seems so far away. And I no longer see her as **The Heap,** so needy and disgusting. I don't see helplessness, only strength and potential.

And the image of the small child sitting next to the raspberry coloured stone is carried with me at all times. She is called **Hope.** She is strong with healthy bones and flesh bursting with muscles that will take her into the outside world. She is trusting, vulnerable and open. Her hands are small, her Shining clear. And I know that all the years of work have been for her. When I look into her eyes I see my own newness, my Shining. I see myself as I was born. Once love of Self is felt then life really begins and there is no changing that. She is filled with the energy of the sun and the gentle beauty of the moonlight and she is me.

EPILOGUE

Very sadly, Libby passed away in October 2018. She had read the manuscript and was very happy that I was finally telling our story: hers and mine. There are no words for the gratitude and love I feel and I will miss her greatly.

It's now 2018. My mother and father have both passed on, I am a seventy-two year old adult and my childhood has become a transparent history.

Co-operation gradually became the norm in my inner world, but I have now accepted our integration and finally come to see that each of these parts of me are real to me but not to the outside world, that they were inside me. With this came a period of grief as I gradually let each of them go.

I now fully understand that no part of my mother, my father or my brother is any part of me and my brain is mine. They have no control over my thoughts, my body, my actions, my beliefs, my feelings, my music, my words, my aspirations or anything else that is mine and in my life.

No-one is inside my head or knows my thoughts. I do not have to temper them to suit anyone else or to keep anyone safe or to avoid punishment. I can think whatever I like and that is liberating.

Time has now passed and I can look back on this journey with some sadness but with a sense of relief and a smile.

I have met my Self. I have accepted my Self. And I like what I see. I am now Rhonda, in all my goodness and all my faults, but it's like meeting a new person and it will take a while for me to get to know me.

Even though I've passed through times of extreme difficulty, throughout the process I have managed to live a fully functional life and many opportunities have come my way. Teaching the piano, the flute, and song writing to individual children; teaching all kinds of music to children in Secondary, Infants and Primary schools; co-ordinating the Australian SING book for the ABC for many years; giving workshops with teachers both here and in New Zealand; the challenge of teaching Music Education in the Education faculties of several Sydney Universities and writing a myriad of children's songs.

Work in music education and in healing through therapy have travelled concurrently and as I look back I think of the times when the terror overtook me and I struggled with each day and it is finally beginning to sink in that I truly survived. I faced the terror. I looked it in the eye and it has finally dissolved.

I am proud of the work I have done in the world and indeed of the inner work I have done that has required determination, resilience and immense support from those around me. It has always been mixed with the satisfaction of learning and with connection.

I am grateful that my music finally pushed its way to the surface and I look forward to moving more often into that wonderful space of creativity where nothing else matters except creating music. The completion of a CD of my music, called "Flight", has been a big but rewarding step into visibility. *

I have been able to connect with others including children through my love of music and through the music I have written and this touches me deeply.

But above all, I'm grateful to my family: my husband, our daughter Nat and our son Kris. Through their love and their support, my healing with Libby, with Richard, with Lisa, and the unconditional love I shared with my dog Prince, I have learnt about trust, about forgiveness and about love.

I feel privileged to have survived the trauma and to have been given the opportunity to live this life and I will be forever grateful that I was able to create an inner family and an inner world in which to escape. Through this I have learnt about humility. Although most of the parts of me have now been integrated into one whole I will miss them and

I will always remember each one and how he or she helped me to come out the other end of a long journey with my sanity intact.

I feel genuine love for my mother and for my father. I do not condone their behaviour but I understand it.

And I enjoy the love of my Self and my Shining which I have finally found.

Rhonda

---

* *I would like to share my music with you and it is available on Spotify and other digital sources. And from my facebook page, and on Youtube: Rhonda Macken Flight. And my Website: www.rhondamacken.com*

APPENDIX 1 – MY SYSTEM

An alphabetical list of the created parts of my Self (alters) who I have included in my book.

Beatrice: was created in order to experience and to contain several memories when very young when the father tied her up in a hessian bag. She also contained the early memory of his triple incontinence as it spilled all over her.

Bernadette: is four years old and was created to contain the memory of being raped with a broom handle.

Bethany: is an important part as she is the child who lived in the turret at the top of the castle. She was the custodian of the moonlight and it was her job to make sure that this thread of moonshine was never broken. It connected her with **Rebecca** in the cave and each of them and the **One who was Born** with the soul waiting in the frozen silence. I first became aware of Bethany when she appeared with **Paula** each in a separate bubble. I now understand that she accompanied Paula, in such a violent situation, to make sure that the thread of moonshine remained unbroken.

At one time, Bethany came to say to us, "I want to show Mary the moonlight that shines onto the floor. The moon that glistens on the deep, deep sea and speaks to the one in the deep, deep silence. It is through Mary that we will come to know our destiny and we will walk on the moors filled with sunshine and life. For if we accept her, then we will have accepted the most feared part of ourselves. But we must be careful, for Mary is very fragile and her mind is scattered."

With the openness of a child she eventually walked up to Mary and extended her arms.

Betti and Rachel: are twins who, like Lucy and Bronwyn (the other set of twins) compliment each other. Betti is in a cocoon and feels sadness as an alternative to fear. She took this sadness into nature to help Rhonda feel safe but she shows no emotions on the outside. Rachel was filled with unending amounts of joy and optimism. Her world is full of created love, fairytale happenings and imagined worlds.

Bronwyn: is Lucy's twin, complimenting her beautifully. "Lucy dreams. I do." She is totally practical, detached and able to take control in the aftermath of any traumatic situation. She remains detached from the feelings of others and also from her own feelings. As the events created intense reactions from most of my internal system, this cold detachment was an essential element in our survival as it enabled someone to take action within a traumatic event. She has immense courage and I am filled with gratitude for her.

Cameo: was created to contain the memory of being strangled and of being smothered.

Emma: is a teenager and the essential part of me who was raped from ages thirteen to eighteen. The mother called her a slut and a whore. In the beginning she talked but no-one listened. It was as though they didn't see her. That she didn't exist. But in our later teenage years she became very angry and feisty.

Emily: was created from Beatrice in order to try and keep us safe in the garage. She was also young and in her child's mind believed that if she became a strong straight line like the tools and the edge of the bench etc that she then could not be put in a hessian bag ever again.

Ezekial: I love Ezekial, the part of me created in order to keep everything at a distance, protected by a proscenium arch, portrayed on a stage that he could observe. We could have drama and violence but as it was just theatre, it was not real. He is theatrical and filled with imagination that he is unafraid to exhibit and which takes me to a very magic place.

Genesis: is bereft of struggle. Her joy is stolen and her love of creation painted over, ready for them to mould their own being in their own image. She has no human spark. She is a non being in a space of nothing.

Genesis is pre-verbal, almost primal. She is there in a human form but there is no existence because she has no knowing. It's as though she died before birth. It's not that she has no potential to feel, she just doesn't know what feeling, thinking or being is. Just like a foetus. And part of her function was to catch the unborn lives and in our child's mind, to protect them. Her name, meaning the origin or the creation and which emerged completely spontaneously and immediately, is apt.

She is numbed by compliant silence.

She contains part of the core or our being, my Self. One way of doing this was to put her in a sealed container in the centre of what **Vigil** describes as 'a big blubbery blob of nothing,' an enormous receptacle and that is Genesis. Her head was never connected to her body and she was incapable of making any decisions or taking any action.

But she was a safe vault for the Self.

Early on, whenever I drew Genesis she was huge, with a tiny, disconnected head, no eyes or ears and her mouth plugged up. But gradually this changed, with a face, a connected head and no gag. Magnitude watched over her.

Fantasy parents: are fairytale parents, each with quite a theatrical and metaphysical name. Each of them seems to be wise and to know about and to understand the wider knowledge of life. They are:

1. **The Ancient One**: an elderly man with a beard and a lantern, who leads me into the lower levels of the castle. The catacombs, the dungeons and the caves. It is his job to guard the embers, the Spirit of the Fire and Rebecca and he knows all the hidden knowledge of this underground world and its significance to the universe.

2. **The Everywhere**: who came into our consciousness very early in the therapy with Libby and became integrated. My first piece of music in this part of my life, a simple almost childlike piece for violin and piano is called "Everywhere".

3. **The Phoenix**: waits, ready to lift us up into one whole, when the time is right.

4. **The Elderly People**: these are seven older people, like grandparents, kind, caring and with plenty of time, who looked after the children. They became invaluable during the times when terror created chaos within our internal system.

5. **Mephistopheles**: was in the deepest black cave, enclosed in a thick walled bubble, tied up with chains. One by one Libby helped him

to remove the chains and finally suggested a hug. "I don't know what that is!" he said but he got one anyway.

6. **Persephone**: is the balance of Mephistopheles. Because she also came from a dark cave she understood the darkness but she had also experienced the earth, its bounty and the spiritual essence of the natural world.

Group of Saboteurs:

1. **Master Cleverness**: was created because it was unsafe for Rhonda to think. To do so would create unbelievable problems, as then reality would be there at all times. That was impossible and unbearable. However, he did this in a vindictive manner, filling the body with a terror that grabbed hold of every sinew.

2. **The Evil Saboteur**: angry in the extreme, fists always clenched, ready to fight. He was created because at one stage everyone had had enough and believed that if Rhonda died that would be good because none of us would have to go through any more.

3. **The Terror**: This was the worst of them all. Like a black swirling mist, turning to red with a central system and thick threads growing longer and more all the time, spreading these tentacles right throughout every inch of my body. My legs, my trunk, my organs then out through my arms and into my hands and fingernails. Then slowly and steadily into my head and my mind. Its possession was then complete. This part remained until I was able to let go of my father.

4. **The Him**: an internalised version of the traumatized father who told Libby and I about the gruesome pictures in full colour that came into his mind almost constantly. He was initially very angry with fists clenched and punching.

Hope: For a long time I knew about the stone but it wasn't until nearing the end of my healing journey that I discovered the small, innocent child called Hope. She and the stone are together, infused with the rose coloured light of the soul waiting frozen in the snow, but which now radiate with a deep red glow. She and the stone are the essence of me. The one who came initially into this life and whose name is Rhonda. That is what it feels like and which creates a wave of gratitude and humility.

Katherine: very angry and snarling, with thick spikes coming from everywhere in her body, even from her vagina, her ears and her mouth.

There was always a thick membrane between Katherine and Rhonda that did not allow any communication. However, she was the balance of Lucy who lived in the circle reality. It was Katherine who lived in the square reality of the home.

Little One: is the emissary for the One who was Born. When I was very young, just born in fact, "the bastard (the insane father) threw Little One down into the dungeons of the castle." She is very, very small and she is a complete circle. He discarded her, but we took a thread from her and created **Rebecca** and even though Rebecca withdrew and remained curled into a tight coil, she was one step further towards life than Little One. I believe that is was the first time we 'split off' from our Self. If we hadn't done this we would not have survived as Little One had no hope of connection with anyone. But Rebecca was just like a seed waiting in the earth for water and light, for nourishment and connection. The psychiatrist, Richard, began this process when he held Rebecca's hands.

Lucy: Oh how wonderful is Lucy, created in order to teach us safely about the outside world. She went to school, to ballet, to the beach, to piano lessons. She played in the street with the kids. She did what others did, copying their actions, what they said and how they said it, imitating their body language, and everything that helped her to function in a world that was totally alien to the world in which we lived at home. This made us appear as 'normal'. She is idealised, with golden curly hair. She sees colours, is perceptive, strong but quiet and caring. She knew nothing of what was happening in the square reality, even to the point where she enabled us to have friends and to experience the reality of others outside our internal worlds.

She and Bronwyn were twins, each complimentary.

Mary: A very important part. She was on her own with no connection to any other parts of us at all, but with a well constructed support system carefully put in place and maintained because if we lost the connection with our father she believed that we would all immediately die. It was Mary who, when we scattered the father's ashes into the sea, tried to follow him.

There are 6 separate parts of Mary, each created to fulfil a unique role.

1. **Mary:** Mary and **Stones** are two equal parts of balancing scales, Mary connecting with the father and Stones being on the outside with

no contamination from the mother or the father. They each knew what they had to do and were solid in this resolve. It was Mary's job to connect but it's this connection with the father that ultimately grew to become a complete identification with him. By the time we were sixteen, in her mind, she was part of him and him of her, unable to understand that she was a separate person. This identification with the perpetrator, called the Stockholm Syndrome, took many years, even after most of the other reasons for therapy had gone, to mend and to finally separate and fully understand that he was dead and no longer part of her nor she of him.

Unlike most parts of me, Mary can think and feel at the same time. She was created from **Ruth** at a time when Ruth was standing right on the edge of sanity, unable to cope with any more and because of our essential need to retain a connection with a parent, was being drawn into the father's insanity with a force beyond her capacity to fight. Hence the **Master Planner's** detailed and complex plan retaining her (our) sanity while at the same time retaining our connection even through his insanity by creating Mary, Mary squared, the square root of Mary (see below) and the diamond. It worked!

She knew about each of the realities and because of this, was considered to be crazy by many of the others in here. However it was she who understood the father's insanity and allowed herself to be fragmented in order to cope with it and to retain the connection with him. This was her ultimate function. And yet she herself was in total isolation from everyone else in the system who all thought she was contaminated and crazy, partly because of her connection with the father but also because Mary knew about both realities. She knew about the world outside the home but also about the reality of the terror, the rape and the violence. Of course, it was decreed that this knowledge was to never be known to the host person; in fact that's why the whole system was created in the first place, so that someone could function in all worlds in comparative safety and in sanity.

When my sister, Kate held my hand, it took me away from having to be Mary as this was a real human connection.

The diamond is a strong shape adopted in order keep the connection with his madness contained by secure and safe boundaries. Only anticlockwise movement was permitted so that the madness was allowed to be as large as it was on the way, but on the way back it was divided again by the Square root of Mary.

2. **Mary Squared**: lives on the right hand point of the diamond, half way between the point of safety and the psychosis. She was created in order to allow the carefully contained insanity to multiply itself and spread into whatever fullness was present, therefore allowing Mary to reach the father. In this way, Mary could retain the connection with the father even through times of his madness. In this way, any insanely intolerable behaviour could be locked away in the top point of the diamond.

3. **The Square root of Mary**: compliments **Mary Squared**. They were both created during the times of not too comfortable maths lessons given by Matt, when we took the concepts he was teaching us and used them to develop a safe system.

Her job was to find the square root of the psychosis, bringing it back to a manageable and containable level.

4. **Mary Centred**: the safety net of this unit. All the other parts of Mary can reach her from any point along the diamond. She is strong, with a calmness that balances terror. She had a lucid and rational at all times and there were occasions when the terror became so profound that she was needed.

5. **Mary Personified**: a strange name, but one that makes sense as her job is to connect with the outside world of people and to take up the front position. To see, sniff the air and feel the warmth of the sun and to be alert when general people are around.

6. **Mary's Spark**: reminds everyone that no matter what happens, while they have breath they still have life and therefore hope.

Magnitude: He is one of my most treasured alters. He is wise and he is kind and like the Master Planner, he knows everything about our system. But unlike the Master Planner, Magnitude looks after us on a spiritual level, aware of our body, our emotions and most of all, our soul that shines with a rose coloured glow, waiting to be reunited with us. He is our guide, leading us in the direction of wholeness.

I see him as a robed figure with a long beard and a staff. His eyes are filled with kindness. He can be and is, firm, setting clear and strong boundaries when they are needed.

I love his language, even though sometimes not fully understanding until a therapy session several weeks later when something emerges and all of what he has said makes complete sense. He often uses words that I have no knowledge of but when I look up the meaning, the word fits perfectly.

Merlin: was the magician who created magic tricks.

Marvin: was the magician whose magic was Truth.

Rebecca: I became consciously aware of Rebecca as a coil. A part who, one by one had withdrawn all her senses, then curled up into quite a tight coil, with no sensory contact with the outside world. No chance of any contamination of or penetration into her world.

She didn't know about caring or about choosing and couldn't see colours. In the early days of co-consciousness, when she was talking to the psychiatrist (although he was unaware of her presence) there was always a back up team of **Emma, Lucy** or **Stones** helping her with the words to say what she needed to.

I think that she's been around since the very beginning of my life, but the withdrawal became complete when Prince was taken away. Even when she began to uncoil, she could not see colours, only black and white.

The first time Rebecca allowed contact with any living soul after that was when Richard, the psychiatrist extended his hands and she took them. Once we began therapy with Libby she gradually began to see colours and with Libby's caring she gradually opened. I now am fully aware of which colours I like, when, and how they affect me.

Rebecca lived deep within a cave beneath the castle, sharing this space with the embers and the Spirit of the Fire who kept my fire of existence alive.

Rebecca was part of a triangle that connected her with **Bethany**, who lived high up in a turret at the top of the castle, and with our soul that waited, safe in the frozen silence. As long as the thread of moonlight (see Bethany) continued to reach her she knew that we were still alive.

Because Rebecca had withdrawn all her senses, she created **Gustav** and **Vigil** to be her ears and her eyes.

Gustav: who came into my conscious awareness quite early in Libby's therapy. In fact he was around almost all the time, and his singing and whistling were everywhere at once. Rebecca knew that when he stopped, the thread of moonlight that connected her to the outside world would be broken.

Vigil: who has many eyes and who kept watch at all times. Hypervigilance is an essential survival skill.

Remember: He knows about facts and about time. Someone had to keep all the facts together in one place --"I'm like a big filing cabinet!" He listens attentively for facts, especially those that tell about horrible things, and then takes them away from everyone else. Especially from Rhonda. She must know nothing, learn nothing, and understand nothing. When she's not functioning well I have to step in and take over for her. I can look people in the eye. I can speak when she's confused and when everyone else is frightened because I have facts and I have no feelings.

Ruth: was the one who was first created to cope with the father's madness and in her child's mind she believed that she could "reach inside him and take it out, then put it within her, that he wouldn't suffer any more and we would all be safe". For quite some time she talked to Libby with her eyes shut as she was too afraid to look in case Libby's eyes were crazy. She was always afraid, always waiting for the terror, knowing it was coming. It was Ruth who came very close to suicide during my therapy with the psychiatrist. Luckily he saw and heard or Ruth would have put us to sleep. "I can feel it already and it feels good."

We knew straight away when it was Ruth as her hand kept constantly tapping. She said that our music comes from deep within the earth.

Stones: A very important part: Stones at all times retained hope. She was the observer, always walking along the edge, head down, kicking stones. Looking in and watching but never part of it. She has no time for trivialities or getting bogged down in the words. She sees the big picture, knowing that we have to search for Knowledge.

She is an individual because she's always been on the outside and alone.

She didn't make any connection with the mother and certainly wasn't linked with the father at all. Stones and Mary (see below and above) are like two equal parts of balancing scales. Stones has absolutely no fragmentation at all. She is completely whole and solid within herself. She is what she is, regardless of what is happening around her.

She walks on the earth and is therefore in touch with 'all that is' and is very grounded.

Stones remained at all times, connected to the inner stone, the essence of our being, I think perhaps the One who was Born. (See Chapter 1 the story of The girl, the Stranger and the Stone.)

And Stones had a hope and an optimism that she never questioned, because she walked immersed in nature. And because she experienced the earth in every moment, its Knowledge lived deeply within her and because of this, she knew about wonder. And therefore knew that 'The One who was Born' still had the God within her.

However, because The Controller decreed, right from the beginning that she was never to be seen, or to interact with any of the others except **Mudlark** (see below), she was never given the opportunity to exercise her 'right of reply'. As an observer, she saw a lot of things happening in the circle reality outside the home to which she would very much have liked to have 'given others an explanation' but had to remain silent.

Stones created the **Earth Mother** (see below).

However, as therapy progressed and my healing became solid, Stones was sometimes brought in to use her mediating skills within the system. But because she was so grounded in our childhood it was vital that she didn't let go of the balancing scales, because if she had, Mary would have tipped over the edge into the father's insanity.

The Co-ordinator: a very important part who was in control of the 'committee' who decided each day and moment by moment, exactly who goes outside, or who does anything, how and what for. He checked continually that s/he was acceptable, behaved in the correct manner.

He also endeavoured to counteract the Terror, which succeeded until well into therapy when I gradually became aware of my history and the many parts of my system.

The **Controller**: is linked with the Master Planner, but he's a wooden figure who observes the whole situation, especially watching in therapy session to see if Libby and me discover how to fit another piece of the jigsaw together. We always knew when he was there because even though I tried to sit normally, he would always change the position of the body so that the right leg rested up on the left knee, and there was nothing I could do about it.

The Earth Mother: knows how to care because she knows about the trees, the gentle water and the wind. And she knows about stroking dogs and washing them clean and holding them when they're frightened. She knows about looking into their eyes and seeing life.

She was created by Stones and she came into our consciousness when Libby was trying to get us to be nice and finally to care for

The Heap. We weren't going to have a bar of this, calling her names and generally treating her with disdain.

We had to look and to watch what the Earth Mother did so that we could learn what 'looking after' means. It took quite a number of years of being aware of the Earth Mother before we could transfer this caring on to The Heap and to **Little One**. This was actually learnt through the teddies that I brought and left at Libby's. After many years of hating them and trying to destroy them, we were finally able to accept them, to treat them well and ultimately to not need them at all once we had love and respect for our Self.

The Heap: She lives in the real world of the violence and the horror, which are the world of the home and the reality of the square.

She is the one whose body was the final recipient of all the filth, the rape, and the physical violence. Even though other parts were in the front line of these events, the physical effects were then passed onto The Heap. Because of this, most others in our system despised her intensely and she was consistently ostracised from ever connecting to or even being acknowledged by anyone else in the system.

She is a crumpled heap, filthy, scratched and bruised. Her mind is glued together with the mortar of fear. She doesn't hear and her dress is torn and dirty and hangs from her body as from a rag doll. Her hair is matted and frames her face with a sense of demented wildness.

Hence, she was totally isolated and loneliness and self-loathing accompanied her at all times.

She was crushed and broken like a limp rag doll. No skeleton or even bones, no features that indicate a being. Now she is a healthy and respected part of my Self.

The Jostler: is an amiable fellow with a cheery smile, so light of foot but slight of hand and ever watchful. He has all the information about the system and our story and is the trusted lieutenant of the system's commander, the **Master Planner**.

His quote: "I am here eternally. Even in death I will take the final piece of the jigsaw beyond the reach of all who search for it." This was his job. To make sure that the jigsaw is never to be put together, the whole picture or story will never be revealed.

This job also assured that the left and right sides of my brain could not be joined and also that the head could not be connected to the body. In other words, the Master Planner had every possible angle covered in order to prevent us coming together and to make sure that we remained fragmented at all times.

This has been highly frustrating over many years, as just as I feel that things are coming together, the Jostler removes the piece of information necessary at that time and there's no way that I can retrieve it.

The Judge: He knew about many realities. Mine and theirs, fairytale and terror. It was the Judge who knew that one day we might live in the reality of others and therefore become visible. Then the body would not be allowed to survive; this was the decree.

It was up to the Judge to know about the reality of others and therefore he learned to "look through the eyes of others." He would know when their reality changed from us being invisible (internal) to visible (external). You see, in my child's mind it was essential, at a moment's notice to look through the eyes of my father in order to try and understand his reality at that moment. To predict what he might do. My childish logic helped me to believe that this would keep me safe.

I now realise that this is what was happening when I was detached and dissociated, looking down at myself with an unsafe person. If I haven't totally vanished, I try to be inside their reality, helping the part of me who is dealing with the situation. But of course, as soon as I place my own eyes somewhere else I still see it from my reality. But this is not to be dismissed just as a child's logic, or a child's fantasy, when the need for that fantasy is essential to her survival.

Often the facts that were given to me, either by words, actions or gestures did not tally with what I saw and experienced. So I had to put myself behind the eyes of others so that I could know that I was not seeing, hearing and experiencing what was not there. That my reality, in the real and violent world was just that. A reality. That the cause of the terror was not coming from me but from outside of me. And the Judge knew this because he looked through the eyes of others, saw and understood more about the outside world.

We always knew when he arrived at a therapy session by his posture and sitting position.

The Mother part: was the internalised ice circle of my mother.

The One who was Born: is exactly as the name suggests. The infant who came into the world but from whom my essence was extracted and held safely at a distance with my soul in order to prevent any possibility of contamination. We finally learnt that she was **Hope**.

Virgin of the Sepulchre (angel of death): For a long time this is the name I knew her by, her function being to take away any being, human or animal who had died. But one day, late into therapy, she corrected this name, telling me she was really the Angel of Death.

She told the reason for this was because the children, living in a dissociated and sheltered reality that kept them from the real and physical results of the madness and the violence, didn't know about or understand death. Therefore, it was essential that the word not be used. So she became the Virgin of the Sepulchre. Even though this was the name that was given by my system, I didn't even know what it meant until I looked it up and found that it's a tomb, and hers is lined with blue velvet, awaiting the gentle placing of a body in its final and safe resting place.

Wicked Witch of the Forest: screams loudly and is very rude to Libby. But she is never nasty or cruel and one of her jobs is to stand up and be counted. To say exactly what she thinks. She also makes parts of me vanish and she's very good at seeing what's coming around corners. She also decoys anyone whose intention to become visible will foil the system.

Right at the end of therapy we realised it was she who felt as though there was always a precipice about to open up in front, beside, behind us. Even during therapy when the terror overtook my life, the chasm was there waiting for us to fall into.

She never thinks and she doesn't feel, she just reacts, which often helps to prevent Rhonda from becoming aware of any horrors. She appeared very early, yelling wildly at Libby and during this therapy she developed considerably.

Yvette/Gang of thugs: were created in order to literally stop my father from killing me during the time in my middle teenage years when my room became an isolated cube. The Gang of Thugs created a connection between the rest of the house in Hope Street and my room. Without them I would have gone insane.

APPENDIX 2

Following is a table of strategies that worked for me in a therapy situation and things that were important in moving forwards, in the hope that perhaps it might be helpful for someone else.

Strategy	Why or why not
Carefully terminate each and every session. To begin, small rituals can bring familiarity and safety	o Reality checks enabled me to be in Adult and in the present before leaving and therefore to close up the emotions of the session and to better function in everyday life. A good way of doing this is to say phone numbers forwards and backwards. o Eg: Accepting an acorn or flower or rock from me as though it was a precious gift. It was. And helped to invite the therapist into my world and therefore to build trust.
Different ways in which to access what is happening subconsciously **1. Drawing**—as a child, with no conscious thought or direction. Right brain drawing.	o Doing a quick drawing in the 10 minutes before a session was always effective and an indispensable way of gaining access to what was causing the fear, anxiety, intense sadness etc. It ensured that the subconscious mind speaks without interpretation or censorship.

2. Writing	o As for drawing, writing freefall without censorship was invaluable. Covering the computer screen or the page I just wrote whatever came without edit. Fear may surface but my motto was 'go with it. Go fearward'.
3. Writing poetry	o This was sometimes the only medium in which certain parts could and would communicate.
4. Writing a therapy diary	o Was invaluable. It was not only a record of therapy but a place in which alters could speak without threat of discovery or repression. It was also empowering and a record if discrepancies should arise.
Writing letters never to be posted	o To a parent or protagonist. And sometimes to an alter.
Writing or talking to something felt in the body	o Eg: Writing to the fear. o Writing to the headache: "Does the headache want to talk?"
Recording therapy sessions	o I found this indispensable, especially as a Multiple, as frequently another part attends the session or 'comes out' in the session and I had no memory of what had occurred. o It has enabled me to learn about all kinds of amazing details about my system. How it was set up and why and how it functions. And to hear their different voices and ways of speaking was validating.

Trust **Each part is about the absolute truth** **And trust gradually builds.**	o Libby always believed what the host or any parts told her. o She was open and ready to listen to anyone who wanted to speak and was aware that it had taken each individual alter a lifetime of courage to come and speak to her. o She treated each alter with respect, but realized that each part had his/her own perception of time, space, matter, therefore any slight inconsistency of story did not mean lack of truth. o And realized that some parts like and trust the therapist, others do not.
The host was not blamed for things that other alters have done	o We found that this can be very confusing particularly if there is no conscious knowledge of that part or no memory of the incident.
Other parts may be present at different times	o I found that if a particular word or idea is understood one week it may not be the next. o And that if an incident is remembered one week it may not be the next.
Ages	o Some parts may be pre-verbal. o My system covered all ages therefore there are very young children, late teenagers and all ages in between. o When a child alter was present, then using adult logic would not often compute with that child.

Knowing the different parts of my system well.	o It was so very reassuring and nurturing to have the therapist know the names and characteristics of each alter. o And genuinely welcomed him/her. o And asked if there' anything they want to say or to talk about or any information they need to ask about.
Using co-consciousness to relay information	o Eg: I hope (an alter's name) is hearing this. o Or "Will you ask (---) to listen to this now? o Or: "Will you relay this information to ---?
Carefully terminated sessions were invaluable.	o Especially when a traumatic memory has surfaced. o Or when I was feeling very vulnerable. o And the possibility to contact Libby was left open if feelings are extreme. As therapy progressed, memories archived and fear diminished I used this safety net less and less.
Ways of bringing me back from an abreaction (see glossary)	o When sometimes going too far into the memory and I was 'losing it' with the terror, Libby tapped L, R, L, R loudly on the chair and with a firm voice said: "Stay here Rhonda. Come back and feel your feet touching the floor." o Having witnessed an abreaction Libby validated the memory as many times as necessary and with genuine feeling, using as many of the same words as I had used in the memory.

Leaving a space between clients	o I never wanted to meet any person who came before or after me. o Of course as Libby became a parent figure, sibling issues came to the fore and to share the parent sometimes brought up very strong and often traumatic feelings.
Unfulfilled promises can be very damaging	o I needed to know that the therapist would always be there for me and would not decide later to terminate. This would have destroyed me as a person who has been traumatized and created Multiplicity as I would have seen it as yet another betrayal. o Libby followed through with anything she said.
We learnt to expect resistance	o That we were dealing with a highly complex and evolved creation that is 'real' and the prominent motivation was to be protected at all costs.
Libby believed: "It is your story, you know what you need to do." She was perhaps a caring and skilled observer We were equal partners in the journey	o It was my story, and when given the time and space and trust and used the tools of listening, writing or drawing I usually discovered what was needed. It was a therapy in which I was permitted to own and to mostly lead the process. o Libby never told me what to do or how to do it. She allowed me, with immense support, to find the answers within myself. o Even bits of information that were revealed 14, 11 or 5 etc years ago would ultimately fit into place in the final jigsaw. The final one whole. o Being a person who has managed, by my own resources to survive severe trauma and to live a functional life, I see myself as competent, creative and determined.

Libby never allowed her own agenda to enter my therapy	o I had enough of my own unresolved trauma and related issues to deal with and am extremely grateful to Libby for her own good mental health. o I found, in a previous therapy that counter transference on the part of the therapist was extremely damaging for me as a traumatized person.
Knowing when I was ready to proceed into a memory	o Eg: Rebecca was quite distressed and curled up on the floor. Libby insisted that she is helped up off the floor by an appropriate part (eg the Earth Mother) before proceeding with e.g EMDR (see glossary) that will more than likely take us into a memory.
Updating each and every part into the present	o Constantly and as many times as is necessary. Included in this information was always 'the father is dead and the mother is very old and frail'. It took a long time for most of us to understand 'dead'.
But-not moving into the present until all the past steps are retrieved and understood	o Not until that part had completed his/her story. o As it helped to provide heaps of information that was essential to the jigsaw and the to the behaviour and belief system of my inner world.
"Patience is a virtue" (a proverbial phrase from the 5th century)	o My 'created system' has been around for a long time and there is very good reason for its complexity and secrecy.
Indicators	o We learnt not to expect that if there's no emotion attached then that issue is resolved.
Not just one method	o There was no one method of therapy that suited every alter.

Libby learnt not to move too fast	o This was a journey, and the processing took time and issues and memories were often needed to be processed over and over again until safe and complete. o As Magnitude said "No-one hurries a tree, so please don't hurry me."
Note taking	o I discovered that sometimes Libby, in her notes, had not gleaned the most important bits from the session. So I suggested that when making notes that she not omit the feelings that had been uncovered and shown. o Libby made her notes available to me whenever I asked. This helped me to know that we were equal travelers on this journey. Her honesty, respect and trust was impeccable
A person who has created Multiplicity has developed constant vigilance	o Libby was aware that I would see through any form of dishonesty on her part. This included lack of genuine belief or feeling. o I was initially also afraid of the effect that the horrible memories were having on Libby and was wanting to shield her from them. However, the professionalism she brought to the therapy soon dispelled this belief.
NB: Libby learnt not ask to speak to a particular part or alter	o It made me feel like an exhibit. o I found in most cases that if and when a switch is spontaneous, that only then will that part speak without intimidation.

Some good sentences	o R: I don't want to hear. L: What would happen if you did hear?
	o R: I don't know. L: But if you did know?
	o R: I can't do that because I feel embarrassed. L: Well you can continue to feel embarrassed or you can get over it and spend this time doing some good work.
	o L: Maybe you don't need to, but are you going to?
Teddies and dolls	o Libby taught me over time, to take them seriously, with respect and care.
	o For the children of my system they were an external representation of my Self.
	o As a child I only had my sister's doll, Betti that I sometimes borrowed.
	o For many years Libby wouldn't allow me to take the teddies home as I would have thrown them out or generally hurt them.
	o It was not until I had been with her for 12 years that I felt enough respect for myself to look after the teddies.
	o Eg. R: Can the teddies stay here for another week? L: Just a moment, I'll ask them.-----Yes, that's fine.
Putting memories or people into the freezer	o I found to be a very effective strategy. Traumatic memories, which can so often spill over into every waking moment, were put, with ceremony into Libby's freezer until I was ready to get them out.
	o This also worked for internal parts who were threatening to harm me. Or my father, who, even though passed on, I believed was still hiding around a corner waiting to attack me.

Objectifying memories	o Often, I put them onto a TV screen and watched as it unfolded. This removed me from full participation in the scene.
Anger work	o It freed my mind and my body. o I used a hose pipe twisted and taped, hit a telephone book while speaking with a voice that came right from my gut. o Libby set this up carefully at first as a very safe event in a safe place with a safe person. All alters involved were purposefully and fastidiously kept safe.
Freedom within the therapy space	o I found that following my body often led into a memory. o Eg: A strong urge to curl up on the floor, or to move the chair forward, or to open the door—was usually a part of me needing to go back into a situation in order to be heard. o One night I woke up with a strong need to have Libby's hands just placed on my back. I followed this up in the next session and immediately Rebecca emerged and gave us heaps of information which led to a much greater understanding of the event, my feelings and of my system.
Longer sessions	o Sometimes a session of 2 or 3 hours brought better results than 3 sessions of 1 hour especially in times of intense memories and emotions when access to the reasons had become difficult and general functioning almost impossible.

Reality checks	o Often distilled panic and brought me into Adult and into the present. (date, time, phone numbers backwards) o Also when still dissociated towards the end of a session this was an essential step to going back into the world.
Several strategies I used to establish co-operation and communication within the system	o A noticeboard set up in the safe place—the banquet room of our castle. o An exercise book that I left open in a particular place in the house. o Round table conferences in the banquet hall. o Drawing my system. I did this regularly and it's amazing the changes over time. o A safe room for children. o Several rooms with locks to contain angry or malicious alters. o Freefall writing. It's amazing the number of alters who spoke while using this.
EMDR **EFT** **Transactional Analysis** **Abreaction** **Gestalt**	o All extremely effective. See the **glossary** following.

APPENDIX 3 – GLOSSARY

Disssociative Identity Disorder (DID): previously known as Multiple Personality Disorder.

Ever found yourself driving in a car but unable to recall the last section of road? Was the light really green? Everyone experiences dissociation to some degree. But there is a long continuum of dissociation. From momentary lack of awareness while driving a car to intense dissociative symptoms that are associated with trauma.

There are seven positions on the dissociation continuum:
- *Everyday Dissociation* : driving a familiar route and arriving at our destination with no memory of the journey. It is also a natural important ability we all use in order to function safely or usefully when sudden trauma occurs (almost watching ourselves help someone injured instead of allowing distress to overtake us). We can also use it to achieve a feeling of calm, sometimes used in spiritual or cultural practices. It also includes out-of-body experiences.
- *Depersonalisation Disorder* - a feeling that your body is unreal, changing or dissolving. Strong feelings that you are detached from your body.
- *Dissociative Amnesia* - not being able to remember important personal information or incidents and experiences that happened at a particular time, which can't be explained by ordinary forgetfulness.
- *Dissociative Fugue* - there is severe amnesia, with moderate to severe identity confusion and often identity alteration. For instance, a person travels to a new location during a temporary

loss of identity. He or she may assume a different identity and a new life.

- *Post-traumatic Stress Disorder (PTSD)* - this person may experience flashbacks, reliving the trauma repeatedly, which causes extreme distress. This, in turn, triggers a dissociative, numbing reaction.
- *Dissociative Disorder Not Otherwise Specified* (DDNOS) - different types of dissociation may occur, but the pattern of mix and severity does not fit any specific dissociative disorder.
- *Dissociative Identity Disorder (DID)* - sometimes called Multi-Personality Disorder (MPD). Someone with DID experiences shifts of identity as separate personalities. Each identity may assume control of behaviour and thoughts at different times. Each has a distinctive pattern of thinking and relating to the world. Severe amnesia means that one identity may have no awareness of what happens when another identity is in control.

DID is the most severe and chronic manifestation of dissociation.

The *Diagnostic and Statistical Manual* (Fourth Edition) says DID is characterised by the presence of two or more identities or personality states, each with its own relatively enduring pattern of perceiving, relating to, and thinking about the environment and the self.

At least two of these identities recurrently take control of the person's behaviour. DID is accompanied by an inability to recall significant personal information.

Professor Warwick Middleton, psychiatrist and director of the Trauma and Association Unit at Belmont Hospital in Queensland, says DID is a serious condition caused by very serious trauma at a young age when the child cannot escape.

"Usually the person inflicting trauma is the caregiver. Sufferers of DID compartmentalise their life in order to survive. it is a hidden compartment but it can be triggered by environmental factors," he says.

The International Society for the Study of Trauma and Dissociation says the dissociated states represent a fragmented sense of identity and different identity states remember different aspects of autobiographical information. There is usually a host personality who identifies with the client's real name.

The different personalities may serve distinct roles in coping with problem areas. The incidence varies greatly between countries but the number of cases has risen significantly in recent years. Possible explanations include a slight correction in the previous tendency to misdiagnose DID as bipolar disorder or schizophrenia, and an increased awareness of child abuse.

Treatment of DID is typically long and challenging but includes working through traumatic and dissociated material and developing more mature psychological defences. The integration of traumatic memories is an essential aspect.

Quoted from the Sydney Morning Herald 29/10/09

Co-Consciousness

This is an awareness by one part (alter ego) of the thoughts of another part in dissociative disorder. There is a continuum. At one end, no parts will be aware of other parts and at the other end all parts will be aware of all other parts. Therapy has enabled me to move from one to the other.

Abreaction:

This is a psychoanalytical term for the vivid, often cathartic return of painful emotion(s) from past circumstances. The patient may have been conscious of the emotion/memory beforehand, or it may suddenly emerge from repression in the subconscious. For Example: A woman in therapy for sexual difficulty recalls being raped in childhood; for the first time, she fully experiences her pain and fear surrounding the incident.

It is also an automatic, unconscious reaction that a person has in response to a stimulus which reminds the person of a situation they have experienced before. As an example, consider a person who has been physically abused who responds to a raised hand by cringing even the though the other person's intent was to brush away a stray thread. Abreaction can also be used to describe the process a therapist uses to desensitize, or help the patient to stop having these automatic reactions. Within the safety of a therapy session, the patient can learn to replace the inappropriate reaction with one that is more suited to the situation.

Transactional Analysis (TA)

A system of individual or group psychotherapy that focuses on personal relationships and interactions in terms of conflicting or complementary ego states that correspond to the roles of parent, child, and adult and the shifting between these. Founded by Eric Berne in the late 1950s.

EMDR or Eye movement desensitization and reprocessing

This is a comprehensive methodology-backed by positive controlled research-for the treatment of the disturbing experiences that underlie many pathologies.

In EMDR, a patient brings to mind emotionally unpleasant images and beliefs about themselves related to their traumatic events. With these thoughts and images in mind, patients are asked to also pay attention to an outside stimulus, such as eye movements or finger tappings guided by the therapist.

For example, in a session of EMDR, a patient may be asked to bring attention to an unpleasant image in their mind, as well as negative beliefs and body sensations associated with the traumatic event. At the same time, the patient is asked to move his eyes side-to-side for several seconds, often following the therapist's hand as it moves from left to right. Afterward, the patient will deep breathe and discuss what was brought up during the exercise. Whatever was brought up can then be used for another exposure exercise. This cycle continues until patient's distress has reduced.

Proponents of EMDR suggest that it works by building new connections between a patient's traumatic memories and adaptive information (for example, positive beliefs) within other areas of the memory, bringing about a reduction in traumatic symptoms.

EFT or Emotional Freedom Therapy

This is a method that was developed by Gary Craig with the desire to help clients let go of negative thoughts, memories, and emotions. This technique involves tapping specific pressure points on the body while recalling painful memories or upsetting thoughts.

During the EFT process, a person is either guided by an EFT practitioner or is self-guided to focus a distressing thoughts or emotions while tapping on certain places throughout the body. These specific spots where the person is instructed to tap are considered points of energy, known as meridians. Instead of using needles as an acupuncturist would, the EFT client is instructed to use one's own on fingers to gently tap on these points. By tapping on these areas and bringing one's awareness to negative emotions one may be able to let go of some negative emotional energy.

I found it an invaluable tool that I continue to use when necessary.

Stockholm Syndrome

In my case this resulted in a complete identification with my father.

When people are placed in a situation where they no longer have any control over their fate, feel intense fear of physical harm and believe all control is in the hands of their tormentor, a strategy for survival can result which can develop into a psychological response that can include sympathy and support for their captor's plight.

Why the Name? The name Stockholm Syndrome was derived from a 1973 bank robbery in Stockholm, Sweden, where four hostages were held for six days. Throughout their imprisonment and while in harm's way, each hostage seemed to defend the actions of the robbers and even appeared to rebuke efforts by the government to rescue them.

Months after their ordeal had ended, the hostages continued to exhibit loyalty to their captors to the point of refusing to testify against them, as well as helping the criminals raise funds for legal representation.

The response of the hostages intrigued behaviorists. Research was conducted to see if the Kreditbanken incident was unique or if other hostages in similar circumstances experienced the same sympathetic, supportive bonding with their captors. The researchers determined that such behavior was very common.

Another more famous case in the U.S, is that of heiress Patty Hearst, who at age 19 was kidnapped by the Symbionese Liberation Army. Two months after her kidnapping, she was seen in photographs participating in a SLA bank robbery in San Francisco. Later a tape recording was released with Hearst (SLA pseudonym Tania) voicing her support and commitment to the SLA cause.

After the SLA group, including Hearst, were arrested, she denounced the radical group. During her trial her defence lawyer attributed her behaviour while with the SLA to a subconscious effort to survive, comparing her reaction to captivity to other victims of Stockholm Syndrome. According to testimony, Hearst was bound, blindfolded and kept in a small dark closet where she was physically and sexually abused for weeks prior to the bank robbery.

What Causes Stockholm Syndrome?

Individuals can succumb to Stockholm Syndrome under the following circumstances:

- Believing one's captor can and will kill them.
- Isolation from anyone but the captors.
- Belief that escape is impossible.
- Inflating the captor's acts of kindness into genuine care for each other's welfare.

Victims of Stockholm Syndrome generally suffer from severe isolation and emotional and physical abuse demonstrated in characteristics of battered spouses, incest victims, abused children, prisoners of war, cult victims and kidnapped or hostage victims. Each of these circumstances can result in victims responding in a compliant and supportive way as a tactic for survival.

www.ingramcontent.com/pod-product-compliance
Lightning Source LLC
Chambersburg PA
CBHW032053090426
42744CB00005B/196

not an option! By the time we got back to his place, I was exhausted. I made a nice nest on the couch and hit the sack. Another great day in the books!

Day 5
Sunday, January 31, 2010

Dang... I've been gone five nights already. It seems like I just got here.

I knew the temperatures at home in Utah were freezing, but we had propped the windows open that night to keep cool, which put me into a rowdy battle with mosquitoes all night. When we woke early the next morning, Lemos and I got ourselves cleaned up and headed to church.

Church was really good, which was not typical of the wards I had been in five years ago. As I sat in the church meetings, I looked around at the crowd and all of a sudden, I saw a familiar face. My mission president's wife was sitting just across from me! I hadn't seen Sister Pexotio in almost five years, so after the meeting we caught up for a bit and made plans to go visit a family that I had taught as a missionary in Florianopolis. After they had gotten baptized, they had moved to Curitiba.

Later that evening President and Sister Pexotio picked Lemos and me up and drove us to visit my long lost friends Mical and Valdamira. They were baptized five years ago right when I was finishing my mission. It was awesome to see them and hear how well they were doing. Mical had been pregnant when I met her, so her four-year-old son really took me by surprise.

I met her on a packed city bus one night when I was super mad about missing the two buses before that one. Normally, I wouldn't talk to girls on the bus on the way home after 9:30 at night, but she wouldn't quit looking at me.

I finally just said, "Hi."

Turns out she was a Jehovah's Witness missionary from Portugal.

She listened to our message about the restoration of the Church of Jesus Christ, she believed in it, was baptized, and the rest is history. My mission president wanted me to write her story so he could get it in the Ensign church magazine.

After visiting our friends, President Pexotio took me by the new LDS temple, which had just been finished, to take some pictures. It was closed, but he knew the gatekeeper, so he got us on the grounds after hours. We walked around and talked about life. It was awesome! After a good night with my old friends, they gave Lemos and me a ride home, where I moved my nest to the floor. I pulled out my bedsheet to use as a mosquito barrier and passed right out!

Monday morning I woke up on the floor at Lemos' house. He was running around getting ready for work, so I threw on some clothes and left with him. I caught the bus to the center of Curitiba with him, and he showed me where President Pexotio worked.

I stopped in and talked to President for a little while. He recommended that I take a tour bus around the city, so I walked to the park, paid R$20 and caught the tour bus. The pass I bought let riders get on and off the bus five times. I almost got kicked off the tour for standing up on the upper deck of the bus. Seeing the city was cool, but after an hour, I was bored. Touristy stuff didn't really interest me.

I looked up cool points of interest in my GPS directory and got off the bus to explore. I saw some cool sites but got kind of sick of all the traffic and people. Toward the end of the tour, the bus drove down a street lined with what seemed like hundreds of motorbike shops. The two wheels in my mind started turning!

Just imagine the places I could go and the cool things I could see if I had a motorbike!

I marked the mega motorcycle street as a waypoint on my GPS and continued on the bus to the center of the city. There I met up with President Pexotio and Lemos for lunch. Nothing like the all-you-can-eat Brazilian buffet! After lunch, I ran by the mall to buy more prepaid phone credits, and once I had my phone all charged up, I set off on foot for the motorbike street. It got really hot, so the five-kilometer walk right after eating a huge lunch seemed like it took forever!

When I got to the motorbike street, I went shop to shop getting prices and asking questions about the laws and regulations for motorbikes in Brazil. I was there for a couple hours talking to people and getting Ideas. My mind was pretty much made up. I was going to have to talk Dave and Brian into using the money we had set aside for flights to buy motorbikes instead!

By Tuesday morning I had seen enough of Curitiba. I woke up early, grabbed my giant pack, said my goodbyes to Lemos, and rolled straight out. A three-hour bus ride later, and a couple hundred kilometers south, I arrived at the Beaches of Picarras, one of my old missionary areas.

I went by my old mission homes to see if the missionaries still lived there. I clapped and yelled outside but nobody answered. I could see missionary clothes on the balcony. I was about to climb the fence and leave my bag there, but I felt like it would be better to just wait and talk to them later. I got a cheap hotel room to store my stuff in and set out on foot to visit some old friends.

It was super hot and I was getting sunburned, so I had to wear a long-sleeved shirt! I was honestly dying. I met up with a few church members and went to a family night with some of them. The church had grown a ton since I was there last. All that missionary work that had sometimes seemed so meaningless had paid off. What a great feeling!

On my way back to my motel, I found my old friend Caio. Caio was baptized while I was in Picarras as a missionary. I found out that he went on a mission, came home from that mission, and baptized his whole family. I was almost overcome with joy. Everything had changed so much since I had served there. Two devastating floods and so many other things had happened in Picarras.

It was late by the time I headed back to my motel, so Caio made sure I made it back safe. My motel room was an absolute furnace! I propped the mini refrigerator door open, cranked the A/C, and put the ceiling fan on high with hopes that it would cool down, and sure enough, my plan to cool the room down had worked. I slept in an icebox! I could almost see my breath when I rolled out of bed.

It felt good to be back on my own, and I was ready to move on. After a leisurely jog down the beach and taking some great pictures, I showered up, checked out of my motel, and took my huge backpack to Caio's house. Caio ditched work, so he and I walked around and saw a few more members and old friends. Still not used to the heat, I was sweating so bad that I had to take a midday shower when we stopped at his place to grab my bags!

I said my farewells and jumped on the next bus to the island of Florianopolis. It was great seeing everyone, but I was pumped to get back to the island where I had lived for six months.

Upon arrival at the island, I called around and found a cheap place to stay. I jumped on a bus to Barra de Lagoa on the far side of the island. Once there, I followed some street signs to a nearby hostel.

The lady working there sold me on staying at the hostel by telling me I could have a bed by the door that had a fan blowing on it. DONE. It was only like $20 a night, so I couldn't complain. The people that were staying there weren't as cool as my personal fan over my bed. It was me and a bunch of rowdy, weird, Eastern Europeans that smoked a lot and never spoke English or Portuguese. I got all set up, locked away my valuables, and went for a short hike. I took some sunset pictures by the lake and checked out some of the "happin places" in town. I was hot and tired. Time to call it a night. That beautiful fan over my bed had been calling my name all day!

2

BRAZILIAN RUMBLE TUMMY

Day 9
Thursday, February 4, 2010

I woke up due to weirdness at like 6:00 a.m. This was the first real hostel that I had ever stayed in, and it shocked me a little bit. I wasn't cool with being around when these weird strangers woke up, so I grabbed some gear and went for a quick run. My quick run turned into a quick 10K, which turned into a massive jungle lakeshore hike. All in all, it was a long hike back. I was way mad I didn't bring a camera! The whole hike was amazing! Tons of super awesome boat houses and an extremely challenging jungle trail would have made epic pictures, but the afternoon heat forced me to head back to the hostel full of weirdos, where I got some food, and showered up.

I had a few hours to kill before I needed to meet Dave and Nian at the airport. Hanging out at the hostel sounded awful, so I took off searching out some old friends from the mission. As I was walking along a road by a huge hill, I heard a loud *whop-whop-whop*. Seconds later, a Policia Militar helicopter, loaded to the gills with killing power and a dude hanging out the door on a harness with a machine gun, appeared from over the hill. It dove straight down at me, turned sideways right over my head so the gunner and I were looking eye to eye, then banked hard and went back around the hill. The whole encounter took maybe twenty-five seconds. I honestly thought Jim Anderson was going to get gunned down by some hell-bent Brazilian helicopter squad!

It was almost time for Dave and Nian's flight to get in, so I took off to go get them. It was about time! I was getting sick of doing cool stuff by myself.

I jumped on a bus and hurried to the airport. I waited for twenty or so minutes and decided I probably had time to run by a bank really quick. Cash in hand, I ran back to the airport. Sure enough, there were my buddies holding a sign with JIM written on it in huge letters! Man, it was good to see them!

We left the airport and dropped off their bags at the weirdo hostel. From there we headed straight to the beach. It was only five kilometers to the beach, but we decided to take the bus. It still took us over half an hour to get there because of all the traffic. As we got our first glimpse of the beach, we all looked at each other in shock. We saw a two-mile span of beach so packed that it was hard to find a place to lay out our towels, but we weren't mad, because we were in Brazil and there were very few ugly people there!

We were all pretty exhausted, so we slothed around for a bit. We had borrowed a surfboard from the hostel so after a while, we decided it was time to give surfing a shot.

Nian went first. Dave and I laughed our butts off as we watched him fight for twenty minutes to get past the first break. We watched him attempt to get a wave and then get hauled in a rip current almost a mile down the beach.

Dave went and didn't do much better.

Then it was my turn.

My first surfing experience sucked! My first paddle out, I got my world rocked by a bunch of fast breaking waves in a row. Then it was my turn to get swept way down the beach by a rip current. Second attempt, I made it out past the break and to the waves, but I must have been in a high spot or something because huge waves were breaking on both sides of me for like twenty-five minutes. I finally caught a wave and got absolutely owned! The force of the wave slammed me so hard that I came up gasping for air and swimming for shore in a panic. That was enough surfing for me.

After swimming hard for that long, we were all wiped out. Being three white boys coming from the dead of winter in Utah, we all got way fried at the beach. Oh, and I stubbed the trash out of my big toe. It hurt super bad and bled like a banshee. We went back to the hostel to shower up, and for the rest of the night we pretty much just took it easy. We bought some grub and watched a group of hippies practice their drum Carnival dance.

Some locals had suggested we hike to a secluded beach on the southern tip of the island for an overnight campout, and that sounded great to us so the next day, we packed up our backpacks, locked them in the hostel storage closet, and headed to downtown Florianopolis in search of supplies for our great adventure. We got into downtown around noon and sat down for a nice Brazilian all-you-can-eat buffet. After we ate ourselves sick, it was business time!

First item of business: find hammocks to sleep in. We scoured the city for two or three hours trying to find ourselves some nice hammocks at a somewhat cheap price. After a long, hardfought search, we found a guy selling hammocks on the street. We gave him the old three-for-the-price-of-two routine. He took our deal, and we had ourselves a nice place to sleep wherever we could find a place to tie up.

We took the hottest, most miserable, two-hour standing bus ride I had ever been on down to the south part of the island. Exhausted from our torturous bus ride, we hit the beach and relaxed until about an hour before sunset. Hoping to get to our campsite before dark, we started trekking east down the beach toward the trailhead. We hit up a small market at the end of the beach to get some final campout supplies. We bought some string to tie up our hammocks and some food and water to hold us over for the night.

As we were standing in line, I felt some bubbles coming up from down deep! A few seconds later, I was hit with an extreme case of Brazilian rumble tummy! I dropped my purchases on the counter and sprinted into the back of the supermarket where I completely destroyed the bathroom. After putting a serious hurt on the bathroom, I decided I would shower off really quick before we started our hike. I was only wearing board shorts so I didn't think it was that big of a deal. Feeling much better, I came out of the bathroom to find out that I was in the supermarket owner's house. There was a lady standing there, and she was not happy! She let me have it! I pretty much just ran out of the store, and we got the heck out of there!

We loaded our food and supplies into our daypacks and hit the trail. It was getting dark fast, so we put ourselves into super hike mode and basically ran up this steep, muddy jungle trail. The hike was supposed to take two hours to get to the top of the hill and an hour down the other side to the hidden, secluded beach. We made it to the top in about an hour. It was just after sundown. The view from the top was absolutely amazing. Just picture this in your mind: a hidden beach with a freshwater lake right by it all surrounded by sand and jungle. We passed a few people coming down the trail. We told them our plan, and they told us that we were crazy for some reason.

It was completely dark by the time we headed down off the top of the hill. We were all extremely sweaty and smelly. Another half hour of hiking, with one small flashlight between the three of us, and we were to the beach! By then, it was pitch-black dark and very creepy! We were supposed to find this Ronaldo guy who was going to show us where to camp. We searched back and forth all along the beach, but all we found were a few hippie campsites—no Ronaldo and no good trees to hang our hammocks on.

I looked at the guys and said, "Well fellas, we might be sleeping in the sand tonight."

We decided to keep walking to the far end of the beach. We were just about there when I noticed a light coming up behind us, and coming fast! We made a quick attack plan in case we were getting jumped and then prepared for the worst!

As the light got close, a man and a boy appeared. The man asked, "What are you doing out here?"

"We're looking for Ronaldo," I told him. "He's supposed to show us where to camp."

He said, "Oh, Ronaldo isn't here, but you can hang your hammocks up under my canopy where I sell drinks during the day."

Awesome! Our new friend led us to the far north end of the beach where he showed us the perfect shelter for hanging up our hammocks.

He said, "My name is Chaverio." Chaverio means key maker in Portuguese. "If you want to come sit by the fire with us in a bit just follow the trail up through the jungle until you get to my camp. If anyone tries to mess with you guys down here, just yell CHAVERIOOOOO! and I will come rescue you!"

We all had a good laugh, and our new friend Chaverio and his son disappeared into the jungle.

After stretching out our hammocks and putting our camp all together, we decided to go see what Chaverio was up to. It took us a minute to find his secret trail in the jungle. Once we did, it was only a short five-minute hike up to his camp.

Needless to say, we were all a little shocked by his "camp." He had a legit Swiss Family Robinson style hut built into the hillside. He had a table, a big mud oven, and a nice shelter complete with a roof made from broken surfboards. On the other end of his camp was a piece of plastic which concealed his shower and toilet. A big pipe coming out of the side of the mountain supplied a steady stream of fresh water. The three of us took turns drinking from the water pipe, and then we all sat around Chaverio's fire telling stories with him and his Argentine friend. Nian accepted some of his "homemade lemonade," and we found out that it was homemade licor. We hung out there for almost two hours. We told stories, laughed, cried, and made some great new friends.

Just before we were about to leave, I took a very refreshing shower in his jungle bathroom. As we headed back down the trail Chaverio yelled, "Make sure to yell CHAVERIOOOO! if anyone comes around messing with you at night or you have any trouble."

We hiked back to our hammocks on the beach and joked the whole time about yelling Chaverio at the top of our lungs. We decided that would be our keyword for distress for the rest of the trip. Once in our hammocks, exhaustion combined with a cool ocean breeze and the sound of waves put us right to sleep.

I woke up on the beach completely confused at probably 4:30 in the morning. Where was I and why was I so cold?

We broke camp and started our hike back out. We were all hungry and still tired, so it was kind of nice to get back to the weirdo hostel for once. We rested up and washed a few things and then set out for the beach again.

On the bus toward the beach we were approached by a nice young lady named Paula. At first, we thought she just wanted to practice her English, but then she invited us to a house party with her and a bunch of her friends. We were way stoked. Chicks invited us to a house party? That's awesome!

We showed up to the party, and it cost money to get in! We were already going to a party on the beach, but Paula talked us into staying, telling us how awesome it was gonna be. So we paid to get in just to find out that Paula, who had conned us into this paid party, was only seventeen years old! What a disappointment. To make matters worse, once inside, we discovered ourselves at a high school party!

Dave and I tore up the dance floor for a minute, but this definitely wasn't our crowd, so we bolted out of there to see if we could catch the last part of the beach party. We stopped to take Nian's picture with a pretty Brazilian girl and headed toward the beach. Right at the beginning of the trail, three dudes in speedos came rolling up the trail toward us. Maybe it was just the speedos, but we all felt a little gay vibe. We continued hiking down the trail and passed probably twenty more guys in more or less than the same dress as the first bunch. Everyone we passed told us that the party was awesome.

At the end of the trail, we burst out on the beach only to see nothing other than dude on dude dance party action! Tons of guys in speedos just getting their bumpty bump on. Gross!

Not our scene, so the three of us took off running down the beach until we found a party with chicks. We chilled there for a bit, but it was kinda lame since we didn't drink or smoke weed. We went to catch the bus back to the hostel and found out that there was an ultimate traffic jam on the only road out from the beach! So…we grabbed a pizza and walked the three miles back to the hostel where we hit the hay!

Day 12
Sunday, February 7, 2010

Sunday we got ourselves all prettied up nice for church and headed out. By the time we got there, I looked like I had just jumped in a pool with all my clothes on! Nothing like 105 degrees in tropical, humid Brazil while wearing church clothes!

We got lost, so we got to church late. When we walked in the back, we found out that it was a stake conference, which is a big meeting of a bunch of wards and branches. The three of us sat in the back and sweated like we had just run a marathon. The stake president gave a good talk, but toward the end of his remarks, he said that the young men of the church need to get married and need to stop vagabonding around. We all looked at each other and put our heads down in shame.

After church we put on some more heat-friendly clothes and jumped on a bus toward the north end of the island. Little did we know that this sweltering, terrible bus ride would have a dramatic influence on the next two and a half months of our lives!

Almost three hours later, we had traveled only twenty miles to the north end of the island.

We hiked to the end of the beach and found a hidden little beach just past some rocks. Let's go! We scaled down the rocks and, once on the beach, we could see a huge rock sticking up out of the water, surrounded by people. It was a huge rock jump. So we swam out to it and threw some gainers and flips. The locals went nuts! They had never seen anything like it.

We talked to these cool kids whose parents owned the place. They said we could stay there whenever we wanted. We got some cool drinks, took a few more pictures, and jumped on another bus toward our hostel. We endured another terribly long, hot, nasty bus ride. We didn't get off the bus until way after dark. As we quietly walked down the lonely street toward the weirdo hostel, I brought it up.

"What do you guys think about buying some motorbikes to get around? I've been thinking about it a lot and, if my math is right, it will even be cheaper than taking buses and airplanes everywhere."

Silence.

Nian just nodded his head with an unreadable frowny face.

Dave finally piped up and said, "Well, we'll have to look into it."

I already had! I told them that either way they decided, I was in on the motorbikes and we needed to make it happen. No more ridiculously hot, long bus rides for me!

On Monday morning, we set out on a research mission. We had a tough decision to make. Should we a) fly and take buses from place to place on our trip, b) buy a car and take it as far as we could and then sell it and fly home, or... c) buy motorbikes and see where the wind took us. Each option had its advantages. Flying was more expensive, but we could obviously cover more ground faster. A car was the slowest means of travel, and we found out that an old crappy car would cost us almost as much as we would spend on three decent dirt or road bikes. We wrote up a big list of pros and cons, figured out the costs of all three options, and finally decided that we were going to go for it!

We checked out of our weird hostel in Barra da Lagoa and set out on foot, with all of our packs and gear, looking for a place to get deals on three nice used bikes. We made our way around the south side of the island. While hiking along the highway, we stopped at like ten different bike shops trying to find the perfect combination of bikes to get all three of us ready to ride!

Turns out good used bikes were kind of hard to come by. We searched high and low and found nothing. I couldn't even find myself a decent place to find a haircut. Nian did manage to find himself a skate park. He "shredded the gnar" with some local druggies while Dave and I enjoyed some snacks in the shade. We had walked five to ten miles and were all super tired. That was enough bike searching for one day. We grabbed the next bus to the Center where we grabbed some grub and caught another bus across the bridge to San Jose where Nian's Mission President was waiting for us.

President Damiani loaded the three of us and our gear into his small car. He loved Nian's long hair! His first comment to us was that we needed to find a place to get Nian's hair cut. He took us back to his place where we had family home evening with his family. It had been awhile since us single dudes had sat in on a family home evening, and it was pretty awesome. Sister Damiani made us some pizza.

As it got close to our time to leave Nian asked, "Hey President, do you think it would be okay if we slept on your back porch?"

His reply was instant. "Absolutely NOT!"

We figured it was because he had an eighteen-year-old daughter that was pretty cute. He loaded us up and took us to a hotel. President talked to us on the way to the hotel and told us the parable of the fast swimming fish and the slow swimming fish. He said too many single people were trying to catch the fast fish and more should catch the slow fish. We didn't know if he was trying to tell us to marry the less cute girls or the easy girls—just kidding!

He also said his excuse for waiting to get married was he hadn't found the right girl. He told that to a seventy (a leader in the Church) one day.

The seventy answered back, "No, you're just not looking in the right places."

Soon after that, he found his wife in an institute class.

We spent the remainder of the wonderful night in our nice hotel watching a Night in the Museum, chasing cockroaches, and manscaping! Haha, good times.

Our night in the hotel was amazing. Air conditioning never felt so good! We slept in as long as we possibly could and then hurried down for the continental breakfast. We got there just in time and got busy eating as much as we possibly could! I would dare say that breakfast was one of the best that I had ever had in Brazil. All the fresh fruit, juice, cake, eggs and everything else you can handle.

We left the hotel and spent some time in search of adventure. We cruised by the bus terminal to talk to the information office and the lady there gave us some good pointers on cheap places to stay and fun things to do during the Carnival holiday. Carnival in Florianopolis is crazy! Florianopolis has a population of around 400,000 people. During carnival, the population swells to around 3 million! It's basically one big party island!

As we left the bus station, a man rolled up in a super crappy car and offered us a hostel for super cheap! Plus he gave us a ride there for free and stopped by a motorcycle shop so we could figure some bike stuff out.

We won't mention that the passenger seat was stuck all the way back and reclined, or that I was the lucky one who got to sit behind it while we were stuck in traffic for two hours! We also won't mention that the passenger door was tied shut with a shoelace, or that the homeboy driving us creeped up on every chick in site, slowly moved his hand to the horn and when the moment was just right, he blasted her with a honk of manhood! As long as she was good looking of course, which was easily ninety-nine percent of the females we saw between the bus station and the hostel.

The hostel was right on the southernmost beach of the island. It was absolutely beautiful! It might have been a little far away from everything, but that's how we liked it. It was calm and peaceful down there and you could fall asleep to the waves crashing right outside your window. There was even a lady from Chile that washed our clothes for us!

We went out looking for a place to eat. A kid passed us on a bike, and we asked him to do a wheelie. He did one forever down the street! We went on our way and all of a sudden homeboy came flying past us in a wheelie again! He continued to show off his wheelie skills till he almost crashed, and then he took off. It was hilarious!

The only restaurant we had seen or heard of was closed, so we asked around to some locals who pointed us in the direction of a small hot dog stand. It was actually really good, and the dude working, whose name was Luis Cristiano I believe, was an awesome dude. He, his wife, and his sister (who had a really fat baby) helped us outline a plan for our trip. Looked like we were in for a great time! We chilled there for a while, and he played some guitar—a few English songs and then some Portuguese country songs. It was awesome.

As we were leaving, we watched a car jump a curb and smash into a cement wall, which was actually somebody's fence. The driver and passenger hurried and switched positions and backed out in a hurry. They went to take off, but I think the car was struggling, so they sat there for a bit, contemplating the situation, and finally took off! We got a good laugh out of it! At least they thought about what they had done. The next day we laughed again when we saw the repair guy laying some bricks and mortar to fix the huge hole in the wall.

After the last couple days of crazy bike searching and bus rides, we were all pretty worn out, so we decided it would be best if we took it easy for a day. The guy that gave us a ride to the hostel had told us about a hidden beach and waterfall that we could hike to. The three of us pulled on some board shorts, grabbed our day packs, and hit the trail stoked for some hiking and waterfall madness.

Our buddy made it sound like the hike was just a little day hike, but the trail proved to be quite challenging. After hiking more than an hour on a poorly marked muddy trail, we finally arrived at the waterfall. It was only a stream of water and the waterfall was only twenty feet tall.

We made the most of it and did some sweet jumps into the small pool of water and swam around a little bit. A small family of Argentines showed up, and we all swam around having fun, except for Dave.

He quietly stood on a tree root about thirty feet above the water. I thought he was just soaking in the moment when he suddenly let out a scream, and boom—GAINER off of a tree root into a tiny pool of water!

He came right up laughing and let out a yell. "I hit the bottom!"

I just shook my head and said, "Dave, your mother would be so mad, but that was AWESOME!"

I moved around to the other side of the pool where I could get a better picture of the jump and started walking out onto a steep rock while holding onto a branch. All of a sudden—SNAP! The branch broke, I slipped, fell to my butt, and started sliding slowly toward the water. I freaked out and tried getting my pack, with all of our electronics in it, off of my back. SPLASH! I went completely under the water, popped out, and threw my pack as far as I could toward Nian on the shore.

The pack got soaked but lucky for us, none of our cameras or the GPS got wet. Mad and embarrassed, I suggested that we go back to the beach.

We hiked down to the coast and made our way along the rugged coastline until we made it to the Pria do Solidao (Lonely Beach). I laid in the squeaky sand while Dave and Nian tried body surfing. By the time we left the beach it was well after lunch time. We grabbed some Guaranás and bread and headed back toward the hostel. Once we got there, I caught the bus to another neighborhood and got a haircut while Dave and Nian enjoyed some beach time. The guy who cut my hair was super cool, so I told him to give me whatever crazy haircut he had. He gave me a mini mullet with eight steps on each side.

After finishing the haircut, he looked at my hair and said, "Muito louco!" which means super crazy.

I caught the bus back to the beach hostel and met up with Dave and Nian. We sat down and had a team meeting. We had been on our feet for the past four days searching the city for some motorcycles so that we could get our butts off of that damn bus! We would have snatched some up the first or even the second day, but the adversary kept putting stumbling blocks in our path!

First, we couldn't take more than 800 reais (400 dollars) out of the bank at a time, and the bikes were costing about 5000 reais (2700 dollars). Then, once we figured out payment, we found out we couldn't buy them without some Brazilian CPF identity number. We broke the meeting and jumped on a bus toward San Jose to go get a CPF number from the city building. That took up the rest of our day, but it all worked out in the end. With CPF numbers and cash in hand, we would be able to get ourselves some awesome wheels that would keep us from having to sweat on the bus like a teenage boy on the "who's the daddy of the baby" episode of the Maury show!

However, while we were on our search for motorbikes, we saw many things, yeah many great and wonderful things were seen and read, especially when we checked our email when we got back to the hostel. Nothing out of the ordinary except for an email in Nian's inbox. It was from Lucia! Nian yelled and started laughing.

Dave and I ran to his computer and read: *Hi Nian, this is Lucia, the daughter of your mission president. You and your friends ate pizza at my house last night. Don't ever tell my dad, but you guys are cute! My friends and I want you and your friends to come out with us tomorrow night! It's hip hop night at the club in Florianopolis and we want to hang out with you guys! Let me know if you can make it! Hugs and kisses! Lucia.*

After reading that, we all laughed and cheered! We were stoked for a night out on the town with some cool girls! We decided that we needed to make our bike purchases happen the next day for sure! There was no way we were showing up to the club on the bus! We rolled back to the hostel and got ourselves some good sleep to get ready for a big day!

3

THE WOLFPACK

Day 16
Thursday February 11, 2010

TODAY IS THE DAY! TIME TO GET A BIKE BETWEEN OUR
LEGS!

All day today, we pulled out as much money from the ATM as
we could, finalized our decisions, and worked on picking up our bikes!

It took Dave forever since the debit card machine wouldn't work.
Finally, he had the guy put his bike on a credit card, and it went through.
Dave and his buddy at the Dinomoto shop went out to a nice romantic
lunch and spent the rest of the morning and early afternoon hanging
out. The mechanic, Michell, put a Dinomoto's sticker on Dave's used
Yamaha TDM 225 and asked him to take pictures along the way and
send them to him so that he and the other mechanics could follow us
in our adventure. They were so jealous, but we would've been, too, if we
hadn't been doing this awesome trip ourselves!

While Dave was gone, Nian and I went to Skin Moto's to get
our new bikes ready to roll! We had gone in several times to talk and
test ride bikes. We were way sick of looking at bikes, so that morning
we went in and offered the lady R$10,000 for a Yamaha XT 225 and

a Honda Tornado 250. Nian called dibs on the nicer Yamaha, so that left me with the Honda that had been wrecked pretty hard. I was going to back out of the deal until the lady let me pull parts off of another Honda Tornado that they had there in the shop to get mine looking and running great!

By the time Dave dropped his romantic lunch date off and showed up at Skin Moto's, Nian and I were taking all the parts off of the crappy bike and putting them on the newer one to make one awesome bike! Dave gave me a hand, and we hung out with another awesome mechanic, Andre. The fool was Brazil's wheelie champion! Medals and trophies galore, but a cool down-to-earth kid.

Nian's bike made us all kind of nervous. It was a 2005, but it only had 5000 kilometers on it. I fought with the owner of the bike shop, trying to get her to tell us what was wrong with it. She said it had belonged to a friend that never rode it. Good enough for me, so we sealed the deal!

When we got done hustling deals, building bikes, and filling up with gas, we borrowed some helmets so we could ride to San Jose to buy cheaper helmets. The hour ride to get there was NUTS! Dave set out weaving in and out of traffic like he had been doing it his whole life. We joined the rest of the bikes on the road and drove in between two lanes of traffic moving at freeway speeds! Weaving through traffic and between buses and semis on our little bikes is what the Brazilians call *TAZAO*! which means awesome, tubular, bodacious, radical, and boner!

But I'm not gonna lie, I was super nervous. Not only for my own safety but more for Nian's, because he didn't have as much experience on a motorbike. I could see him in my rearview mirror passing in between two semis at full speed! Little did I know, this sight and feeling would become a common one! By the time we made it to San Jose, the parts stores were all closed, so Nian and I bought some decent helmets from the Yamaha dealership and paid R$250 for them, which I thought was a bit much for a cheap helmet.

It had been a long day, so we celebrated our bike purchase by eating some awesome all-you-can-eat pizza! We rode the bikes back to our south island hostel, showered up, and headed out on our new rides to go clubbing with Lucia and her friends!

We weren't supposed to use her name in this book because we wouldn't want Nian's mission president to find out that his daughter met up with us to go to the club! Haha, I believe that qualifies as looking for a wife in the right place, right? Right Nian?

We were so stoked and finally felt cool as we pulled up to the club on our sweet bikes! We were dressed as if we were going to a Vegas club with the Rockwell watch guys during supercross in Las Vegas. When we met up with Lucia and her friends and got in line, we found out that we weren't dressed for the occasion. I had a flat brim hat on while Dave and Nian rocked bandanas. We had to take them off and hide them until we got inside, where we found out just how out of place we were.

Everyone was way dressed up and way better looking than we were! Good times at the club and tons of beautiful Brazilian girls. We made the most of it and got crazy dancing out hearts out! We found out the hard way that they don't dance the same as we do in the US. We didn't care and had a great time!

By the time we left, we were all completely soaked with sweat. We grabbed some grub with Lucia and her friends, traded our sweaty shirts for jackets, and rolled on back to the south part of the island. It was after 4:00 a.m., just a few short hours before sunrise, when we got back to the hostel. We were super tired, so we passed straight out! We needed some good rest to be ready for the weekend!

Let's just say we slept in as long as we could on Friday morning. Everyone said the north part of the island was where we would find the real party, so once we were all awake and done messing around on the beach, we decided it was time to leave our south island hostel and head north—but only after stopping at our moto shops and getting our bikes all tuned up of course! The last thing we needed was to break down out in the jungle somewhere.

We packed up all our gear, strapped it on our backs, and hit the road! First stop was at Dinomotos where Dave had bought his bike. The guys there helped us change our filters and oil, and then they gave our bikes a general overall inspection. We ran by Skin Motos and grabbed some parts and stuff for Nian's bike and my bike. It took us a couple hours to get everything ready to roll, but as soon as it was ready, we grabbed some food and rode north!

We rode up to Ponta das Canas, which was only fifteen miles away. We found a nice place with cold A/C to crash for a couple nights. We ditched our gear, showered up, and hit the streets once more!

The north end of the island was completely different from the south. In the south, everyone drove crappy old cars or rode bikes. In the north, everyone drove Porsches or Lambos and lived in mansions.

We had rolled out looking for a good time, and that was exactly what we found. There were supermodels and awesome cars everywhere! We parked our bikes by a mall and set out on foot, talking to people and having fun. We grabbed some pizza and decided to explore more on the bikes. We rode west into some neighborhoods of mansions, and that was where we found *As Festas* (the parties).

We rode past a giant house party. There were $100,000 cars on both sides of the street and a solid line of super models trying to get into this house. Dave, Nian, and I slammed on our brakes and instantly turned around! We parked our bikes between a couple super cars and casually got in line to go into the party.

Once again, the three of us were very underdressed for the occasion—so underdressed that they wouldn't even let us in. We figured they kept us out because they were certain we would steal all their chicks! We chilled outside with the bouncer, trying to make friends with him so he'd let us in. Homeboy had bigger arms than any human ever born! His arm size to head size ratio was way off. Giant arms and a tiny head. It was insane! We talked to him and tried picking up on chicks for a cool hour.

"Hey, there's a party at Posh Club tonight. You guys should

check it out," one pretty girl said.

We weren't having luck at the house party, so we saddled up and rode on over there. We stashed the bikes in a dark parking lot, but as we were walking away, I got a strange feeling about leaving them there.

"We should go back and move the bikes closer to the streetlight," I said. "They'll be safer there."

We moved the bikes and went to the club. It cost over $500 to get in! Depressed at the cost of the club, we turned around and went back to the bikes.

When we showed up at the parking lot, we noticed some cops about fifty yards down the road from where we had parked our bikes. As soon as we sat on the bikes, the cops flipped their lights on and raced toward us!

They nervously got out of their car and asked to see our documents and the documents for the bikes. Of course we didn't have them because the bikes were not registered or titled in our names and we left everything else back at the hostel. They got super pissed and started drilling us on what we were doing.

The three of us did our best to make friends with the officers and to deescalate the situation. Turns out, a car had been stolen in the dark parking lot where we had originally parked our bikes. Some people in a house nearby said they saw three dudes messing around near our bikes. The cops had pulled the spark plugs out of our motors so when we showed up we wouldn't be able to take off.

I sat back and thought, *Oh boy, we've only had our bikes for a day and a half and we're already about to get arrested!*

When they realized we weren't the three bandits they were looking for, the nice officers replaced our spark plugs and apologized. Two nights after having bikes and the cops were already all over us! We almost went to jail! It was a good scare. Needless to say, the three of us were very glad we had gone back and parked under the lights on the road in a rich neighborhood!

We were a little bummed that the party was so expensive, but we met some people that told us about another party the next night in the same club that would only cost $30! We were in for that! Except for Nian. Nian didn't want to go. He and Dave got in an argument over it, which Dave won. Now Nian was in for the party as well!

We woke up late the next morning. The previous night was nuts and we were all pretty worn out, so we got some rest. Sleeping on decent beds and with a cold air conditioner running might have also had something to do with us sleeping in.

Other than the Carnival party we wanted to hit up that night, we didn't have anything planned until the next morning. The Carnival party didn't start until 10:00 p.m., and it wasn't cool to show up until midnight, so we had some time to kill.

The three wolves of the Wolfpack, which we had started calling ourselves due to Dave's awesome truck stop T-shirt with three wolves and one ghost wolf on it, grabbed their day packs and headed out on their new bikes.

We left Ponta das Canas and rolled over to Praia Brava (Mean Beach). It wasn't that mean. We were going to try surfing again, but the waters were packed, so we decided to hike around the northernmost point of the island.

We headed north from the beach and climbed up a steep hill until we were high above the beach. The trail was muddy and proved quite difficult in flip flops. At the top of the trail, we found an awesome hippie village that was built inside a series of caves and rocks. We decided that we could easily live there for a while, but since we had bikes now, we should probably stay near roads.

We settled into the hippie village to pass some time, but all of a sudden, Nian jumped up and yelled, "I'm going to poop my pants!" as he ran into the bushes. Five minutes later, Nian walked out of the bushes with his head down, looking like a very somber fellow.

Still laughing from his dramatic exit, Dave and I asked him what his deal was.

He told us how a family walked around on a different trail just as he was dropping and squatting to poop. They totally saw him serve up a healthy portion of poop soup in the woods!

We all decided that it was time to eat, so we trekked back to the beach and to the bikes. I had heard of another awesome hidden beach hike to the south of us, but after two hours of riding in unbelievably bad traffic and scorching heat, we ended up just stopping at a corner market and eating junk food. I felt bad for getting us nowhere, so I paid for everyone's food. We abandoned the hike idea and headed back toward our motel.

Once again traffic was nuts and we soon found out why. There was a huge roadblock ahead of us. Feeling like we were above the law, we rolled our bikes up on the sidewalk and tried getting around the human roadblock. As we got closer to the roadblock, it started looking more like a Mardi Gras party. As we rode through the crowd, we naturally got funneled through the middle of the party. That was when we discovered that this party was actually a transvestite parade.

Hundreds of dudes dressed up like chicks! *What the hell?* Nian put his head down and gunned it right through the middle of them!

He was almost through the middle of the group when a guy ran up, rubbed his chest, and said, "Hey there, beautiful!"

Nian took off, and then it was my turn. I floored it through the huge group of intimidating she-dudes. A guy ran out at me. Not wanting the same groping that Nian got, I didn't even slow down. As he got close to me, I swerved and barely missed hitting him head on! My mirror clipped him—or her—and shattered everywhere!

Dave rode through right behind me. He rolled up next to me, and I yelled, "Freak man! That was a new mirror! What just happened?"

The three of us raced out of there! We still had some time before it got dark, so we headed back down to the beach and got our ultra relaxing chill on. Our spot on the beach provided some great sunset pictures, and sundown meant it was almost party time!

We rolled back to the pad where we got showered up, then headed back out to find some power food that could sustain us through an all-night party! We wasted a couple hours walking around asking hot chicks where the party was that night. We found that if we spoke in very broken Portuguese then the girls liked us more. We also discovered that most of the babes, as Nian called them, spoke decent English.

It was around 10:00 p.m. when Nian started freaking out because we weren't at the Posh Club party yet. Dave and Nian argued about whether we should go at 10:00 or midnight. Nian won this argument, I laughed, and we headed off toward Club Posh. We got there in decent time and bought our $30 tickets.

The "party" we were attending was actually a Kaskade concert in a super fly Brazilian event venue. It was nuts! We were some of the first people to show up. Naturally, Dave and I made fun of Nian for wanting to come early. We marveled in the parking lot as we were suddenly surrounded by amazing cars and beautiful women! I'm not a huge electronic music fan, but it was awesome watching Kaskade in Brazil. I never knew it, but he's a Latter-day Saint, and he went to school at BYU in Provo, Utah.

The concert got going, and the three of us set out to meet some girls. We tried doing this in the same way we used to do it in the States, which was completely wrong. We tried every tactic we knew to meet girls at a party and nothing proved to work. We later learned that if you want to meet a girl, you just grab her and make out. If she kisses you back, then you're money. If she doesn't kiss you back, then move on to the next one. Definitely not something we were used to—or would have had the guts to do!

Turns out our mechanic friend, Andre, was selling drinks at the club, so we got all the discounted Coke Classics we could handle. We partied hard until 4:00 a.m., which was when I lost track of Dave and Nian. I searched everywhere for them and finally found them sleeping in the back of the venue against the wall. Poor guys were all partied out! I was against coming to the party early, so I stayed another hour just to prove my point.

Sometime after 5:00 a.m. we headed back toward the motel.

The ride home was interesting. There were hookers everywhere! We, of course, honked our horns and rode straight at them.

Nian yelled once, "Dude! That chick was way fine!"

We laughed and broke the bad news to him. "Nian, that was a tranny!"

By the time we arrived, it was starting to get light, so we showered up and packed our gear. We had told the motel people that we were leaving that night, so we wanted to be gone before they got up that morning. The three of us, tired as ever, tied our bags to our bikes, said a prayer for protection and guidance, and headed off into the early morning mist!

Injury report:

Jim's bad stubbed toe - healed.

Kiley's torn up foot - healed.

Nian's broken heart - healed.

Jim's broken tooth - not healed.

4

GHETTO RAIN GEAR: BARATO SEMPRE SAI CARO

Day 19
Sunday, February 14, 2010

There we were! Finally out on the open road! I had my GPS tied onto my handlebars with a piece of string, the small city of Picarras plugged in as the destination.

We soon found out that our bikes weren't as fast as we had thought they would be. My bike was a 250cc, so it was slightly faster than Dave's and Nian's 225cc bikes. We were by far the slowest ones on the freeway, but that didn't matter! We rode along the coastline freeway honking, swerving in and out, and all around having a great time! I kept wanting to stop and take pictures. The sunrise over the ocean with the island of Florianopolis in the background was absolutely amazing! We rode through tunnels, around cliffs, and along beaches. The speed limit was 120 kilometers per hour, but Dave's and Nian's bikes had a hard time going faster than 105 kilometers per hour.

I had gotten a little ahead of the guys. I slowed down so they could catch up. They rode up to me and gave me the Brazilian hand signal for eat so we pulled off in the big beach city of Balneário Camboriú. We rode into the city and parked on the beach. We were all dead tired after staying up partying all night.

It was Sunday, so we tried finding a church, but it was almost 11 a.m. We figured that we had already missed it. Nian ran off taking pictures of a train parade. Dave and I kicked it on a park bench and watched some super old dudes play bocce ball. When Nian came back, happy about taking pictures of his train parade, we headed to a churrascaria.

A *churrascaria* is an all-you-can eat Brazilian barbeque restaurant. We ate ourselves sick! That ended up being a terrible decision. The three of us were now in a full-blown food coma and wanted nothing more than to get some sleep! I told the guys to stay strong for another hour until we got to Picarras, where I had friends that would let us nap at their houses.

We rolled up to Picarras and went straight to my friend Caio's house. He invited us to stay there, and he put some cushions on the porch so we could take a nap. Dave jumped in the hammock while Nian and I crashed out on the cushions. I woke up sometime after dark. Had I really taken a seven-hour nap? We were still way tired and it was pouring rain, so we hung up more hammocks and camped out at Caio's house for the night. He was awesome to us. His family fed us and made sure we were taken care of! I even found out later that he had stayed up most of the night standing guard over us and our stuff while we were asleep! What a great guy!

After sleeping for more than half a day, we woke up early the next morning. We kicked it with Caio for a bit and got some breakfast down by the beach. We were feeling way fresh, so we got an early start back on that open road! We rolled along the coastal highway as far north as we could on our way to Porto União, which is another city where I lived and served as a missionary.

Right before we headed inland away from the coast, I tried taking a shortcut that I had found on my GPS. Let's just say, I got us lost in a jungle swamp. The guys got mad at me and made me promise that I'd take us straight to the freeway. Once on the freeway, we were headed straight west. The scenery and ride were impossible to describe! Wide, curvy, smooth roads through forests and farmlands! So amazing! We stopped at a roadside store in the middle of a banana farm in the mountains. I bought the guys some sugar cane juice and freshly picked finger size bananas. Absolutely delicious! We won't even talk about the store owner's hot daughter! My goodness! Too bad she just talked about her boyfriend the whole time.

We hate other guys' girlfriends, so we fired up our hogs and hit the road!

It was such a beautiful day! We enjoyed blue skies and smiles all around. About an hour and a half out of Porto União, we visited a kid Nian baptized on his mission who was serving his own mission in a city called Rio Negro. We went to the store, bought some ingredients, and made a healthy meal of spaghetti at the missionary's house. Then Nian said his goodbyes to his mission buddy and we kept on route for Porto União.

Right after we left Rio Negro we were hit with a wall of rain! We hadn't really planned on rain. What were we thinking? It rains every day in Brazil!

The three of us took shelter in a small roadside bar. We were there for almost an hour. If we wanted to make it to Porto União by nightfall, we had to get going! So, we suited up with trash bags over our gear and bodies and grocery sacks on our feet (which made Nian look like a girl) and kept on truckin!

It got dark before we thought it would. Suddenly I was wet, cold, pissed, and the awesome road we were on turned into a trashy, pothole, two-lane highway. Foggy conditions and continuous rain didn't help our travels either! The three of us rode hard until after 10:00 p.m., which was when we rolled into Porto União.

We were planning on surprising my good friend Sister Leni by showing up at her house when we got there. I had met Leni on my mission. She had gotten baptized into the Church, and we were hoping that after surprising her, she would invite us to stay with her. After calling her a bunch of times with no answer, it started pouring rain way hard again!

It was almost 11:00 p.m. So... now what?

We rolled past the only other place I could think of, the missionary's house where I had lived five years before. We parked on the street, and I crept around their house to see if they still lived there. I poked my head up and looked through the window. Turned out, the missionaries did still live there!

I knocked on the door, which they answered completely confused. I explained our situation, and they were kind enough to let us sleep on their floor. We parked our bikes in their garage, brought our soaked gear inside, sprawled everything out on the dirty floor, and crashed out! What a long day. We were all completely worn out. What had we gotten ourselves into?

You can probably guess what our first item of business was the next morning. If you can't, then you should get better at guessing. We bid adieu to our generous missionary hosts and hit the road toward the dollar store. We weren't going any farther without rain gear! Why we thought it was a good idea to buy rain gear from a dollar store, I don't know. Since the start of the trip people had been telling us, "Barato sempre sai caro" (cheap always comes out expensive). Forget being soaking wet on the road! Our cold, wet ride to Porto União sucked so bad! After getting on our sweet new rain gear, we were off to find Leni's house for lunch. After some searching, we found her house.

Having the opportunity to baptize Leni was one of the highlights of my mission. She is still way active in the church and is an awesome example of faith! She's the only member of the church in her family and still holds true to the faith! Turned out, she had had the young woman of the church over for a pajama party. That was why she hadn't answered my calls.

She cooked up the best barbeque I have ever eaten. It was so awesome to finally eat some home-cooked food! After lunch, her daughter Ana and a friend took us on a drive to the countryside and showed us some awesome waterfalls and farms near where they grew up. It was still sort of rainy. That made for some awesome waterfalls. The highest one was probably eighty feet tall.

We hiked to the top and Ana said, "Make sure you don't fall in, cause if you fall off you'll die for sure! There's tons of rocks at the bottom."

We were all standing by the edge of the river watching the water fall off the edge when all of a sudden, I heard Ana start yelling. I looked up. Nian had his shoes off and was already fifteen feet out into the swift river!

I yelled, "Nian! Get your butt back over here! I am not going to fish your soggy body out of this river and then tell your mother that you were being an idiot while on my watch!"

We finally coaxed him back to shore and headed back to Leni's house. We enjoyed a nice cup of hot cocoa and saddled back up on our bikes. We rode to the outskirts of the city and up the city's Cristo Hill right at sunset! SO Pretty!

When we got back to Leni's house, Ana was insistent that we go out to a last night of Carnival party with her and her friends. We were tired, but it would be against our Wolfpack biker gang creed to turn down a party!

We splashed on some cologne, jumped in with Ana and two of her friends, and hit the town! It was a super rowdy party! Not quite as fancy as the parties we had attended back in Florianopolis, but we still had tons of fun. There was a band playing the whole time, and there were hundreds of people yelling, drinking, and dancing. I got sick from all the smoke, so we went back to Sister Leni's house and had an amazing night's rest in soft, clean beds!

5

PEACE OUT, PARAGUAY!

Day 22
Wednesday, February 17, 2010

The next morning, we broke the bikes out super early, geared up, said our goodbyes, and started out on the next leg of our travels. According to my GPS, we had a 560-kilometer journey inland to make it to the town of Foz do Iguaçu on the border of Brazil and Argentina. We were headed to see the biggest waterfalls in South America! We were stoked!

We rode hard for 500 straight kilometers through the prettiest mountain range and farmland I have ever seen! All of our bikes were jetted for sea level and hated crossing the higher elevation mountains. As we started to climb the mountains, they all started choking for air.

The first leg of the ride was super cold and windy, but as we got closer to Foz do Iguaçu, the weather started acting in our favor. As we came up over the mountains, my bike was struggling for air, which led to an over consumption of fuel, so I was almost completely out of gas.

When I thought I should be out of gas already, I bowed my helmet and said a silent prayer. *"Heavenly Father, thank you for letting us be on this awesome journey and please let us find a gas station before I run out of gas!"*

Just as my bike started sputtering, we rounded the corner and there it was: a tiny, one pump, dirt floor, gas station! I said another prayer of thanks while we fueled up our bikes and bodies.

We made it to the state of Paraná where we found smooth roads and blue skies. We also found another thing we hadn't anticipated on our trip: toll booths. We hadn't planned hundreds of dollars' worth of tolls into our budget!

We made it to Foz do Iguaçu right at sunset. We found a nice happenin' hostel that had good air conditioning and crashed straight out! We had just ridden a hard 350 miles for over ten hours. Such a long ride! I think my butt was paralyzed—or perma-numb! Time for some hiking, waterfalls, and a day or two of R&R!

We woke up refreshed after sleeping in a freezing cold room of heaven. It felt so good! We were soon on our motos and on the road! We set our course for Argentina but stopped along the way at the Three Frontiers, where the countries of Argentina, Paraguay, and Brazil all meet up. Then we crossed the river into Argentina.

We stopped in the middle of the bridge that separates Brazil and Argentina and took some awesome pictures. Nian almost got hit by a speeding car, so we saddled up and rode down into Argentina toward the waterfalls.

It was kind of expensive to get in. I convinced a guy that since we had Brazilian CPF identity cards, we should get to pay the local rate. All three of our passes, food, and drinks were less than one pass for an American would have cost us. We were always trying to hustle a deal!

The falls were absolutely incredible! I couldn't even describe how big they were. We jumped on a bridge and walked across to the Brazilian side of the river. It was almost a mile across! It felt good to go on a long walk after such a long day in the saddle.

After walking miles upon miles just to take pictures of a waterfall, we were all starving. We decided to splurge and eat at the park. We grabbed our food and sat down, and here came our new friends, the coatimundi.

In the Pursuit of Life

The coatimundi looked like weasley housecat raccoons, and they weren't shy. Ten or twenty of them surrounded our table and started begging for food. So we fed them, even though we weren't supposed to. Feeding one turned into a wild feeding frenzy! We grabbed our packs and got out real quick! There were signs everywhere saying that you're not supposed to feed them. The last thing we needed was to get in trouble in Argentina!

After all afternoon at the park, it got way too hot, so we grabbed our motos and cruised around Argentina for a while. We tried talking to cute girls, but that didn't go so well due to none of us speaking fluent Spanish. After getting shot down by the Argentine girls, we crossed the bridge back to Brazil.

It was early afternoon and we had a few hours to kill before dark. Why not stop by Paraguay?

We followed the river north for about ten miles and then crossed the Ponte de Amizade (the Friendship Bridge) into Paraguay. Unless you go there you'll never understand how crazy it is to ride across this bridge! It's unreal! There are two solid lanes of buses and cars, people walking everywhere, and two steady lanes of motorcycles weaving in and out of the madness! I ended up pointing the mirrors on my bike inward to avoid getting them broken on a car or bus! I had been riding motorbikes for almost twenty years and the five minutes it took us to get across that bridge easily earned the title of the craziest ride of my life!

I don't even know how to describe Paraguay. As you leave the most disorganized bridge crossing ever, there's no visa check station, no entry procedure, and the nice paved roads turn into a mixture of dirt, old crappy asphalt, giant pothole laden, smokey mess! As you cross the dusty mess, you pass through a line of mean-looking military police that are armed head to foot with shotguns, AR–15s, and pistols. I swear I saw one of them with a grenade.

I guess thousands of Brazilians go to Paraguay every day to buy cheap electronics, drugs, illegal cars, and other stuff. We went over for a while just to check it out. It almost seemed like there were no rules. Traffic circles were so crazy! It got dark fast, so we got the hell outta there!

After another wild bridge crossing, I told the guys to wait on the highway while I rode down by the river to take a picture of the sunset over the river. I cautiously took my camera out and made sure that there wasn't anyone around that could rob me.

I took a couple pictures, but I needed to change my camera to a low light setting to get the perfect shot. As I was messing with my camera, I had a distinct feeling come over me. Right then, the thought popped into my mind, *You need to get out of here! NOW!*

I knew that if I didn't get out of there, something bad was going down! God didn't want me there, and I immediately knew that! I had a crazy feeling there was something or someone after me. Everywhere you looked there was porn, drugs, hookers, and all around filth! The whole area around that bridge was completely evil. I stuffed my camera in my pocket, fired up my bike, and ripped up the hill as fast as I could to meet up with the guys.

We raced back to the hostel as fast as we could. We tried hanging out with the Europeans at the hostel, but we were beat. We turned the air conditioning as cold as it would go and slept like kings!

So, there we were the next morning, at the hostel packing up from our Iguaçu adventure. While eating breakfast, we overheard someone say that you could buy iPhones in Paraguay for fifty bucks! We were suckers for a sweet deal, so we saddled up and headed back over the Ponte de Amizade.

Again, we came face to face with what could be the eighth wonder of the world. Traffic was backed up for miles and miles before the bridge. Luckily, we had bought motorcycles, so we could evade such problems! As we were weaving in and out of traffic, hopping up on medians, cutting across lawns, and rubbing shoulders with other moto riders, we got separated. I cut around a bus. When I came around the other side, Dave and Nian were nowhere to be seen!

I rode around into the taxi drop-off lane and rode all the way up to the river. I tucked my ears back and rode up a super steep dirt hill and came to rest right at the start of the bridge. Traffic…evaded.

I raced through the madness on the bridge and waited on the Paraguay side for my guys. There were thousands of bikes passing in the middle of hundreds of cars and buses so the odds of me seeing them were slim. I waited there until all the fully armed police guys made me nervous.

I thought to myself, *Where would I go if I lost one of them?* It came to me instantly: the gas station where we had gotten gas and food yesterday! I raced over there as fast as I could, praying the whole way that they would be there in one piece. I pulled in just in time to see Dave run out the door with a huge smile, holding a cheap soda pop and some candy.

I rolled up and yelled, "HEY! What the heck bro? You guys left me in the heat of the battle! What happened?"

Dave calmly replied, "I took Brian off the freeway and down into a neighborhood where we flew down the street, to the frontage road, up the side grass hill and jumped back on the freeway right before the bridge, cutting in front of all the traffic! We cruised through the Brazilian checkpoint into what I can only describe as this: if you were to take two motocross races and line the hole shots up directly across from each other and then drop the gates! It was AWESOME! Imagine a four lane highway (same size as a two lane back in the good ol' U.S. of A.) with two rows of cars coming, two rows of cars going, extremely close to each other because in between the coming and going you have two lanes of motorcycles coming and going! We're flying down the middle, elbows tucked and clippin mirrors! We make it to the other side and a dude with an AR–15 pulls me over, asks me for some bike documents and identification. Once he saw the American flag flying proud on the back of my pack and confirmed that I was American, he saluted me and told me to have a good time! Then it was back to the races, cruisin' down the road with the throttle pinned. When you come up on a roundabout, there are no stop signs, no yield signs, it's every man for himself, hammer down, as fast as you can go, and praying for the best! You just get thrown into the mix and hope you come out in one piece on the other side. We made it through, and raced straight to this here gas station, bought a couple liters of cola, some snacks and such for $1.50, and now here you are!"

I just looked at him and grinned.

"You thought up that description the whole way over here didn't you?" I asked.

But it was funny because I would have said the exact same thing when trying to describe this place to people!

After hours of being hustled by little kids, and creepy guys trying to sell us drugs on dirty streets that were packed shoulder to shoulder with dirty people, we found out that the fifty dollar iPhone was a fake piece of junk! It literally looked like a kid's toy with Apple stickers on it. We were pissed!

Feeling defeated, we made the most of our trip and bought some cheap blankets. As we walked back to our bikes, a kid approached me selling 124 gig thumb drives for $5.00. I figured it was a scam, but I rolled the dice and bought one. The kid took my money and quickly disappeared. I opened my thumb drive only to find out that it was filled with hot glue! Darn kid got me!

Feeling more defeated, we got back on the hogs and fought the traffic back out of the filthy streets. I've never been offered to buy drugs and filth so much in my life. Peace out Paraguay!

We were already loaded up with all our gear, so after crossing the bridge back into Brazil, we rolled straight out! We were headed east for Curitiba and had to make 650 kilometers before nightfall. It was balls to the wall for the Wolfpack!

It was a beautiful sunny day, so we jumped on the freeway and rode hard for probably three or four hours. As we rolled through a small town, I looked back to discover that Dave was gone! Nian and I pulled over and devised a plan for our search party. I would wait on the side of the highway while Nian went back to look for Dave.

Half an hour later I was just about to give up hope. That was when Nian came back with the bad news.

He popped his helmet off and said, "Dude, we're going to have to haul if we want to make it to Curitiba before nightfall! Dave has a flat tire!"

We flipped around and backtracked until we found him pushing his bike along the freeway. We had a small emergency can of Fix-a-flat, which we were convinced was a rip off. Turns out, we didn't get ripped off! It saved our eternal bacon. I put the whole can of Fix-a-flat in Dave's soggy tire and told him to pin it until he got to the next little town.

Once there, we asked around until we found a little bike shop that was open. We wasted almost two hours working on Dave's tire and eating junk food. I also bought an insulated pop can holder and fashioned it to my handlebars.

Genius! I thought. *Why didn't I think of this sooner?* But as it turned out, trying to drink out of a can while riding a dirt bike at seventy miles per hour proved to be tricky, and I usually ended up with Coke Zero or energy drink all over my face!

Back on the road, we put the hammer down, stopping only for fuel for another three or four more hours. If we made killer time, we could still make it to Curitiba a little after dark!

It was on this stretch of road that Dave and I put down the sweetest, bike-to-bike candy pass of all time! I had a bag of M&M's that I was munching on. Dave did a hand signal saying that he wanted some. I floored it and got thirty or forty feet ahead of him. I let off the gas and held out the open bag of candy as far as I could. Dave hit the gas and came flying past me, simultaneously grabbing the candy and dumping some into his mouth, all done while riding at seventy miles per hour! We thought it was cool, and you would have, too, if you had seen it.

One of the most epic/scary mental pictures of my life was taken on this stretch of road. What I would have given for a helmet camera!

Picture this: the three of us are riding as fast as we can on two-lane roads somewhere in the mountainous farmlands of southern Brazil. We're making our way up one side of a huge mountain and we're almost to the top. There are thick pine trees on both sides of the road and there's a decent number of semi trucks fighting the same battle with gravity that we are. Our bikes are jetted for sea level and the air is extremely thin, so our motors are choking out like crazy. Dave and I are limping along while taking leaps of courage to pass the struggling semis. Right as our motors are about to blow up we can see the top of the mountain in sight. We look back to make sure Nian's okay. There's Nian, going as fast as he can right down the middle of the highway. He's laying his body as flat as possible on his bike in order to avoid any extra wind drag. Not more than five feet behind him is the first of a line of six monstrous, smoke-billowing, overloaded, semi trucks! Nian, a true motorbike legend, maintains perfect low wind drag form, and doesn't let them pass!

Dave and I both started laughing uncontrollably and slapped a huge high five while riding seventy kilometers per hour! What an epic moment! I would have given anything for a picture of Nian holding his ground against six semis!

We started down the other side of the mountain, and it was smooth sailing. I was stoked! Everyone could finally keep up with me, and we were making great time. As we rode down the ridgeline of the huge mountain, we caught a glimpse of an amazing sunset. Of course we stopped and lost another half an hour of daylight goofing off and taking pictures. It was worth it. We got back on the bikes and decided that It would be best if we found a nice place to stay an hour or two outside of Curitiba. Even if we rode super fast the whole way, we still weren't going to get there until almost 11:00 p.m.

As it was getting dark, we continued working our way down this mountain we had just crossed. I saw something going on in my rearview mirror. It looked like a strobe light. I slowed down and discovered it was Nian flashing his lights. He was freaking out about something. I pulled over, and he came flying up and made an uneasy stop!

I lifted up my helmet and said, "Dude, what now?"

He explained that his bike wasn't going very fast, and his throttle was acting kind of weird. I hopped off my bike and busted out my Leatherman multi-tool. In a few seconds, I had his throttle taken apart.

I held a frayed wire up to his face and said, "BOOM! Broken throttle cable! Now we're really jammed up."

I rigged Nian's cable directly to his carburetor. That way, once he got going, he could pull on the cable with his hand to give the bike gas. My GPS showed that there was a little town not too far off. We were back on the road.

I jumped on my bike and put my foot on Nian's passenger foot peg. I got going and pushed him along in front of me. Once we got to a decent speed I yelled, "Nian! Pull on the cable!"

He did and started along great. But who was I kidding? Nian was a BMX rider at heart. I kept forgetting that he'd never really been on a long motorcycle ride before. He was all over the place and doing his very best not to crash. I waved him over, and we traded bikes. I rode his busted, slow bike until we arrived in the tiny city of Laranjeiras do Sul thirty minutes later.

We parked in front of the local bar and ordered some pizzas. After filling our tummies with delicious Brazilian pizza, we asked around to see if anyone knew who owned the local moto parts store. It was Friday night in a small town. Any parts stores would definitely be closed, but we figured that someone would know the owner and that he would open up and help us.

What were the odds that we ran into the moto club president, who also happened to be really good friends with the parts store owner? Our new friend ran to find us a throttle cable while we fed pizza to the town drunk. Some forty-five minutes later, our buddy returned. He had five different throttle cables in his hand. What do you know? None of them fit Nian's bike!

By this point, I was getting a little upset. "Let's just call it a night," I said. I sent Nian and Dave out looking for a motel while I pulled out my Leatherman and worked on figuring out the broken throttle cable.

I asked all over for a piece of wire, and everyone turned me down. I was walking through the parking lot back toward our bikes and saw some wire laying on the ground. I pulled it out of the mud to see if it might work. It was a piece of wire from a burned tire. I kicked back some more mud and grabbed a bunch of the wire. I ran back over to the bikes and got busy working on a fix. Somehow, using this old burnt tire wire, I ended up lashing Nian's throttle cable back together. We were back in business!

Nian and Dave soon returned and reported that they had only found one place to stay: Motel Romantico. Which of course means "romantic whore house" in Portuguese. I wasn't stoked to stay there, but WHATEVER! I was tired and I didn't care. We got to the nasty motel and started unloading our gear.

Suddenly, a furious lady ran over to us yelling all sorts of nonsense. She was under the impression that there were only going to be two people sleeping there, Dave and Nian. She wanted me to pay for my own room. I rarely get upset, but I let this lady have it! She was being really stupid! I think she was just mad when she found out that Dave and Nian weren't gay lovers coming to stay in Motel Romantico.

Up until that point, my bike had been 100% awesome, no issues or problems. As we left Motel Romantico, I accidentally kicked my blinker off as I jumped on my bike in a fit of rage! We were still four or five hours from Curitiba. Awakened from our scuffel with the whore house attendant, we decided that we were good to keep riding for a little while. We hadn't been on the road for more than twenty minutes before mother nature decided to literally rain on our parade. Luckily it was light rain and it broke after it got the three of us sufficiently damp.

We rode for another hour or two. That was when our good idea to keep riding didn't seem so good anymore. I was cold and so tired

I was falling asleep at the handlebars! I dozed off once and that was enough! We saw a rest stop and decided setting up camp in a sketchy forest was better than falling asleep at the handlebars and dying.

We pulled into a small grove of trees in the middle of the rest stop. This was perfect. I believe Nian used the words, "Dude, this is Hammock Heaven!"

I parked my bike between two big trees and shined my light back and forth. "I like this spot, but I call I don't have to sleep by the biggest spider web and spider I've seen all trip!"

We all laughed and tried to find a way that we could hang our hammocks up in sort of a triangle. Our idea was to sort of "circle the wagons" and keep our bikes and gear inside the hammock triangle. We figured a robber would have a harder time wheeling our bikes away if he had to go through us first. I started tying up my hammock ropes when I saw Dave just out of the light from my headlamp.

"DUDE!" I yelled. "You're right where that killer big spider was!"

Dave slowly turned around. As our eyes focused in the weak light from the head lamp, we saw it! Dave had walked through that gigantic spider's web and now had the most pissed off, gnarly eight-legged, furry, ferocious beast of a spider on his chest, ready to take Dave's life for destroying his kingdom. Dave calmly looked down, slowly grabbed his bundle of rope, and brushed the monster of a creature to the ground. Let's just say Dave's five-inch wide size eleven skate shoes won that battle! No better way to cap off an awesome eventful day than a deathmatch with a monster spider in the middle of the night!

As we got ourselves all wrapped up in our new Paraguayan blankets, Dave said, "I shouldn't have killed him. I bet all of his spider friends and family saw the whole thing! We're screwed."

Suddenly I wasn't tired anymore. The thought of spiders revenging their king's death on me while I slept raced through my mind! I pulled the top of my hammock closed and prayed that we would be watched over by our guardian angels as we slept. The three amigos then rode their hammocks all the way to the lovely valleys of New Snoozerton.

6

WHITE MR. T AND THE CONCRETE ARK

Day 25
Saturday, February 20, 2010

We woke up with the sun beating down on our faces and flies bothering us like crazy! We rolled/fell out of our hammocks and found ourselves in what appeared to be some sort of nature park. I was shocked how good I had slept. We explored the park until we saw the giant sign that read, "The Garden of Gethsemane." That was honestly what this little rest stop nature garden was called! A little strange, but whatever! We all decided that it was a little too sacrilegious for our flavor, so we started packing up our camp.

I walked around until I found a bathroom. As I opened the door, I prayed, *please, please please!* Sure enough, a shower! Dave and I took awesome polar-ice-cap-freezing-cold showers. Nian went last. He got all soaped up and the water shut off on him! Dave and I had a great laugh! Nian was so pissed that Dave and I had used all the water.

Once two thirds of us were feeling pretty clean, it was back on the path to Curitiba! It took us longer than planned. We ended up rolling in there around noon. Once in town, we topped off our gas tanks, and I called my buddy Bernardo Lemos. He didn't answer, so

I plugged his address into my GPS, and we cruised over to his house. Once there, his landlord remembered me from when I had stayed there three weeks before. She let us in, and we parked our bikes in the yard.

As we were unloading our soggy gear, I glanced down at my odometer. We were almost up to 2000 kilometers already. That's over 1200 miles!

Tired from our travels, we all passed out in the heat on the floor in Lemos' house! We were so tired it wasn't even funny. By the time we woke up from our naps, it was almost dark. Lemos had just gotten home. We all packed up and headed out for some more amazing pizza. Back at Lemos' house, the food coma combined with the heat hit us hard. We sprawled out on the floor and passed out gain! I guess we weren't used to this riding all day and never sleeping thing.

Lemos woke us up early to get ready for church. We pulled on our scrubby, dirty, somewhat nice clothes and walked to church. By the time we got there, us three Americans were all soaked with sweat. I think we all said the phrase, "Isn't this why we bought bikes?" at least once. Church had already started when we walked in a couple minutes late.

It was an instant staring contest between Dave and every pretty girl in the place! I guess we looked somewhat out of place. Three white boys, two with long hair and the other with a goofy haircut.

About halfway through church, an older lady walked in and sat down next to us. It was my mission president's wife, Sister Pexotio! It was great to see her again. After church, she invited us to go to visit my Portuguese friends, who had been baptized while I was a missionary, and we set a time for later.

We all complained as we walked home from church and then complained again as we walked to lunch. Lemos was terrified of motorcycles. There was no way we could get him to ride with us. We couldn't ditch our host, so we dealt with it and walked.

Lemos took us to his favorite restaurant. It was another all-you-can-eat churrascaria. Once again, we all ate ourselves sick. After eating three days' worth of food, the hot walk back to Lemos' house was horrible. We napped out again and slept until a call from President Pexoito woke us up. He was on his way to pick us up for a family night with my Portuguese friends.

Dave, who served his mission in Portugal, instantly hit it off with them. Afterwards he said, "Their Portuguese accents were music to my ears. Took me back to my Portugal days."

After family night, President took us back to Lemos' house where we crashed out again! We couldn't seem to get caught up on our sleep! Side note, I was pretty sure we were going to be obese by the time our trip was over. Our diet pretty much consisted of gas station food, pizza, and all-you-can-eat restaurants.

The next morning, we finally woke up refreshed and ready to go. We had one more visit to make while in Curitiba, and then we were on the road! We said farewell to Lemos, packed up our bikes, and cruised over to my friend Caio Moreno's house.

Caio and I had met as missionaries five years earlier. I was excited to see him. When we got to his apartment, we found something else that we were excited about, more food! We chatted it up about what we needed to see and do at our next destination in São Paulo, ate a ton of delicious pancakes, and got on the road as quick as we could. We wanted to make it to São Paulo before nightfall. Curitiba was good to us. While we were there, we easily put on a few extra kilos and loosened up our belts a notch or two.

There we were again, the Wolfpack, back on the road! Every time we packed up and headed out, it was a great feeling. Unknown adventure around every bend! We rode nonstop for a few hours with the great city of São Paulo plugged in as our destination. The Wolfpack was coming up quick on São Paulo and making great time!

We pulled off for gas in a city called Jacupiranga. We all stopped on the road and looked up. Directly above us, we saw this giant sign that read, "Caverna do Diabo" (The Devil's Cave) with a big arrow pointing west. There wasn't even discussion as to if we were going or not. The only thing we worried about was finding headlamps and climbing rope for a great spelunking adventure.

After some asking around we stumbled into the local hardware store. We bought a bunch of gear for cave diving and a huge chain to lock our bikes together while we were in the cave. We were ready to roll! We took a quick left and headed northwest for about sixty miles!

That took us to a small town called Eldorado. We stopped for a bit to grab some adventure snacks and get more cave info from the locals, who gave us the skinny on huge waterfalls and caves all along the road to Caverna do Diabo. We were just about to ride toward one of the waterfalls when the heavens opened up and poured rain killer hard on us. We hunkered down in a gas station, suited up in our cheap rain gear, and kept on course for the waterfall and cave.

Before getting to the cave and about an hour before sunset, we saw a small, hand-written sign for Cachoeira Meu Deus (My God Waterfall), so we pulled back a barbed wire fence and started cruising down a dirt trail.

When I say trail, I mean trail. This was a legit mountain ride. I felt like I was riding my dirt bike in the mountains of Utah. We rode until the muddy little trail turned into a stream. Dave and I grabbed board shorts, and the three of us hiked about a mile up the stream and through the green Brazilian jungle. It was getting dark fast, but the sound of a roaring waterfall was calling our names. It was almost dark by the time we found it, and it was awesome! A one-hundred-and-sixty-foot waterfall crashing down right in the middle of the rainforest! So legit!

Dave tried to swim and get behind it, but it wasn't happening. Nian, who had been too lazy to dig out his swimsuit, jumped in in his underwear and also got denied by nature's powerful force! We were convinced that there was an awesome cave with tons of treasure behind the waterfall, but nightfall kept us from finding it.

We hiked as fast as we could back down the slippery trail toward our bikes. By the time we got to the bikes we were hiking by moonlight.

The spiders were out in full force, which left all of our faces covered with webs. Such a terrible feeling!

Dave's bike had tipped over in the mud while we were gone. Unfortunately, the visor on his helmet was broken beyond repair. We got on the bikes and headed down the trail toward the road. Dave soon found out that he was rolling flat tire number two for the trip! We busted out another can of Fix-a-flat and once again got him back up and rolling.

I rode ahead of Dave and Nian and ended up waiting for them at the bottom of the trail.

When they finally got there, I said, "What took you so long?"

"Well, did you see those cows back there?" Dave asked. "We stampeded that whole herd of cattle back down to the fence and barely avoided getting kicked by some jackass/burro that hates motorcycles!"

I just laughed, put the gate back up, and we all rode off. We rode for another hour until we came up on the town of Iporanga.

As we crossed a rickety old bridge and came into town, I lifted my helmet and yelled, "Hey! This place gives me the heebie jeebies!"

We rode through a thick cloud of fog and turned onto the main street of the little town. We slowly rode up toward the bars and stores that were still open. Once again, I voiced my concern about how weird the place was and how I didn't trust any one of the town drunks, who were all now watching us. That was when I looked over at Dave. All Dave was wearing was a pair of board shorts, water shoes, and ten feet of chain coiled around his neck with a huge padlock we had bought to lock our bikes up. All 220 pounds of Dave Kiley was looking pretty mean at that moment!

Dave fearlessly rode up to the first group of drunks and said, "Hey! Where's a good place three motorcyclists can camp for the night?"

A tall slender guy jumped up and ran over to us. He introduced himself as Lineus and then went on about how he was a "tourist guide" and that he was our "friend" and that he was there to "help us."

Once again I voiced my opinion. "Guys, there's a 79% chance

this guy kills us in our sleep and sells our organs in Paraguay. This feels like a super sketchy situation to me!"

Dave, with the huge chain still around his neck, and looking like the white Mr. T, didn't even flinch. We listened to Lineus's pitch about how he would help us find a campsite, watch over us while we slept, wake us up early for breakfast, help us fix Dave's flat tire, and guide us through all the craziest caves that most people would never be able to find. By this point we were all listening.

I was still a little sketched out about the whole camping by the river thing, but the idea of exploring hidden secret caves was screaming our names! All of this waterfall adventuring and craziness had us all feeling pretty hungry, so we sat down for a burger at a place that Lineus recommended. We held a Wolfpack council and came to the conclusion that we trusted this Lineus fellow. We finished our burgers and followed him to what he called a "safe campsite."

It was a small model of Noah's Ark made out of concrete right on the creepy river that we had crossed while riding into town. We parked our bikes inside the ark and hung our hammocks in the entrances.

Lineus continued telling us cave stories until we had our camp set up. As he walked away, he told us he would be at the top of the hill all night to watch over us. We laid in our hammocks and joked about getting mugged, and that was when it happened!

THUMP! My string busted and my hammock slammed to the earth! I was so pissed! There's nothing worse than getting body slammed when you're feeling relaxed and falling asleep. Nian and Dave both laughed hysterically. I tied my hammock back up with double ropes and crawled back in. After a few minutes it got quiet, and we all started drifting off to sleep.

Out of the darkness I heard some rustling and a loud THUMP followed by a slurry of swear words in Portuguese! I was sure we were getting mugged! I jumped out of my hammock ready for a brawl! Turned out, it was just Dave's hammock ropes coming untied and his hammock of solitude crashing down to the earth.

In the Pursuit of Life

We had another good laugh and tried our best to sleep through the loud drone of tree frogs and mosquitoes. I believe at one point someone asked if there was a car alarm going off. By that point, we were all dead tired, so we prayed that we wouldn't be killed in our sleep and then drifted off to Snoozetown.

Around 4:00 a.m. we were surprised to find out that we were sleeping in a ghetto farmyard. I woke up startled and ready to brawl again because there was something moving around by Dave. As my eyes focused in the misty darkness, I saw that it was just a damn donkey sniffing around Dave's stuff. I yelled and spooked it off but surprisingly didn't wake up Dave. He and Nian were two of the soundest sleepers I had ever met. I tried sleeping for a couple more hours, but it was useless. We were surrounded by what seemed to be millions of very ambitious roosters!

I wasn't exactly happy about it, but I mustered up some ambition, and around 6:00 a.m. I rolled out of my hammock ready for some serious cave spelunking. As the sun came up, our buddy Lineus came to wake us up and then showed us where we could get some breakfast. We scarfed down some sweet bread and candy and then he took us to a shop to get Dave's tire fixed. Once we got Dave's bike rolling, we were off to the caves!

Lineus decided to ride on back with Nian, which he quickly learned was a suicide mission! It was a wild ride for both of them! Old Nian held it together and just gave him a few good scares. We rode out of town and then half an hour up dirt roads into the jungle. Most of the road was washed out due to record-setting rainfalls. Why we decided to go on a random cross-country motorcycle trip during record rainfalls, I will never know.

After Nian scared the living shart out of Lineus, we finally showed up at the Ouro Grosso Caves. We donned spelunking helmets while Lineus gave us a quick crash course into cave diving. He told us to put on jeans for safety's sake, and that was pretty much it for the safety course.

A short fifteen-minute hike and we were deep within the earth. Caverna Ouro Grosso was awesome! It was literally a small hole in the ground in the middle of the jungle, which opened up into a mile-long cave. We would have never known about it if our buddy Lineus hadn't taken us there.

We hiked/climbed up a river inside the cave for more than an hour. We finally came to a waterfall that we couldn't get up since we didn't have ropes or harnesses. Next time, we for sure weren't going to forget our ropes and harnesses. There was still another 1200 meters of cave that we didn't even explore.

We left the Ouro Grosso Cave and went over to the Caverna do Diabo. The four of us hiked around in it, but it was a nature hike compared to the last cave. Lineus then took us up to one more cave. It was cool but it reeked bad from all the bat guano. There weren't any crazy climbs or waterfalls, so we were soon bored and wanted to see more. Almost the second we walked out of that cave, the skies opened up and poured down drowning rain. We found a pavilion where we could wait out the rain, but it didn't stop forever. We showered up and situated our packs. We were all so stoked for the last big cave. Lineus had been raving about it all day. It was the Caverna Casa de Pedra (The House of Rock Cave).

Our excitement was crushed when we found out that our cave diving/spelunking adventures had suddenly come to an end. Lineus said it had rained too much for us to go into the Caverna Casa de Pedra. The Caverna Casa de Pedra has the biggest cave opening in the world and has a steady river flowing through it. If the water inside the cave is too high you can get trapped and die in there, as many have done. The cave is almost two kilometers long and drops over one hundred meters over its length. You enter at the top and come out on the other side of the mountain. We were all still game to do it, but Lineus told us that it was a terrible idea.

We each gave Lineus $10.00 for his guiding services, thanked him for showing us a great adventure, and dropped him off at a bus stop. It was time to let our horses run back toward São Paulo. All rain geared up, we rode off into the clouds.

After riding through the mountains and muddy roads for a couple hours, we stopped to spray the mud off our bikes, fill up with gas, and get goodies in the small town of Apiai. Then we took an awesome mountain road full of curves and fun/dangerous semi truck passes toward São Paulo. It finally quit raining just as the sun was going down. After three or four hours of solid hardcore riding we were almost in the outskirts of São Paulo. We stopped at a bar for some food and met a drunk guy that sang/mumbled a whole Beatles song without a word of either English or Portuguese!

We were all ready to call it a night around there somewhere, but we couldn't find the hotel or a campsite anywhere! According to my GPS, we were only seventy kilometers from São Paulo, so we pushed on into the night. Probably not the smartest idea, but off we went!

Upon arrival in one of the biggest cities in the world, we got some gas and asked some cops where we could find a good place to stay or camp. They advised against camping out and said we should get a hotel near my friend Guisti's house.

Once again, here came the rain. We pushed onward in the rain for another three hours looking for a hotel that would let three people sleep in one room. It was impossible. Every hotel we tried wanted to charge us a fortune. We were all mad, tired, and wet.

Finally, around 3:00 in the morning, we found a place. I went in and told the attendant I wanted the cheapest room possible. We parked our bikes in the garage and we ran our stuff up to the room. Turned out, we had gotten ourselves into a brothel-like motel, where you can get rooms by the hour. Let's just say there's a big difference between a motel and a hotel in Brazil. This place was really gross.

As I prepared to spend the night, sleeping in my rain gear, due to the nastiness of the place, the security guard showed up at our door and demanded that I go down to the front desk. I went down tired, wet, and upset. The attendant wanted me to pay for another room, saying that three of us couldn't stay there. I gave her a piece of my mind, but she called my bluff on the Wolfpack absolutely NOT leaving at 4:00 a.m.

Needless to say, I got my money back, we grabbed our gear, and headed back out on the streets. We rode aimlessly as it was kind of pointless to get a room at that time of day. All of a sudden, I recognized the hood we were in, Praca do Se. My buddy had shown me a picture and told me that it was one of the most dangerous areas in all of São Paulo. There we were, three white boys, riding around on big wheels at 4:30 in the morning! Way crazy!

We stopped on a street corner and bought at least fifty shots of hot cocoa that a lady was selling to people that were starting to go to work. We decided that it was a bad idea to lay down and sleep in the homeless park, so we pushed on to my buddy Guisti's house where I had stayed when I had first arrived in São Paulo exactly a month before. We made it to Guisti's dad's house around 5:00 a.m. The sun was starting to show a faint glow on the skyscraper skyline. We pulled onto the sidewalk and leaned our bikes up on the wall outside of his house. We decided that we could wait until a respectable hour, like 7:00 a.m., before knocking on the door. Within seconds we were all leaning our heads on the wall. A few seconds later, and the three of us were fast asleep, sitting on our bikes with our helmets on!

7

BRAZILIANS DON'T TRUST US WITH THEIR DAUGHTERS

Day 29
Wednesday, February 24, 2010

We had been asleep on our bikes for maybe an hour when I heard someone yell in English, "HEY YOU! HEY YOU! HEY YOU!" I jumped off my bike ready for an altercation! The person yelled again. "HEY YOU! HEY YOU!" A few seconds later, the person I was prepared to battle for my life with walked around the corner!

It was a nice old man looking for his lost dog—looking for his lost dog named HEY YOU! I couldn't believe it. The old man had woken Dave and me up, but Nian seemed to have slept through the whole thing. We were so tired that we didn't care if we got robbed, mugged, or killed. I wanted more than anything to get my body horizontal. Completely numb and bent out of shape, Dave and I got off our bikes, laid down on the sidewalk, and slept like hobos for another hour and a half (helmets still on and everything).

"Elder? Elder? I'm looking for an American Elder."

It was my buddy Guisti's sweet mom waking us up, calling us by the title we had gone by as missionaries. I looked down at the clock on my bike. It was 7:30 in the morning! We had just survived sleeping on the side of the road in a super dangerous city!

Gusti's mom invited us into their house. I don't really remember what was said. I was so tired. Everything was fuzzy. All I remember was Guisti's dad telling us that we couldn't stay there because his married daughter was there for a few days because her husband was out of town. I told him we just wanted to please take a nap, which he was fine with. They forced us to shower, of course. Weird, I thought we smelled great after days of camping and non-stop freeway riding in the rain. Our soggy shoes needed to be burned! They were downright gross at that point.

We took our naps, which turned into the three of us waking up at 3:00 p.m.! It felt great to sleep in a bed again! We just chilled with Gusti's family and washed clothes for the rest of the day. It was pretty awesome! Brother Guisti cooked up a super delicious churrasco dinner!

After dinner, Nian found an address for a kid that he had baptized on his mission in Manaus, Brazil. He was currently serving a mission in São Paulo just north of where we were. The three of us jumped on our bikes and set out to surprise him. After more night riding and rain riding through sketchy parts of town, we were unable to find the missionaries' house. Fortunately, Nian had written down a phone number, but when he called, it was brother Guisti's cell number! Nian and Dave argued about whose fault it was that he had the wrong number.

We rode back to the Guisti residence and in the end, Brother Guisti did end up inviting us to sleep at his place. By sleep at his place, I mean he locked us in his garage where we slept on small cushions on the floor. We weren't mad at all. It was dark, cool, and we got to keep an eye on our bikes all night. Brazilian people really don't trust us around their daughters. I wonder why.

Injury Report:

All previous injuries: healed

Nian: millions of flea bites

Whole Team: lots of bug bites, rashes, and soggy feet.

We got on the streets early in the morning in search of the missionary Nian had baptized. Massive confusion led to more investigation. After some serious research, we finally found out that Nian's buddy was serving in a different city about an hour north of where we were. We jumped on the crazy, congested, eight-lane freeway and weaved in and out of traffic until we got there. We finally met up with Nian's buddy at his house and then took him and his missionary buddies out to lunch. After lunch guess what happened? It started raining!

We geared up again and made the crazy ride through traffic back to the Guisti's house. It was time to get back on the road. We said a sad goodbye to our good friends, the Gusitis. They were so great to us! They fed us, washed our clothes, and basically treated us like family. Such amazing people!

Once we were all geared up, we set our course for South São Paulo where Dave's mission president, President Amorim, lived.

Nian and Dave decided to go all Nascar through the traffic. A car cut me off as I tried to follow them, and I got left behind. Lucky for me, I had my GPS with the address to President Amorim's house plugged into it. Even with my GPS guidance, it still took me a couple hours to find the place.

Dave had told us that President Amorim was pretty well off. As I pulled into his neighborhood, I could see what Dave was talking about. My surroundings were suddenly transformed from a dirty, congested, concrete jungle to a very pleasant gated community that looked more like a botanical garden than a neighborhood. After some persuasion, I talked the heavily armed guards into letting me into the gated community. I circled around the beautiful streets and sure enough, there were Dave and Nian. I was convinced they would be lost for a day or two, but to my surprise, they beat me there!

President Amorim's gated community kind of reminded me of a wealthy Florida subdivision. His house and neighborhood were unbelievably beautiful. All the houses were huge, everyone drove awesome cars, and there were armed security guards everywhere. I even saw a gardener trimming the grass along the sidewalk with a pair of scissors! I´d live there in a second! We had pizza with his family, got showered up, and told stories with President Amorim for a couple hours. We all fell asleep on his couch, and it was game over for the rest of the night!

Day 31
Friday, February 26, 2010

"Good morning" someone whispered. We rubbed our eyes and learned that the maid had woken us up for breakfast.

Breakfast was a beautiful spread of fresh fruit and cinnamon roll type bread. We cleaned up really quick and it was time to ride! With our packs tied to the racks on the back of our bikes, we were ready for the road again! Rio de Janeiro was our destination goal by nightfall.

As we were leaving, we casually mentioned to President Amorim that we were just going to find a place to camp in our hammocks when we got to Rio. He freaked out!

"Boys, if the gangsters and robbers don't kill you, the snakes and spiders will! I won't allow you to camp out around Rio! My brother lives there. He has a nice house that you will stay in. Promise me you will stay there and won't camp out!"

The three of us promised to accept his offer of a nice place to stay. President Amorim gave us his brother's cell phone number and told us to call him when we arrived in Rio. We thanked President Amorim for his hospitality and the Wolfpack made tracks!

We had been riding toward Rio for a few hours when I realized that I hadn't seen Dave for a while. Nian and I pulled over and waited on the roadside. No Dave. The two of us decided to keep on course. We figured Dave would eventually find a payphone where he could call me on my cell phone. After a couple hours, he finally called. He had missed a turn and ended up riding up into the mountains where he finally ended up in the city Campos de Jordao. He was easily three or four hours behind us. It was getting late. There was no way we could make it all the way to Rio before dark.

I pulled out my GPS and picked a town between our current location and Rio de Janeiro. Nian and I were about three hours south of the beach town Angra dos Reis which was three hours south of Rio. I told Dave we would stop and stay at the first hotel in Angra dos Reis and that he should meet us there. If for some reason we weren't there, find a payphone and call my cell.

Nian and I jumped back on the highway and headed northeast as fast as we could. Just as it was getting dark, my GPS took us on a shortcut which ended up being a dirt road into the middle of nowhere! It felt like we were riding up a mountain canyon road in Utah. We were maybe a half an hour down this back-road shortcut when the ultimate wrath of all rain storms unleashed its fury upon us!

We slammed on the brakes and threw on our rain gear as fast as we could! We saddled back up and coasted along at maybe ten miles per hour while using our left hands like window wipers to get the rain off of our helmet visors. We were all rain geared up, grocery bags on our feet and everything, but it didn't matter! I was completely soaked from head to foot! After two more hours of rainy, windy, muddy, mountain roads we made it to Angra dos Reis.

Nian and I grabbed some grub and called President Amorim's brother in Rio to let him know we weren't going to make it to his place that night. He gave us a destination address for when we arrived and made us promise that we'd stay in a hotel.

I was pretty irritated from all the rain and tiredness. We were sitting in a parking lot trying to figure out our situation when suddenly my bike tipped over, smashing my mirrors and scattering gear everywhere! I lost my temper and snapped on Nian. He gave me a sad puppy dog face, which made me immediately ask for forgiveness.

We found a nice little hotel right by the water, took a hot shower, and spread all of our soggy gear out to dry.

I looked at Nian and asked, "Where is Dave and why isn't that fool calling us?"

We were in the first real hotel you came to in the town, so hopefully he'd find us! We hoped for the best and tried to stay awake in case he showed up or called. Exhaustion overtook us and we both fell asleep with the lights on while sitting up waiting for him.

When we woke up in the morning, Dave was there! I thought he was a goner for good. I guess he had fought the same drowning rainstorm that Nian and I had battled. Somehow, he found the little hotel in the middle of the night and talked the attendant into giving him our room key. We were happy to see him!

I'm not gonna lie, our room smelled exactly like a cheap zoo on a hot day! All the wet gear and soggy shoes made the room super rancid!

We ate an unbelievable free breakfast at the hotel and went on one of the prettiest rides ever though landslide central. Record rains were causing landslides everywhere! After a nice morning of adventure, we showered up and hit the road toward RIO!

The highway between Angra dos Reis and Rio was absolutely gorgeous. We weren't making good time at all because we kept stopping to take pictures. We also stopped at Ilha Grande (Big Island) on the way there. We debated getting a boat out there but we decided that it was too expensive. We contemplated putting our gear in trash bags, filling them with air, and swimming out there, but that was an all-around bad idea!

As we rolled into Rio de Janeiro, our lifestyle changed dramatically! I had President Amorim's brother's address plugged into my GPS. It took us right to the middle of Itapema Beach, which is one of the fanciest, most expensive beaches in all of Brazil.

I said, "There's got to be some sort of mistake. There's no way he lives here."

We found the exact address and rang the doorbell. A man with an extremely deep voice answered on an intercom.

"Who is it?" he said.

"We're the Americans your brother sent."

The deep-voiced man came back on the intercom. "Wait there. I will come escort you in."

He came down, let us in the gate, and showed us where to park our bikes in their underground, guarded, garage. We grabbed our gear off of our bikes and crammed into an elevator with him.

The second we walked into his house he stopped us and said in this thundering voice, "Lets go over the rules, boys! Rule number one: Take a shower! IMMEDIATELY! Rule number two: make your beds when you get up in the morning! Rule number three, don't go down to the beach alone. The gays might try to kidnap you. That is all."

We agreed to obey his rules as we walked through his apartment in shock! We went from being bums who camped on the beach in hammocks to staying in an awesome penthouse overlooking one of Rio's most beautiful beaches. Manuel Amorim, the owner of the penthouse, his wife Marcia, and the maid Carmen treated us like kings! After getting to know them for a minute, we wasted no time obeying rule number one.

Shower time! This shower was easily one of the nicest I had ever seen. The whole thing was made from Brazilian Cherry hardwood and had a giant shower head that almost drowned us! We washed some clothes and took some very refreshing naps!

Night one in Rio, we were about to call it a night around midnight, but recharged from my power nap, I decided that I wasn't tired. I talked the guys into going out to check out the city with me. I had met a guy on the plane a few weeks earlier who had told me if I ever went to Rio I had to check out this place called Lapa! Apparently it was the happening place.

I punched LAPA into my GPS. The GPS processed my search and showed that there were two streets named Lapa in Rio. Hmmm… We took a wild guess as to which one was the right one and followed my GPS guidance for the next thirty minutes. Just as we were about to arrive at our gambled-on destination in the outskirts of town, we discovered that we had guessed wrong. We were riding into a giant *favella*, which is a Brazilian ghetto!

As we pulled up to the address the GPS took us to, there were five dudes sitting on the sidewalk smoking crack. We were definitely on the wrong side of town at the wrong time of day! We were about to ride out when we heard loud concert music. We stopped, and rode around the block, where we found out that the neighborhood was having a huge concert/party all night. We parked our bikes by some cop cars and partied in the ghetto and watched the concert until it got over. We were all getting creepy feelings from the place so we loaded up and rode back toward town.

Around 2:30 in the morning we found the actual Lapa Street that we were looking for. We went into a sports bar to enjoy some Guaraná. They were showing the UFC fights, so we sat and watched the fights until 3:00 or 4:00 in the morning. Famous Dave fell asleep at the table in our restaurant. That was our cue. We called it a successful day and went back to Manuel Amorim's penthouse for the night.

Day 33
Sunday, February 28, 2010

The next day was Sunday, so of course we got some good church time in. After church, we jumped on our bikes and went to the famous hill/rock/cable car, Pão de Açucar (Sugarloaf Rock). We rode a cable car up to the top, and Nian played with some monkey things. We took a bunch of pictures and realized that this wasn't our kind of adventure. Way too many tourists for us! While we were there, it started raining and didn't quit. The relentless rain really put a damper on the rest of our day. We called it an early night and got caught up on some much needed laundry and sleep.

Day 34
Monday, March 1, 2010

We woke up the next morning refreshed and ready to roll! There were two things we really wanted to see and do while we were in Rio: visit the giant Cristo statue and hang glide off of the Gaieta Rock! We finished our breakfast and looked outside. Blue Skies! It had finally stopped raining!

We obeyed rule number two and made our beds, then grabbed our bikes and got ready to roll. Just as we were leaving, Manuel's personal security guard, Francisco, stopped us. He told us that the Amorims had called him to come take us around the city and to ensure that we were safe.

First, we headed to Rociha, easily one of Brazil's most dangerous and famous ghettos. Francisco wouldn't even let us get out of the car. We took some pictures on the move and headed up to Gaieta Rock in search of a place to go hang gliding. The second we got there, it started pouring rain. We had a counsel amongst the Wolfpack and decided that we weren't meant to hang glide.

On our way back to the Amorim's house, we asked Francisco if he knew of a good place to get gear and extra parts for motorbikes. He said he knew of the best place in town to get cheap stuff, and the four of us headed that way. We had to wait in a line in the rain for nearly half an hour to even get in the store. This place was like the soup Nazi of moto gear! You step up, tell the guy what you want, then move to the side to pay and get your stuff. The three of us basically emptied our pockets and loaded up with gear! We all got new rain gear, yellow glasses for night riding, rubber boots, and a bunch of other odds and ends that we had broken or might break along the way.

When we were all geared up, Francisco took us back to the Amorim's place where we were greeted with a bomb lunch! The second the rain broke we were on the road, ready for our ride up to the Cristo statue!

The GPS took us through some pretty sketchy ghettos, but we were soon riding through the clouds and fast approaching the giant statue of Christ. We parked our bikes and ran all the way up to the statue! Once at the top, we were again struck with disappointment! Half the statue was covered with scaffolding and being prepared for renovation.

We fought our way through waves of tourists and managed to take a couple pictures. On our way back down, we took our time and had fun taking more pictures.

It started clouding up again, so we raced back to the Amorim's! We ate some grub and headed out on foot to kill some time. We walked up the beach and made our way over to a monstrous mall in search of a bowl of acai. We found our favorite snack and then walked in the rain back to Amorim's penthouse.

We were all extremely sick of the rain! We were watching the news that night and found out that a lot of Rio de Janeiro had been flooded and that there were landslides covering up roads everywhere! We all looked at each other and decided that we had seen enough of Rio de Janeiro for the time being. The last thing we wanted was to get clapped up in a natural disaster! We washed the last of our dirty clothes and got our packs ready for the open road. Hopefully we could ride our way out of this wet madness! If we couldn't, at least we now had nice rain gear and rubber boots to make the rain riding less miserable!

Day 35
Tuesday, March 2, 2010

We woke up in the morning and ran over to the balcony. We had been in Rio for almost four days, and we were all feeling the itch to get back on our bikes! The weather had finally cleared up! We said our goodbyes to the Amorim family and ran down to the garage.

Soon we had our bags wrapped in plastic and tied onto our bikes. On the road again! But the second we crossed the bridge leaving Rio, the rain showed its evil face and wailed on us! We stopped and wrapped ourselves in our shiny new rain gear thinking we had finally dodged a bullet. False! For the next six hours straight we endured the ultimate beat down from the heavens! I had the small beach town of Guarapari plugged into the GPS and was hell bent on getting there. It rained and rained and rained. Before we knew it, we were almost nine hours into the 500-kilometer ride that was only supposed to take us six hours. We were all wet, tired, and mad!

Just after sundown, we hit the mother of all traffic jams. We were on a two-lane highway that was completely stopped. We only waited for a second before we started weaving our way up to the front, where we saw a terrible sight: an overturned semi tangled up with a small car. There on the road, we saw our first dead bodies of the trip. As we rode past the gruesome scene, we all held a small moment of prayer in our hearts for the deceased and their families. I'd be lying if I said I didn't pray that we wouldn't die while on our travels as well!

As we rode away from the carnage, I had a terribly uncomfortable feeling. These feelings, which had become familiar, made me nervous. I slowed way down and focused on seeing through the rain while staying a safe distance from the truck ahead of me. Unless you've ridden in the rain at night, you'll never know how hard it is to see. Especially when every twenty seconds, you're passing a semi truck headed the other direction.

All of a sudden, the heavy rainstorm we had been riding in for hours, turned into the ultimate monsoon! I had on yellow dishwashing rubber gloves and was using them like windshield wipers to get the rain off of my visor. And remember, poor Dave had been visorless since his bike had tipped over on his helmet while we were hiking the Meu Deus Waterfall.

I guess Dave was getting frustrated with how slow I was going. He raced past me, and Nian followed right behind him. Road conditions turned from bad to worse. There were huge bumps and potholes everywhere. We were following a big semi truck which produced a blinding wall of rainwater spray. That made seeing the road even harder! Dave was right behind the semi. Suddenly the semi jerked to the left! I saw Dave's taillight go four feet in the air and then disappear. Nian's taillight also disappeared. I struggled to see what happened but a split second later, I was in the same mess!

The road had swerved hard to the left. I hit a small curb and took air! I ducked and just missed smashing my head on a road sign. Luckily, I landed back on the road and came to a screeching halt. I threw off my helmet and frantically looked for Dave and Nian. Down a grassy hill I saw Dave standing by his upside-down bike.

I yelled, "DAVE! You alright?"

"I'm okay!" he called back, and we both started yelling for Nian.

Out of the dark, we heard his voice. "Awww, crap!"

I ran down through the grass to find Nian lying next to his bike just behind a guard rail. We got him stood up and calmed down, and made sure he was okay. It scared me to death, because if something were to happen to Dave or Nian, I would have held myself completely responsible.

Turned out, the semi we were following had blinded Dave for a split second. He went off the road, hit a curb, and launched into a grassy median. Nian hadn't really been watching the road—he had just been following Dave's taillight. After Dave had wiped out, Nian was right behind him. Nian's front tire hit the guard rail, but somehow he whipped around and his bike came to rest softly in the grassy mud on the opposite side from where he had hit.

We were all pretty shook up. Once we got Dave and Nian back up on the road, we cautiously coasted to the first gas station we could find. We parked under the gas station canopy to get out of the rain. It also gave us a good chance to look our bikes over and to hold a small Wolfpack meeting.

Nian and Dave wanted to tie up our hammocks there at the gas station, but I really wanted to get to a hotel before we called it a night. It was only another thirty minutes away, the rain had almost stopped, and the area around the gas station was way sketchy. After some intense convincing, I talked the guys into riding another fifty kilometers to the next beach town.

Once there, we all felt way better! We found a super cheap place and woke up an old lady that let us in. We had been on our bikes in torrential downpours for more than twelve hours; we were very tired boys. The nice old lady let us stow our bikes in her garage. Once our bikes were secure, we dragged ourselves up the stairs to our room. Dave laid down in his soaked clothes and rain gear and fell immediately asleep. Nian and I took some quick warm showers and passed right out, but only after saying our prayers and thanking the good Lord that we were all still alive, of course!

8

THE VOLCANO

Day 36
Wednesday, March 3, 2010

The smell of swamp mud woke me up. Well, I wished it was swamp mud I was smelling and not our gear. I couldn't stay in there with that smell, so I snuck out and went for a jog while Dave and Nian slept. I ran down to the beach, got a Coke, and relaxed for a bit. After hanging out for a couple hours, I ran back and woke up the boys.

We got some breakfast and assessed the damage. By some sort of miracle nothing was broken. The only bad thing was that all of our freshly washed clothes were now soaked! It was a nice sunshiny day, so we decided that we would get as much distance behind us as we could.

With blue skies, we were rolling hot on our journey to the city of Salvador. But what do you know, after a few short hours on the road, the dreaded rain came again. We put our heads down for a while and pushed through it, but finally, it hit so hard we couldn't go anymore.

We stopped and sheltered up at a truck stop to let the downpour pass over. We hung out with the locals and ate some food. As we waited, the downpour turned into a full-blown monsoon! After holding another Wolfpack counsel, we decided that we had learned our lesson about night riding in the rain. The truck stop had showers, so we got cleaned up and ready for bed. The toilets in this joint were pretty crazy. They were just a piece of porcelain that had traction bumps on it so you could squat on it and poop through a hole. That was interesting.

I bought the guys a round of hot chocolates, and we hung up our hammocks. Dave asked our new friend, the gas station attendant, if he would keep an eye on us during the night. The last thing we needed was to get jumped while we were sleeping! We joked for a minute and listened to the drone of tree frogs as we hung there under the store's wraparound porch and called it a night.

Somehow we all slept great! Like every morning when we camped out, we woke around 4:30 a.m., this time to the sound of 10,000 roosters! Sleeping in was never an option.

Weatherwise, this seemed to be one of the best days for travel so far. We were feeling great and ready to put some distance behind us! Once on the road, we were lovin' it! We took our shirts off, put our headphones in, and enjoyed our nice ride through the Brazilian countryside. We were making great time, but sure, enough there was always some kind of problem to slow us down.

We had been riding for four hours without stopping, and we were all pretty low on gas. My GPS showed a small town about twenty-five kilometers up ahead. I had been on reserve for ten kilometers already, so I was starting to get nervous about running out of gas. I cruised ahead of the guys in search of gas. I raced around a corner and saw a couple cops. Shirtless, I stood up, saluted, and blazed right past them! They both had really confused looks on their faces and just watched me blast by.

A few minutes later, Nian and Dave came cruising along together. When they came around the corner, the two cops were standing in the middle of the road waving for them to stop. The cops can stop you for no reason there. The boys pulled over to see what they wanted. The cops wanted to see their bike documents, passports, and other paperwork. The tough-guy cop told them that they couldn't drive without a Brazilian driver's license. Then he gave them a spill on how they were going to confiscate their bikes and a bunch of other bullcrap.

The boys stood their ground and talked their way out of a bad situation. After almost an hour of intense discussion, the cool cop brought back their documents from the car and told them that they were good to go. Tough cop was wrong, and we were legit.

During this whole confrontation, I had continued up the highway looking for a gas station. I was so close to empty, it wasn't even funny. I was putting up hills and then cutting my motor to coast on the down hills. I was praying I'd make it to a gas station! Almost twenty minutes later, I sputtered up to a gas station. I filled up my bike and set up shop at a roadside acai shop while I waited for the guys. I had managed to evade the cops, but I suffered the wrath of an intense sunburn while waiting for Dave and Nian. We gassed up their bikes and pushed on.

We rode for a few hours until we were suddenly smashed by a microburst of rain. We stopped under an overpass and got our rain gear on (except for Dave, who had ripped his rain gear while getting laid out and rolling through the grassy field a few nights before). The Wolfpack was drenched, even with our gear on, and Dave was getting worked over with no gear on. I had all my rain gear on, and it seriously felt like I was getting sand blasted by small marbles!

We pushed through the rain and the pain. I looked back, and the boys were nowhere to be seen. I backtracked and found them in a gas station hiding from the rain. We fueled up, dumped the rainwater out of our rubber boots and ate more unhealthy gas station food. I got bored and struck up a conversation with a trucker. Somewhere along this chat with my new friend, I noticed a map of the state on the wall.

I pointed at the map and asked, "Hey where should we visit around Salvador before we leave?"

Without hesitating he yelled, "You have got to go to Morro de São Paulo! It's an island forty-five minutes off the coast that is a nonstop party every day!"

Turned out, going that route would save us 150 kilometers on our journey as well. It was decided. Once the rain slowed up a little, we took his advice and headed out with our sights on going to Morro de São Paulo. We continued our journey until late in the night. At some point along our rainless night ride, we turned back and realized Dave had turned up missing again. Nian and I hung out for a cool thirty minutes until we decided to go back and search for him.

Dave's sprocket was completely rounded off. We gave him a push start and limped his bike to the city of Valença. The whole city had a sketchy, fish smelly feel about it. We grabbed some grub and found another cheap place to stay for the night (this one wasn't as nice as the last one). We got in our room, killed all the cockroaches we could find, and then fought over the top bunk. We got all our wet stuff spread out to dry and started drifting off to sleep.

Nian started shifting around on the bottom bunk. I heard a loud CRACK, and then I came crashing down! My bunk had broken and landed on Nian! We all had a good laugh, fixed it, and got back to bed.

After spending the night in the roach-infested dive in Valença, we put our bikes under a guarded shelter and jumped on a 7:00 a.m. party barge headed for the island of Morro de São Paulo. Paradise Island here we come!

A short forty-five minutes later, we were there! After fighting with the locals about paying their ridiculous "port tax," we were soon on the beach. We had endured a lot over the past few days, and it was time to take a serious break! We found a cheap place to sleep and ditch our bags, threw on some board shorts, and hit the beach.

I believe Dave's description of this magical moment went something like this:

"Now close your eyes and imagine this: you're laying in your hammock, tied up between two palm trees on the point of an exotic island—sun shining, blue sky—and you're just basking in the shade of the palm trees. You get up and walk into the blue ocean—perfect temperature, little fish swimming through your legs. You walk up the white sandy beach, get yourself a big bowl of acaí with honey and strawberries and head back to your hammock. You look down, and you are wearing nothing but a cut-off Jesus T-shirt and a pair of swim trunks, and then you realize, *Hey, I'm Dave Kiley and I'm living the dream!*"

The Wolfpack took it super easy for a few hours. The only thing on our minds was hammocks and happiness! We all kind of did our own thing for a few hours and just relaxed. As it started getting late, I found Dave and Nian. They were talking to a pothead who was carving faces into palm roots while selling dope at the same time.

I asked the boys, "Hey, have you had like ten people invite you guys to a party tonight and then offer you crack or sex?"

They looked at me funny and nodded their heads.

I laughed and said, "Dude, this place is beautiful, but it's evil as all get out!"

We watched the sun set and headed back to the room to get ready to go to the beach party that all the locals had been inviting us to attend. All showered up, we still had almost an hour before the party was supposed to start. We cranked the A/C in our room all the way up and were soon fast asleep!

I woke up at 2:30 in the morning and realized that we had missed the party! I ran down to the beach and sure enough, the party was still bumpin'! I grabbed a couple Cokes and hung out with a rowdy crowd until the sun started coming up! As the party crowd dispersed, the drug dealers and hookers moved in. They were everywhere. I turned down easily thirty or forty solicitations for drugs and sex. It was really gross.

I sat my butt in the sand and took pictures of the sunrise until almost 8:00 a.m. That's when I heard a shrill yell from someone running down the beach!

It was Dave yelling, "Nooooo! I missed the party!"

We kicked it for a bit, woke Nian up, and the three of us went for a nice run on the beach. Once we finished our good workout, we grabbed another bowl of delicious acaí and showered up. I was kind of tired from the all-night dance party, so I turned the A/C in our room down to ice box mode and took a quick nap. I woke up six hours later completely confused. Had I really slept all day? I guess I was a tired fellow.

I wandered around the island for a couple hours looking for the rest of the Wolfpack. I finally found them in the ghetto looking for somebody that could put their hair into cornrows. The Wolfpack hit the beach for the next few hours. We were finally just relaxing, and it felt great! We made friends and fooled around until it was almost dark.

A group of girls ran up to us and asked, "Aren't you guys going to the Sunset of the Bats party?"

We had no idea what they were talking about, but we were soon following them up a monstrous hill on the north side of the island! I guess we were going to a pre-party where everyone gets wasted and watches thousands of huge bats fly off into the sunset. We were only a couple hundred yards from the top of the hill when God changed our plans. It suddenly clouded up, and within a minute or two, we were surrounded by thunder and lightning! A couple minutes later, it was an absolute downpour! Rain wouldn't leave us alone!

We rounded up the girls and ran back down the hill to a restaurant. What was probably going to be us watching tons of people get wasted turned into a nice group dinner date. Half the girls were from Argentina and spoke English; the others were Brazilian. It monsooned for almost an hour and then suddenly quit. As soon as the rain let up, we made plans to meet up with the girls later and then hustled back to our place. We had finally found some cool girls to hang out with! All our hard work was paying off!

On our way back to our place we decided we had better stop and get some caffeinated beverages so we wouldn't be drowsy while we hung out the ladies. We ducked into a little corner store and found a 2-liter energy drink called "THE VOLCANO!" The three of us passed it around and chugged the whole thing down!

We got cleaned up and met up with our Argentine ladies for a nice 11:00 p.m. dinner. I guess that's how they roll down here. After our second dinner date, the three of us and four girls headed up the hill to this wild club. It was fun, but we don't drink, so we didn't really fit in. We just did our thing for a couple hours and had fun dancing like Americans while everyone else watched us. Around 3:30 in the morning, I went to the bathroom. As I circled around to use the urinal, I looked over and saw three dudes lined up to snort cocaine off of the bathroom sink.

I thought to myself, *This isn't our kind of party! It's due time that we get the heck out of here!*

We grabbed the girls and headed out. As we started down the hill, one of the girls pointed out a drunk dude that was laying on a big brick wall. On the other side of the wall was a straight thirty-foot drop off to the ocean. The guy was trying to stand up and kept falling.

The girl said, "Wow that's so sad!"

I was ready to get back, so I said, "He'll be alright. Let's get back to the place before things get weird."

Dave acted like he didn't even hear me. He walked straight over to the drunk guy, picked him up, and started walking down the dirt trail with him on his arm. I grabbed his other arm and we worked our way back down to the beach.

I looked at Dave, shook my head, and said, "Dave, I don't know how you can see the good in even the worst people."

Just as I said that, our new friend, Nesto, started throwing up all over us! I bailed out, but Dave just stood there and took it.

By the time we got to the beach, our drunk guy was somewhat coherent. He told us where he was staying and what his friends' names were. We couldn't find either, so we laid him on a beach table and sat there making sure he didn't die until his friends got back from the club. Just as the sun started lighting up the horizon, Nesto's buddies showed up and carried him home.

Glad that his life was off our consciences, we hung out on the beach and took pictures of the sunrise. Somehow, the sun reenergized us. All three of us headed out on a Wolfpack run around the island.

We ran some four miles down the exotic beaches until we were all so tired we couldn't stand it anymore. We jogged/walked back to our main beach, swam around for a bit, ate even more acaí, and then passed out in our ice box cold room!

Day 40
Sunday, March 7, 2010

Sunday morning we rolled out of bed. Check that, it was late Sunday afternoon. There wasn't an LDS church on the island, so we decided that we'd take it easy in respect of the Sabbath day.

After eating our daily, deep dish of acaí we headed out into the ghetto looking for a good place to get a haircut. On our way up the hill into the ghetto, we saw a kid with an awesome haircut run out of a store.

I yelled at him, "Hey! Where did you get that awesome haircut?"

He yelled back, "Legal did it. He lives just over the hill. Ask around over there and you'll find his place easily."

We thanked him and set out for this guy named Legal ("Cool" in English). Of course, our whole conversation on the walk to his barber shop was about how jealous we were that our nickname wasn't Cool. Once at Legal's barber shop, I got another haircut, but much to Dave and Nian's dismay, he didn't know how to do cornrows. Legal gave them a lady's number that would come to our place on the beach to weave their hair.

The three of us strolled back over to the beach and took full advantage of "The Day of Rest!" We kept ourselves horizontal on the beach until our skin couldn't possibly take one more minute of sun. While getting our beach on, we managed to meet quite a few cool people. We got some food with some of our new friends and rolled back to our motel.

Dave and Nian had Marina come by and put their hair into cornrows. As she started on Nian's hair, the ultimate thunderstorm of the week unleashed its fury and knocked the power out. We laughed at Nian because of his half-cornrowed hair. Nian started getting frustrated. I finally broke down and held a flashlight for Marina to finish his weave. The best part about it was she did Nian's rows to the side, which somewhat made him look like a girl! Dave didn't waste any time to let him know it either!

Soon, we were all cleaned up and ready for the nightly party. By the time we were ready to hit the streets, it was well after midnight. Life on the island had our sleep schedule all messed up—except for Nian. He had fallen asleep while Dave and I showered. Poor guy was all partied out! All slicked up and looking way American, Dave and I headed up the hill looking for the party.

That night's party was all the way at the top of the hill in an outdoor club. The first half of the party was awesome! The DJ played tons of American music. Dave started talking to a couple cute Chilean girls. He waved me over and much to my surprise, they spoke English. These girls were cool. The best part about them was, in Spanish, they both had cute little Latina voices, but in English, they both spoke with a deep monotone man-ish voice. We didn't care. They were cute and cool. We hung out with them for the rest of the night and, once more, retired to our beach to watch the sunrise. Nian staggered out of our room and joined us for our daily breakfast bowl of acaí.

With our lack of sleep and bloodshot eyes, Dave and I looked at each other. We both knew what the other was thinking. We nodded our heads and agreed, *It's time! Let's get outta here!*

9

THE WOLFPACK SEPARATES
TO TAKE DOWN A KILL

Day 41
Monday, March 8, 2010

After breakfast, we carried our tired selves back to the hostel and packed up our gear. Soon we were ready to roll. We said our goodbyes to the great people of Morro de São Paulo, Dave held back tears as he hugged all of the nice girls he had met, and we caught the boat back to Valença. We got our bikes out of the parking place, washed them up good, and were soon on the road headed toward the city of Salvador!

We took a shortcut to Salvador by loading our bikes on a ferry. That cut about 300 kilometers off of our trip. As the ferry shoved off, this is what Dave had to say about our short stay at Morro de São Paulo:

"That island was sweet! Nothing better than three days of paradise, sunny beaches, tropical storms in the afternoons, beautiful women, and crazy techno dance parties every night from midnight to sunrise! Who cares if we didn't get much sleep there, if any. Except one of us, who couldn't hack the party that last night. Hmmm, I just can't seem to remember who that was. Can you remember, Nian? Every morning walking home in the twilight and watching the sunrise, sometimes carrying drunk Argentines home, and sometimes dodging the island's lonely prostitutes. Then going for a quick run on the beach and putting up the hammocks for another round of serious relaxation. We got our hair did, somebody got their mack on with a Brazilian chick, also can't quite remember who. Nian, can you remember? Man guys, if we weren't only halfway to Manaus, I would have loved to have stayed with the great people of Morro and partied for a few more days, but we really need to start covering some ground or else we won't be home for at least a year! Which I guess wouldn't be so bad. Maybe we'll go back and put in some job applications to run their parties next time we're down here! Those last three days were awesome, but I'm ready to get back on the road!"

Nian and I just looked at Dave. "Wow, Dave, that was deep."

An hour later, our ferry arrived at the city of Salvador. By now it was getting late. We tried to get a room in the same place where Dave's Chilean princesses were staying, but the hostel didn't have a secure place where we could park our bikes. That was a deal breaker for the Wolfpack! Bike security was always a very high priority.

After some wheeling and dealing, we found a nice place that was also super cheap. We turned the A/C down to Arctic chill mode and crashed hard! All of us fell asleep so fast—didn't go out to eat, didn't go hang out with the pretty Chilean girls we met, nada! I guess staying up all night for days on end had finally caught up to us!

Our three-man biker gang woke up after a twelve-hour recovery coma, feeling all rested up and ready to roll! As we ate breakfast we scouted out our next leg of the trip on my GPS. What would be our next destination? There were a few big cities on our path going north.

"No more big cities," I said.

We had overheard some travelers on Morro de São Paulo raving about a beach town called Pipa. I plugged "PIPA" into my Garmin and pulled up a route that avoided major highways while following the coastline.

I announced, "Well guys, looks like Pipa is well over 1200

kilometers away. Might even end up being 1500 kilometers if we have any unexpected detours. There's no way we'll make it there today."

That's when Dave piped up. "Time to get crazy! What were we going to do? How about riding non-stop until we get there!"

I studied our map and said, "Dude, with food and fuel stops there's a good chance that it takes us twenty-four hours to get there."

That's when Nian jumped up and said, "Let's do it! It will be epic, and we're not scared of staying up all night!"

It was settled. We were going to try and ride 1200 kilometers only stopping for food and fuel.

We grabbed our gear, topped off our fuel tanks, and jetted out! We rolled about an hour up the coast until we got to the little town of Lauro de Freitas. We pulled over and decided that if we were about to pull a twenty-four-hour straight stretch, we had better be getting our bikes tuned up right now! It was gonna be intense. Throttle pinned, twenty-four hours straight, flying up the coast at a cool fifty-five miles per hour!

We found a cool little shop called Moto Racing and worked out a deal with them to give all three of our bikes a full tune up. My brakes were pretty much gone, Dave's bike was getting ridiculously hot, and Nian's bike was deathly slow. We told the mechanics to get everything tuned up great for as cheap as possible, and they got to work. We chilled in their air-conditioned office watching Nitro Circus videos for almost two hours.

The whole process was taking much longer than we expected. We patiently walked down the street and ate a massive lunch, expecting to have our bikes ready to roll as soon as we got back. Not the case. Turned out, the whole inside of my wheel had come apart. The bearings around my axle had blown up and were eating away the aluminum on my hubs. The owner of the shop spent almost five hours rebuilding my wheel. It would have been cheaper to just replace the whole wheel and tire. I was pissed. I hated spending unnecessary money, and I was keeping us from making progress on our epic ride.

Right around 5:00 p.m. our bikes were washed up, tuned up, packed up, and ready for some serious travel! So there we were, on top of the world, crisp cool night, and we were flying as fast as we could up the highway!

We were approximately 11.4 kilometers into our 1200-kilometer trip. I looked back, and Dave was missing. Nian and I stopped and waited for him. After waiting for a few minutes, I got the worst text ever from Dave!

Bike's broke. Come back.

"Well this is just awesome," Nian said.

We rode back until we found Dave pushing his bike back toward the shop where we had just finished a full day of tune-ups and repairs. I put my foot up and used the old technique that my dad had taught me back on the farm, where the guy with a good bike pushes the broken down bike with his foot on the passenger foot peg. We pushed all ten kilometers (which might not sound like much but is actually quite difficult and very taxing for the guy pushing) back to the bike shop, and what do you know—closed for the night!

Dave finally managed to get ahold of the shop owner. He came and opened the door, we stashed Dave's bike inside, and we rode doubles until we found a cheap hotel.

As we threw our packs into the room in a fury of defeat, someone said, "Remember that time we were going to ride 1200 kilometers straight and we made it exactly 11 kilometers?"

We laughed at ourselves. Once again, with the A/C turned down as much as possible, we three kings had pleasant dreams!

Day 43
Wednesday, March 10, 2010

After spending a wonderful night in Lauro de Freitas, in what was easily the nicest hotel we had slept in the whole trip, we ate a bomb breakfast and rushed to the shop to get them going on Dave's bike.

It was in there for maybe an hour when the mechanic came back with the results. It had a blown motor! We all looked at each other with a grim sense of reality. Turns out, the cam shaft and bearings were completely fried! We had a decent knowledge of motors and fixing them. It didn't really make sense that his motor blew ten minutes after getting what was supposed to be a full lube change and tune-up. Something was wrong. We were convinced that the mechanics forgot something or sabotaged his bike in some way.

But there was nothing we could do about it now. We had to just eat it and get it fixed. Hours passed. We were all sick of sitting in the Moto shop. We had now burned almost two days at this place. Dave was bummed about how much it was going to cost. At the beginning of our adventure we had all agreed that if any of our bikes died, we would split the cost to get it going again. Splitting the repair three ways made it a little less painful.

The mechanic rolled Dave's bike out of the garage sometime around 4:00 p.m. We paid the man and wasted no time getting ourselves right back on the road!

Feeling much better about life, we hauled tailpipe as fast as we could away from that wretched bike shop! Our bikes were running great, and we were all rested up. The time had finally come to ride the 1200 kilometers to Pipa! We all cheered as we raced past the ten-kilometer mark where Dave's bike had blown up the last time. We were once again on top of the world! Crisp evening air, no bugs, smooth roads though groves of palm trees, and awesome tunes pumping in our headphones were the only things on our minds!

About an hour after dark, I looked over at Nian, lifted my helmet and yelled, "Where's Dave?"

Hoping he had found an awesome cave or maybe stopped to make friends with some chicks, we headed back to find him. We found him coasting along the side of the highway about fifteen minutes back. NOOOOOO! ANOTHER BLOWN MOTOR!

We all yelled and cursed those idiot mechanics! Our rage levels we're extremely elevated! Unbelievable! We were about 120 kilometers from the shop where we had spent the last two days getting crappy work done. Our only option was to return and make them warranty Dave's motor.

I tied a stick to our climbing rope and attached it to the rack on my bike so I could tow Dave to the next town to the north. Once there, we would find a place to stay and call the shop to let them know that they needed to come pick up and fix Dave's bike.

Soon after it got dark, we casually rolled through a military police checkpoint. It was no big deal at this point; we had passed similar checkpoints every 200 kilometers since we had started our trip. We maybe made it five kilometers past the checkpoint before the sirens came blaring! This big cop pulled us over and got all up in our grills about something stupid! He was all kinds of nervous!

We played dumb and tried to calm him down while at the same time cussing him in English. The last thing we needed was some power trip, highway patrol officer giving us guff, but as it turned out, it was a blessing in disguise.

We didn't know it, but the next city down the road was 130 kilometers away. We would have all run out of gas and been way farther away from a moto shop. Not to mention, towing Dave's bike with a stick on a rope that far would have sucked really bad!

We ditched Dave's broke down bike at the roadside police station. I took Dave's pack, and Dave road doubles with Nian back down the highway to a small town called Conde. Now we were on a mission to find a campsite—in the dark. After thirty minutes of searching, I was getting the feeling that we were going to have a hard time finding a good place to tie up our hammocks that wasn't super sketchy.

The fat boy inside of me carried me to a bakery where I bought some delicious cake-like bread. I asked the baker where we could hang up our hammocks.

He replied, "Dude, on THE BEACH! It's pretty safe down there, and there are plenty of places to hang up your hammocks."

I grabbed my snacks, and we headed toward the sound of the waves. As we got close to the beach, the streets turned from cobblestones to sand.

I got my speed up and plowed my heavy bike through a huge sand dune! I looked back just in time to see Nian wreck into the same dune with Dave on the back! We parked our bikes and split up in search of an awesome campsite on foot.

"Guys, I found a good one!" Dave yelled.

Nian and I came running back. Dave had come across an absolute work of wonder. It was a cabana-looking lifeguard tower about halfway down the beach. Angels built this knowing that we needed a place to stay! It was honestly perfect. Three posts perfect for hanging up our three hammocks and a roof to keep us dry in case we got some rain. We soon were swinging in our hammocks enjoying the nice ocean breeze and listening to the waves crash on the beach. There couldn't have been a better way to finish off an extremely sucky, disappointing, day! As we drifted off to sleep, we all joked about how we were on top of the world!

I woke up to the most amazing sunrise ever! Nian and I basked in the wonder of it while trying to wake up Dave. He was out! We got up, went for a good jog, worked out, took a shower on the beach, and tried to figure out how to get Dave's bike back to the shop to get fixed.

We rode through the small town of Conde and asked around until we found the best local bike shop. This shop was really low key. It was actually pretty ghetto but for some reason, we trusted them more than the last shop with all their professional equipment and such. Dave jumped on with the owner of the shop and rode back out to the police checkpoint to get his bike. Half an hour later they came rolling back in. The owner was using the push on the passenger foot peg technique to get Dave's bike back to his shop.

As they rolled up, Dave tore his helmet off and yelled, "Dude! That was nuts! He was pushing me going like 100 kilometers per hour!" He laughed, and we could tell he was having a good time despite his misfortunes.

After a short assessment on the crappy bike, we found out that a gasket had blown and most of Dave's oil had leaked out. So there we sat. We didn't know if we were going to have to head back to Lauro de Freitas to get it fixed at the same shop or see if our new buddies could get it going. We decided to try and have these guys fix it so we could stay on the road. After working on it for a bit, the mechanic came out with a confused look on his face.

He explained that the oil filter had been put in backwards. He said that the filter being in backwards had probably messed up the oil flow and caused the motor to blow both times. Dave was not happy! The mechanics got everything straightened out and started Dave's bike up. It seemed to be running great.

We held a Wolfpack conference and decided that we would risk it and keep going. The thought of waiting in the shop at Lauro de Freitas to get the motor overhauled again made us all cringe.

We strapped on our gear and hit the road headed north once more! We took it very easy to see if everything was running okay. We were around 100 kilometers up the road when Dave pulled over and stopped. I just shook my head in disbelief.

Dave pulled off his helmet and said, "Guys, I hate to do this to ya, but I think my motor is going out again."

There we were, 250 kilometers from anywhere. Our options were limited. Dave's motor was jammed up for the third time. What should we do? These were our options: We could try to push his failing motor to go another 100 kilometers to the next small town. We could pay over $200 for a tow truck to take it back to the moto shop that had already screwed us twice. Or, we could try to hitchhike a ride for Dave and his bike with a truck driver back to where we got the bike fixed before and force them to fix it for free!

Dave made the decision. He was hell bent on hitching a ride with a truck driver. We grabbed some grub and flagged down the rustiest, slowest, truck we could find. The driver was super cool and even helped us lift Dave's broken dinosaur of a bike into the back of his truck. Nian and I jumped on our bikes ready to follow Dave and his trucker friend back to the shop in Lauro de Freitas.

Dave came around the truck and said, "Guys, you've probably seen on The Animal Planet where a pack of wolves splits up to corner whatever it may be chasing and then make an easier attack and kill. I think that's what our Wolfpack needs to do right now. You guys continue north until you get to Pipa. I'll go get my bike dialed in and will meet you there as soon as possible!"

There was no time to talk it over. Dave had made up his mind, and his trucker buddy was anxious to get going. Now came the sad part.

Dave jumped in the cab of the rusty old truck and said, "Well, if this guy takes advantage of me... I love you guys!" Then they pulled away. Slowly. Very very slowly.

Nian and I just looked at each other. Nian won't admit it, but he was holding back tears. That's when we realized we had just sent our good buddy off with a random trucker.

I looked at Nian and said, "Well, I think he'll be fine. Dave has been doing lots of pushups and crunches lately. He could fight off a soggy truck driver if the dude tried taking advantage of him!"

Nian and I decided we didn't need to rush to Pipa anymore. We might as well go slow to give Dave more time to catch up. We planned out a nice scenic route that took us up the coastline. The two of us flipped around and hit the road going north.

First stop would be Acaraju, where we planned to get lunch and grab some cash out of the ATM. We had been riding for maybe an hour when our nicely paved road turned into cobblestones that led down into a river. We'd have to take another ferry.

As the ferry arrived, Nian and I dug through all we had but only scrounged up $1.50. We had given Dave all the cash we had to get his bike fixed, and now we didn't have enough to cross the river. I somehow managed to get us on the ferry without paying. As the ferry chugged across the river, we made friends with the attendant. As we disembarked, I tried handing her our little handful of change that we had left. She smiled at us, shook her head, and waved for us to go! What a nice lady!

We raced forty-five kilometers across a palm tree covered island (with a minor pit stop to pump up my flat front tire) to catch another ferry on the other side back to the mainland. We had to get there before dark if we wanted to catch the last ferry of the day.

As we got close, I could see cars driving up the loading bridge. We made it to the ferry with seconds to spare! They were getting ready to lift the drawbridge as we pulled up. The attendant waved us over, so we ripped up the bridge and onto the ferry. As the ferry shoved off, the lady came to collect the $20 ferry fare from us. That's when we broke the bad news to her. We only had $1.50. She was very angry! She took our remaining handful of coins and agreed to let us go this one time.

Once back on dry land, we rode up the coast to Acaraju, where we got fresh pockets of cash at the ATM and kicked it for a bit. After some deep convincing, I talked Nian into keeping on the track toward Pipa. I took a wrong turn somewhere, which put us into some really ghetto small beach town. It was actually kinda creepy, and we didn't have Dave there to scare everyone off by riding around shirtless with the chain around his neck.

Just after sunset, as we looked for the road out of town, my front tire blew completely out. I asked like thirty people where I could get it fixed and finally found someone that changed/fixed tires in his garage at his house. We were there for a good two hours shooting the breeze and fixing my tire with this guy and his family. As we were leaving, the grandmother of the group piped up and said that we should check out the beach Lagoa Redonda.

She said, "It's amazing! There are giant sea turtles everywhere! The beach has even been on TV!"

We didn't put much thought into it. With my front tire all fixed up, we paid the man, said thanks, and rolled out headed north. About thirty kilometers later, I saw a sign with an arrow pointing toward Lagoa Redonda.

I stopped and said, "Hey, I think this is the awesome turtle place that the old lady was talking about."

We took the road and headed in that direction. The road quickly turned from nice pavement to rough dirt, and then led us aimlessly twenty-five kilometers to nowhere. At the very end of the road, there was a small river and a small lunch shack, which was strangely open at midnight. The lady working at the shack said that if we crossed the river, we would be able to ride straight down to the beach, where we would find a secluded campsite easily. She assured us that the river wasn't too deep and that the bottom was hard.

A few minutes later, Nian and I sat side by side staring down into a dark, fast flowing river.

Nian looked at me and said, "You talked to the lady that told us to come this way. You go first!"

"No way! You go first!"

Nian dug in his heels and stood his ground.

I took off my dry socks, lifted up my helmet so I could see better, and saddled up on my bike. The river was about twenty yards wide. I circled around, got my speed up, and plunged straight into the dark water! After a big initial splash, the bottom leveled out. Lucky for us, I gambled right. The river was only two feet deep.

After we both made it through the river safe and sound, we plowed through sand dunes and palm groves (which almost blew up our bikes, as they didn't do so well in the soft sand) for the next fifteen minutes. The end of the dunes put us right on the hard sand of the beach. We took off to the north along the ocean, looking for some palms close to the water where we could hang up our hammocks.

Nian and I discovered that the hard sand beach was smoother than most of the highways we had been on over the past week! We weaved back and forth cheering and laughing while going as fast as we could on hard packed sand. We were having a great time! Nian loved trying to run over the crabs that would suddenly appear at the edge of our headlights! After almost forty-five minutes riding up the beach, we were both almost completely out of gas! I had been on my reserve tank for what seemed like forever! We had gone almost thirty kilometers up the beach, were running on fumes, and were pretty much lost.

I slammed on my brakes and flagged down Nian. The overwhelming darkness made it almost impossible to find a road or trail that would take us back to a main road. It was time to circle our wagons and set up camp. A short search produced a small grove of palm trees. We leaned our bikes against the trees, hung our hammocks up, prayed that the good Lord would protect us from harm, and listened to the sound of waves crashing on the sand as we settled in for another terrific night's rest in God's beautiful great outdoors.

10

THE HOLIEST HOSTEL IN TOWN

Day 45
Friday, March 12, 2010

We woke up around 4:45 a.m. Not by choice, but because that was when
the sun peeked over the horizon. As my eyes focused, I looked around
and realized that we had camped directly in the middle of paradise!
Our hammocks were tied up between two lonely palms overlooking a
long, beautiful beach bordered by a big blue ocean! After taking in the
greatness for a minute, I felt something fall on me.

Expecting to see a leaf, I looked down at my Paraguayan blanket.
It was covered in bees! I slingshotted out of my hammock expecting to
be attacked by the swarm of pissed-off bees I had just kicked off of my
blanket. Thankfully, there were no bees flying around me. I cautiously
walked back to my hammock and peeked inside. It was full of motionless
bees. I poked one with a stick. *They're all dead?* That was when I looked
up at the palm tree above my hammock. Directly over my head was a
gigantic swarm of bees on one of the palm leaves! *AHHH!*

I woke Nian up, and we quietly packed up to get out of there as
fast as we could!

My bike had tipped over in the deep sand (which broke another one of my mirrors) while I was trying to park it the night before. There was a random wooden post buried right next to where I had tipped over, so I had pushed my bike over to it and leaned my handlebar on the post for the night. As I was packing up my gear, I looked down at a small sign on the post that read, "Sea Turtle area." We had been joyriding and camping all night in a Giant sea turtle nature preserve! You'll get in more trouble in Brazil for messing with a sea turtle than you would for killing a human! We both felt it was best to get a move on!

We mounted up and plowed through more deep sand until we found a trail that led to a soccer field. A small foot path by the soccer field led us to another endless dirt road. By now, we were both almost bone dry outta gas! After what seemed like forever, we puttered into the very small river/beach fishing town of Ilia dos Flores. We asked the locals where we needed to go to find the nearest gas station. Everyone we asked gave us different directions to stations that were too far away.

As we were losing hope, a young kid walked by and overheard us getting directions to the far away gas station. He politely sat and stared at us until we were done getting the directions.

I looked down at him and said, "Hello, little buddy."

His eyes lit up as he replied, "My dad sells gas at our house! Follow me!"

Nian and I looked at each other and then followed the shoeless little guy around the neighborhood. He ran into a half-finished house. We pulled up and parked out front. A few minutes later, a sleepy-looking dude wearing only a swimsuit came staggering out of the house. He was holding four 2-liter Coke bottles full of gas! Turned out, this guy's secondary source of income was selling bootleg, black market gas out of his living room! He had a couple hundred 2-liter bottles filled up and stacked in his house.

I looked at Nian and said, "That can't be safe, but you've got to do what you've got to do to survive!" We had a good laugh and paid the man double. He definitely saved our bacon and we were very grateful!

After getting fueled up, we asked around to find out how to get ourselves out of town. Everyone said that we should ride inland for an hour or two, then get another ferry across the river. Once across the river, we could take the highway to get to the city of Maceo.

As we were about to drive hours out of our way, another guy told us that we could go to the fishing port down the street and pay guys to take us across the river on a "small ferry boat." That sounded great to us. We seriously drove circles forever until we found the fishing port. These people spoke with a Portuguese accent that Nian and I had a hard time understanding. Directions were getting difficult, but we finally found the fishing port.

There were no "small ferry boats" like the man had described. Nian and I sat on the riverbank and watched an old lady wash her horse as we thought about our options. That was when I heard a faint hum coming from across the river. A minute or two later, two guys in motorized wooden canoes pulled up and landed their vessels next to the lady with the soapy horse. Without saying anything to us, one of the guys got out of his canoe, walked over to us, grabbed my bike, and started wheeling it toward the water.

I looked at Nian and said, "They can't be serious!"

They were serious all right! Turned out, the "small ferry boat" the guy was talking about was actually just two if his buddies' little fourteen-foot wooden fishing canoes. Instead of riding hours out of our way and paying thirty bucks for a chartered ferry, we gave these good fellas four dollars to risk our lives and our heavy bikes in wooden canoes! It took five full grown men to help us lift our bikes into the canoes. We were then given some small strings to tie our bikes upright in the vessel.

That was easily one of the top three most intense boat rides of my life! We may have only gone thirty minutes with a three horsepower outboard motor, but my super heavy butt and super heavy bike had this guy's little canoe pushed to the limits! Every wave we hit, I thought we were going to the bottom! It was way nuts, but we loved every second of it!

After thirty minutes of pure stress and sweat, thinking that we were going down, we finally made it over to the other side!

All Nian and I could say was, "I wish Dave were here. He would have loved this!" We had probably said that exact phrase fifty times since losing Dave the day before!

Surprisingly, after our awesome journey in canoes across the river, our day only got more exciting. The beach we landed on was calling to me.

I looked at Nian and said, "Nian, let's cruise the beach again."

He wasn't too pumped on the idea. He wanted to find food, and he knew the crabs wouldn't be out in the daytime for him to try and run over again, so it wouldn't be as much fun as it had been the previous night. Due to my convincing ways, I managed to pressure Nian into doing it. He only agreed to ride the beach with me after I promised that if we didn't find food in exactly thirty minutes, I would pay for his lunch of choice.

We hit the hard-packed beach and put the hammer down! We were flying down the sand as fast as we could go! We were cruising along, cheering and laughing at 100 kilometers per hour! I raced past a huge lump on the sand and slammed on my brakes. It was a huge dead sea turtle!

We checked it out, and it was still kinda fresh with bugs eating it and stuff. Nian was really disappointed that we couldn't keep the shell and become one of the newest members of the Ninja Turtles. Our frowns soon turned upside down when we found a huge, awesome turtle skull right next to the shell.

Soon after, I found another smaller turtle skull, and Nian decided that if we were a real biker gang, we would call ourselves "The Turtle Skulls!"

All we needed was one more skull for Dave. We'd be the toughest guys around with turtle skulls tied to the front of our handlebars!

I'm sad to say that the big skull fell off of Nian's bag somewhere along the way, so we were down to one small skull. I thought I might make a necklace out of it or something.

After beach cruising and turtle shell hunting, Nian and I found a nice little restaurant on the beach. It was exactly thirty-one minutes since I had made my promise to him, so I bought his food and we hit the road hard toward the city of Macieo.

For some reason, I hated Macieo. Maybe because my bike fell over right when we got there and broke my mirror again! I couldn't believe how many mirrors I had gone through on the trip! I might as well have just taken them off. So, after more convincing, I talked Nian into continuing another 250 kilometers up the coast to Recife. We wrapped our fingers around our throttles and made great time!

The ride was super hot and smoky. It was sugar cane harvest season. A lot of the farmers were burning their fields after they had cut their crops. The roads were also covered with loose stalks of sugarcane that had fallen out of trucks, which was super sketchy to ride through!

After a long, hot, scenic ride, we finally arrived in Recife. It was pretty much dark by the time we rolled into town. We stopped at an internet cafe to look up a place to camp or stay and to see if Dave had written to us. No word from Dave, and no decent, cheap, hostels online. As I studied the map of Recife, I noticed, in very tiny writing, *LDS Temple!*

I looked at Nian and said, "Dude, let's go see if we can find a place to camp somewhere around the temple grounds! Temples are usually in pretty safe neighborhoods."

Nian almost yelled, "That's a genius idea! Why not try to stay at the holiest hostel in town?"

Twenty minutes later, we were outside the temple gates! I sheepishly went up to the guard and asked him if he knew of any good campsites nearby.

He gave me a strange look and said, "I don't think camping around here is a good idea. You'll probably get robbed and killed. Who are you guys and what are you doing here at 10:00 at night?"

We explained ourselves and our situation.

The guard replied, "Well, if you're a member of the LDS church and have a current temple recommend, you can just stay in the temple's onsite hotel. It costs $2 a night. Do you want me to call and get you a room right now?"

"Yep! We absolutely do!"

We couldn't believe our good fortune! The Church had a very nice hotel built right behind the temple for members to stay at when they were in town going to the temple.

Smiling ear to ear, Nian and I rode our bikes down into the lighted, underground, guarded, parking garage. We grabbed our packs and were escorted inside. The receptionist didn't know what to think of us—two vagabonds, with smoke-blackened faces, trying to check in to the Church's very nice hotel. We got in our room and found out that we were in the cleanest, nicest place we had stayed in so far! I was so ready to sleep in a big, soft, clean bed! Not only was it an amazing room, but it was also super safe and super cheap! The two of us agreed that guardian angels were looking over us. We said our grateful prayers, took an amazingly hot shower, talked about missing Dave, and slept off the pains of an extremely adventurous and exciting day!

We slept like angels in the Lord's hotel! It was extra nice to wake up and look at the beautiful temple right outside the window. I was really lucky and got to go in for a session.

I spent a few hours in the temple while Nian got some wash done and picked mangoes around the temple grounds. When I got out of the temple, I found Nian, and that was when we got the bad news. We were getting kicked out of the temple hotel! But not because of our bad behavior this time. They were closed on Sundays. We had been planning on staying at the temple and waiting for Dave to reunite with us, as staying at the temple was super awesome and cheap! But once we finished washing everything that we owned, we set out in search of a new cheap place to stay.

We had a hard time finding a place that satisfied our needs, which were a) a safe place to park our bikes, b) super cheap, and c) free breakfast. We found a place down by the beach that wasn't bad, but they were completely booked. After some serious convincing, we finally talked them into letting us sleep on the ground in the washroom for $4. Not the greatest setup but it would do for a day.

Turned out, the guy that worked at our new hostel had served an LDS mission in São Paulo. He took us under his wing and promised to help us find a church to attend the next morning. Once we had our lodging secured, we decided to take full advantage of the nice warm weather and try our hand at surfing again. We pulled on some swim trunks and headed to the beach, but our plans quickly changed when we saw the huge signs warning, "DANGER! No Swimming! Shark Attack," everywhere along the beach!

Not wanting to surf with the sharks, we spent the rest of the day going to flea markets and sifting around Recife. We got back to the hostel just before dark and discovered we were staying there with a very weird crew. When I say weird, I mean WEIRD! It was pretty uncomfortable there, so we hit the streets to find something to eat.

We had been living the homeless life for a few weeks now. Nian and I both agreed that it was time to splurge again. We set out on foot looking for the best restaurant in town. After walking almost four miles down the beach, we found the most amazing Tucanos type churrasco restaurant for way cheap! We were there for a couple hours just hanging out and because of that, we ate until we were sick! I just couldn't say no when the waiter would come around and say, "More Filet Mignon anyone?"

The restaurant finally kicked us out, and we set out walking the four miles back to the hostel. About a mile into our walk, I found myself lying face up on the ground. I had eaten so much that it made me dizzy when I tried to walk! It took Nian and me two hours to get back to the hostel. Our long walk turned out to be a good thing because by the time we got back to the hostel, all the weirdos were gone or asleep.

Nian and I stole a fan and hit the floor. We had chosen a bad night to eat ourselves sick. It was super hot and humid. We laughed at each other because of our misfortune. We both tried to lay in front of the fan and somehow, we finally fell asleep.

Miss you Dave... COME BACK SOON!

Day 47
Sunday, March 14, 2010

Let's just say we didn't sleep so well. Everything was fine until we were both lying on the same mattress at 3:00 a.m. trying to kill each other for the fan. It was so hot! We woke up soaked with sweat!

After eating our free breakfast, we took ice cold showers and headed off to church. When we walked into the church, we found out that the air conditioner was broken and it was a million degrees inside the building. But we were pleasantly surprised when we walked into the room where the priesthood meeting was being held and discovered that the good Lord had blessed us with ice box temperatures. We stayed in the rooms with A/C and enjoyed the best three hours of church that we had sat through in a long time.

After church, we put our feet up and relaxed at the strange hostel for a few hours. There was supposed to be a young adult fireside at the church that evening (a fireside is a meeting just for young adults with a good speaker who is often funny). We decided we would stick around for that and then hit the road going north and see how far we could make it that night. We had been planning to stay in the heat box hostel again, but we got a super gay vibe, which facilitated our decision to leave.

We packed up our gear and hit the road to find the fireside at the church. After an hour of searching, going to five churches that were all dark, getting lost in a ghetto and doing a sweet ghetto hill climb on our bikes, Nian ran out of gas. I pushed him to a gas station where both of us blew the plumbing out of a gas station bathroom! Our big dinner the night before raged in our stomachs. We gave up our search for the church fireside and decided we'd hit the road headed north out of Recife. As soon as we rolled out, we drove past the chapel where the fireside was. It had just gotten over. Bad luck!

We saddled our iron horses and rode north for just over two hours to João Pessoa. I wasn't paying attention, took a wrong turn, and we ended up in a ghetto side of town. Our trusty GPS showed that we could take a shortcut across a river to get back to the freeway. Otherwise, we were going to have to backtrack half an hour to get there. We slowly rolled through the ghetto little town and, according to the GPS, we were only two kilometers from the freeway. I got confused when our roads turned from cobblestones to dirt road and then from dirt road to a path leading down a hill to the river. We cautiously rolled down the hill and up to the riverbank.

Nian hopped off his bike and said, "Dude, I can see the freeway over there. All we gotta do is get across this bridge."

The bridge Nian was talking about was made out of two 1" X 5" pieces of wood nailed to a rickety framework! This thing was SUPER sketchy! All the wood and handrails were busted up and extremely untrustworthy. The sketchiest part of the whole situation: the water was basically a huge river of POO! One wrong move and we'd be in for a long night trying to get our bikes, our gear, and ourselves, out of a poo river.

Nian walked across the bridge as I looked at the maps on the GPS. I had ruled out the idea all together. No way I was going to let Nian attempt that. I had been riding motorbikes since I was nine years old, and it made me nervous!

Nian walked back from the other side of the bride and said, "Dude, it doesn't look too bad. There's one spot that's kinda broken but we should be able to make it."

Without looking up from my maps, I half kiddingly said, "Nian, if you think you can make it, go ahead."

Next thing I know, Nian fires up his bike. I looked up just to see Nian fearlessly fly up some makeshift planks onto the bridge!

I yelled, "NIAN! Whatever you do, don't fall in the river!"

He calmly rode across the rickety structure until about halfway across the sixty-yard bridge. His handlebar hit one of the broken handrails and sent him swerving! My heart sank! I couldn't help but pray, *Lord, please don't let Nian put it in the river!* I held my breath until he finally made it across to the other side.

Nian almost made us have a smelly night of poo river diving. There was no going back now. I charged the Tornado up the planks and onto the bridge. I was a little more cautious than Nian had been. I eased myself along until I had made it across safely. Right as I got off the bridge I rode a wheelie up the hill while both of us cheered!

We soon discovered that the other side of the Poo River didn't provide the best access to the main highway either. We rolled through a ghetto and out into a field. While watching our backs to avoid getting mugged in the ghetto, we searched around for a road that would lead us to the freeway. After twenty minutes of searching we found a little dirt trail that seemed to lead in that direction. We followed the trail about four kilometers into a field, found the main road, and then couldn't find anywhere to get onto it. Finally, after an intense search, we followed a bulldozer trail that led us through some 300 yards of jungle and to a little bike trail that we followed up to the freeway.

Once on the freeway, we breathed a breath of relief and offered up prayers of thanks! Another hour and a half of good hard riding and we were there! We had finally arrived at the quaint little beach town of Pipa.

It was well after 2:00 a.m., so any hotel or hostel would definitely be closed. After driving the whole city, asking the town drunks for advice, and getting completely lost, we finally found a decent place to camp at "Lovers Beach" on the outskirts of Pipa. I surveyed the skies, licked my finger, put it in the air, and told Nian that it was going to rain.

He said, "No way!"

I politely guaranteed him that it would rain and made an executive decision that we were going to find a place to stay or camp where we wouldn't get rained on. I wasn't really comfortable camping with Nian on "Lovers Beach," either.

Fun fact: When we were in Morro de São Paulo, some British dude asked a group of us if we thought it was going to rain. Someone said, "Ask the Americans. They know eeevveryyythininggggg!"

I confidently told him, "I guarantee it will rain tomorrow, probably around 3:00 p.m."

I saw the guy two days later. He came straight over to me and congratulated me for predicting a massive rainstorm which started at 3:30 p.m. on the day that I had said. It was funny!

But it was still going to rain and we needed to find a place to sleep. As Nian and I got on the bikes to ride back into town, I tipped over in a huge bush and couldn't get out. I got way mad and took off. As I rounded the corner headed back to town, something caught my eye.

It was a hammock under a nice porch. I looked closer and saw that it was a cool looking hostel. I jumped off my bike and slowly went inside. I yelled for someone to attend us, but it was pretty quiet. Nian and I decided that we would just sleep under their porch and get a room in the morning. We started unpacking our blankets and situating our bikes so they wouldn't get stolen.

I heard some strange voice coming from inside the hostel. A sixty-year-old lady came out with a wasted look on her face and said she was working there. I asked if we could get some sleep and get a room in the morning. She said no, but after some good convincing, we talked her into letting us get a room for the night instead. I apologized for waking her up.

She replied, "Don't worry about it. I was just getting ready to go out to meet some friends."

What sixty-year-old lady goes out to meet friends at 3:30 in the morning? After some more good haggling, we talked her into letting us sleep under the front patio for free.

We were looking forward to a big day of swimming with the dolphins and doing nothing the next day. We talked about how much we missed Dave, hung up our hammocks, and passed OUT!

Oh and by the way, not more than an hour after I predicted rain...torrential downpour!

We were surprised the next morning to find out that we were sleeping in the place where breakfast was served. Looking completely homeless, we tiredly rolled out of our hammocks and ate a killer good breakfast for $2. As more people showed up to eat, Nian and I discovered what we were dealing with. We were surrounded by chicks!

Somehow the heavens had smiled upon us, and we were staying in a hostel with ten pretty girls. We just looked at each other and laughed! The girls were actually pretty cool and cute for once. After breakfast, we put our gear in a room and headed out for some adventure with the girls from the hostel. They took us down to the beach and showed us where the dolphins came in to swim.

Nian and I ran into the water and waited. Without fail, the dolphins showed up a few minutes later. We swam our hearts out trying to get close enough to touch them. Our attempts to ride a dolphin failed, and we were soon worn out from swimming so fast. Swimming with the dolphins wasn't a big deal if you ask me. It sounds so much cooler than I thought it was. Nevertheless, scratch that off our list! Swimming with dolphins...CHECK!

We spent most of the day on the beach. I easily took four nice naps in between sessions of swimming with the dolphins. We all got some food and headed back to the hostel. Nian and I took another good nap. By the time we woke up, it was almost dark! Apparently, we were very tired boys. When we slept in our hammocks, I usually slept with one eye open in anticipation of someone coming to mess with us.

Half awake, we walked down onto the big patio in front of the hostel. That was where we found our ten new girlfriends living it up. They were all completely wasted! I looked at Nian and laughed.

They ran over to us and yelled, "Yeah! Let's party!"

Tiredly, I looked at them and said, "We don't drink, but we're down to party with you!"

Confused, they spent the next three hours trying to get Nian and me to drink with them. They were unsuccessful in getting us to drink, but we were successful in getting an awesome dance party started! Nian and I danced with drunk chicks until 3:00 in the morning. That's when the cops showed up and told us to turn the music down. Soon, all the chicks were passed out. Nian and I decided to do the same.

We worried about Dave and his whereabouts for a bit, and laid down for a well-deserved night's rest in an actual bed!

Our accommodations consisted of a room with six beds in an open loft overlooking the dirt road right in front of the best beach in town. Since it was completely open to the town and weather, we got woken up at like 5:00 a.m. every day, but it was so awesome! Just down from our place there was a 150-foot cliff over the beach that you could hike halfway down and watch the most amazing sunrise ever!

But we missed the next sunrise, and when we woke up from being in a coma for almost twelve hours, we realized that we had missed breakfast, too! Brazilian breakfast is easily our favorite meal of the day. We had missed out on fresh fruit, fresh juice, delicious breads, cakes, eggs, and of course chocolate milk!

As we sat in our room, mad that we had missed breakfast, we could hear a peculiar accent coming from downstairs. A couple had shown up while we were sleeping. We went down and that was when we met Liam and Colette from Scotland. These two diehard travelers had been on the road for eighteen months circling the globe! They had gone all the way around the world, gotten engaged in Machu Picchu, and had some of the most awesome stories that I had ever heard!

Nian and I explored the town for part of the afternoon and ended up on the beach. Nian convinced me to rent another surfboard and give surfing another try. The outcome was no different than the first times. Paddling out through the breakers almost killed us. Every wave almost drowned us, and after an hour of trying, we had only gotten up once for a few seconds. Maybe surfing just wasn't our thing, and I was okay with that.

Exhausted and frustrated, we returned our rental board, grabbed a Coke Zero (which I drank like water) and headed back to our pad. For the rest of the evening, we chilled with the whole crew at the hostel (which consisted of Me, Nian, Liam, Colette, Neto—which is the guy that owns the place—and the ten other girls). We all went out, bought grub, and cooked up some delicious dinner. Of course, the girls bought a ridiculous amount of alcohol, too. Pretty soon, dinner had turned into them getting wasted again. We busted out our laptop, plugged in some party music, and turned the whole hostel into an instant dance party!

The party lasted until around 2:00 a.m. We were notified that the cops were about to be called again, so we shut the music down. Our drunk friends convinced Nian and me to be their designated driver/ moto taxi drivers for the rest of the night! Soon, we were riding triples all around town for more "fun" and dancing!

One of the girls from the hostel and I went on a romantic beach walk. We ended up sitting on the beach talking. I was about to kiss her when she started digging through her bag. I pumped the brakes on the kiss when she pulled out her lighter and lit up a smoke.

Gross! Hard pass! I thought.

By 4:00 a.m. Nian and I had all our drunken friends gathered up and safely back to the hostel.

The hostel was only $10 a night. It was super rustic and open, and the owner had a dog named Lelo that loved us. We were still waiting to hear from Dave to find out if he was okay and what his plan was. He had messaged us saying he had gotten his bike fixed and was on his way. Our Brazilian phone service was super unreliable. I kept getting stacks of texts from him all at once. I told him where we are staying, but the place was hard to find. I had a hard enough time finding it with the GPS. Hopefully, when he got there, we could all kick back and relax for a few days! Knowing Dave, he had probably made some friends, got a good paying job, and didn't know how to break it to us that he had started a new life!

11

JIM TIME

Day 50
Wednesday, March 17, 2010

I woke up to some strange commotion coming from downstairs in the hostel. Our shared room had a big open wall and balcony that faced the street. I sleepily walked out on the balcony and looked down to the street. My heart stopped!

DAVE! He's alive and he's back! I woke Nian up, and we both ran down to the street!

"Dude, Dave! Where have you been?"

The next two or three hours were spent eating an amazing breakfast while swapping stories and introducing Dave to all our new friends.

Dave had gone back to where we had gotten our bikes fixed, and they wouldn't help him so he had to get it fixed from another guy.

We got Dave a bed at the hostel and swapped stories for a couple more hours. That afternoon, the reunited Wolfpack went back to the beach so Dave could swim with the dolphins. It was a beautiful day and there were tons of dolphins. Dave went out in the water and swam with the dolphins for hours.

After Dave finally came in, we started making friends with some local kids. Before we knew it, we were engaged in a full blown, multi-nationality soccer game! Scottish Liam jumped in, and we played hard for more than an hour. We played five games to five goals. I'm proud to say our American/Scottish team won three of the five games. After soccer, we were all tired and thirsty. We grabbed some ice-cold Guaraná drinks and headed back to the hostel.

Back at the hostel we hung out and made up funny songs while Dave played guitar. I will admit that freestyling lyrics while Dave jammed on guitar was one of our favorite downtime activities on the trip. We did it for hours on end sometimes.

As we were laying in hammocks and singing the afternoon away, Liam ran in the room and yelled in a Scottish accent, "IT'S SAINT PATTY'S DAY! Let's go get food and cook up a feast!"

Liam passed out food assignments and we all went to the store to get our stuff. Of course, the chicks from the UK came back with only booze. After an hour or two, we had put together a traditional, Scottish St. Patty's Day feast! We all ate until we were sick.

Some speakers came out and we found ourselves right in the middle of another insane dance party! That party lasted for an hour or two, and soon we were all at one of the clubs in town continuing the party. After a couple hours of that, all our friends were so drunk that they weren't fun, so the Wolfpack decided to call it a night. We rolled our motos back to the hostel and hit the hay!

Dave and I rose with the sun the next morning and grabbed an early breakfast. We both decided that we were feeling fat, so we hit the streets in search of an energy drink and a gym where we could lift some weights. We soon found both and got a great workout in. Nothing feels better than working out after you've been out of it for a while.

We grabbed some delicious egg sandwiches as we left the gym and rolled back over to the hostel. Once we got there, it was time to do nothing but chill and relax for a bit. The next few hours were spent laying in our hammocks with Dave playing the guitar and all of us making up more funny songs. We ate a late lunch and decided that we would give surfing another shot.

We told everyone that it was beach time, grabbed our shorts, and headed down the trail to Lovers Beach. It didn't take long before we had haggled our way into renting some more surfboards. We took off in a dead sprint for the water, and the battle was on! Lovers Beach was well known for having the biggest, best waves in the area. We figured that if we were going to learn how to surf, we might as well do it on the best waves possible.

I've never felt so wrong in my life! Thirty minutes later, I had finally succeeded in getting past the surf. Every time I got close, I would get pounded by two or three huge waves, flipped upside down, and swept back in toward the beach. Once past the surf, I watched guys get up and ride waves in while I caught my breath and rested for a bit. I waited for the perfect set of rollers. After what seemed like forever, I found my wave. I paddled as hard as my short, stocky, arms would allow, and quickly popped up to my feet. I got a huge grin on my face when I realized that I had finally conquered surfing. I had figured it out!

Less than five seconds later, the wave dumped me forward and then rolled me end over end several times. I popped up and gasped for air! I reached up and touched my scalp, which was now throbbing with pain. I looked at my fingers, and they were bloody. My board had hit me in the head and opened me up pretty good. That was it! I swore off surfing. I swam back to shore and turned in my surfboard.

I was exhausted, so I laid down on a towel and passed out! I woke up freezing cold as the sun was going down. We watched the sun go down, grabbed some showers at the hostel, and enjoyed some of the best homemade custard I had ever eaten before calling it an early night.

I woke up just after sunrise to find Dave's and Nian's beds empty. *What the heck?* They had woken up early to watch the sunrise on Lover's Beach. How romantic. Dave met a hippie on the beach that made him a bunch of trinkets out of wire and inspired him through his peace talks about the Earth life.

I ate breakfast with our hostel friends and headed to the gym for another much needed workout. After attempting to get rid of a few pounds, it was time for another good day of chillin' at the beach!

As I was riding back to the hostel I thought, *I'm going to do my own thing today. I need some Jim time.*

Dave, Nian, and I have been together for almost two months. It didn't matter who it was, after being together twenty-four hours a day, seven days a week, you start getting on each other's nerves. Besides, they failed to invite me to watch the sunrise this morning. I turned around and headed out for some solo exploring.

Feeling good about my decision, I tore off toward a jungle road that I had found on my GPS. After a short ride, I was there, flying up this trail on my bike and feeling great. I hadn't gone more than twenty minutes up the tiny dirt trail when a thought came into my head. *I wonder how long it would take me to walk back to the hostel if I broke down? I'm fifteen miles away. I can walk three or four miles per hour. It would take me four to six hours to walk back.* I realized that I had put myself into a moderately sketchy situation.

I immediately flipped around and headed back toward town, but when I got there, I still wasn't ready to meet up with everybody. I casually explored around the town and then went over to the main street to buy some batteries and other essentials that I'd need once we got back out on the open road.

As I walked from the hardware store to the supermarket, Dave and Nian spotted me. I pretended to run from them, but they soon caught up to me and chewed me out for ditching them all day. I told them about the awesome trails I had found, and we made plans to all go ride there the next day. The three of us walked down to the dolphin beach and back, and by then it was almost time for dinner.

It was our turn to cook dinner for the rest of the hostel crew. What better meal could three American guys cook for a bunch of foreigners than big juicy steaks and burgers? We bought all the essentials for a real American style barbeque and headed for the hostel. As we pulled up and parked our bikes, we weren't surprised to learn that the rest of the crew was already pretty drunk. That didn't stop us from cooking up a legit barbeque dinner.

Dave was standing by the grill cooking, and I was shuttling meat to the serving area. I put down a plate of steaks, which everyone dished up fast. Just as we were all about to dig in, a loud, pissed off sounding Liam ran out onto the porch and yelled in a heavy Scottish accent.

"DAVE! WHAT THE F*** WAS THAT!"

Pause…

We all thought we were about to see our drunk Scottishman friend run out to put fists on Dave. Just when the tension was at an absolute climax, Liam finished.

"DAVE! THAT IS THE BEST F***** THING THAT I'VE EVER PUT IN ME MOUTH IN MY ENTIRE LIFE!"

We had expected a fight. Liam's intense compliment caught us all by surprise! We all laughed until our stomachs hurt!

After eating an uncomfortable amount of food, we attempted another dance party with our drunken hostel friends. Our party only lasted a few minutes before the cops showed up again and shut us down. Our friends weren't ready to call it a night yet, so we all walked down to the bar district where they got blackout wasted and us three sober Americans drank Cokes and laughed at funny situations. By 2:00 a.m. we were all too tired to have any more fun, so we took ourselves home and tucked ourselves in for the night.

Our last day in Pipa was nothing short of amazing.

We woke up early and set out for a nice trail ride on our bikes. Somehow, a short trail ride took us fifty kilometers down the beach, and I found myself out of gas—again! We took care of it by draining some of Dave's gas into a water bottle and pouring it into my tank. We rode south in search of a mystical lighthouse that someone had told us about. We crossed a couple ferries, passed though some really old beach towns, and ended up on the hard-packed sand and cruising up the beach again.

Nian and I were going as fast as we could just laughing and soaking up the experience. Dave on the other hand, would get going as fast as he could and see how far he could drive out into the shallow surf. We tried convincing him that it was a bad idea, and he finally believed us when he got his spark plug wet and his bike wouldn't start again until it was dry.

While searching for this lighthouse, we found another giant dead turtle, we all hit vultures on our bikes, Dave got hit by a monster wave and found himself up to his seat in ocean water, and we all got some good sun. After riding forever up a sand dune and almost blowing up our bikes, we finally found the lighthouse. It wasn't as special as we had thought it was going to be, so we jumped on the coastal road and headed back to Pipa.

On our way home, Dave crept up on the side of me at like four miles per hour. As I was turning, I saw that I was going to hit him. I bailed off to avoid us both getting wasted. Luckily, we were going pretty slow. I landed on my feet and stopped, and Dave didn't even wreck. My first wreck of the trip and the only bad thing that happened was my brake lever got a little scratch. Thank goodness!

As soon as we arrived back at the hostel, Neto yelled, "You need to get to the Madeiro beach, NOW!"

There was a nest of giant sea turtles hatching! We dropped everything, grabbed a couple people each, and headed to the beach!

As I was running out, Neto yelled to me, "You're crazy! The cops are gonna bust you for riding with three people without helmets."

I ran back and grabbed helmets for the two girls riding with me, and we headed for the beach after the others. We were almost there, but as I rolled over a hill—COPS! I slammed on my brakes, turned around, and went back over the hill to drop off one girl. After I dropped her off, I rode right back over the hill and past the cops. Nian and the others were all stopped, talking to the cops. They had no helmets, were riding three, and doing it in flip-flops. For some reason, I had my shoes on as well. I dropped the one girl off at the beach, rode back past the cops, grabbed the other girl from her hiding place, took her to the beach, and then dropped off my extra helmets for the others that were waiting at the police checkpoint. Long story short, we got everyone to the beach and none of us got tickets!

Once on the beach, we ran down the trail toward the water where there was a group of fifty or so people gathered and waiting for the baby turtle nest to hatch. Turned out, it had already hatched and there were only three turtles in the nest. The turtle specialist went to the next nest just to check on it, and it was hatching at the exact same time! The specialist opened the nest and it had over one hundred baby turtles in it! It was pretty awesome watching them struggle their way down the beach to the water. Truly an act of God.

After we finished saving the baby sea turtles, we went back to the hostel, showered, and we all went out to eat for our last night out in Pipa. All-you-can-eat pizza was a bad choice on such a warm day and so late at night. Needless to say, we didn't end up leaving like we thought we would. After eating, we ended up going out dancing with the whole hostel crew again and having an equally amazing time as every other night in Pipa.

We had been surrounded by amazing people during the whole trip! We had been to some of the most beautiful places on Earth, but what would be most ingrained in my mind was how amazing the people we met were! It seemed like everywhere we stopped, there was somebody there waiting to take super good care of us! Pipa wasn't an exception by any means.

Our time in Pipa was relaxing and more fun than we could have hoped for from one of our last beach visits on the Atlantic Coast. During the six days we spent there, we slept great, went to the gym, ate better than we did on the whole trip and for cheaper, attempted surfing a bunch, swam with the dolphins, and made friends that we would remember forever!

It was real awesome Pipa, but in the morning, THE WOLFPACK RIDES!

12

WE WERE (NOT) GETTING ROBBED!

Day 54
Sunday, March 21, 2010

Sunday morning, the three of us woke up as early as we could, said our sweet, sweet goodbyes to all of our new best friends, and hit the road once more! A couple short hours in the saddle, and we were in Natal.

We made sure to make it there before 10:00 a.m. so we could find ourselves a place to go to church. We searched for a bit and managed to find an LDS chapel. As we walked in, we got a lot of strange looks. I guess three big, dirty white guys dressed semi gangster just walking in off the street wasn't normal to them. We got our weekly church meetings in, grabbed some food, and got right back on our iron horses ready to run!

We rode some 530 kilometers, which seemed like forever, through rain, smoke, and wind. Finally, around 9:00 p.m., we pulled into Fortaleza. All three of us were wet and completely exhausted! We grabbed the first cheap, sketchy, motel we could find, locked our precious bikes up in their garage, and got some sleep.

The next day was bike fix up day!

For the past couple weeks, we had been asking people where

we could find cheap parts nearby. They almost always told us to wait and buy everything we needed in Fortaleza. We got out of our sketchy motel and headed downtown. After searching forever, we finally found it—motorcycle parts heaven! Both sides of the streets for miles were lined up with bikes and bike shops. My time had arrived for a new set of tires. I guess that's what you do after 9000 kilometers of pure, unadulterated South American adventuring on a used bike. After some serious homework, we discovered that we were soon going to be doing thousands of miles on the dirt roads of the Trans-Amazonian Highway from here on out.

I rolled into the tire store and said, "I need the biggest, meanest, knobby, street tires you have."

An hour later, the Tornado rolled out looking like a regular off-road dirt bike. The three of us also made a necessary investment and put performance exhaust pipes on our bikes. For some reason, Nian's bike was a full twenty kilometers per hour slower than mine and Dave's bikes. We loaded up our packs with spare parts and tools, bought new rain gear, fixed Dave's visor on his helmet, and started getting Dave's rebuilt motor inspected. Just as we were trying to finish up our maintenance tasks, it got dark and the shops were closing.

We got some food and decided we'd finish up our bikes in the morning, and then we'd get straight on the road! We weren't stoked to hang out in Fortaleza at night. Fortaleza had a huge problem with prostitution and sex trafficking type stuff. Not wanting cute Nian to get kidnapped and sold into sex slavery, we hurried back to our sketchy motel and got another room while we waited for the shops to finish up a few small repairs on the bikes.

In the morning, we got all our gear packed up and jetted straight into town. Once back at the repair shops, we got the bad news. Dave's motor was all messed up—AGAIN!

What the heck!

We wanted nothing more than to be on the road, but the last thing we needed was to be in the middle of the largest jungle in the world with a bad bike. Dave hung out with his bike mechanics while Nian and I explored Fortaleza. After hours and hours of walking around and killing time, I got a text from Dave.

It's about ready to roll!

We hustled back over to the repair shop, made a few last-minute adjustments, Dave traded a mechanic his T-shirt for a hoodie, and we got on the road! Our plan from there was to ride a little way up the coast to the beach town of Jericoacoara. People had been telling us about this amazing beach town for a month. We had to at least check it out. We figured we would go up there and enjoy the beach for a day or two and then head inland toward the Amazon. But to tell you the truth, we had seen enough beach. We were ready to get into the jungle!

The three of us held a silent prayer in our hearts that Dave's bike wouldn't blow up as we rode north. We only had five hours to ride until we would be sitting on beautiful, white sandy beaches. It was soon completely dark and a little bit rainy. After getting gas, I looked back, and somewhere we had lost Nian along the way. We were only half an hour from our destination. We waited for thirty minutes before deciding Nian was a big boy and he'd get there, so we kept going.

Dave and I headed toward the beach town, took a wrong turn, and ended up in the middle of some huge sand dunes in the middle of nowhere! Keep in mind that our bikes are awful in the sand. We pushed our bikes to the limit as we fought to get through more than a mile of soft sand. Once through the dunes, we stopped in the middle of a dirt road to figure out what was going on.

By this time, it was almost 2:00 a.m. As I looked at my GPS, I heard a door slam! Just as I looked up, some really old dude ran out of his house in his underwear! Not knowing what to do, I asked him how to get to Jericoacoara. He yelled a bunch of gibberish, and all I understood was that we needed to take a fifteen-kilometer trail through mud, sand dunes, and beach to get to the city.

Just as we were about to get going, another old man jumped out of the bushes directly in our path! He was obviously drunk, holding a two-foot knife, and looked like he had never taken a shower in his whole life! He yelled a bunch of nonsense and then asked us for a ride into town.

Dave and I just looked at each other and bailed outta there! The next half hour was one of the most physically demanding rides of the trip so far! We were basically riding along a trail through sand dunes that followed the beach. Dave and I both wrecked five or six times. Having our huge heavy packs tied to the back of our bikes made them super top heavy. This made it almost impossible to keep our bikes upright when we lost momentum. We were both getting pretty frustrated when we finally broke out of the dunes and hit the beach. The beach was covered in hard sand, which made riding a dream!

From there, we could see the lights of a small city far off in the distance. We were there! We both yelled for joy as we weaved back and forth riding down the beach.

We were riding side by side when, all of a sudden, we rode through a wet spot in the sand, a deep stream of rainwater running into the ocean. We both hit it at the same time, which, of course, soaked both of us! Normally this would have been pretty funny, but neither of us smiled this time. We had put up a hard fight to get to Jericoicoara, and we both wanted to be there already.

As we pulled into the town, we were surprised to find out that the streets were all pretty much just soft beach sand. We leaned our bikes on some palm trees and set out on foot in search of Nian. We were hoping he had gone around our sand dune sidetrack and beat us there. It only took us twenty minutes to cover the whole town. No sign of Nian. As we enjoyed some fresh mango juice, a lady came up to us and offered to let us stay at her motel for $5. That sounded great to us! We sent Nian a message letting him know where we were, said our prayers, and hit the hay!

A loud knock got Dave and me right out of bed!

It was the lady that owned the motel. She was way nervous about us being in there after checkout.

In the Pursuit of Life

Thanks to a dark room and cold A/C, Dave and I had slept for almost ten hours. We told the lady that we'd pay for our room for another half day and we hit the streets again in search of Nian. We ran to an internet cafe and checked our messages. Still no word from Nian. We both feared the worst: Nian had actually gotten kidnapped and sold into sex slavery.

As we walked back toward our motel, we saw a dark figure racing toward us from down the dusty, sandy street. A few seconds later, we could tell it was Nian! We breathed a huge sigh of relief. As he pulled his helmet off, he was already laughing.

He yelled, "Guys! I almost slept in a whorehouse last night!" (NIANS STORY.)

Now that we had found Nian, we were ready to get on the road toward the Trans-Amazonian Highway that would lead us through the jungle and eventually to Manaus. As Dave and I walked with Nian back to the motel to gear up for our epic ride, a strange wind began to blow.

I looked around and said, "It's gonna rain, boys!"

Dave and I tucked Nian in at the motel so he could get some sleep. After we had put Nian down for his nap, we put on some board shorts and headed out in the rain. Starving from being so worried about Nian, we got some lunch and hoped that the rain would slow down. It just got heavier. Trying to kill some time, we found a gym and made friends with the owner. We pumped up some sweet music in his gym and he let us work out for free. After an hour of serious exercise, it was still pouring!

We splashed in puddles for a bit and went to check on Nian. Once we got back in the freezing cold room, Dave and I were soon fast asleep.

BOOM, BOOM, BOOM! Annoying bang on the door. It was the owner wanting us out of there again. It had finally stopped raining. We geared up really quick and pushed our bikes out to the street. The owner ran outside, freaking out about us owing her more money. After debating the situation in English, we decided that she was ripping us off. We all laughed, started our bikes, jumped on, and busted it out of town!

I don't think any of us realized how late it was when we jumped on to ride. About an hour into our ride, it was pretty much completely dark and very foggy from all the evaporating rain. After another hour, we had made it just about 200 kilometers.

As we got gas, a cool gas station attendant made us a bunch of pastels and other food. He told us we were crazy for riding at night and talked us into camping out there at the gas station. He said we shouldn't worry because he'd be awake all night and he'd make sure no one messed with us or our stuff.

Just to the side of the gas station there was a covered gazebo/ picnic area. We organized our stuff in the middle of the shelter and hung our hammocks around the poles. Worried that someone would try to shank me in the middle of the night, I tied my hammock as close to the roof as I could. Nian gave me a boost into my hammock, I pulled my Paraguayan blanket over my face to keep the mosquitos off, and within a few seconds, I was fast asleep.

Day 58
Thursday, March 25, 2010

It was 3:00 a.m. I was fast asleep with a cheap blanket tied around my face. All of a sudden, I was awakened by men yelling in Portuguese! I tore the blanket off my head and saw three guys yelling and running around through the middle of our bikes and gear! One of my worst fears had come true!

WE WERE GETTING ROBBED!

I slingshotted out of my high hammock, ready to throw down! Fists up, I was expecting the men to either come at me or run away. They did neither. They just continued jumping and yelling in the middle of our small camp.

In Portuguese, I yelled, "What's going on?"

They responded, but I couldn't understand what they were saying. Turned out, they were trying to kill a rat! The three men beat a giant rat to death with sticks and then casually walked back over toward the gas station.

My heart raced at an exploding rate as I laid back down and tried to sleep. I had thought it was finally time for the three of us to get into the brawl of a lifetime! We joked about it all the time, but none of us actually hoped we would ever have to fight it out. Unless I was completely tired, when we slept out in our hammocks, I never really slept very well. I was always very comfortable, but I couldn't help but sleep with one eye open. It was hard to get a good, sound night's sleep when the only thing on my mind was the thought of some thug cutting down our hammocks and stealing our bikes—or even worse, the thought of getting shot in our hammocks while we slept. After what must have been hours of tossing and turning in my hammock, I finally managed to calm down and get a little bit more sleep.

As I tossed and turned, I opened my eyes and noticed the dim crack of light along the horizon. I looked at my cell phone which was conveniently plugged in right by my hammock and the light switch. It was 5:00 a.m., and we were going to cover some serious ground that day!

I rolled over, switched on the light and yelled "Bom Dia!" which means good morning.

As soon as we had our hammocks rolled up and tied to our bikes, we hit the road. It was going to be our big day! We were going to try and put somewhere between 1000 and 1500 kilometers behind us. That would be our longest day on the bikes by far!

Around 100 kilometers into our epic ride, Dave's bike started leaking serious oil. Lucky for us, we noticed it right as we were passing through a small town. Soon, we had Dave's bike in a mechanic shop and torn completely apart again. The three of us grabbed some food and walked around the little town. Nian and I washed our bikes and some three hours later the mechanics had Dave's bike going. Maybe we needed to quit making lofty goals for the distance we would ride. It seemed like every time we did that, Dave's bike had motor problems!

We were back on the road! It was now afternoon, and we knew that if we wanted to make it to the town of Teresina by nightfall, we had better hustle! The next 400 kilometers were non-stop, hardcore riding. That meant passing everyone we overtook on the road, regardless of road conditions and traffic situations. The further and further we got from the beach, the more things started looking like we were in the jungle. The thought of riding through the heart of the Amazon seemed to call out to us and drove us to keep riding, even though we were tired and sore.

We had been on the road for probably five hours when I looked around and couldn't find Dave. Great, we lost him again! I sent him a text message and told him that we would wait for him at the first gas station we came to in Teresina. Nian and I rode on, but not before we stopped and cut the claws off of a dead sloth that had turned itself into roadkill!

Right before dark, Nian and I pulled up to the first gas station in Teresina. We waited for half an hour or more.

I looked at Nian and said, "If Dave was coming, he would have been here by now. Do we ride back and find him or ride on to meet up with him down the road?"

We decided to ride on. I sent Dave another text letting him know our plans.

Nian and I weaved ourselves through the city and finally figured out how to get across this huge river and to the west side of the city. Following my trusty GPS, we followed a main road and rode as far west as we could without leaving the city.

I stopped and checked my text messages while Nian rode up ahead about a mile. No reply or word from Dave. I rode up to where Nian was stopped and took off my helmet.

THERE IT WAS! THE END OF THE PAVEMENT! The Trans-Amazonian Highway is a 5000-kilometer road that cuts across the Amazon rainforest. Only parts of it were paved. This part wasn't. We had no idea what we were in store for, and what was worse, we had no idea what had happened to Dave. As we watched the Amazonian sun set over a giant dust cloud and 200-foot-tall trees, Nian and I chugged some Guaranás while waiting to hear from Dave.

My phone rang! It was a strange, unknown number. It was Dave! Somehow, he had passed us and had ridden almost two hours down the dirt road that Nian and I were about to embark on. Once he had ridden into the jungle, his cell reception had gotten lost. He had ridden on until he had found a pay phone. He told us that he had a flat tire and was about to tell us the name of the little village he was in when…

Silence. The last little bit of credit on my prepaid phone ran out!

Nian and I made an educated guess as to where he was, and we made dust down the dirt road!

After riding over 150 kilometers down the dusty dirt highway, I was ready to call it a night. Every corner either revealed a strange person, a cow, or another crazy animal in the road. As we were about to give up hope and set up camp in the jungle, we puttered into a little trucker restaurant shack. I saw a pay phone and figured Dave must be close.

We rode around the shack and saw Dave's bike parked on the side. He was just sitting at a big table having a grand ol' time while eating with the eight women that lived and worked there.

Nian and I were soon eating as well. We weren't having as much fun though. We were both mentally exhausted after riding so far in bad conditions.

After eating, we were going to hang up hammocks and sleep there. One of the ladies was being very friendly with Dave. Too friendly. I didn't think Dave noticed it, but Nian and I sure did. I got up and walked around back looking for a bathroom. I opened four or five doors to see if they were the bathroom. Behind every door I opened was a small room with a bed in the corner. I got weird vibes and decided to abandon my search and pee in the trees.

I went back inside, and the Wolfpack talked the situation over in English.

I looked at Dave and said, "I know these ladies are very nice and very friendly. Do you find it at all odd that there are eight decent looking ladies living here without any men? Bro, these nice ladies don't make a living off of their cooking. I just went into the back looking for a bathroom. All I found was love shacks!"

Dave still insisted that we sleep there, but Nian and I refused.

We thanked the nice ladies, paid them for our food, and headed out in search of a tire shop. We hadn't been out of the sketchy ladies' little roadside restaurant for two minutes when some kid came by and said, "Hey, my uncle has a tire shop that will be open first thing in the morning. Why don't you come sleep at my house? Nobody's there and we've got hammocks already hung up."

I felt uneasy about doing that, but we all decided the three of us could punk this kid if he tried anything.

As we walked Dave's bike over to this kid's house, I asked, "Hey, do you have a shower, by chance?"

He assured me that they had a great shower. This sounded amazing since I hadn't showered in a couple days and Nian and I had just eaten each other's dust for the last 150 kilometers. We pushed our bikes through a gate and onto the back patio of this kid's house. Quick surveying informed us that a) the house was made of mud and was still under construction, b) it had a good grass roof that was pretty much enclosed, and c) it had a door. Good enough for me, just as long as this kid didn't pull a gun on us!

We walked inside and sure enough, it was just as he described it—three small bedrooms and one door. Oh, and for some reason, there was a satellite dish on top of the grass roof. The whole house reminded me of an old pioneer-built grain barn on our farm where I grew up. Inside, there were four hammocks hung from the rafters. Nian immediately called the one he wanted to sleep in, next it was my turn, and it was Dave's day for last pick on sleeping privileges.

Fun fact: After only a week into our trip, it had seemed that Dave and Nian were always fighting over what bed they wanted to sleep in. I didn't think either one cared, but they just loved to argue. Ever since then, we had been taking turns deciding who got to sleep where.

Our new buddy lit a bunch of candles, and the little mud shack was soon glowing. We gathered our things inside by candlelight and got ready for some sleep.

Our buddy said, "Oh, do you guys want to take a shower?"

I accepted his offer and followed him out into the darkness. We walked about fifty yards from the mud house. My buddy walked under a small lean to where he twisted a light bulb that was hanging from two bare wires for some light. As my eyes focused, I quickly learned that our new friend and I had different definitions of what made a nice shower.

We were at the family well house. Our friend dropped a bucket with a rope tied to it down a hole.

Splash!

He pulled it up, handed it to me, and said, "Turn out the light when you're done."

He then turned around and disappeared back into the darkness.

I stripped down and poured a bucket of freezing water over my head. I dropped the bucket in the hole and pulled it back up full of water. I sat the bucket down and tried to soap up my now muddy body.

Just as I was about to rinse off and get out of there, I heard a lady start yelling from a neighboring house about thirty yards away. She was super mad! She thought I was a stranger out there stealing water at midnight. There I stood, completely naked as this old lady walked closer and closer while giving me a good tongue lashing!

I assured her that I was friends with the kid at the other house, and she finally went back inside.

I quickly finished my "shower" and hurried back to the shanty so Dave could have his turn at the well-bucket shower. I told the guys about my naked confrontation with the angry neighbor lady and we all had a good laugh!

I wrapped up in my little Paraguayan blanket, laid down in my hammock to go to sleep, and just then realized how awesome this situation was! Four hammocks tied up in a makeshift mud shack, crickets singing, strange animals yelling in the jungle, candles burning, and three amigos swinging and smiling while falling asleep!

Once again, we were rudely awoken at 5:00 in the morning! I heard a loud thud that was immediately followed by moans and groans. Dave's flashlight cut through the darkness. I looked over at Dave standing in the doorway to one of the little rooms.

He shook his head and said, "My hammock broke. How did the biggest guy get stuck with the kids' hammock?"

We fixed it and tried going back to sleep, but it was no use. The loud drone of roosters meant we were already up for the day. We packed our gear up while our new buddy and host ran over to his mother's house and then ran back to inform us of the good news. We were invited to breakfast!

As we walked down the path toward his mom's house, I looked up and realized that we were going to the house where the old lady had come from to yell at me during my shower.

I looked at Dave and Nian and jokingly said, "You guys can just go ahead and thank me for this amazing breakfast. This is the old lady that saw me naked at the shower last night. She liked what she saw and is now going to treat us really nice!"

We had a good laugh and sat down around the table on her front porch. I had only been joking, but she was actually super nice and overly friendly toward me! Every time she said anything to me, Dave and Nian laughed.

Breakfast consisted of one hardboiled egg, some couscous, and one little cup of warm, raw milk. Nian wouldn't touch eggs, so he just walked away. Dave and I told him he was being an ungrateful guest and demanded that he eat the egg. Dave and I thanked our hosts and apologized for Nian's rudeness! These people had offered Nian more that they should have, and he had just walked away from it. The next four hours consisted of Dave and Nian arguing about whether what Nian did was morally acceptable or not.

We loaded up our gear and wheeled Dave's bike across the street to our buddy's uncle's tire shop.

Soon, we had Dave's tire fixed and we were hot on the road! Right through the heart of the Amazon! It was a beautiful day, and we were loving it! Not more than twenty kilometers into our day, I looked down for some GPS guidance and saw an empty void where my GPS should have been!

"I lost the GPS! NO!"

It must have bounced out somewhere between breakfast and where we currently were. I immediately raced back to the little village where we had slept. I spent over an hour searching and scouring the sides of the road. It was useless. I had lost a $500 electronic device on a dirt highway in Brazil. If it didn't bounce off into the jungle, someone definitely stopped and picked it up. It was gone forever. Our guiding light and ultimate road map was gone. That hurt a lot. I was in a bad mood for a little while.

For some reason, my eagle scout preparedness skills had prompted me to pack a second GPS. I pulled it out and tied it to my handlebars. This was an old Garmin automotive GPS that I had packed just in case we ended up buying a car. The automotive GPS worked, but I hadn't downloaded the South American maps to it before I left. I was only able to see major roads and cities. The GPS I had lost had every little detail on it.

Mad about our loss, I suggested that we get some ground behind us, so we rode on! The further we got down the dirt road, the more and more it felt like we were embarking on a jungle safari. It was hard to stay on the road with so much exotic roadkill to stop and see! So far, we had already seen three dead anacondas, one dead alligator, three dead sloths, a bunch of dead monkeys, and other animals that we were unable to identify. We were around 10,000+ kilometers into the trip. Only 2000 kilometers more, and we would be in Manaus!

About an hour before dark, my rear wheel started to shake really bad. After assessing the situation, I couldn't believe my eyes. My sprockets and chain were already completely worn out! I had burned through a new set of sprockets and a chain in less than two weeks!

As we fueled up, I pulled out my tools and tightened my chain. We talked to the gas station attendant who recommended that we set our destination for the small town of Porto Franco, which was about an hour up the Trans-Amazonian dirt highway. Once there, we could probably find some sort of motorbike parts store.

We were soon in Porto Franco and trying to hustle a deal with the local bike mechanic. It took the guys a couple hours to find the parts and get them put on our bikes. In the meantime, we got some food and enjoyed some delicious "Jesus" brand guarana drinks. As soon as my bike was ready to roll, we were back on the road! It was soon dark. Right about then, we learned the hard way that in the jungle, darkness also brings on intense fogginess. It was so foggy that I had to use my left hand as a windshield wiper to keep the moisture off of my helmet visor.

We rode on into the misty darkness for what seemed like forever. I was getting to the point where I was going to fall asleep at the handlebars when we saw a faint light. We had finally made it to some sort of civilization where we could find an okay place to camp without worrying about jaguars or anacondas teasing us in the middle of the night. The road we were on took us down a huge hill and, finally, we popped out of the forest just to find that the city I thought we had found was just a small village on a river.

As we pulled up to the river, there seemed to be something missing. There wasn't a bridge! Lucky for us, we showed up right as the last ferry of the night was about to cross over to the other side. We gave the guy some money and rode aboard. Twenty minutes later, we were across the river and in another village.

We split up to look for a nice place to hang up our hammocks. I found a little schoolhouse on the outskirts of town that looked pretty decent. I started planning hammock situations while I waited there for Dave and Nian. All the trees around the school were too far apart for hammocks or they were too close to the dirt highway for comfort. Then I saw it. The water box!

Most buildings in Brazil have a huge water box on top of them where fresh water is stored. The water is pumped into the box and then the gravity of the water flowing all the way down from the top of the box provides water pressure for the house. This particular water box was probably thirty feet tall and built on a 10' X 10' framework of timbers. It was perfect.

Dave and Nian rode up and saw the work of wonder. Soon, all three of us had our hammocks tied up toward the top of the water box and we tiredly joked about getting mugged or getting carried away by mosquitos. We covered ourselves with bug spray, wrapped blankets around our smelly bodies, and listened to the spooky sounds of the jungle as we drifted off to sleep.

13

THE SHORTCUT MADE OF MUD

Day 60
Saturday, March 27, 2010

Waking up in a hammock in the middle of the jungle is one of the craziest experiences ever. You open your eyes and expect to be at home in bed, but when reality sinks in, you are hanging thirty feet in the air in the middle of the jungle. It always makes for a good time!

We actually slept in for once. We would have slept longer, but school bells soon had us up and trying to get out of there before anyone could come get mad at us for camping on school grounds. We commenced our daily routine of wrapping up our hammocks, attaching all of our belongings to our bikes, changing nasty clothes, and brushing our teeth. After finally sleeping good for once, we were all feeling great!

Once we were all loaded up, we spun our wheels and started hustling down the dirt road! We hadn't gone more than half a mile when I looked back and Dave was stopped. I looked again but this time longer. When I looked back in front of me, Nian had slammed on his brakes.

Oh Shoot!

A split second later and I slammed into him! I bailed off my bike, rolled, and slid to a dirty stop on the dusty road.

I was pissed! Not only at Nian, but also at myself. My shoulder, elbows, knees, and hands had pretty bad road rash on them. I stood up, calmly dusted myself off, picked up my bike, and rode off in a fit of internal rage.

I rode as fast as I could until I arrived at the next village. There was a gas station there. I pulled in and busted out my first aid kit, washed out my wounds, and got myself all doctored up. I was still pretty mad, but a bunch of Brazilian gas station candy made all my anger go away. After fueling, feeding ourselves, and getting washed up, we were soon back on the road.

By now, it was apparent that we were far, far away from any big civilization. Towns that we passed got smaller and smaller, and the trees around us got bigger and bigger. The views and scenery at this point of the trip were absolutely amazing! Giant trees, huge rivers, small villages, crazy birds, and luscious greenness were around every corner.

After a few more hours on the trail we were all hungry. A break in the jungle revealed a fishing village next to a massive river. After taking some awesome pictures on a rickety wooden bridge, we befriended some of the villagers and bought some drinks and snacks from them. Before long, we had become great friends with the village river folk.

After about twenty minutes I was catching fish with some kids while Dave and Nian paddled around the river in a wooden canoe that the villagers had carved out of a giant tree. I looked out and noticed that the canoe was about three quarters of an inch out of the water! I guess the villagers didn't realize that Dave and Nian were almost double their size. Luckily they didn't sink it, because our new friends cooked up some fish for us and made sure we were plenty full for the rest of the day. What a beautiful place! We all agreed that we could spend a week or two there, but we had to ride on.

We said goodbye to the river folk, jumped on our motos, and rode another few hundred more kilometers down the Trans-Amazonian dirt road highway.

Right as the sun started slipping below the horizon, I pulled over on a hill and said, "You guys feel that? It's about to open up and pour rain!"

We quickly strapped on our rain gear and prepared for our highway to turn into slippery mud! We decided we'd hustle to the next gas station or rest stop. Around 10:00 p.m. we found shelter at a small bar/truck stop on the side of the road. Soon, we had made friends with the owner who kindly invited us to hang our hammocks up under his front porch balcony where his pool tables were. This nice old bar owner let us take freezing showers, made us food, and sold me a giant snake-killing machete. We hung out with the locals and had some good laughs.

Sometime around midnight we climbed into our hammocks to call it a night. Just as we were drifting off to sleep, I heard lightning crack off in the distance! A few minutes later, we were engulfed in an unbelievable storm! Wind, lightning, thunder, and deafening rain on the roof kept me up for another couple hours.

The sound of rain beating down on a tin roof almost drowned out the drone of the tree frogs, but we were clean, dry, and safe! Once asleep, we all slept great in our hammocks. I woke up early and noticed that it was still a drowning downpour, so I went back to sleep. The rain didn't really slow down until after 9:00 a.m., when the downpour became a drizzle.

After some discussion, we finally decided that it probably wasn't going to stop at all. We wrapped everything we owned in plastic bags and got ready to hit the trail. Everything was awesome except for one minor mishap. My rain gear was nowhere to be found! I had left it at a gas station more than 400 kilometers back. I put on this bright purple poncho that our friend Liam had given us in Pipa, and we rode out.

After a good hour of riding hard down the muddiest roads ever, I was completely drenched and covered with mud! I was getting super cold, so the second we came across a small town, I set out looking for some new rain gear. It was 11:00 a.m. on a rainy Sunday morning, and we were in a tiny town in the middle of the Amazon. Any store that might have sold rain gear was definitely going to be closed, but I was set on finding some gear. The silly purple poncho just wasn't cutting it.

I scoured the entire town frantically, asking everyone if they knew of anyone or anywhere that would sell me rain gear. More than an hour of searching and I found a moto store with the back door open. Lucky for me, the guy lived in his store. He opened up his shop and sold me the only rain gear he had, which also happened to be really nice and exactly my size. Once again, my prayers were answered in the form of a miracle.

I didn't want to get the inside of my new rain gear muddy. We stopped at the nearest gas station, and I showered the mud off of myself in the nastiest, smelliest gas station bathroom I had ever experienced in my entire life! We were in business and back on the road!

We rode way hard through mud and rain all day. The roads were nuts! Nian got his front tire caught in a rut as we were climbing this crazy big hill and somehow ended up backwards and upside down in a mud puddle. He was pretty shook up, but some words of encouragement got him back on the road. We slowly made our way around stuck semis, giant puddles, and small rivers all over the road. Every time we stopped for gas or food, people would tell us that we were out of our minds!

Every single person would say, "You're crazy! What if you break down out here? There's no stores to fix your bikes! You don't ride at night, do you?"

"Yes."

"No way! You're crazy! You're going to get robbed!"

Every time someone said this, we looked at each other and smiled.

We rode through jungle, rivers, fog, and mud, broke down, fixed our bikes, saw the most amazing sunset of our lives, and finally, Sunday night, we made it to the small jungle town of Uruará.

We rolled into town completely exhausted. After a little searching, we found another gas station/restaurant/rest stop that let us hang our hammocks up inside their restaurant for the night. We took a shower at the gas station and set up camp. We were all starving, so we went into town.

Little did we know, this little Amazonian town in the middle of the jungle was nothing short of pure craziness! We rode down the main street along with what I guessed were 500 of the town's youth population on motorbikes. We asked a guy what was going on, and he informed us that everyone goes to the main road every night and just does laps around the town's central park. It was crazy! I felt like I was in a Motocross race!

After taking some laps with the other 500 riders and getting some food, the Wolfpack took it back to camp and got some good rest for our upcoming day.

We were kicked out of the restaurant encampment pretty early the next morning. We gathered up our gear and headed into town to find a hardware store. I needed to wire up a cigarette lighter plug on my bike so I could charge my automotive GPS while we were riding. Up to that point, I had been turning it on and off to conserve the battery.

I struck up a conversation with a nice guy at the hardware store. He asked where we were going. I told him that we were planning on riding another 1500 kilometers to the Southwest toward the town of Porto Velho. Once there, we were going to ride the remaining 1000 kilometers north toward Manaus. The guy just looked at me like I was out of my mind!

He said, "Why are you going the long way to Manaus? You should take the shortcut. Once you ride out of town you are going to pass a store on your right. Turn right at that store. Continue on this dirt road for 210 kilometers and you will arrive at the city of Santarem on the Amazon River. Once at Santarem, you are going to want to find the river port. Every couple days, there's a river boat that sails up the river from Santarem to Manaus. You can pay them to put your bikes on the boat, and then you can relax until you get to Manaus. I must warn you though. You definitely don't want to break down while you're on the 200-kilometer shortcut through the jungle. There are jaguars, snakes,

Indians, and a hundred other things that can kill you out there!"

The wheels in my head were turning 100 kilometers per hour! I thanked this nice fellow for the advice, gathered up my electrical supplies, and hustled outside to share this new information with the Wolfpack! The decision was unanimous!

"WE'RE TAKING THE SHORTCUT AND SAILING UP THE AMAZON!"

We set out in search of supplies and spent the next few hours getting ourselves ready for this extreme 200-kilometer ride through the jungle. We got Dave a new chain and sprocket, outfitted ourselves with handy new fanny packs, enjoyed some Amazonian food, relaxed for a minute, and then we headed down the road toward "The Shortcut."

We found the little store that my friend had told me about, turned right, and headed down the dirt road right through the middle of the jungle! People we had talked to while getting parts in town had said that it was a rough road but that we'd fly right across it with our bikes. We had no idea what we had signed up for!

We busted out the first 100 kilometers no problem! Well, one problem. No more than ten kilometers into our ride, Nian tried riding across a thin ridge of mud in the middle of a massive puddle. Needless to say, he ended up upside down and backwards again!

Around every bend there were monstrous puddles, gigantic eight-foot diameter trees across the trail, and crazy slick muddy spots! All in all, we had made pretty good time up to that point. At about the halfway mark, we took a break to oil our chains and rest our soggy butts.

When we turned our bikes off, we heard the craziest sounds ever! We were surrounded by howler monkeys. They were screaming like gorillas all around us! Pretty nuts! I felt like I was in a scary movie!

We ate a small snack and set out of the second half of the shortcut. This was where things got crazy! The next twenty kilometers took us over four hours to get across! The road was fifty yards wide and was made up of pure mud and quicksand! Some of the puddles were over four feet deep! There were trees across the trail that were over eight feet in diameter! It took all three of us to help each other creep, lift, push, pull, and drag our bikes across this swamp!

I kept getting nervous because every few hundred yards we'd cross a six-inch trench weaving across the trail. All I could think was, *That must be one big snake to leave a track like that! I don't want to meet that guy.*

The mud got so bad that we all just put on our swimsuits and drove right through the middle of it! After the super swampy section of the shortcut, we were all excited just to ride fast again.

Dave was clipping along at a decent rate when his front tire slipped into a puddle. He had assumed that the puddle wasn't more than six inches deep. It was, in fact, almost two feet deep. Dave's front tire stopped immediately, which caused his back end to flip around and slingshot Dave from his bike.

I slammed on my brakes, threw my bike down, and ran over to the scene. Since we were only wearing board shorts, Dave was chewed up pretty bad. We used what water we had to wash out his road rash, but we didn't have near enough. We needed to get him washed up quick so he didn't get infected. Jungle infections are no joke!

Soon after Dave's mishap, I went to put my foot down as we were riding around a corner and the ground just sunk away beneath my foot. It twisted my knee backwards and all the weight of me, my bike, and gear pinned my bad knee backwards underneath my bike. I was certain that my leg was about to break. Good thing my buddies Dave and Nian were right behind me or I would have been in major trouble!

After more than seven hours of pure intense riding, we finally made it to the other side of the jungle. The shortcut trail will forever go down in history as the craziest ride of my life!

Right before crossing a foot bride back to civilization, we found a massive abandoned mango grove. We ate mangos until we were almost sick. We pushed our bikes onto the foot bridge and rode to the other side. After riding thousands of miles on muddy dirt roads, we had made it back to pavement! Nian got down and kissed the ground.

Night was fast approaching, so we got our gear together and hustled the next fifty kilometers to Santarem. Nian ran over a massive lizard and stopped to take some pride pictures. All the running over crabs on the beach must have been good practice. As we got to Santarem, we searched out the river boat but only after getting our bikes washed up and detailed.

We worked our way onto the boat where we made friends with the captain. He said we could crash on the boat that night as it didn't leave until the next afternoon. We hung up our hammocks, showered the mud off for like thirty minutes each, and crashed out!

We had logged over 3000 kilometers in the past week, and we definitely felt it! Now we were going to take a three-day boat ride/nap up the Amazon to Manaus. It would be nice to rest up for a bit!

MOTO TEAM...OUT!

Day 63
Tuesday, March 30, 2010

We slept great the first night in the port. We had heard that Santarem was supposed to have "the most amazing freshwater beach in the world," so we woke up early and rode in that direction. We stopped for some breakfast and to get our bikes looked over. As we ate, lo and behold, here came our archnemesis for this whole trip, Torrential Rain! And how it rained. Seriously, the roads became rivers in the matter of five minutes.

We waited out the rain for over an hour. As the time our ship was supposed to sail got closer, the downpour slowed to a drizzle. The three of us grabbed our now clean bikes and raced back toward the port. Three days is a long time to be on a boat eating only rice and beans, so Nian and I bought some food while Dave hustled over to the boat to buy our boarding passes.

Completely loaded with cookies, chocolate wafers, delicious

juices, and other goodies, Nian and I headed for the boat to meet Dave with our tickets. Upon arriving at the boat, we were greeted by four angry policemen carrying machine guns. They made us park our bikes and proceeded to search our gear. As they performed an inspection on our bikes, they found that Nian's license plate was broken off.

In Brazil, a bike's license plate has to stay with the bike for the life of the machine. They even put a wire lock on it to make sure that it never gets taken off or tampered with. Needless to say, they were very unhappy with Nian and his broken license plate. They started giving us some serious guff, which was not good because our boat was scheduled to leave shortly. I learned that three of them were in an English class, and we were soon laughing and having a good time talking about how cool their guns were. It was a close call, but we made it to our river barge just in time.

We lifted our bikes onto the bottom level of the boat and then hoisted them down into the gallows for the rest of the three-day ride.

As we boarded, we discovered that a few more people had joined us for our three-day river trip. By a few people, I mean like 350 more people! We pushed our way through a colorful, rainbow, spider web of hammocks and people and finally found our stuff. Instead of having staterooms, this cruise ship just had thousands of hooks and one big open floor. There were three rows of hammock hooks all spaced about a foot apart. The night before, we had shared this big open floor with maybe ten or fifteen other people. All of us had taken plenty of space to spread out our gear and sleep comfortably.

Nian's and my hammocks were now a foot apart, and a family of seven had squeezed in between Dave and me. The lady right next to me was way bigger than I was, and her ninety-year-old feeble mother was right next to her. Our stuff was scattered all over the place. We all looked at each other and thought to ourselves, *awesome!* Here we were, ready for a comfortable boat ride up the Amazon, and suddenly it felt like the packed inside of a crowded city bus. As the barge shoved off and steamed upriver, we laid down in our hammocks and attempted to settle in for a long ride.

Nian and I fell asleep. When we woke up, there were people jammed up—touching us—all around us. I was honestly shocked. It was around 7:00 p.m. and everyone was hustling around for dinner.

The Wolfpack went up to the top deck and enjoyed our dinner of cookies and Guaraná. We talked and relaxed on the top deck until sometime around 11:00 p.m. Hopefully we were tired enough to fall asleep with strange people touching us on each side. We dropped down to the hammock deck and attempted to squeeze into hour hammocks. I woke up the ninety-year-old lady sleeping next to me. She just rolled over and stared at me. I laid down in my hammock and stared right back at her until I finally fell asleep!

Night one, I don't think any of us really slept at all. It turned out, I had hung my hammock under an extremely bright nightlight. Dave and Nian both got up to go to the bathroom in the middle of the night and were confronted by an unfriendly scene. The guy with his hammock right next to the bathroom door had thrown up chunks of his dinner of chicken and rice all over the place. The guys found out that it was vomit by walking through it. The worst part was that Dave was barefoot! I still think Nian was grossed out more.

The drone of the ship's motors woke me up somewhat early. I scrambled up to the main deck where I enjoyed a breakfast of fresh fruit and fresh juice. We had been on the boat for almost a day, and I thought I had seen pretty much everything. We spent most of the day sleeping, playing cards, and watching the jungle pass by.

A bunch of people scrambled up to the top deck, so I followed suit and climbed the ladder up to the roof of the ship. They had all gone up to take pictures of *Encontra das Águas*. This means the meeting of the waters. This is where the Black River and the Amazon meet. There is a definite muddy line in the water that goes on for miles. They told us that it can even be seen from space.

Soon after passing the Encontra das Águas, we discovered that we were surrounded by freshwater dolphins that ranged in color from black, grey, blue, and pink. At times, they swam alongside us for miles. The dolphins were cool to watch. We saw some of the most amazing sunsets, sunrises, moonsets, and moonrises of our lives while on the boat. All of them occurred over the river, which made it that much more mystical.

After a while, I found out that some people had gone down to water level and slept in the cargo area. I grabbed all my gear and jumped right on that idea. Down on the cargo level, the whole back was full of crates of mangoes (which we were free to eat, I guess) (and were DELICIOUS), bananas, mamão, lemons, many other fruits and veggies, chickens, and a dog. The front of the boat was open and quite fresh. I hung my hammock so I could lay there and watch the Amazonian jungle pass by.

I had spent almost the whole first two days searching the riverbanks for sloths and jaguars, but we mostly saw cows, chickens, and river people, all of which were very interesting, but sloths and jaguars would have been so much cooler. The river was almost overflowing, so the shorelines were full of trees falling in the river, and the effects of erosion were everywhere. As it got late, I laid in my hammock watching the moon set over the river.

I smiled, shook my head, and thought, *What on earth am I doing? I am one lucky guy, and I live the best life ever!*

I hung a blanket up over the annoying nightlights, and the loud rumble of the ship's motors hummed me off to sleep. Night number two in the cargo area was a lot more relaxing than night number one in grandma's lap.

14

A LIFE-SIZED SILHOUETTE PORTRAIT OF NIAN

Day 65
Thursday, April 1, 2010

Once again, we arose with the sun. We took our hammocks down, tightened up our packs, and prepared ourselves for arrival into the Port of Manaus! A few minutes before disembarking, our old friend Mr. Rain showed up in full force, and once again made things complicated for the three-man Wolfpack. We rigged a pulley to the roof of the boat and hoisted our bikes out of the gallows. Lifting them out of the boat was a lot easier than we had expected. There were probably thirty guys trying to help us for money. I offered them five bucks to leave us alone. It just made it worse.

We soon had our bikes off the boat. We pulled out into the rain and were about to ride through a big steel gate to get out of the harbor when a guy came out screaming at us. Apparently we had to pay $25 each for a port tax. We had no money, so we spent a sweet twenty minutes trying to talk our way out of paying. I finally broke and went to an ATM while the guy detained Dave and Nian.

Upon arrival in Manaus, we were just happy to be back on dry ground. The riverboat was a cool experience, but the three of us had a hard time sitting still for that long. We got some lunch while we made a game plan. While we enjoyed some non-boat food and planned, we left our bikes at a shop so they could take care of some repairs that were necessary after the Shortcut trail ride.

Once they were repaired, Nian gave me an approximate address of where some of his friends lived in the city. I punched it in my GPS, we suited up in our tattered, muddy rain gear, and rode east through the city. Almost two hours later, we were finally on the other side of the city. My GPS took us through every scary, dirty ghetto possible! After a long, stressful ride through ghettos and industrial parks, and just after dark, we found one of Nian's old mission areas.

Relieved to be alive and at our destination, we stopped in and visited a couple families that Nian had known as a missionary. The second house we visited belonged to Brother Edivaldo and Sister Marta. Before we even had a chance to get our rain gear off, they insisted that we sleep there. The three of us looked at each other, smiled a little, and thankfully accepted their generous offer.

As a missionary, Nian had baptized their family of four. As you walk in their front door, the first thing you see on the wall in their living room is a life-sized silhouette portrait of the family and Nian. These people absolutely loved Nian!

After a full day of madness, the three of us were all too tired to even function. Sister Marta made us a delicious dinner of sandwiches and hot chocolate.

We must have smelled horrible because they were persistent that we shower before we went to bed.

We had all declined three or four times when Edivaldo finally said, "If you guys don't shower, you're going to have to sleep outside."

Though super tired, we finally broke and took a well-deserved bucket shower in their front yard. All three of us were completely out of clean clothes, so they let us borrow some pajamas. Everyone we met looked at us funny because we smelled like mud and mold. Inside all of our packs there was a rancid plastic sack of wet, muddy, sweaty clothes!

As soon as we were clean and dry, Edivaldo and Marta made us a place to sleep in the kids' room while their two kids slept on the couch. We three amigos laid down on mattresses and were almost instantly fast asleep. It had been almost two weeks of only sleeping in hammocks, so it was great to sleep on a mattress and in a house again!

I woke up in the morning more refreshed than I had ever felt in my entire life! As my eyes focused on the clock, I was shocked when I realized that we had slept for almost ten hours! We were three tired amigos. As we stumbled out of the bedroom we were greeted by Edivaldo, Marta, and the rest of their family.

Edivaldo had taken the day off of work, and their whole family had been up for hours washing our dirty, rotten, stinky clothes in a wash basin on their front porch! I have never been so grateful as I was for their kindness! What amazing people! It felt great to have clean clothes, but I was sure embarrassed. We had been stuffing our rained-on dirty clothes into plastic bags and carrying them around with us in the heat for weeks. One of Dave's leather belts had completely changed color from the mold it had grown on it while in one of these bags of wet dirty clothes. Gross! I couldn't feel anything but love for these people! I had been fully prepared to throw all my clothes away and buy new ones. To wake up and see all our clothes drying in their front yard was an absolute blessing.

Without even skipping a beat, Marta fixed us a big breakfast. I felt bad because this humble little family was giving us so much. We cleaned up our breakfast mess and sat down on the couch while waiting for our clothes to dry. Of course we all fell asleep again, only to be woken up when it was time for lunch.

We ate lunch at Marta's mom's house next door, and it was amazing! We had been living off of gas station food for the past couple weeks, so to eat a home-cooked meal was a real treat. By the time we finished lunch, the blistering hot Manaus heat had already completely dried out our recently washed clothes. We all sorted out our wash and readied ourselves for a fun night down on the riverwalk.

Edivaldo and Marta had contacted a lot of the people Nian had known while there as a missionary and invited all of them to meet us down by the riverwalk. I was excited that we were finally going back out on a leisure ride and not just riding to make it to the next city.

Nian, Dave, and I were getting our bikes ready when Edivaldo came out and asked, "Who is the most experienced on a motorbike?"

Nian and Dave both pointed at me.

He turned to Tiago, his sixteen-year-old son, and said, "Tiago, get a helmet. You're riding with Jim. Ok, who's the second most experienced rider?"

Nian and I both pointed to Dave.

Edivaldo said, "Marta, you're going to ride with Dave."

Dave and I both looked at each other and questioned whether or not we should tell Edivaldo that Nian had very little experience riding with someone on behind him. We jokingly said that if we said a prayer, everything would be alright. So we said a quick prayer and were on our way!

Tiago, who was riding with me, was having the time of his life! Nian and Edivaldo led the way while the other four of us followed close behind. We had been racing in and out of traffic for more than an hour when we finally started to get close to the west side of the city. Our surroundings started looking less like a huge Brazilian city and more like the Amazon rainforest we had imagined. We finally arrived at Ponta Negra (The Black Point). Ponta Negra was a long neighborhood in an upscale side of town that had a nice riverwalk. It was also where the new LDS temple was being built in Manaus.

We ditched our bikes, met up with about fifteen other people, and walked down to where the temple was being built. There was a huge wall around it and a massive steel door keeping us out. We climbed up on the wall and looked in. All we could see were footings and bricks. A way nervous security guard saw us up on the wall and asked us to leave. Just our luck! From there, we set out to take pictures by the mighty Rio Negro.

As we were walking along the river, I remembered that we still hadn't figured out any information on selling our bikes so we could fly to Machu Picchu.

I grabbed Edivaldo and asked, "Hey, what's the easiest way for us to sell our bikes here in Manaus?"

Edivaldo looked at one of the other guys, and they both laughed hysterically. He proceeded to tell us that Manaus was home to the three biggest bike factories in South America and that they employed thousands of people from all over the city, including quite a few of the church members.

I slowly looked at Dave, who then looked at Nian. We all knew exactly what that meant. More than a month ago we had decided that if we couldn't sell our bikes in Manaus, we'd try to ride them to Machu Picchu and sell them in Peru.

After Edivaldo quit laughing, I posed my second question. "Do you think we'll be able to sell them in Peru?"

This only made him laugh harder. Edivaldo told us how dangerous the road was between Manaus and Peru. First of all, it was expensive and time consuming to get on a ferry boat to get across the Rio Negro. Once on the other side, we would have to travel over 2500 kilometers of uninhabited jungle, full of dangerous animals and dangerous road conditions.

We told him we had already gone through that and would be perfectly fine.

He frowned. "What are you going to do about the bandits? There are bandits everywhere along that stretch of highway just waiting to rob people making the long trek from Manaus to Peru. Once you get to Peru, how are you going to get across the border without having your bikes licensed and titled in your names? The border patrol there is going to arrest you for either being bike thieves or smugglers. If it were me, I wouldn't go to Peru."

Nian, Dave, and I got really quiet, really fast! The more I thought about it, the more of a terrible feeling I got about riding to Peru. We walked back toward our bikes in silence.

At a park near the end of the riverwalk I took a deep breath and said, "Alright! Wolfpack team meeting! Right now! Okay guys, what are our options?"

Dave shrugged and said, "Well, we can sell our bikes for basically nothing here or risk it and ride on into Peru."

I looked at Nian and asked him what he thought. Nian shrugged too, made a huge frowny face, and shook his head back and forth as to indicate that he didn't know/had no opinion on the matter, his signature response.

That's when I said, "Guys, what if we keep going? I'm not talking about riding west to Peru. What if we ride north! I haven't said anything, but I've been looking at maps and my GPS for the last couple days, and we are only like 3500 kilometers from Colombia. We could be there in a week if we took it easy. I know we'll still have the problem getting our bikes across into Venezuela, but I feel like we'll figure it out, just like we've done the entire trip!"

"What do we do once we get to Colombia?" Dave asked.

I grinned, and Dave knew exactly what I was thinking.

He shook his head and said, "You're not thinking what I'm thinking, are you?"

Smiling from ear to ear, I nodded and said, "Boys, how awesome would it be if we figured out how to ride all the way home?"

Dave immediately said, "Way more awesome than anything I've ever done! In fact, probably the most awesome thing I've ever heard of *anyone* doing!"

Nian was now smiling and handing out plenty of high fives to Dave and me.

I said, "Okay guys, so here's the new game plan for the trip. We ride north as far as we can. If we get stuck somewhere, broken down, lost, homesick, robbed, or whatever, we ditch the bikes with the nearest LDS family we can find, and fly home, or we sell them for parts and fly home."

We all agreed that even though everything was still up in the air, we had a pretty decent plan! It felt good to have a plan, as we hadn't really had one for most of the trip. As we rode back to Edivaldo's house and ate dinner, I could feel that our new, extremely tentative game plan breathed a new breath of life into our trip!

Day 67
Saturday, April 3, 2010

We woke up late to find out that it was General Conference for the LDS Church, which only happens twice a year! There are three two-hour meetings on Saturday and two two-hour meetings on Sunday. It is broadcasted worldwide to most LDS church houses, and we were going to be late!

We munched down a quick breakfast and ran the half mile or so to the chapel. The three of us struggled to understand the Portuguese translator for more than an hour.

Just as we were about to fall asleep, Edivaldo asked, "Why don't you guys go into one of the side rooms with the American missionaries and watch it in English?"

We jumped on that opportunity right away! The talks were awesome, and we were all enlightened.

When the meetings were over, we ran back to Edivaldo's mother's house, where we proceeded to stuff our faces again! I sure do love myself some Brazilian rice and chicken. As we finished up our lunch, it was just about time to head back to the chapel for the 2:00 conference session. We fought off the food coma and walked the half mile to the chapel.

This meeting was much different from the first. We sat in a now hot, humid room and fought off sleeping for the entire two hours. Nonetheless, it was still a great meeting.

We had two hours to kill before the 6:00 meeting, so we set out on foot and visited a bunch of families and friends that Nian knew. Just before 6:00, we met up with Edivaldo and went to our last meeting of the day. We were spiritually fed for another two hours.

Upon arriving back at Edivaldo's house, we found that all of our packs and gear had been emptied and washed, and all of our belongings were now neatly organized into piles on the floor in the kids' room. I shook my head and just wondered how these people could be so generous. We had barely changed out of our church clothes when we were invited to eat again.

As we sat down at the table, Dave leaned over and whispered in English, "Hey, do you think they're going to eat us? I'm kind of getting the feeling like they are fattening us up so we'll be more delicious!"

We laughed and ate a typical dinner of bread with plenty of butter, ham, eggs, chocolate milk, rice, and beans. As we cleaned up the food, I couldn't help but laugh again when I realized that everything we ate was a pure weight gainer! After dinner we sat around watching TV and joking with Edivaldo. I couldn't have been more grateful for such a relaxing day!

Day 68
Sunday, April 4, 2010

Sunday, Sunday, Sunday! The Lord's day of rest.

The three of us slept in the next morning. However, we were up in time to eat a good breakfast and make the hike to the local church where we watched the 10:00 a.m. session of General Conference.

Around noon, some of Nian's mission friends invited us over for a huge lunch. We ate like kings and had some good laughs with more great people.

After lunch, we tiredly walked back over to the church for the last two-hour meeting of General Conference. The Wolfpack sat down for the meetings and fought off sleep the entire two hours. We were spiritually uplifted and grateful we had a chance to take a break from riding to attend the meetings.

We spent the rest of the evening riding through neighborhoods and visiting Nian's friends. We ended up at a fun family's house where we played games and ate dinner. Just as it was getting late and we were getting ready to leave, it started raining super hard. We had left our rain gear at Edivaldo's house, so we stayed and played games for a while. The mother of the family insisted that we sleep there on their couch, but we wanted to make it back to Edivaldo's place. The rain let up a little, so we made some makeshift rain gear out of trash bags and hustled back over and called it a night.

The rain woke us in the morning. It was coming down! We had been in Manaus for five days. The Wolfpack was starting to get the itch to get out in search of more wild adventures. Due to flooding rains, those adventures were going to have to wait for a day or two. It was raining so hard that Edivaldo and Marta's kids stayed home from school. We spent the majority of the morning catching up on emails home and playing with the kids.

Lunchtime came and the rain still hadn't slowed up. We ate a big meal at Edivaldo's mom's house and ended up asleep on her couch. We woke up an hour later covered in toys, all wearing funny sunglasses, and we all had suckers in our mouths. The kids had been messing with us and taking pictures of us on our cameras the whole time we were asleep. These kids were the coolest!

Late in the afternoon, the rain slowed to a drizzle. We threw on our rain gear and tried to head into town in search of supplies and parts that we would need for our adventures into Venezuela and beyond. About halfway into town, the drowning rain returned. We flipped around and retreated back to Edivaldo's neighborhood, where we spent the remainder of the evening visiting and eating with more of Nian's friends.

The Wolfpack was ready to ride! The weatherman was forecasting heavy rains again the next day, so we were hoping to get saddled up and riding north by Wednesday.

When I opened my eyes on Tuesday morning, I was surprised

with a strange silence. No rain pounding on the tile roof! We ran out and thanked the Lord that we could see blue skies!

We gave Edivaldo's kids a ride to school and then gave Edivaldo a ride to work. He filled us in on the best places to get parts and supplies around Manaus and also told us about a wild botanical garden we could check out if we had time to kill. We were about to be riding into unknown territory. We spent the majority of the morning and early afternoon making sure our bikes were one hundred percent dialed in and ready to go. We also loaded up on a few spare parts we might need along the way. Who knew if we would be able to find parts for these Brazilian-made bikes once we left the country.

As we were going over our motos, a young mechanic noticed something strange on Nian's Yamaha XT225. The small rubber sleeves between the carburetor, the air box, and the motor were all deteriorated and cracked. Our mechanic buddy searched out some parts while the three of us ate a nice lite lunch of açaí bowls. Our poor bodies couldn't handle any more huge meals for a while! Everywhere we went, the humble people of Manaus tried to fatten us up with delicious feasts!

As we walked back from lunch, we saw the mechanic test riding Nian's XT225 around the block. He was flying! Maybe even going faster than Nian had gone the entire trip. Finally, a moto mechanic had good news for us! The cracked rubber boots were letting excess air escape between Nian's carburetor and motor. This was cutting Nian's power by at least 20%. Grateful for his discovery, we paid the mechanic and gave him a healthy tip on top of that.

We had a few hours to burn before we needed to pick up Edivaldo from work, so we decided to check out the botanical gardens. The ride to the gardens was better than Christmas morning for Nian! He was finally able to keep up with us. He cheered and laughed as we raced in and out of traffic and up a jungle trail to the gardens.

The gardens were interesting. After hiking around for an hour or so, we realized that it was probably a little mellow for three young adventurers such as ourselves. Nonetheless, we were determined to see a live sloth in the wild. Our searches led us off the designated path. Getting off the path only got us covered in giant spider webs and huge ant bites. That facilitated our decision to abandon our search for sloths, and we hustled back to our bikes.

We picked up Edivaldo from work and zigzagged through rush hour traffic back to his place. It was hopefully our last night in Manaus. Edivaldo put the word out that we were leaving and soon had a going away party put together. We headed over to a neighbor's house, where we were met by many of Nian's friends. We spent the rest of the evening eating, laughing, and playing games.

It started pounding rain just as we were getting ready to head back to Edivaldo's house for the night. The very friendly lady that owned the house insisted that we sleep there. She was a single lady that had four attractive daughters around our same age. It wasn't the best situation. Thankfully, Edivaldo shut that idea down fast so we didn't look like the bad guys! The Wolfpack loaded up and headed back to our basecamp, where we gathered our gear into our packs and readied ourselves to get up and ride out in the morning!

15

O PRESIDENTE

Day 71
Wednesday, April 7, 2010

The day we had been dreading had finally come. It was time for us to leave Manaus.

Once again, we enjoyed an amazing breakfast with Edivaldo and his family. I definitely put on a cool five to ten pounds while we stayed with them. The people of Manaus treated us like kings! They were honestly some of the most amazing, kind people in the world. Everyone we met in Manaus was so awesome!

Soon, our three-man wolfpack had our gear tied to our bikes and we were ready to roll north toward Boa Vista! Edivaldo, Marta, and family were all crying their eyes out. That wanted us to stay for a few more days!

Just as we were about to drop their kids off at school, we heard an old familiar sound. A quiet rushing sound followed by a WALL OF WATER! The rain was back! It seriously started downpouring the second we were about to start riding. Soon, we had our rain gear on, Edivaldo and Marta's kids dropped off at school, and we were on our way out of town!

As we were riding out of Manaus we passed a sign that read, "Military Zoo." A lot of people had told us that the zoo was super cool. We couldn't resist the chance to see a sloth that had evaded us in the wild, so we pulled in to check it out! The three of us sat in the rain and joked with a security guard while we waited for a military training routine to get over so we could enter the zoo. With as hard as it was raining, we were the only ones there. By only ones there, I mean the only ones there! It was just us and the animals.

For the first few minutes, we cautiously walked around the park and kind of felt out our situation. Upon discovering that we were completely alone, we started having more unsupervised fun with dangerous Amazonian animals than anyone should ever have!

The first cool animals we found were the ocelots. They looked like cute miniature jaguars. We called them over and tried feeding them candy we had in our pockets. They loved it and were purring like house cats. Dave had the sleeve off of one of his shirts that he was waving inside their cage. All of a sudden, one of the small ocelots went nuts! It snatched the sleeve out of Dave's hand in a split second! In two more seconds the three ocelots had torn his sleeve into a million tiny shreds!

This zoo was everything we could have asked for in the Amazon! Without a guide, the odds of seeing any of these animals in the wild were pretty minimal. We spent the next couple hours playing with monkeys, sloths, snakes, gators, and a bunch of other animals that I couldn't even identify.

Hands down our favorite part of the zoo was the panthers and jaguars. The black panther was the best. We found the back side of his cage and called him until he ran over and bit down on the cage wires. As he was biting down around the metal, I reached out and touched his razor-sharp tooth! Who's done that? I would say very few people. From that point forward, Dave and Nian called me "Bagheera," who is the wise old black panther off of *The Jungle Book*. The rain started letting up a little bit. Around noon we decided it was time to hit the road.

I pulled up my GPS and typed in Boa Vista, which is one of the other cities where Nian lived as a missionary. We figured it would take us about ten hours to cover the 800 kilometers to get there, so we suited up in our rain gear and set out, determined to make it to Boa Vista to sleep. You can only guess what happened next.

No more than thirty minutes into our ten-hour ride, the heaven's floodgates opened up! I had seen record-setting, flooding rainfall in my life, but this was the worst rainstorm I had ever driven in. The fact that going over fifty kilometers per hour felt like a thousand bullies giving you red hands after a gym class shower meant we were going pretty slow.

We had been drowning in the rain for almost half an hour when Dave rode up alongside me and gave me the cutting hand across the throat sign that meant *shut it down*. I looked again, and Dave didn't have a visor on his helmet! I had forgotten that he had lost it again. That whole time, he had been trying to ride with his hand up in front of his face so that the stinging rain didn't cause serious damage to his face! We held up under a gigantic tree and waited another half an hour for the wall of water to pass. If we were still going to make it to Boa Vista by night, we were going to have to fly!

The rain clouds soon turned into blue skies and we discovered that we were riding right through the heart of the Amazonian rainforest again. The road was half pavement, half dirt, and was full of huge death trap potholes. Around every bend we scared up big flocks of red macaw parrots. There were more exotic parrots flying around than any other kind of bird. I wished I could have spent two weeks exploring all the adventurous territory that we passed, but we were set on making it to Boa Vista even if we had to ride all night!

At around 4:00 p.m. we crossed the equator. I slammed on my brakes, and we walked over to check it out. The whole trip we had been talking about doing all the equator tricks where you pour water out of a bottle and see which way it swirls or balance an egg on its end. We had taken some pictures and started getting ready for our experiments when a big bus pulled up and stopped.

The bus door opened and out poured a whole traveling circus of transvestites! There were probably thirty dudes dressed like chicks walking in our direction.

More frightened than I had been at any time during the whole first part of the trip, I looked at Dave and said, "Now what?"

Without missing a beat, Dave sternly said, "We get the hell out of here, that's what!"

Nian and I had no arguments. The equator was cool and all, but not cool enough to get kidnapped by a bus full of nasty trannies! As the chicks/dudes walked over to where we were, we jumped on fast, got a fist full of throttle, and got outta there!

We rode like tireless jungle warriors for almost ten hours. I pulled up the maps on the GPS and we had only covered 500 kilometers! I guess we had spent a little too much time at the zoo. It had been dark for almost two hours and the three of us were getting tired and hungry. Soon, we pulled into the little town of Rorainópolis.

Usually, when we would make decisions about the trip or the course we would take, it was an epic tooth-pulling party to get Dave or Nian to make any kind of decision. It got so bad that we started assigning Nian to make decisions when it was his turn.

We stopped in the town for gas, and while filling our tanks I asked, "So do you guys want to camp out here tonight?"

At almost the same time, Dave and Nian said, "I'm in!"

We picked up some groceries and goodies and set out in search of a nice dry campsite. On the edge of town, right next to the jungle, we found an old abandoned tire shop. We had our hammocks up in record time, and we all joked about getting mugged until it almost wasn't funny anymore. The guys soon fell asleep, but I lay awake for what seemed like hours. There was something about the drone of tree frogs and distant howler monkeys mixed in with the buzz of mosquitos and other crazy jungle sounds that kept me awake. After a while, the pounding rain returned, and soon I was sound asleep.

The second the rain stopped, the jungle came alive! 4:30 in the morning in the jungle is a crazy time of day! How do I know? I was awake. I've never heard such a thing in all my life. I lay in my hammock for more than an hour just listening to how crazy the sounds were. By 5:30, it was starting to get light. I woke up the rest of the Wolfpack.

As we rolled out of our hammocks, we realized that we had camped next to a swampy area. I pulled up my shirt and checked out my lower back. I was covered in one million mosquito bites! The mosquitoes there were the size of small birds. They had been eating up through our hammocks and Paraguayan blankets the entire night! All three of us looked like we had chicken pox. Literally every inch of skin that was in contact with the blankets was covered with bites! We broke camp super fast, geared up, and were soon back on our mission to make it to Boa Vista at a decent hour.

The ride was equally as awesome as the day before! It was even more special because we finally weren't riding in the rain! We had blue skies and a nice tailwind. We must have remembered to say our prayers before we left camp that morning.

The rest of the ride to Boa Vista was unbelievable! There were tons of huge flocks of parrots, dead gators, and other crazy animals all over the road. We came out of the jungle and into some savanna looking planes. Once there, Boa Vista was just around the bend.

My bike's tires had been wobbling and acting funny. After some basic diagnostics, we determined that it was my brakes. Once in Boa Vista, for some reason, it took us forever to find a bike shop. As my bike was getting new brakes, we got some grub and had another team meeting.

We had raced two days through the jungle to get there, and none of Nian's contacts that we were going to visit were home. Dave and I nominated Nian to make the decision.

"So Nian, what's it gonna be? Do we sit around here and wait for someone to get home, or do we set sails for Venezuela?"

Nian made a frowny face and shrugged his shoulders.

By the time my bike was out of the shop, we had all decided

to keep going north. As we rode out of Boa Vista, I could have sworn I was riding through southern Texas. I couldn't believe how fast the terrain and landscape changed from rainforest to high desert. A long, hot four hours later and we were climbing a huge mountain range in another epic rainstorm.

The Venezuelan border was just on the other side of this huge mountain we were riding up. I had been on reserve for more than half an hour. Nian was way behind me, and he got way worse gas mileage than I did. He was for sure out of gas. I sputtered into the first gas station in the small town of Pacaraima on the Brazil side of the border, filled up, and filled up a pop bottle to go rescue Nian.

Dave showed up just as I was about to go back. He took my bottle of gas and went to rescue Nian while I went over to the customs building to get working on the paperwork we needed to do to get our passports stamped and get us into Venezuela. Before I knew it, the three of us were cleared to go into Venezuela and were riding north into the Venezuelan highlands.

I couldn't believe how different Venezuela was from Brazil. Gas there was so cheap! We stopped at the small town of Santa Elena de Uairén, where Dave volunteered to pay for our fuel. He filled all three of our tanks for like twenty-five cents! Gas was five cents a gallon! It might as well have been free. Everyone there drove huge gas hog trucks, Jeeps, and classic Chevy cars.

As it was getting dark, we rode just over 100 kilometers into Venezuela. We wanted to get some ground behind us before we set up camp. About an hour after dark, we were rudely stopped at a military police checkpoint. They were not happy! We had a long dispute in broken Spanish, which we definitely lost. They sent us back to the border to get Venezuelan insurance and permission paperwork to drive in the country. We flipped around and rode the hour and a half back to the border.

Wouldn't you know it, about twenty minutes before arriving, we were welcomed by a drowning rainstorm! We took shelter for a bit but it was useless. We were drenched! After a little hard work, and a lot of soggy gear, we found a place to stay for the night. The guy suggested that we keep our bikes inside our room. We thought that was weird, but apparently, there was a big bike robbery problem there. We crammed our motos into the room, took our turns calling who got to sleep on what bed, took hot showers, opened and hung up all our gear, and called it a night.

Day 73
Friday, April 9, 2010

The Venezuelan motor vehicles department said we needed to get Venezuelan driving insurance and a release/permission to take our bikes from Brazil to Venezuela. Who would have thought we'd spend the whole next day working on meaningless paperwork!

I felt like the border people were just messing with us. Nothing was working out for us. We went to the insurance place. Their internet was down, so they made us wait four hours for it to come back online. The Venezuelan driving permission papers were just as hard to figure out. We were all getting depressed. Finally, at 5:55 p.m. it was looking like we weren't going to be allowed to operate a motor vehicle in Venezuela. I walked outside the office to where Dave and Nian were relaxing.

Heartbroken, I gave them the bad news. "Guys, it looks like we're not going to get into Venezuela with our bikes."

From behind me I heard someone say, "Hey, are you guys Americans?"

I looked back to see a tall Brazilian guy from the highway patrol. He said, "My name is Vladimir. I think I can help you guys."

This guy just straight looked like a movie star! He was dressed in normal clothes but had a huge badge and gun on his belt. After learning more about our situation, he demanded that we follow him. Once in his office, he jumped on his computer and started typing really fast. Soon, he had made us some counterfeit papers that said we were legal with Brazil and that we were okay to ride into Venezuela. He signed and notarized all the papers and sent us back to the Venezuelan motor vehicles office. They accepted our fake paperwork without even thinking about it.

We thanked Vladimir and jumped back on our bikes! After all of our fiascos and running all over tracking down paperwork, we were almost completely out of gas again. We buzzed over to the gas station just to find the workers locking the gate. Turns out, the gas stations closed at 6:00 p.m. and were only open on Wednesday through Friday. All the gas stations were communist government owned and highly controlled.

There was no way we were sitting around this dumpy border town for five days waiting for the government gas station to open up! Needing fuel in a bad way, we started riding around neighborhoods asking around if anyone had an extra gas can sitting around that they'd sell us. After talking to probably fifteen people, we found out that there were people who sold underground, black market gas. Everyone thought we were from the government, so it was hard finding someone that would admit they had any for sale. We asked all over the ghetto side of town for anyone who'd sell us some gas. Nobody had any, but they always seemed to know someone who did that lived eight or ten blocks away. We were led to three or four houses that usually sold black market gas, but no one would sell us any.

Dave yelled into a house asking them if they had any gas that we could buy. They yelled back and said that they didn't, but an eleven-year old girl overheard Dave asking for gas in his broken Spanish.

She ran over and said, "My grandpa sells gas. Follow me!"

She led us around the block to her grandpa's house. It was now well after dark, and I was feeling super sketched out. I thought to myself, *There's a 73% chance we get robbed right now!*

The little girl's grandpa heard us pull up. He ran right out and nervously said, "Kill your motors, turn off our lights, and push your bikes in the backyard!"

I looked at Dave and Nian and said in English, "Are we about to get kidnapped?"

Nervously, we pushed our bikes into this guy's backyard. He turned out all the lights around his house and filled our bikes up from some big five-gallon cans. He explained that it was illegal to sell black market gas, and that if he were to get caught, he'd be in big trouble with a bad communist government.

Once we realized that they weren't going to kill us and steal our bikes, we were having a good laugh with this guy. Soon, there were eight people standing on the back porch of their house just staring at us.

A fourteen-year-old girl curiously asked, "Where are you from?"

Dave, who spoke the best Spanish out of the three of us, said we were from Utah.

A lady stepped out of the shadows and asked, "Mormons?"

Dave, Nian, and I all looked at each other and smiled! "Mormons" was a nickname for members of The Church of Jesus Christ of Latter-day Saints. It turned out she was a less-active member of our church! What were the odds? Before we knew it, we were all inside sitting around their kitchen table eating a feast of Venezualan arepas with them. This family was so awesome! They loved us! We hung out and ate with them for over two hours, and our new Mormon friend drew out a map for us to get through Venezuela in the safest manner.

It was getting late, so we thanked them for their hospitality and for their fuel. We started packing our gear so we could get on the road.

Our Mormon friend shook her head and asked if we were crazy. She said, "You can't leave this late. You'll get robbed for sure!" She called her husband and asked if it was okay if three American Mormon boys crashed at their house. He was fully supportive, so we followed her and her two kids to the other side of town where she conveniently had two extra mattresses in their front room.

Once again, we saw the hand of God on our trip. What were the odds of getting led to a house with a member or our church inside after all we had gone through at the border and trying to find gas? What a great experience!

It was my turn to dibs what bed I wanted, so I chose the single mattress while Dave and Nian shared a full mattress. It was pretty funny watching those two argue about how the other one was taking up too much room on the mattress. As I drifted off to sleep, I said my prayers and thanked the good Lord for watching out for us and for allowing us to meet more great people who helped keep us safe.

When morning broke, we grabbed some quick breakfast with our new friends and by 6:00 a.m., we were on the road! It was chilly and foggy in the Venezuelan highlands. As the sun came up, it burned off the fog and graced us with some sunny weather. The highland Venezuelan countryside was amazing. Rolling green hills as far as the eye could see!

As it got warmer, we stopped at a huge waterfall to remove some of our warm clothes and take some pictures. The waterfalls there were unreal! There were literally thousands of them all along the way. The one that we didn't get to see was Angel Falls, which is the highest waterfall in the world. Next time for sure. After resting our minds for a bit, we jumped back on for another four hours of intense riding.

The three of us were making excellent time when we came up to another police roadblock. As we got closer, we discovered that it was a military checkpoint and that we were driving right through the middle of a military training facility. We tried to do our usual routine where we would slow down, stand up, salute as we rolled by, and keep on going without stopping.

Our foolproof plan didn't work so well this time. We tried talking our way out of getting searched, but soon we were inside of their checkpoint holding cell with a large, dark Venezuelan guy that was yelling at us in Spanish. He ordered three soldiers to push our bikes into the back where they could search all of our belongings and told us we weren't going anywhere! The big leader of the guards informed us that they were going to detain us and keep the bikes because we didn't have international driver licenses. We repeatedly showed him our Utah driver licenses and said that US driver licenses are automatically international driver licenses. They weren't budging. They were legitimately out to get us!

Throughout our trip, we had had lots of hang ups and bumps in the road, like breaking down, getting lost, not having money, and so forth. This was the first time on the trip that I thought, *It might actually be over.* These guys were way serious and by the looks of our situation, they weren't about to let us go.

The main angry military guys left us with some guards while they went to a meeting. The guards were all about our same age. After talking to them for a while, they actually turned out to be pretty cool. We hung out and joked with them for more than an hour. When the main military leader guy came back, we were all laughing and having a good time while the guards fed us some crazy Venezuelan fruit that tasted like uncooked dirt. We soon had the main guy in on our jokes, but he still wouldn't let us go.

I pointed to the assault rifle that one of the leaders had over his shoulder. I made an approving face, nodded my head, and said, "Muy Fuerte!" which I thought meant very strong in Spanish.

He smiled and got a gratified look on his face.

I then pointed to the big dark leader of the bunch and said, "This guy looks like President Obama."

Silence.

My joke may have just sealed our fate. I immediately broke the awkward silence that I had created. In broken Spanish, I said, "I'm going to call you O Presidente."

The whole group of guards erupted, and the big leader got a look of sheer pride on his face.

We spent another half an hour befriending these guards, who had been completely hostile to us no more than an hour earlier.

All of a sudden, O Presidente looked at us and said, "You can go."

We all three smiled, thanked them for their understanding, got our bikes out of hock, and we hit the road once more! No doubt, all three of us had a prayer in our heart as we rode away, thanking the Lord for getting us out of another sticky situation.

As we motored through Venezuela, the landscape went from green grassy plains, to jungle, to savanna, to desert. Every terrain you can think of, we rode through in Venezuela. We were a good ten hours into Venezuela when something went missing: Dave's wallet! We quickly circled back in search of it! Our prayers were again answered when he found it sitting at the last gas station we had stopped at for gas. It was nothing short of a miracle that it was still there with all of his money and cards intact.

We rode hard for another few hours until it got dark. Without a map, we quickly got lost in a city called Ciudad Guayana searching for a big bridge which was supposed to be our landmark passageway to the north part of the country.

Tired and hungry, we stopped at a small supermarket for some local food. By now it was well after dark. The three of us sat on the front steps of the market and ate our snacks. As people passed by us, we asked for directions on how to get out of the city.

Almost every person we asked shook their head and responded, "What are you guys doing here? Get the hell outta here! It's super dangerous, and you're all going to get killed!"

Needless to say, we dropped everything and split out of town! Forget getting jammed up by Venezuelan robbers!

Three hours later, we stopped at a small town called El Tigre for gas and goodies. After fueling up, we rode over to a small restaurant and parked our bikes on the sidewalk next to two policemen. Just as we were getting our helmets off, one of the cops immediately jumped on our case.

"What do you think you're doing? Don't you know that it's illegal to ride motorcycles after 9:00 p.m. in this part of Venezuela? It's almost 1:00 in the morning! What do you think you're doing?"

We pleaded ignorance and told them our story. As most people did, they soon warmed up to us and rode away, but the whole encounter left me with a very uneasy feeling.

The streets were pretty much empty and there weren't any threatening people around, so Dave and I went into this open-front cafe to grab some juice and sandwiches while Nian stayed by the door to watch the bikes. Dave and I were just about done eating when a guy with a long knife in his hand came in, leaned over, and half whispered something to Dave.

Neither of us understood what he said, but we were pretty sure he either said, "I'm going to steal your bikes," or "Someone's gonna steal your bikes."

My uneasy feeling now felt like an absolute warning! Wide-eyed, we looked at each other and without speaking, dropped our food, and ran to the front of the cafe!

As I approached our bikes, I did a quick scan of our situation. Across the street, there were now three guys standing on the sidewalk watching us. To my right, there were two more guys standing there watching us. To my left, were five or six more guys and two recently parked cars with people in them that hadn't been there before.

The three of us slammed our helmets on our heads, jumped on our bikes, and raced out of there! As we were riding off, I looked back. The two cars were following us. Hoping it was just a coincidence that they left at the same time as we had, we put the hammer down and went as fast as we could to get out of town!

Just as we were about to leave El Tigre, our road was blocked and we were waved to pull over into a police checkpoint. The cops grabbed us and pulled us inside their office.

I'm one hundred percent sure that the two cars were following us out of the city. I'll admit that I was getting nervous. I have no doubt in my mind that they wanted to rob us or harm us in some way! For once, I wasn't bothered by the corrupt cops giving us problems. In fact, I felt like they actually saved us from an awful situation!

The cops wanted money and were very upset when they found out that we didn't have any. Dave did most of the smooth talking since his Spanish was the best. I understood most of what they said but spoke just a little Spanish.

Every time they asked me for money, I just smiled and said, "Si?" and then laughed a little. Then I laughed more because it was funny to see them get confused. After some twenty minutes of smooth talking and giving the cops all the candy we had, they finally agreed to let us keep on our way.

As we were about to pull away, one guy asked where we were going.

"Colombia" I said and pointed north.

The cop told us we were going the wrong way.

He said, "If you go north to Colombia, you'll have to ride along the coast past Caracas, which is the most dangerous part of the country. You'll for sure get robbed and probably killed. You should go back into town two kilometers, take a right on Highway 15, and go 1000 kilometers through the mountains and countryside until you get to Maracaibo. Once there, you'll be almost to Colombia. That route is all farmlands and small towns. It will be much safer and a better ride."

I had a very distinct feeling that we needed to listen to this guy, so we didn't even question the cop's advice and cautiously rode back toward El Tigre. We found Highway 15, took a right turn, and quickly motored off into the darkness headed west!

About ten minutes down the highway, I had the strangest feeling overcome my whole soul. I honestly felt, and know, that someone was waiting to ambush us just north of the police checkpoint in El Tigre. I remember being on the verge of tears thanking my Heavenly Father for sending those cops to stop us where they did. This story would have had a much sadder ending if they hadn't.

It was a dark and dreary moonless night. As we rode west on Highway 15, I looked up and thought, *Few times in my life have I ever seen this many stars.* It was a dark, lonely road, so the three of us bunched up and rode on into the night!

Sometime around 3:00 a.m. we pulled off to grab some goodies. As I parked my bike, I felt my back tire getting a little shaky. Upon further inspection, it turned out that my sprockets and chain were completely worn out again! I couldn't believe I had ruined a full chain and sprocket set in just a couple weeks. We busted out our tools and tightened my chain as tight as it would go. As I pulled back onto the street it was still slipping on the sprocket teeth. We were in the middle of nowhere. We asked a guy if there was a bike shop nearby, and he said the only place I would find parts was 500 kilometers in either direction.

We had to make my current setup work. Nian and I got busy and took the rear end of the Tornado apart while Dave slept on the sidewalk. Once apart, we moved my chain tensioners all the way in and started working on taking some links out of my chain. It was risky. If we damaged my chain beyond repair, we would have to leave my bike and ride the 500 kilometers to the nearest bike shop. We pulled the masterlink off my chain and laid it out flat on the sidewalk. We found a big nail, which I held with my Leatherman. Nian found a huge rock and a short piece of small steel pipe. The two of us spent the next hour beating on that nail with the big rock! We tried everything we could think of to get the chain links apart! Just as we were about to give up, we saw one of the links start to separate. I wedged my Leatherman in between the two links and held the nail as tight as I could over the small pipe.

I looked at tired Nian and said, "Alright Nian, grab your rock and hit this nail as hard as you can! Please don't break my hand!"

Nian landed one last clean blow on the nail and the chain links blasted apart! We had successfully shortened my chain a couple inches. It was soon back on my bike and all snugged up. We woke Dave and got back in the saddle. Even tightened up, my chain still slipped if I tried going more than seventy-five kilometers per hour, so we slowly limped down the road.

It was about 4:00 a.m. when I found myself riding alone in the early morning fog. I thought, *That's strange, they must have stopped so Nian could do one of his emergency bathroom visits or something.*

I waited about twenty minutes until I could see their headlights coming toward me in the distance. I then jumped back on my bike and continued westward. After a minute, their headlights disappeared again. I thought, *If I'm going this slow they'll catch up to me easily.*

I kept limping my bike down the road. An hour or so passed, and they still hadn't caught up to me. I was about to turn back when I remembered my chain situation. As light started to appear along the horizon, I looked at my GPS to assess the situation. I was pretty close to a small city called Valle de Pascua. I figured I could wait for them there and maybe even find myself some parts to fix my bike.

16

THE MOTO CLUBE SAVES
JIM'S ETERNAL BACON

Day 75
Sunday, April 11, 2010

Just as the sun was rising over the Venezuelan prairie, I coasted into the police station at the entrance of Valle de la Pascua. It was a calm Sunday morning and there was just one young guard on duty there.

I tried talking to him for a minute, but all I managed to communicate to him was that I needed to wash my hands, which were completely black from working on my greasy chain the night before.

I cleaned up as best I could and laid down in the shade next to the freeway while I waited for Dave and Nian to roll up. I waited there for almost two hours. I figured they must have stopped to sleep somewhere. Logic would say that I should have been exhausted, but for unknown reasons, I wasn't tired.

Impatient, I jumped on my bike and headed into the town. Soon, I had searched the whole city for a bike shop, internet cafe, and/or a Latter-day Saint church. To my dismay, I found none of the above. I returned to the police checkpoint to inquire whether or not the guard had seen Dave and Nian. The guard shook his head and shrugged his shoulders.

Bothered by his response, I limped on, stopping at each city to see if they had a Latter-day Saint church or a bike shop that was open. I wasn't having any luck, but the riding between the small towns was amazing; jungle, farms, lakes, and exotic roadkill kept me quite entertained. Sometime around 11:00 a.m. I came to the city of San Carlos, which had an LDS church.

I parked my bike around the back of the chapel and walked up to the building. Just before opening the door, I looked down at myself. I was wearing a black jacket, T-shirt, green shorts, and tall red soccer socks. I wasn't very well dressed for church, but this would have to do. I opened the back door and walked in.

It turned out that the back door was actually the front side door to the chapel. There were sixty or seventy people staring right at me. I hesitated but walked in and found a seat. I was soon greeted by a man who started treating me like I wasn't a member of the church. I made it clear that I was a member, and we shared a quiet laugh. I caught the last forty-five minutes of the sacrament meeting. It was awesome participating in Spanish.

After the meeting, one of the members informed me that there was no bike shop in the city, but he did show me where I could find an internet cafe. I stopped in there and wrote Dave and Nian an email informing them of my plans to ride on in search of parts. I then tightened my chain once more and got back on the road in search of a town with a bike shop.

From San Carlos, I headed north and rode until around 5:00 p.m. I had been riding for almost ten hours and had experienced zero luck finding a bike shop that was open on Sunday. I was starting to get nervous that I wouldn't make it to Maracaibo, which was a bigger city that would for sure have the parts that I needed.

By now, my extreme lack of sleep was starting to catch up to me. I tiredly pressed on until my chain was slipping on the sprockets so bad that I couldn't get my speed up anymore.

Somewhere in the outskirts of the city of Barquisimeto, I pulled off on some grass to snug my chain up one last time. My rear sprocket's teeth were all gone. It looked like a bumpy circle. As I was tightening my chain to the breaking point, I looked up and saw two bikers coming my direction. They rode past me and then immediately turned around and pulled over next to me.

There was a skinny fellow on one bike and an older guy and a lady on the other bike. As they stopped, the older guy asked if I was alright.

In my broken Spanish, I did my best to tell them my situation of being separated from the other guys and having a bad chain and sprocket.

The older fellow yelled his reply, "YOU ARE CRAZY! This is the worst part of town! You shouldn't even be stopped here. Someone could steal your bike at any second. You need to come with us! I'm the president of the Motorbike Club in the city. Our club has a mechanic. Follow us, and we'll take you to his house. You can stay at his house tonight. Tomorrow, we will help you fix your bike and get you back on the road!"

I felt way sketched out by the whole predicament, but I didn't really have many options at that point. As I pulled out to follow them, I took another look at the lady on the back of the president's bike. Sure enough, she had an open bottle of beer in each hand.

I laughed at my situation and followed them through the city to their mechanic's house. They called him "Vitamina," which means vitamin or smoothie in Portuguese. The president introduced me to Vitamina and told him my story.

Vitamina was probably in his mid-forties. I would guess he was around 5'5" tall and maybe weighed ninety pounds soaking wet. I was instantly invited into his house and almost forced to take a warm shower. I must not have noticed, but there was a good chance that I didn't smell very good.

Before I knew it, I was all showered up, and at a biker gang pool party and barbeque! The moto clube ALPHA ROAD LARA instantly inducted me into their club!

Mind you, I hadn't slept since 5:00 a.m. the day before when we left the Brazil-Venezuela border! I did my best to answer questions and talk to people, but my tiredness and the speed at which they spoke made understanding anything very difficult.

After eating one of the best meals of my trip, I found a couch to lie down on by the pool. I simply couldn't stay awake any longer. Just as I was about to drift off to sleep, I was surprised by an angry old man yelling at me in Spanish! I understood nothing he said and lay right back down after he left. Before I could fall asleep, Vitamina and Nassar, who was another member of the biker club, came and grabbed me. They informed me that the old man who was yelling at me said he was going to call the police and that we should probably leave. We jumped on our bikes and rolled out!

It was probably 10:00 p.m., so I figured we were going back to Vitimina's house and calling it a night. Nope! I was wrong. They took me straight to a karaoke bar where they got wasted and I slammed Coke after Coke trying to stay awake! We left the bar sometime after midnight and rode the town! I found this pretty funny because they were both super drunk and riding double with little Mr. Vitamina driving.

Our little joy ride stopped being so fun when I again realized that I was deathly tired and that I was having a hard time keeping up with my sprockets grinding so bad! They bought me an amazing Venezuelan steak sandwich at like 1:00 a.m., and then the three of us finally headed back to Vitimina's house. Sometime after 2:00 a.m. I finally found myself a bed to lie down on. I had been awake for forty-five hours straight and had ridden more than 1500 kilometers! Being in a real bed never felt so good! The next day, Vitamina and I were going to get me back on the road so I could meet up with Nian and Dave!

To my dismay, I was awakened somewhat early. I had really been hoping to get more than six hours of sleep. I enjoyed some fruit and juice for breakfast. I had hardly finished eating when I looked out the window to see Vitamina out in his yard with my Tornado up on a block. He had already been up for a couple hours working on it.

It didn't take the two of us long to tear the rear end of my bike completely apart. We cleaned the whole bike and made a list of all the replacement parts I needed to find. Right before lunch, Vitamina and I set out riding doubles on his big cruiser bike to try to find all the parts I needed to get the Tornado up and running again. I'm not going to lie, I felt a little weird riding around on the back of this little man's big cruiser bike. I couldn't help but smile.

After several trips to multiple stores, waiting for the country's afternoon siesta nap to get done, and some rain delay, Vitamina and I soon had the Tornado fixed up and running like a champ!

Dave called Vitimina's cell phone and we planned to meet up at the Colombian border sometime between 9:00 a.m. and 11:00 a.m. the next day. I tried leaving that night, but my new moto crew wouldn't let me. They said it was too dangerous due to potholes in the road, thugs, and of course, rain!

It was raining so hard that nobody wanted to go out to party that night! Vitamina's family cooked me some Venezualian arepas, rice, and beans. There couldn't have been anything better than eating an authentic Venezuelan dinner right then. We all talked and hung out for the rest of the evening. I was still pretty tired from the day before, and I wanted to get up and get on the road really early! I packed all my gear and hit the hay at my first possible opportunity.

Four in the morning and my alarm was blasting. I hopped out of bed and peeked out the window. The rain had finally stopped! Five minutes later, the Tornado was ready to roll. I was excited to get back on the road and meet back up with the guys! I woke Vitamina up and said goodbye. He gave me a bandana with their moto clube logo on the front and told me to always take it with me on rides for good luck. I agreed, thanked him for his help and kindness, tied the bandana on my head, and rolled out as fast as I could.

There wasn't a lot of traffic that early in the morning, so I made super good time! I rode as fast and as hard as I could, stopping only for gas. It was about 500 kilometers from Vitamina's place in Barquisimeto to the Colombian border. I really had to hurry if I wanted to get there before 11:00 a.m.

About an hour from the border, I crossed a massive bridge near the city of Maracaibo. As I exited the bridge, I noticed a big group of people looking at something. I slowed down and rode around the group for a better look. They were staring at a dead person laying on the sidewalk! I couldn't believe it! I hated that. Nothing puts me in the dumps like seeing a dead body.

The last 100 kilometers to the Colombian border were super ghetto. All the roads were covered with trash. Nine out of ten cars were huge 1970s rusty old Chevys! I saw one old Chevy towing another one with a ten-foot tree tied between their two bumpers. It was pretty funny. Traffic was bad for the last couple hundred kilometers, and it was noon before I got to the Colombian border. I rode around for a few minutes looking for the guys. They were nowhere to be seen.

I was ready to head into town and send them an email, when these two ragged guys jumped out in front of me! Thankfully, it was Dave and Nian and not two random thugs trying to rob me! They had just about given up on me and were about to cross over the border into Colombia.

We hugged, laughed, shared our stories from the past two days, and drank homemade mango juice that Dave had bought (which we thought got us all sick). A few minutes later and we had successfully gotten our passports stamped and were out of Venezuela!

None of our bike documents were in our own name. Each time we crossed a border and had to go through immigration/customs offices we would all sit there nervously praying that the workers were feeling generous and would let us cross. Back together again, the three of us rode across the border into Colombia knowing that we had to go through the customs office there. What do you know? We got held up at the border again. We were interviewed, harassed, bothered, asked for bribes, and finally, four hours later, we were on our way!

Once in Colombia, we rode northeast as fast as we could while it was still light. Our next destination was the port city of Cartagena, which was about 500 kilometers from the border. Colombia gave me a strange feeling. Road conditions were pretty bad, and everything was dusty and dirty. Crossing into Colombia put us into a different time zone, which meant it got dark earlier.

We finally left the hot dry dusty desert of eastern Colombia. As things around us started looking more tropical, the roads turned from horrible to awesome, so we kept on going. It was probably around 11:00 p.m. when I looked in my rearview mirror and saw a flashing light coming up behind me. I shook my head and thought, *Now What?*

Turns out it was only Nian. He flagged me and Dave down, stopped his bike, and sprinted off into the jungle. A minute or two later we heard a faint yell come from the trees.

Dave yelled back. "What?"

Nian yelled again, louder. "Throw me the toilet paper!"

Dave and I laughed, and Dave yelled back, "We don't have any!"

Nian moaned.

We laughed some more and got him some TP. Once Nian was all flushed out and cleaned up, we were back on the road!

Around 3:00 a.m., I was following Nian through a small farming village when all of a sudden I saw his tail light go crazy. I soon found out why. He had swerved frantically to miss a huge cow! Dave and I both dodged it, and we pulled over. Nian's close call with a cow got me all flustered and killed my desire to ride any further.

We were sitting there talking on the side of the road for probably five minutes when I asked Nian what he wanted to do.

No reply.

I looked back at his bike and said, "Nian?"

No answer.

Then I yelled, "NIAN!"

A faint reply came from the trees. "What!"

He had snuck back out in the trees to use the bathroom again. Dave and I shared another good laugh. I walked off the road a little bit and looked out into the dark field where Nian was serving up a healthy portion of poop soup.

As my eyes adjusted to the darkness, I could see a slight shimmer of light coming from the whole landscape. I studied it closer and finally realized that it was millions or billions of fireflies lighting up the entire countryside! No moon, few stars, and fireflies tracing every tree, field, fence, and hillside. What I saw was truly a sight that film can't capture. Believe me, I tried to film it. I wish everyone could have been there to share it with us. It was one of the most amazing acts of the Good Lord's great nature I've ever seen! It was so awesome that we rode up the highway another few kilometers until we found some nice trees on the side of the road to hang our hammocks in. We were all dead tired. I had been on the road for almost twenty-four hours. We quickly tied up our hammocks and watched the fireflies until we were fast asleep.

Day 78
Wednesday, April 14, 2010

The next morning, I woke up and realized that we had slept right on the side of a major highway. We got about three or four hours of sleep. As I forced the sleep out of my eyes, I looked across the street and saw ten men standing there looking at us.

I yelled, "Nian, Dave, wake up! There's some sketchy dudes looking at us!"

The second I rolled out of my hammock, all the guys took off. It was really weird. I felt like if I were to have slept another five minutes, the group of them might have tried something. I didn't know what, but I said my prayers and thanked the Lord for waking me up when he did!

We wrapped up our hammocks and headed toward the city of Cartagena. We put the hammer down and rode nonstop until we made it there. Upon arriving in the city, we were pleased to find that it was an old pirate town, full of castles, fortresses, and old rusty cannons. We rode as far as we could and were soon at the boat harbor. We splurged on junk food at a gas station and found a place to use the internet so we could get on Google Maps and find out what our next destination was.

That was when I discovered some potentially trip changing news. I rolled my chair back out from the computer I was using and said, "Hey guys, turns out, there's no roads that connect Colombia to Panama. This might be the end of the road for us." I searched deep into blogs and other traveler websites and found that we only had a few realistic options to get from Colombia to Panama.

1. Ride 200 kilometers through the Darian Gap death jungle which only one man had successfully crossed with a 2-wheel-drive Rokon motorcycle and the help of ten Indians in canoes.

2. Try to get on smugglers boats and ferries from near the guerilla territory in Colombia.

3. Pay $2000 per person to fly across with our bikes.

4. Put our bikes in a shipping container and wait a month while they went from port to port.

5. Try to find someone who owns a sailboat and pay them to sail us four days across the Caribbean to the San Blas Islands and get dumped off right in the middle of Panama.

We weighed out our options, grabbed some American-style breakfast, and set out looking for a sailboat captain that would let us hitch a ride over to Panama.

We started out by sifting through all the marinas and ports asking all the boat owners if they knew anyone that was sailing over to Panama anytime soon. We had been searching for hours. We were tired. Just as we were about to give up, some fisherman sent us over to the main boat harbor to find a man they called "Captain Pedro."

We found Captain Pedro's boat, but he was nowhere to be found. We set up shop next to the harbor office and waited for him. I found a warm shower right on the dock, so we all took a nice long shower while we waited for the captain to return.

It was getting pretty late when someone ran up to us and said, "Here comes Captain Pedro that you've been looking for."

I looked up and was a little shocked by what I saw. A tall, dark older man with somewhat greying hair, wearing long khaki shorts, tan boat shoes, and an unbuttoned long-sleeved white shirt. This guy looked like the stereotypical sailor. He walked up to us and asked if we were the guys that were looking for him.

We explained our situation and, almost without hesitation, he agreed to sail us across for $800 each. After learning the price, we sat down and hashed through what seemed like hours of haggling. When all was said and done, he agreed to sail us across for $400 but we had to work for him while we prepared to sail and help out while out on the water. We had ourselves a boat! Even if it did cost us over a million Colombian pesos, it wasn't really that much for a four-day sailboat ride to the exotic San Blas Islands and Panama, all the food we could eat, fishing, sailing lessons, getting the bikes across the sea, a nice bed to sleep in, and basically everything we'd ever dreamed of!

Captain Pedro showed us the ropes around the ship. There were three small rooms. The three of us had one room to share, and we agreed to help find more people to fill the other room in exchange for the cheap fare. We put our bags in our room and headed into town.

First stop was the laundromat! Each of us had a huge sack of filthy clothes! Our clothes hadn't been washed since we left Manaus a week before. Some of them were pretty rotten.

Cartagena was super awesome! Lots of the streets in the main old town were built in the 1500s, and they were only wide enough for one car. I assumed that it looked a lot like Spain or France would. We explored for a few hours and saw the town for most of the night. We stopped in at a couple hostels and did our best to recruit some more shipmates for Captain Pedro. After hours of good exploring, we took 'er back to the NIGHT HAWK II (which was the name of our ship) and called it a night!

17

SHIPWRECKED IN THE CARIBBEAN

Day 79
Thursday, April 15, 2010

I woke up completely confused! Where the heck was I, and why was I so hot?

I remembered that I was sleeping in the tiny forward cabin of a sailboat with another full-grown man. Dying of heat, I quickly changed into some board shorts and my running shoes and got the heck out of there! To my surprise, I had slept almost a full eight hours for once! Usually, once I woke up, going back to sleep is never an option. Dave and Nian were still in Sleepytown, so I left them a note that said I was out running and that I would return.

My run through Cartagena was an eventful one. I stuffed my headphones into my ears and headed off toward the old pirate fort part of town. I needed to get a haircut and needed to find a place to get some Brazilian money exchanged into Colombian pesos. There were a lot of travelers and hostels in that part of town, so I figured I wouldn't have too hard of a time finding either of those services.

I was maybe a mile into my run and just outside of the big stone walls of the pirate fort part of town, when a large, dark man stepped out in front of me with his hands out. I stopped fast and pulled my headphones out of my ears. As he got closer to me, I saw what he had in his hands. In his left hand was a massive bag of marijuana and in his right, what must have been cocaine. I stopped fast and looked for a way around him.

In English, the man said, "You want weed, cocaine, or hookers? I've got whatever you want brother!"

I simply replied, "No thanks, I don't smoke, and I'm in a hurry."

Our brief conversation must have drawn some attention because in a matter of seconds, there were ten to fifteen big guys all around me trying to sell me any kind of drug I might have wanted. I made it perfectly clear that I didn't want any of their drugs. After that, the first big guy chewed me out for being in a sketchy part of town and told me that I should leave.

I agreed, stuffed my headphones back in my ears, and sprinted away from them. At about that same moment, I looked down at my phone and thought, *Wait a minute. What kind of place is this? It isn't even eight o'clock in the morning, and I've already been hustled by drug dealers!*

A few more blocks into my run and I found a barber shop. A nice lady cut my hair and sent me further into old town Cartagena to find a place to exchange my Brazilian money. I ran up and down the pirate fort looking streets until I found the place. I swapped my money and headed northeast along the wall of the fort. From the fort, I ran up along the beach for a couple miles and watched teams of guys net fish with a cast net. From there, I headed back in the direction of the boat. Another mile later, and I found myself in the middle of another ghetto part of town. From the ghetto, I could see a big hill with tour buses going up and down from the top.

Curiosity got the best of me, and I was soon hiking straight up the side of the hill. By the time I made it to the top, I was so dehydrated I could hardly walk straight. I bummed a drink of water off of a street vendor, took some pictures, and headed straight back toward the boat. By the time I got back to the boat I was so tired I could hardly even run.

I took a quick shower and crashed out below deck on Captain Pedro's boat.

Late in the afternoon, footsteps on the top deck of the boat woke me up. I climbed up topside to find Dave and Nian sorting out all of our freshly washed clothes. Nothing felt better than putting on clean clothes after wearing the same greasy, stinky, clothes for days on end. Feeling fresh and clean, the three of us decided that we had better celebrate our successes before we sailed off the next day.

The next three hours were spent racing around on the cobblestone roads of the old pirate town. Right as we were about to head back to the boat for the night, we passed a huge building with a big neon sign on the front. A casino!

We all looked at each other and laughed. Before we knew it, the three of us were sitting around a blackjack table with some of Cartagena's elite. We each played $20. Nian and I were out fast, but Dave was on fire! My head couldn't concentrate on gambling because the hand that Dave was using to place his bets was the same one that had gotten chewed up when he had hit the dog back in Venezuela. Every time Dave would place a bet or hold on a good hand, I would laugh at his big bloody, bandaged hand out on the table. He looked like a true pirate. After a good win, Dave cashed out and we headed back to the boat.

As we pulled up to the marina, we could see a big figure waiting for us. As we got closer, I could make out Captain Pedro. Before we could park, he told us to kill our motors and quickly push our bikes into a dark alley that led out to the docks where the Night Hawk II was tethered.

The captain grabbed us and quietly explained that it was extremely illegal to ship bikes on a private sailboat. Once again, the three of us looked at each other and smiled while thinking, *What have we gotten into now?*

My bike was first. I was instructed to wait in the shadows until there wasn't anyone around. As soon as the coast was clear, I hopped up and pushed my bike down wooden docks to the Night Hawk II. Captain Pedro, Dave, Nian, and a couple dock hands were there waiting for me. Captain Pedro unhooked the cable that ran to the top of the sailboat mast while I tied a thick piece of rope around the whole middle section of my bike. The Captain clipped his mast cable to my rope and started cranking on the hand winch that lifted and lowered the mast. Before I knew it. my bike was being swung out over the water. The four of us wrestled it over the front part of the boat and positioned it nicely on the deck in front of the mainsail mast. I tied it up tight with some small ropes while the guys repeated the process with Dave's and Nian's bikes. Once we had all the bikes safely secured to the front of the boat, we covered them with our big plastic tarp that we had bought to use as a tent. After all our hard work in the humid heat, we were absolutely exhausted. Captain Pedro went out to party, and the three amigos fell asleep on the top deck of the boat!

The warm Colombian sun woke us up the next morning. *I could get used to sleeping on the deck of a sailboat*, I thought. We were getting ready to head off into the city when Captain Pedro showed up with an old car that he had borrowed from someone. He said he needed our help buying food for the trip, so we all hopped in, and we raced to a massive supermarket on the far side of town. Counting the captain and his wench/helper lady, the three of us, and three random travelers we had recruited from the hostels, there were eight of us sailing over to Panama. This meant we were going to need quite a bit of food and supplies.

I don't think any of us were quite prepared for the markets. First we went to the fruit market. Captain Pedro jumped out of the car and disappeared into a huge tent. We followed close behind. Once we got inside the tent, we found out that it was actually a building that was probably the size of a football field. This place was massive! It was completely filled with every kind of fruit you can imagine. First, we bought a fifty-gallon burlap sack full of pineapples, another full of mangoes, and others full of other delicious fruits! We were soon all completely loaded with fruit. We returned to the small car and repeated the same process at the vegetable and bread markets.

Then we went straight to the supermarket, where we ended up spending over a million pesos on all sorts of food and candy! We were just throwing everything we wanted into the cart! It was a great time. I was glad Captain Pedro thought a lot like we did when it came to buying food for a trip. By the time we were done shopping, the captain's little car was more than overloaded with food. Somehow, the four of us managed to still get in, and we headed back to the boat.

We spent the next few hours doing some minor repairs around the boat. Captain Pedro was pumped that we were willing to help him work his boat. He lined us out with tasks and headed back into town. What a cool guy! Just before sunset, the captain returned with his wench. They were both so drunk that they could barely stand up.

Captain Pedro stumbled onto the Night Hawk II and yelled, "DAVE, UNTIE THE LINES AND LET'S SET SAIL!"

We hoisted the sails and pulled out of the port. It was amazing! Our bikes tied to the front of the sailboat, us getting some sailing experience, and eating the best food ever, which was all cooked for us by the captain's wench! I couldn't help but smile!

As we literally sailed off into the sunset, Captain Pedro went below deck to get his GPS wired up straight. As he ran down below deck, he yelled for his wench to hold the wheel. After watching her put us ninety degrees off course three different times, I relieved her of her duties and eased myself into the captain's chair. I got the hang of it in like thirty seconds and had us due on course!

Drunk Captain Pedro came up from below deck, looked at his instruments, and said, "Wow, you really know how to captain a boat! Are you good to navigate us for a little while? I'm super tired from partying all night last night!"

I replied, "ABSOLUTELY!"

So he said, "Okay then. You're first mate for now! I'm gonna take a nap for a bit. Just make sure you keep us on the bearing. Also, keep an eye out for shipping containers floating in the water, and make sure we don't get hit by an ocean liner ship!"

The nap he spoke of turned into him finishing off a couple more bottles of booze and passing out on the top deck. I leaned back in the captain's chair, put my foot up on the wheel, and enjoyed that I could see every star in the sky as I sailed us off into the night!

Sailing at night was an awesome experience, but the rocking of the waves and not being able to see anything but stars made it a tiresome task. I did my best to stay alert and to keep us on course. Sometime around 3:00 a.m., I started getting super tired. As my eyes were getting heavy, I heard a deafening horn blast! I jumped up just in time to see a gigantic ocean liner ship coming toward us! I turned hard to the port and gave the big girl plenty of room to pass us on our starboard side. As she motored past us, I couldn't help but stare in awe. That ship was MASSIVE! All lit up from bow to stern, it looked like a floating city. The giant vessel disappeared as fast as it had appeared. It was shockingly fast!

My encounter with the monstrous ship had woken me back up. Another couple hours behind the wheel, and I was about to fall asleep when Dave and Nian woke up. I showed them the basics around the helm, and the three of us switched off captaining the vessel for the rest of the night.

Sometime around 10:00 in the morning, Captain Pedro finally woke up! He lumbered around for a bit, checked the GPS, congratulated us on being on course and being good sailors, and proceeded to cook a delicious breakfast.

Once we were done with breakfast, I was one tired sailor. Manning the helm all night had taken a toll on me. I decided that it was just about nap time. Before lying down, I dug up a spool of fishing line and a big metal spoon that was stashed in one of the storage compartments on the Night Hawk II. I slowly let the lure out behind the boat as we sailed along. I watched the line for a while with no luck. I really wanted to catch some fish. I left the lure in the water and tied the line off to a cleat on the back of the boat. Struggling to keep my eyes open, I retired to the bottom deck for some shut-eye.

I was soon woken up by Nian looking for my pliers. Turns out, Dave and Captain Pedro had hooked and pulled in a monster Tuna while I was sleeping! Nian needed my pliers to get the hook out of the fish's mouth!

I was mad that I had missed out on the tuna catching action for like four seconds. Tiredness overtook my anger, and I passed out again.

When I finally woke up from my extended nap, dinner was set. We were having fresh-caught tuna! Captain had chopped it up and fried it up for us. It was seriously some of the best fish I have ever eaten! It was amazing that one tuna was just big enough to feed all eight of us really well!

Pretty soon, it started getting dark again. It was time for Captain Pedro to get hammered drunk, and I was up to pilot the boat. The second night, Dave, Captain Pedro, Nian, and I all took our turns at the helm.

Captain Pedro was one unique guy. My Spanish swear word vocabulary increased one hundred percent while we were on the boat with him! He truly took the phrase "swore like a sailor" to a whole other level.

After my turn at the wheel, I went and lay down right on the very front tip of the bow and tried falling asleep. The moon and stars were so bright that I couldn't even keep my eyes closed. After two hours of lying there awake, we hit a huge wave and my pad slid all the way over the edge of the boat! The only thing that kept me from going in the water was a tiny cable. If I would have been asleep and lying completely flat, I would have gone overboard! Getting lost at sea was really low on my priority list! I got myself better situated on the bow and started drifting off to Sleepytown.

All of a sudden, a strange noise and loud splashing woke me up. I looked around but couldn't see what would be making that much commotion. Just as I was about to lie back down, I looked down into the water which was all lit up with moonlight and starlight. I could faintly see fifteen or twenty big white figures right below me at the bow. One rose up and made a huge splash! It was a pod of dolphins!

There were tons of them! I lay on my stomach over the bow for the next thirty minutes trying to get one to jump up and touch my hand. There were dolphins on both sides of me doing all kinds of jumps and tricks all around the wake the boat was putting out! I hate to sound like a sissy, but it was absolutely magical! Words can't describe what I felt while watching such amazing creatures dance in the starlit waters around our boat. After a while, my dolphin friends left, and I finally got some sleep while Dave and Nian piloted the Night Hawk II for the rest of the night.

Day 82
Sunday, April 18, 2010

By the time I woke up Sunday morning, we were only ten miles away from the San Blas Islands. After a quick breakfast of fresh fruit, I took the wheel and piloted us most of the way in. As the islands came into sight, Captain Pedro took the helm for the last little bit due to low tide coral reef dangers, which was really funny, and you'll find out why very soon!

We needed to stop in the small island immigration office to get our passports stamped before we could offload on the mainland. Captain made some phone calls and found out that they were closed until the next morning.

With an extra day to kill, we sailed the Night Hawk II between two paradisiacal islands and Captain Pedro yelled out, "Drop the anchor boys!"

We did as we were told, which brought us to our new home for the night. As the boat stopped in the calm Caribbean waters, the Wolfpack was ready for a swim! The three of us started doing flips and diving off the top of the boat! The water was probably about forty-five feet deep, and we could see all the way to the bottom! So blue and so clear!

Captain pulled a big bag full of snorkel stuff out of a storage locker on the boat, and we spent the next few hours diving around the reefs and swimming our hearts out. There were so many amazing colorful fish, sting rays, and huge conch shells. We snorkeled over to one of the nearby islands, where we were immediately greeted by Indians eager to sell us necklaces made out of miscellaneous things they had found on the tiny island. We each bought one and returned to snorkeling around the tiny island.

I was swimming along in the shallows, following some colorful fish, when I noticed someone in the water in front of me. I poked my head out of the water. There was an old Indian woman standing waist deep in the water about twenty-five yards in front of me. I quietly paused and waited for her to leave. She stood there motionless for a good thirty seconds. The old lady started doing a swimming motion with her arms pushing water behind her.

I thought, What the heck is she doing? That's when it hit me! She was taking what we call an "aqua duce!" SHE WAS POOPING IN THE WATER!

I panicked, turned around, and went full Michael Phelps Olympic swimmer until I was out of sight. That was a close call! After we felt how bad our sunburn levels were, we all headed back to the boat.

Captain Pedro was already busy cooking us up a huge meal! We all ate really well. After dinner, the captain loaded us up in the dinghy and motored us over to another small indigenous island. We explored while he stayed on the boat. It looked exactly like an island would look in my mind if someone were to say, "Okay, so you're on a deserted island." Just palm trees and a few Indian huts where they hung out during the day. Pedro said all the Indians lived on a bigger island a few miles away.

We walked all the way around the island, which was when we got a great idea. Let's sleep on the island!

Needless to say, Captain was soon dropping us off again with our hammocks, ropes, and blankets. We trekked through the fading light to the east side of the island. There, we found two palm trees growing out over the water on a forty-five degree angle. Dave and I shinnied up each tree, and we tied all three of our hammocks up over the water. The two trees made the perfect triple hammock bunk bed! Our sleeping setup looked like it should have been on a postcard!

Lying in our bunk hammocks over the water was one of the most surreal moments of my life! Every star in the sky was out and sparkling like a mega firework that was millions of miles away. Small waves and light sounds of the islands were all we could hear. It was hands down one of the most amazing campouts of our adventure. Knowing that we were the only people on the island made the experience unbelievably relaxing. Words can't describe the feeling I had while lying in my hammock thinking about the grandeur of God and all his many creations. It was one of the most unreal, peaceful, spiritual feelings of my life. Tears come out of my eyes once or twice every ten to fifteen years. I didn't cry that night, but I was very close. I wished everyone I loved could have been there to share the unspeakable beauty with us! The light wind swung our hammocks and rocked us until we were enjoying the most magical night's sleep of our lives.

A loud wave woke me up around 2:00 in the morning. I opened my eyes and looked out over the Caribbean. As my eyes focused, I could see a giant, lit up figure out on the water. It was a mega yacht! I rolled over in my hammock and said, "Hey guys, wake up. Either Jay Z or an Arab oil tycoon came to say hi to us." We had a good laugh and quickly fell back to sleep.

The Wolfpack slept like kings! Totally refreshed, we woke up as the sun rose over the Caribbean. We rolled up our hammocks and walked around the tiny island looking for Captain Pedro. Just as we rounded the corner closest to where we had been dropped off, the Captain was beaching the dinghy. We loaded our gear up and motored back out to the ship.

Back on the Night Hawk II, we ate a quick breakfast and got ready for the last few miles of sailing before we were back to dry land.

Captain yelled, "HEY BOYS, HOIST THE ANCHOR AND LET'S SET SAIL!"

We were a short ten miles from the port where we would be unloading our bikes. We anchored off shore and took the dinghy to the small island with the immigration office where we could get our visas and passports stamped.

As we sat on a bench waiting for the office to open, Captain Pedro came up to Dave, Nian, and me and said, "Gringo amigos, thanks for everything, guys! I have been doing this for a long, long time. I've never had such an awesome group of people on the boat. I am really going to miss you guys. Here you go."

He gave us each twenty-five American dollars! He paid us for all our work on the boat! We couldn't believe it! Everywhere we went, people were trying to get extra money out of us, and he had just given us a refund!

He then handed us a pink piece of paper and said, "Here are my three cell phone numbers. Call me if you ever want to sail the Caribbean again. Next time don't worry about money. Just call me, and I'll take you and your friends or family for free!"

He got a little choked up and gave all three of us a sturdy brotherly hug. What an awesome dude!

Soon, we had our documents stamped and were back on the boat and sailing around toward the port where we could unload our bikes. One of the European guys that was sailing with us saw some dolphins. He ran back to the helm and asked the Captain if we could go back so he could get a picture of them. Captain Pedro did a loop and sailed right through the huge pod of playful dolphins. It was pretty cool.

When he looped around, we got slightly off course. I was on the front deck uncovering our bikes when I felt a huge jolt. Then BLAM! Scraping sounds and I'm lying on my back on the front deck of the Night Hawk II!

The next thing I heard was Captain Pedro yelling, "Puta! Meirda!" and other Spanish swear words I didn't understand! Over and over again! A slurry of Spanish swear words were the only thing that came out of the Captain's mouth for the next hour!

Turning back to see the dolphins had caused him to run the Night Hawk II aground on a shallow coral reef! Just when we thought the trip couldn't get any crazier, there we were, SHIPWRECKED IN THE CARIBBEAN!

Captain Pedro jumped in the dinghy and tried pushing the Night Hawk II backwards off the reef while Dave reversed the motor turning back and forth. We were stuck. Our ship wouldn't budge!

Soon, out of nowhere, an old Indian man showed up in a motorized canoe that had been carved out of a huge wooden log. He dropped a huge rock for his anchor, tore his shorts off, and dove in wearing only some skimpy, worn out underwear and a snorkel. I grabbed a snorkel and dove in to follow him.

When I got under the boat, I discovered that the Night Hawk II's rudder was blocked by some huge rocks from behind. Some of the rocks were about half my size.

So what did we do? The old Indian man and I came up for air and regrouped. He gave me a hand signal that we were going back down. He took a couple deep breaths and said, "1... 2... 3..." Then both of us swam down under the boat, each grabbed one side of a huge boulder, and walked it along the bottom away from the boat! It was pretty awesome and very scary!

The waves we're rocking the boat deeper and deeper onto the reef. We were hurrying as fast as we could as the tide was going out. If the tide went out much more, the Night Hawk II would be left high and dry, so we panicked to free it as fast as we could! It took the old man and me about half an hour to move all the huge rocks from behind the rudder.

Exhausted, I dragged myself back onto the Night Hawk II. That was when I saw the madness that had overtaken us! More Indians had showed up with bigger motorized canoes and outboard boats. Somehow, Captain Pedro had tied four motorized boats up to the back of the Night Hawk II. They all floored it at the same time as Pedro pushed the front with the dinghy and Dave ran the Night Hawk II motor in full reverse!

The result of this attempt to free our vessel off the reef was pure craziness and chaos! Boats were crashing into each other, clothes-lining each other, and almost sinking to the bottom themselves! It was SO CRAZY! When that didn't work, Captain Pedro decided that the only way to get the Night Hawk II free before the tide got too low was to shed a lot of weight. He needed to get us and our heavy bikes off of the boat ASAP.

Puzzled as to how this was going to work, we did what we were told and untied the bikes and hooked one of them to the winch line that connected to the top of the mast.

We hoisted each bike up in the air, swung them out over the water, and lowered them into the Indian's motorized wooden canoes!

Once again, we all looked at each other and thought, *Is this really happening?* We put Dave's bike, Nian's bike, all our bags, and ourselves in one big canoe. My bike went with four other guys in a smaller canoe.

Once we were all off the Night Hawk II, the four motorboats began pulling again, two dingeys pushed from the front, and Captain Pedro was at the helm going full throttle backwards. They battled at it for a few minutes, and finally the Night Hawk II lurched backwards! One more big pull and she was free!

We were a hundred yards away already. We heard Pedro yell a loud slurry of swear words and then, "ESTOY LIBRE!" ("I'M FREEEEE!") So awesome! He then stood up at the helm and yelled, "ADIOS AMIGOS!" ("Goodbye Friends!") as he waved goodbye with both hands.

The Wolfpack was already on its way to the mainland. The canoe ride was super nerve-racking! I was squatting on the bottom holding tightly to each side. The water was only four inches from the top of the canoe! One big wave and we would definitely sink!

Twenty minutes later, we were going up a river inlet with Indians everywhere. The boat drivers took us to their friends' "port." We unloaded our bikes and were informed that we had to pay them fifty American dollars for transporting each bike. We only had the seventy-five dollars that Pedro had given us, so we turned up our negotiation skills. I gave them fifty dollars and told them that was all we could spend. They were PISSED! I was ready for a good old-fashioned fight.

We tied our gear and packs on our bikes and told them, "Sorry, we don't have any extra money." After thirty minutes of arguing, one of them left and returned with an army dude dressed in camo and carrying a machine gun! Once again, they demanded more money! We couldn't turn back now. The three of us talked over the situation in English.

I looked at Dave and Nian and said, "Guys, let's try and trade them stuff to see if they'll let us go!"

We opened up our packs and started offering them random items that we could replace easily. After a long, tense negotiation, they finally accepted our 100-foot climbing rope, a pair of rubber boots, a bunch of candy and snacks, and a small bottle of cologne as payment.

Their leader signaled for us to get the heck out of there. We fired up our machines and rode out of there as fast as we could! The road from the coast going inland was intense! We put the hammer down and raced down jungle dirt roads through mud, mountains, and deep rivers for the next two hours. Panama's mountains were so pretty! After a wild mountain ride, we finally made it to asphalt.

I looked down at my GPS and sure enough, we had made it to the Pan-American Highway! The Pan-American Highway, also known as Highway 1, runs from Southern Panama all the way to Alaska. A short 7000 kilometers up the highway would put us at the US border! At 3:00 p.m., Monday April 19th, WE HIT THE ROAD FOR THE ULTIMATE RIDE HOME!

18

THE PAN-AMERICAN HIGHWAY (P.S. I HATE YOU, HONDURAS)

Day 83.5
Monday, April 19

We were happy and feeling great as we headed north up the Pan-American Highway. Once again, we were on some nice, big freeways. Panama uses the US dollar as well, so it was cool to buy things in dollars. About 200 kilometers up the highway we found ourselves lost in Panama City, one of the most modern cities we had visited in the past couple months. I would have told you that we were in Florida. We circled around Panama City for a couple hours and finally found the way out of town.

Soon after leaving the city, we crossed the Panama Canal. That was super awesome! You could see how much work went into building it. After crossing the canal, we rode west-southwest for what seemed like forever! Sometime after dark, the highway headed back northeast. The Wolfpack trekked on up the highway.

After hours of riding we made it to the Costa Rica-Panama border. We were pumped to get into Costa Rica to find a nice campsite. As we crossed the border, we were informed that the Costa Rican customs didn't open until 7:00 a.m. We could get out of Panama but couldn't get into Costa Rica until morning. So we found a couple of nice poles and fence posts right in front of the customs office and hung up our hammocks to get a few hours of shut-eye. We wrapped up in our Paraguayan blankets to keep the bugs off us, and around 3:00 a.m., the jungle sounds whisked us off to sleep.

Day 84
Tuesday, April 20, 2010

On Tuesday morning, we were woken up a little before 5:00 a.m. There were already people lined up at the border fighting to be the first to get into Panama to go to work. We broke camp and jumped in line to get into Costa Rica. Little did we know, we were almost two hours early. Finally, 7:00 a.m. rolled around, the office opened, and when our turn to get stamped into Costa Rica came around, we had to go a mile back to Panama to get our passports stamped there. We had to wait another hour in line there, and then we were back to the Costa Rica customs office.

Once again, we made it to the front of the line, where we were informed that we needed our yellow fever shot cards or we weren't going into Costa Rica. The lady just told us that we were out of luck and that we had to go back to Panama, get the shot, wait six days, and then we could enter the city. We were super mad. I went back up to the front of the line and asked if I could get a copy of the card faxed or emailed to them. They said that was okay, so we got to work.

I searched around for a pay phone and called my sweet Mother collect.

"Hey Mom, can you send me my yellow fever shot card?"

"Jim...you don't have your yellow fever shots."

I said, "Well, that's not good. I'll figure it out. Hope all is well, and I love you! Talk to you later, Mother Dear!"

Ummm... shoot. Now what?

There was no way we were going to sit around for six days

waiting for a shot to take effect. I thought through our options and had an idea. Immunization cards are pretty simple. I could make them! All I needed was a computer and a printer. I had my mom email me my immunization card. We found an internet cafe and got to work.

I printed off my old card and wrote a date from a year ago in the yellow fever section. We photo-copied it, and I took it back to the Costa Rica immigrations office. Turns out, Panama stamped my passport with the wrong stamp so...back to Panama, then back to Costa Rica. Finally, they stamped me into Costa Rica! Then it took me two more hours to get our bike paperwork all finished up and done. Dave and Nian just got on the internet, found some shot cards on google images, changed the names, printed them off and got stamped into Costa Rica like a charm!

Around 2:00 p.m., we were finally on the road in Costa Rica. What a headache! We are three very clever bandits!

Once in Costa Rica we just rode HARD! It was a super pretty country, but we didn't have time to stop and see the sights. Next time, I guess! We rode a few hours through some hot jungle, which was amazing. We were headed north along the Pacific Coast. Suddenly, the road veered back to the southwest. That took us up into some mountains and through some pineapple farms.

We rode through a small rainstorm and stopped for gas and goodies in the small town of Cacao. As we left the town, we hit a stretch of nice curvy roads. We were having a blast flying up the mountain on awesome paved roads when, all the sudden, our bikes started running way crappy! We were at such a high altitude that our bikes were choking for air. Suddenly it started getting chilly and started to drizzle a little. That was strange because just hours before we had all been cursing the blasted jungle heat. Nian and Dave stopped to put on their rain gear. I reluctantly stopped and put mine on as well. I had been under the impression that it would just drizzle a little and we'd be high and dry soon.

Little did I know, five minutes up the mountain road—Boom!

An ultra-freezing rainstorm awaited us! I had on three shirts, two jackets, and all the other warm clothing I could possibly squeeze under my rain gear. Twenty minutes up the mountain road, my bike was going twenty miles per hour at full throttle, and I was FREEZING! Like teeth-chattering freezing! I would compare this coldness to the time I fell through the ice while ice fishing. SO COLD!

The little mountain that I thought we would pass soon turned into one of the highest mountains in Costa Rica! We pinned our bikes and rode as fast as we could (twenty-five miles per hour) until we were out of the mountains. As we headed down the other side, the clouds broke a little and we were able to see just how amazing the place was. We all stopped just before San Jose and told each other how cold we were over and over again.

Back on the road, we were soon in the middle of San Jose. My GPS only had a couple major roads on it, so I just kept us going in the general direction and followed the flow of traffic. Miraculously, we made it right through the city—during rush hour—with no problems. We did get put onto a nice toll road that wasn't cheap, so we begged the attendants to let us through! It worked about half the time. It got dark, and we rode until we were close to the Pacific Ocean again. We got some gas, got some wild Central American energy drinks, and hit the road.

The stretch of road from San Jose to the Nicaraguan border was kinda sketchy! Lots of transvestites and truckers. Needless to say, we didn't stop except for some roadside police checkpoints. The cops there were super cool. One of them gave me his address and wanted me to come back and buy his beach property.

Around 3:00 a.m., we arrived at the Nicaraguan border. We were stopped by the border police and told that we needed to wait until 7:00 a.m. for customs to open.

This campout was a little different from the rest. As we crossed the border, the roads were dirt and the whole area was extremely gloomy and unkept. There was a huge parking lot full of trucks and a few people walking around. The wind started blowing, and it was looking like it was going to rain. We arranged our hammocks under a little roof next to the customs office. I pushed my bike up under my hammock and tried to get some sleep. I woke up three or four times throughout the night to keep an eye on some creepy people that kept walking around us. I didn't get much sleep, but it sure felt good to lay down for a bit!

As morning broke, I awoke and found out that we were being watched by three shady-looking guys! It was probably around 6:00 a.m. It was starting to get light and we had been asleep for a few hours, so hopped right up and asked a dude what he wanted. He didn't even move, just stood there and looked at me, and then slowly walked away.

We broke camp and once again started the research process of finding out how to get through customs and on our way in Nicaragua. I went to the office first, fought off all the money changers as usual, and then got in line to get my passport stamped. While I was waiting, I plugged in my phone to get it charged enough to listen to my tunes. I got stamped in and went and rode around until I found Dave and Nian. We talked over our situations and decided to find a shower and get cleaned up. We were all black from road grime!

Oh shoot! I forgot my phone!

I ran back over to customs and...GONE! I ran around frantically asking who took it! Nobody said anything! I was heartbroken. Seriously, so bummed out! I asked two more people if they had seen it and nothing. As I was walking out, some guy walked up to the counter and said something to the guy that I had asked first. He put his head down, walked over to a filing case, and grabbed my phone and charger out. Another prayer answered!

We found a truck stop and took poops in holes in the nastiest crapper we had ever seen! We got showered up, and after getting all our bike paperwork done and getting our bikes and gear sprayed for invasive bugs, we were once again on the road!

We rode up the west shore of Lake Nicaragua. The landscape and scenery were amazing. The only thing wrong with the picture was the

BUGS! I looked down, and my knees were black from splattered bugs! I had bugs all over in my leg hair and just all over for real! Our visors were pure bug guts! Except for Dave's... He didn't have a visor! That sucked so bad!

Nian ran out of gas, so Dave and I rode five kilometers to the next town, filled up, and Dave took a water bottle full of gas back to Nian.

When they got back and got filled up with fuel, I had bought a lunch of American-style fried chicken and Monsters. We sat down and ate the BEST fried chicken of our lives! The owner overheard us say just that and responded to us in English. Turned out he lived in Silver Springs, Maryland, ten miles from where I had lived for the last three summers. We finished our lunch and some old war veteran dude gave us detailed directions in English of how to get through Nicaragua the fastest. We cleaned the bugs off of ourselves and rode hard once again.

Soon the dude's directions had taken us in a super big loop and we were headed back toward the road where we had started. While somewhat lost, we did pass through some super awesome volcano mountains and really cultural small towns. As we passed through one of them, I thought, *I bet there are LDS missionaries in every one of these towns.*

Not more than two minutes later, low and behold, two American elders walking right at us! I locked up my brake and screeched to a halt. We talked to them for a bit, got better directions, and continued our volcano mountain ride down to the Pan-American Highway. A couple more hours up the Highway and we were in the middle of a desert surrounded by volcanoes.

Our bikes were burning up, and so were we! The heat was unbearable! We bought tons of water and got all fueled up at the first gas station we came to. Back on the road, we busted it up the Highway toward Managua. Once there we stopped to pee and there was a stalled car.

I hopped off, and we all helped this dude push his SUV to the top of the hill. As he thanked us and hopped in his car, I noticed that he had a huge pistol in the back of his jeans. Guess helping him was the right decision. I never told Dave and Nian this, but I took us on a long detour to keep us out of the city after I saw that dude's gun. It just gave me bad vibes. The detour took us right past Lake Managua, which also had tons of huge volcanoes!

It was such an awesome landscape. After four or five more hours of burning up in the desert, we were close to the Honduras border. About fifty kilometers from the border, we stopped, got gas, and spent every dime we had of funny Nicaraguan money on drinks and goodies. Another hour of riding, and we were at the Honduran border.

Once again, the border crossing and customs area was super ghetto and full of fools trying to "help us" and rip us off by exchanging our money. We simply told them the truth, that if they wanted to "help us" with our paperwork for free, they were more than welcome to. We were truly OUT of money! I had used my safety $150 that I kept in the back of my passport and we had spent everything else on junk food.

Nian and I wanted to use the bathroom but couldn't because it cost money! We turned in our Nicaraguan driver licenses and got ready to go into Honduras. Twenty minutes later, we had our passports all stamped and we were ready to go. Then some guy told us that we had to wait for the Motor Vehicle people to get out of a meeting before we could get permission to drive in Honduras.

Then came the bad news. It was going to cost each of us over fifty American dollars to get the permission. The worst part about that was we were only going to be in Honduras for a couple hours. My GPS said that it was only 280 kilometers across the whole country, so we waited around for an hour and fought with people about not paying due to our no money situation. Finally, the boss lady came out of a meeting and we were invited to go in and talk to her. That's when we found out how big of trouble we were really in.

The nearest ATM was forty kilometers into Honduras. We couldn't ride there, because we didn't have permissions yet. We also couldn't go back into Nicaragua because we had already turned in our Nicaraguan driver permissions. We were really jammed! She said that some guy would give us a ride to the ATM and back for a hundred dollars each! NO WAY! Not only was that too much money but also too time consuming.

All of a sudden, Dave says, "Is this your money?"

He's got a huge wad of money in his hand! I would guess probably more than a thousand American dollars! He found it sitting on the floor in the boss lady's office!

She claimed it and was even more ruthless with us! I was starting to get worried again that this was the end of the road!

NOW IT STARTS GETTING CRAZY!

As we walked out of that lady's office with basically no options, the wind started blowing very strange. I looked around and realized that it was about to storm HARD!

I walked out to my bike and said, "Fellas, pack your bags and get your rain gear on NOW!"

We got geared up for the rain in like five minutes! It was strange because we had a crowd of about twenty people watching us that all knew our situation. Just before we were all ready to go, the heaviest rainfall ever began to pound down on us! As a literal wall of water overtook us, I knew that God wanted us to keep going, and that he was opening up the gate to Honduras for us.

I push started my bike, as I had been doing ever since my starter went out in Panama. Dave and Nian were right behind me and we FLEW PAST THE BORDER PATROL GATE!

The rain was so heavy we couldn't even see the road! Someone yelled as we blew past, but there was no stopping now! The super heavy rain suddenly quit five minutes after we had BLASTED the border! I was actually mad that it stopped raining, because that meant the frequent road stops and patrols would all be functioning normally.

We passed another police checkpoint after another twenty minutes. My heart was pounding out of my chest. There was a good chance the border patrol had called the checkpoints and told them to keep an eye out for three bandits who didn't pay to get permission to drive in Honduras. I stood up on my pegs, saluted the officers with one hand, and honked my horn a few times with the other hand.

They looked at us, confused, and never bothered stopping us! We passed five more patrol stations using the same technique! We followed the Pan-American through Honduras, getting lost here and there along the way, of course. We stopped and got ourselves some ultra energy drinks, got on all our cold weather gear, and headed for the El Salvador border. That's when it happened—stopped by a police roadblock!

Oh shoot! I thought to myself. We all fumbled through our stacks of papers and showed them some random wet documents we had picked up along the way and then acted like we didn't know what they were talking about! They really only stopped us because people were getting mugged and/or murdered on the bridge just down the road from us. So in a way, like so many people along our way had done, they were watching over us. They finally let us go.

It was probably around midnight before we got to the El Salvadoran border. We got in the middle of a huge line of trucks and went as fast as we could to avoid getting stopped by the Honduran exit customs. Worked like a charm! We all thanked the Lord for our safe passage through Honduras.

Once in El Salvador, we used a different tactic on the customs guy. We just talked about how awesome El Salvador was, how excited we were to eat the food, and what we needed to see while we were there! Pretty soon, we were good buds, and he sent us on our way. He mentioned something about getting permission for the bikes, but we never saw another government building so we just kept on going. The GPS once again took us on a sweet unneeded one-hour detour. Soon it was raining again, so we geared up and made good time through El Salvador!

We did stop in one small town to munch down some pupusas. So delicious! We got to San Salvador around 2:00 or 3:00 a.m. and soon we were again lost! After more energy drinks, gas, and directions, we were hot on our way. We flew through some territory that I assumed was really pretty, but the darkness ruined all of that! At around 4:00 a.m. we finally arrived at the Guatemalan border!

We rolled in there super confident and cool, sure that we were once again on our way! There was a big bridge separating the two countries and that bridge was blocked by a gate and like ten guards. We told them some story about why we didn't have our permissions to drive in the country and, of course, they didn't buy any of it. We begged them forever to let us through, but finally we agreed to hang up our hammocks there and get some shut-eye and wait for them to call the other border in the morning.

The bathrooms were locked, so Nian and I peed off of a 200 foot bridge. It was pretty funny!

As we walked off the bridge we heard Dave yell, "BOMBS AWAY!"

A few seconds later we heard a faint splash followed by laughter. Dave had just dropped a huge poop off of the bridge! The Wolfpack had a really good laugh! Soon we were all camped out and sound asleep swinging in our hammocks! That was honestly one of the longest, most eventful, hottest, coldest, and most mentally draining days of my life!

Day 86
Thursday, April 22, 2010

4:45 a.m. and I was wide awake! I think I only slept an hour or two. Two reasons why. First, the night before Dave had bought me a RAPTOR energy drink (which rocked my world). Second, there were ten million birds making squawking sounds as soon as the sky showed the slightest signs of light. I was so mad!

I got up, took my hammock down, and packed my bike up. It was still only 5:00 a.m., so I tightened my chain up, straightened my headlight, and did some other minor tune-ups on my bike.

I took a shower out of a hose, went for a small hike, and by that time it was almost 6:00 a.m. I went and talked to a guard at the post. I asked if we were good to cross the bridge into Guatemala. He gave me a big smile and thumbs up and said we were good to go. So I went and rousted Dave and Nian out of their hammocks, they broke camp, I push started my bike, and we rode off.

Dave and I rode past the guards honking and saluting as we went past. As usual, Nian was a couple steps behind us. One ornery guard came out and put his hand up. Nian stopped. By this point I was across the bridge. I saw freedom and wasn't turning back! Dave made it as well. We rolled up to the Guatemalan customs office. I started my paperwork while Dave went and looked for Nian. By the time they calmed the guards back down and made it across the bridge again, I had most of my paperwork all taken care of. We streamlined Dave's and Nian's paperwork, and soon we were on the road in Guatemala.

The minute we crossed the river from El Salvador, our surroundings went from semi-jungle sub-tropical to super desert! At around 9:00 a.m. we got some gas, oiled our chains, drank energy drinks, tested the gas station's plumbing, and hit the road!

We rode to a small town called Cuiaba. There, a guy told us that our best route was to head south until we were on the Pan-American Highway again. An awesome scenic ride through mountains and down curvy roads led us back to our main road. We went through a small town called Taxisco and the next leg of our journey seemed to take forever!

The scenery in Guatemala was amazing! Hot to cold, desert to jungle, mountains to plains, city to farmland. We passed Escuintla and continued up the Pan-American. Once we reached Mazatenango, we could almost taste the Mexican border, which meant we were in the last country we needed to get to before arriving in the States.

We were all so focused on the journey that we didn't really pay much attention to much else. The road signs started counting down the distance from the Mexican border. Ninety kilometers. Seventy-five kilometers. Sixty kilometers. Fifty kilometers. Once we started getting somewhat close to Mexico, traffic slowed and a never-ending line of semi trucks appeared. We all looked at each other like, What the heck? We seriously passed probably twenty-five to thirty kilometers of straight semis lined up all along the side of the road. Once we got closer to the front of the traffic jam, the cars, trucks, busses, and people had the road completely packed. We bobbed and weaved our way to the front of the jam.

BOOM! Another wrench in our gears. Human roadblock!

No way across—unless you went back and around, which was more than a 200-kilometer detour! They were blocking the road to protest other countries doing business in Guatemala or something. They had been there since 8:00 that morning.

I simply told them that we were Americans and that we were going to cross. I rode up to the line of people and was about to lift their rope and push my bike under when some dude that spoke broken English told me that it wasn't a good idea. So we waited for thirty minutes with no progress.

Being so close to Mexico made me super inpatient, so I walked across their barricade and into the little village on the side of the road. I was looking for a trail or even somewhere I could cut a fence and we could sneak past. I walked up a road and down a long driveway. There was a huge gate open, so I walked in. Inside the gate there was a big five story house surrounded by what looked like a fortress-type wall. On the inside of the wall were like forty garage-looking things.

First thing that came to my mind was, *Hmm... What a strange car detailing place.* Inside all the garages there was a sign that read, "Half price on your birthday." I was so confused. Some kid ran out of the big house, hopped on his little scooter, and headed my way. Then it hit me. It was a massive whore house! GROSS!

The kid rode up to me, so I stopped him. I asked him how to get around the roadblock and sure enough, he knew a way. He couldn't explain it, but he said for a few bucks he would show us the way. He gave me a ride back to the crowd and we ditched his scooter. We pushed back through the crowd to Dave, Nian, and our bikes. Nian and I didn't have enough room for the kid on our bikes, so Dave was nominated to give him a ride. He saddled up with Dave, and the four of us rode twenty kilometers back down the super traffic jam road.

We then took a right, which took us through some small, creepy, eerie little town. We went through the town, turned down some side road, went through a backyard, and then into the jungle. The whole time, the kid was telling us to slow down and be quiet. Like we had to be super sneaky or something? I thought we were going to be like ten minutes on this little side road. Nope.

We drove almost thirty kilometers through dusty jungle roads! Parts of it were intense! I felt like I was riding trails in American Fork Canyon with my buds again! After forty-five minutes of crazy trail rides through jungle, rivers, and rocky mountain trails, we finally popped back out on asphalt. The whole time, our new buddy was sitting on Dave's backpack full of Caribbean giant seashells.

All Dave could say was, "That sucked! I could feel his nuts in my back the entire time!"

We got a good laugh out of that! At one of the steeper parts of the trail, the fatness of our buddy made Dave's sprocket slip and stripped it out pretty bad. We dropped our buddy on the side of the road and gave him seven dollars. He was pumped and so were we.

Thirty minutes later, we were at the Mexican border. We went through the whole customs process again, I got searched for some reason, and we were soon on the road again!

19

JIM RIDES ALONE

Day 86
Thursday, April 22, 2010

Mexico. The last obstacle between us and our beloved home country.

For some strange reason, the second we got into Mexico, I got this feeling of *Ride as fast as you can. Don't stop for anything or anyone unless you absolutely have to!*

The customs people told us we had to ride to the next city and buy a refundable permission to ride in Mexico for four hundred dollars each rider. Haha—NOPE! We just got the heck out of there!

The feeling of caution didn't leave me, even until we needed to stop for gas and money. My cards were shut off, Dave had lost his wallet back in Colombia or Venezuela somewhere, and Nian didn't have very much money on his card. We sifted around Huixtla, Mexico until I found a pay phone, called my bank collect, and got my card reactivated. We got some food and got a game plan together.

The only game plan we could come up with was keep riding until we couldn't ride anymore! So, we did exactly that! We rode until we arrived at Arriaga at around 2:00 a.m. On the way there, we were riding down the freeway and passed a parked truck. Somehow some idiot left a twenty-foot pole sticking out of the back of the truck and into the road. I saw it in the nick of time, swerved, and ducked! Inches from ruining my trip! Dave and Nian weren't much farther away from the same tragedy! I said prayers of thankfulness to be alive.

We found our next gas station, where we got some food and decided that it was too cold and we were too tired to continue on. We made buddies with one of the pump managers, and he said he would watch over us if we hung our hammocks under one of the carports behind the station. As soon as I got myself somewhat horizontal, I was OUT! I still had a nervous feeling about Mexico, so I hung my hammock up almost touching my bike. I knew that it was going to take a lot to wake me up, so if someone was wanting to take my bike and bag, they were going to have to get me out of the way first!

Soon after falling asleep in my hammock at the gas station, I was woken up by someone kicking my hammock. It was Nian. He and Dave were almost all packed up and ready to hit the road. Turns out it wasn't soon after falling asleep. We had slept for almost five hours. It really felt like I slept for five minutes! I was so tired!

After a few minutes of disorientation, I was ready to roll. We loaded up on gas station goodies and energy drinks and we were off! The gas station we had camped at was somewhere between Arriaga and Tonala Mexico. The three-man motorbike crew rode maybe twenty minutes northwest, where we came to a fork in the road. The GPS had us going almost completely west but road signs and directions we had gathered from the gas station wanted us to go north. I stopped and contemplated the decision.

We had been told that the toll roads were the safest way to get through Mexico and the signs ahead of us said that the toll roads were to the north. So north it was. Little did we know, we were about to take one of the biggest detours of our trip!

From Arriaga heading north, we took one of the most amazing mountain roads winding up through the desert of Chiapas. It was just barely light and kind of foggy. As the sun came up, this scene was exactly how I had pictured Mexico as a child. Desert and deserted but gorgeous all at the same time. Our three-man wolf pack rode in formation, as fast as we could, through hairpin turns, going up the mountainside. All I know is the area around Terra e Liberdad, Mexico, was breathtaking!

When we arrived at the top of the mountain, there came another fork in the road. We looked at the basic GPS map, looked for signs that would lead us to Mexico City, and finally asked for more directions.

Dave asked some old man but didn't trust him, so he asked a couple guys walking down the roadside. For some strange reason, both people told us to head back east toward Tuxtla Gutierrez. An hour or two later we found ourselves in the middle of Tuxtla Gutierrez. It was a huge city laced with first world stores, Walmarts, fountains, and other interesting stuff.

We stopped at a stoplight and the guy selling newspapers on the side of the road caught my attention. He had a huge piece of wood with all the major newspapers attached to it. Every one of them had pictures of a lady that had been brutally murdered. I got a sick feeling and was bummed out for the next few hours. Ehh. I hate that!

As we rode out of Tuxtla Gutierrez, we paid a toll and asked the lady which way we needed to go to get to Mexico City. She told us to continue on the highway we were on. We pressed onward. Suddenly, the green oasis we were driving through turned into pine trees and jagged mountain passes. We climbed to over 8100 feet of elevation and our bikes that were jetted for sea level didn't like it! I had my bike pinned at full throttle and was only going fifty kilometers per hour. Our bikes were sputtering and choking from thin air until we coasted into San Cristobal. I was absolutely frozen as well! It blew me away how many times we went from blistering hot to bone-cold temperatures!

In San Cristobal we got gas and hit the mall in search of a map. Not buying one right off the bat in Mexico was a major mistake. We got our map in the mall and as we walked out to our bikes, we asked a security guard where we needed to go to get closer to Mexico City. He pointed us northeastward, and we headed out of town.

We were supposed to take the main road down past Zinacantan. Somehow we ended up in the middle of a bunch of Indian villages in the highlands near San Andrés Larráinzar. The roads were almost perfect for road bikes. The next five hours of riding were all hairpin turns. I drug my foot peg like five times. That's quite an accomplishment when it sits almost a foot and a half off the ground. We were lucky because the roads were actually really nice. The views from up there were indescribable—sheer green mountains with farms cut into them, cliffs everywhere, laced with rivers, and dotted with small humble homes. There were Indian farm ladies wearing goat wool skirts leading goats everywhere. We only saw a couple men. We figured that they were in the fields.

A couple hours into the mountains we stopped at a waterfall and asked for directions. We were eating a snack when Nian realized that we hadn't showered for a couple days. So of course he got naked and jumped in the river! I also washed up and we got back on the road. After making great time going downhill and making a few scary passes on a two-lane mountain road, we finally made it out of the mountains and back to somewhat of a main road. We were somewhere around Teapa. From there we rode north toward Villahermosa. The road going north was super hot and full of banana groves. It was nice to be back on flat ground, though.

A couple hours to the north and we were just outside of Villahermosa. We were all out of gas and super dehydrated. We fueled up and sat in the air conditioned service station for more than half an hour! It was honestly unbearably hot! After a good break we got back on the road. The road toward Cardenas was pretty slow going. We hit some traffic and when we finally got back on the freeway, Dave didn't dare go over eighty kilometers per hour for fear of blowing up his bike.

I rode on the far shoulder trying to get some shade from the trees planted in the median. I was miserable. Between Cardenas and Coatzacoalcos we got stopped at police and military checkpoints every fifty kilometers. We were stopping at our fourth checkpoint when our whole trip took a MAJOR TURN!

The way we got through checkpoints in Mexico was to act like we only spoke English. The cops would yell at us, asking for documents and licenses. We would give each other confused looks and say, "You speak English? English? Inglishesh?" We played it off super dumb, even though we understood more than ninety percent of what they were saying. Finally, most of them would give up and just let us go after five or ten minutes.

At this particular stop, it was all military and they weren't nice. After twenty minutes and me showing them all the moldy clothes and junk inside my pack, they were going to let us go. They weren't happy about us not having Mexican driving permission though. As I was tying everything up, Nian leaned his bike over and put his exhaust pipe on my bare leg! I screamed as it sizzled my flesh!

"NIAN! OW! FREAK! YOU JUST BURNED THE CRAP OUT OF ME!"

Nian said, "Oh. Sorry, dude."

No more than thirty seconds later, he leaned his bike over on me and once again scalded my leg with his exhaust pipe!

"GOSH DANG IT, NIAN!!! OW! AHHHH!"

Now I was livid! Driving slow for the past few hours and the high temperatures had been building up frustrations. After the second branding on my leg, instead of saying things to Nian that I would regret, I just grabbed my bike, push started it, and rode off down the road in a fit of fury! I rode maybe twenty minutes and stopped. I waited until I could see them coming a few kilometers back and started riding again. I could see them in my mirror every few minutes, but I was still a little upset so I stayed out front.

I passed through two construction zones and stopped at the next fork in the road to wait for them. I took off my shirt and waited. I sat there for more than twenty minutes. No riders passed by. So I rode a couple kilometers back to the last gas station. They hadn't seen the guys, so I got gas and started riding backwards down the edge of the freeway.

About half way back to where I had last seen them, I got stopped by some cops, hassled by those cops, and they made me get over to the other side of the freeway to keep going back. I rode almost all the way back to the military checkpoint looking for them. No Nian and Dave.

So I got back on the freeway and headed out as fast as I could! About ten kilometers back toward where the cops had stopped me, there was a short portion of road construction. Suddenly, the semi truck that was directly to my left decided that he needed to make a sharp left-hand turn and that he didn't have enough room to make his full turn. So he came all the way over into my lane and forced me off the road into the gravel.

I slammed on my back brake. My brake lever bottomed out. My back brakes were COMPLETELY GONE OUT! Now, I had two choices: keep riding off the side of the road and slam into a cement barricade or hit my front brake in gravel. It was pretty much a toss-up, so I decided to hit the front brake. That of course slingshotted me to the ground! Right next to a turning semi trailer, mind you.

I felt the sting of road rash all along my left side. I looked to the right, and right next to me were moving semi trailer tires. As fast as I hit the ground, I hopped back to my feet and grabbed my bike, almost before it even stopped sliding. I pushed my bike off the road onto a sidewalk. By this point I was cursing myself out loud while thanking God to be alive in my mind.

Keep in mind, I had my shirt off trying to get some relief from the intense heat, so my shoulder and side were pretty roughed up. I used one of my water bottles to wash out my road rashes and put my shirt back on. I had broken another mirror and bent my shifter pretty bad. It took me a second to get the bike back together. As soon as I did, I was back on the road trying to catch up to the boys.

Another five kilometers down the road, and the same cops stopped me again. They hassled me some more, but they hadn't seen any bikers go past. They let me go after some good convincing. I got on the road going as fast as I could to catch up to the guys. Right then, I had a thought come into my mind: *YOU'RE GOING THE REST OF THE WAY HOME ALONE!* Then I thought, Why? *No that's silly. I'll find the guys soon.*

It was getting dark, so I decided that I had better get to a hospital soon! The last time I crashed a motorbike in Mexico, I had gotten a bad infection, so I really wanted to get my road rashes washed out.

I rode into Acayucan, Mexico around 10:00 p.m. and rode all around town looking for a hospital but ended up going to an internet cafe instead. I sent the guys a message telling them to meet me in Veracruz. The guy that owned the internet place spoke some English. He gave me perfectly detailed directions of how to get to the local Red Cross station.

I hopped back on my bike and raced over there. The Red Cross staff took me right in and got me all cleaned up! Whatever they used stung like crazy! It seemed to work great though. The fact that the whole visit cost fourteen pesos (just a little more than a dollar) was awesome, as well!

It was almost midnight before I got out of the Red Cross. I headed back toward the internet place, but I soon figured out that the streets were all one-way streets, and I was lost. I rode through the middle of the town, around a carnival and huge crowd of people, and ended up stopping at a pharmacy to get some more bandages.

As I was leaving the pharmacy, I asked a couple people if they knew where I could use the internet. Nobody would help me. I was starting to get a little freaked out. It was super creepy there! I backed my bike back into the street and got ready push start it. Three teenage kids walked out of the pharmacy. I looked at them and thought, What an interesting crew. There's the tall, skinny pretty boy with his hair slicked back, the funny troublemaker with tattered clothes, two ponytail looking things coming out where his sideburns should be, and his hat on upside down, backwards, and folded in half, and the momma's boy with a huge helmet on, shirt tucked in, and a cheesy smile on his face.

After I had looked them over, I got a feeling they were sent to help me. They walked straight over to me and asked me what the heck I was doing. They told me how dangerous it was where we were and told me that they would take me to the only internet place that was open and then to the freeway.

Momma's Boy and Troublemaker hopped on one scooter and Pretty Boy on another. They buzzed through the town while I followed close behind. As we got off into some neighborhood, my mind kept going through scenarios: *Okay, if they try anything, first I grab my two foot Brazilian jungle knife, then I take the biggest one first, and so on.* Then the thought came to my head (for those of you who know who the Three Nephites are) *What if these are the Three Nephites sent to get me out of trouble?* I remember getting cold chills and having a super calm feeling come over me. Right then I thanked God for sending good people to always get me out of tight places!

The Three Amigos took me to an internet place. I checked my email. Nothing from Dave and Nian. From the start of the trip, the plan for if we got separated had always been to get on the internet and message a meeting place right away. I was a little upset that they hadn't written to me. I left the internet place and the Three Amigos were sitting out front watching my bike and gear for me. We jumped on our bikes and they led me to the freeway on-ramp. I got off, thanked them for their help, and they rode off. As they rode away, I once again got the feeling that I was saved by the grace of God.

Back on the road! By now it was after 1:00 in the morning. I rode north toward Veracruz on one of the nicest freeways I had ever seen. There were very few cars, and I could see every star in the sky! Pretty amazing. I stopped for gas at around 2:30 a.m. There at the gas station, I found a good guy that was more than happy to give me some advice.

I asked him for the best roads toward the United States and where the best place to spend the night was. The guy said I had two options to get back to the US: straight north up to Texas, or northwest to Mexico City, then up to Mazitlan, and then up to Arizona. He said that the Mexico City route was the safest and had the best roads.

I figured Dave and Nian would go that way as well so I decided that would be my best route.

The guy told me that if I went any farther than Orizaba that I would freeze to death, so that's where I should spend the night. I thought, Freeze to death? It was almost 3:00 a.m. and I was still sweating. I push started the Tornado and headed north. Two hours later, I was only about fifty kilometers from Orizaba, and I was so cold! I shivered uncontrollably for the next thirty minutes, but being super cold was probably the only thing that kept me awake.

I got off the freeway in Orizaba and looked for a hotel. Maybe five minutes down the main road I passed like twenty cop cars and tons of cops running around a building with guns drawn and yelling! I rode past thinking, *What in the heck is going on? What a crazy day!* I didn't even slow down until I was inside a hotel parking lot!

The first three hotels were full. I finally found one that had an open room for ten dollars. I checked in and limped my broken, frozen self into the room. After taking one of the most deserved showers of my life, I redressed my wounds and lay down. As my head hit the pillow, I realized that I had to get back up and shut the blinds. The sun was coming up! It was almost 7:00 a.m.! I had been on the road for almost twenty-six hours and I was EXHAUSTED!

Before lying back down, I realized that I would be ungrateful if I didn't kneel my road-rashed knees on the floor to thank GOD for still being ALIVE! I did so, lay down, and was instantly asleep.

20

MEXICO TO UTAH IN TWO DAYS? (NOT) IMPOSSIBLE!

Day 88
Saturday, April 24, 2010

I woke up a frantic mess at 10:30 a.m. I had no idea where I was, what was going on, or why I was so sore. I collected my thoughts, realized that I had only been asleep for a couple hours, and went back to sleep. A couple hours later, and I was up.

I packed all my nasty dirty clothes and put on my second-to-last clean shirt. I went to the hotel office and talked them into letting me use the hotel computer. Still no email from Dave and Nian. I was still rollin' alone in Mexico. I tied all my gear up on my bike and hit the road, but not before stopping and downing a Monster, of course.

I was definitely feeling the measly four hours of sleep. I topped off my gas tank and hit the freeway! I was surprised to find one of the most scenic motorbike rides I had ever been on. The freeway was winding and full of trees. I was wishing I had a super bike so bad. It was such an awesome ride. The road wound back and forth up to around 8700 feet elevation. Once my bike got up to the higher elevations, it began sputtering and choking due to the thin air.

Once I got over the mountains, I realized that my back brakes were completely gone and that my back sprocket was almost worn out again. I stopped and tightened my chain. I looked up and saw an awesome mountain: Pico de Orizaba. Little did I know, it is the highest mountain in Mexico at 18,500 ft elevation.

The views from up in the Mexican mountains were unreal! I had always thought that Mexico was full of nasty cactus desert. Not true.

I rode as fast as I could toward Mexico City. As I came down out of the mountains, a strong wind slowed my roll down to about fifty kilometers per hour and killed my gas mileage. I ran out of gas, but luckily I had filled up a Gatorade bottle the night before. I coasted into a town called Puebla. I filled my tank and set out in search of a bike shop.

I got the run-around all over town. People ran me back and forth for almost two hours looking for bike parts. I found a little shop that sold me a battery and some mirrors. They sent me to the Honda shop to find the rest of the stuff that I needed to fix my bike. I finally found the Honda shop and started talking to some guy about what I needed. An older fellow came up to me and asked me if I spoke Portuguese. I guess he had a Brazilian mother. Turned out he spoke English, Spanish, Portuguese and three other languages. Also turns out that he owned the Honda shop. We chatted it up for almost half an hour. He had lived with a Latter-day Saint family in the US, lived in Sweden, and been all over the world. He was closing his shop because it was Saturday and they closed early on Saturdays. He sold me all the parts I needed for super cheap and got me back on my way.

I checked my email before I got back on the road and what do you know, Dave had written me. They were ahead of me again. They were fixing Nian's bike closer to Mexico City. Dave told me to check my email in Toluca, which is just past Mexico City.

I got a new spark of excitement, grabbed some grub, and hit the road. The closer I got to Mexico City, the more ghetto my surroundings became. I tried keeping my tracks straight but without proper maps and someone to help navigate while I drove, I soon found myself lost in southeast Mexico City, surrounded by chop shops and ghetto!

I worked my way east, trying to get as close to Toluca as I could. Soon my eastbound road ended and sent me north. This sent me into one of the nicest upscale metropolitan cities I've ever been to! There were sushi bars and steak houses on every corner. Instead of being surrounded by trashy old cars, I was surrounded by BMWs and Benzes. It was a night-and-day difference.

All of a sudden, my chain came off as I drove down a busy street! It locked my tire up and brought me to a dead stop in the middle of traffic. Luckily I wasn't run over. I forced my bike to the side of the road and spent the next half hour trying to unbind my chain. Finally, with the help of my handy Leatherman, I was able to free my wretched chain. Back on the road again.

I asked people next to me in traffic which way I needed to go to get to Toluca. Not one of them would even talk to me, but a street sweeper sent me east through the center of the city. I would have told you that I was in Washington, D.C. There were monuments and parks everywhere. Tall trees and flowers were on every corner and in the median of every street. It was simply beautiful.

I finally asked a soccer mom in a nice car what way I needed to go to get to Toluca. She said she was headed there and that I could follow her. I followed her through the heart of Mexico City. I would have told you we were driving through Denver. There were mansions in the pine trees, Best Buys, and shopping malls everywhere. As the soccer mom led me onto the freeway, I once again felt like God had sent me an angel to get me out of a bad situation.

The road between Mexico City and Toluca was so pretty. It was a giant pine tree forest that never seemed to end. Once again, I was almost out of gas, so I coasted down to the first gas station before Toluca. I got some gas, had another drink, got made fun of by some kids, looked for internet without luck, and got back on the road. Another hour or two, and I was in Toluca.

I checked my email and hadn't received anything from Dave and

Nian. From Toluca, I had two choices to get to Guadalajara. North or south? A girl in one of the toll booths told me that going north was safer and that the roads were nicer.

Once again, I began a wicked battle with a hard headwind. I got behind a big bus and stayed ten feet behind it for almost an hour. When I got out from behind it, I realized that I was pretty dizzy from the fumes! My surroundings were still way pretty, and it was evening so it wasn't super hot. All things considered, I was feeling pretty good. As I left the small town of Ucareo, I started coming down the hill toward Lake Cuitzeo. It started getting cold and the sun was almost down, so I pulled off to put on as much warm/dry clothing as I had. I piled on three layers, then my sunday clothes, and then I witnessed one of the top three most amazing sunsets of my life!

I watched the sun go down until it was almost completely dark. As I rode past the lake, I wasn't excited to find out that the whole distance of the lake was pure bugs! These weren't just mosquitoes either. These were like small dragonflies. As I passed the lake, I was now mad thanks to the terrible film of bug guys on my visor and all over my stuff. I wiped as much as I could off and pressed on.

By the time I made it to Guadalajara, it was super late. I found an open internet place just to find out that Dave and Nian hadn't written to me. I wrote 'em and told 'em to meet me at church in Mazatlan Sunday morning. I fueled up and tore outta there.

I hadn't even been on the road for an hour and my chain came off again. I managed to get it back on and cruised slow to the next gas station. There, I got some food and a drink and started feeling all strange. I got dizzy and wondered if I was going to pass out. I laid down on the sidewalk outside the gas station store and wondered if I was going to die. I closed my eyes for about ten minutes and started feeling better. I think I just needed some real food in my system. Too much gas station candy wasn't treating me well.

I topped my tank and talked to a guy that lived in a wood shack behind the gas station. He was fixing a tire and said that he'd let me use some of his tools to shorten my chain. I had tightened it as far as I could, and I was to the point where it was just going to break my sprocket if it kept going with it that loose. I put my bike up on a stump and tore it apart. I was super excited to find that the bearings, brake, and hub in the back wheel were all completely worn out.

It took me about an hour to get the bike apart, cut a link out with an old nail and a big steel hammer, and get everything back together. Once I got it back on the road, I was flying! It felt so good. It was probably 3:00 or 4:00 in the morning, and I was feeling great!

As I came down out of the mountains toward the coast, it got cold, and I mean COLD! I was doing leg lifts and jumping on my pegs. I even stopped and ran with my rain gear on! The night never seemed to end!

I was probably thirty or forty miles from the next town when I ran out of gas. Once again, my Gatorade bottle of gas saved my bacon. As I rolled down getting closer to the town, I got stopped at a toll booth. I had started just driving around their gates and not paying them because they were wicked expensive. This time I got stopped by a gun. They were determined to make me pay, and I wasn't about to spend my last few pesos on a toll. I was worried that the gas station wouldn't accept my card and I would be out of luck if I used my pesos on the toll.

After arguing with these toll workers for more than twenty minutes, I turned around and drove out the other toll exit without paying! I was waiting to hear bullets fly past my head, but I must have gone unnoticed.

I was then on the old highway. I sputtered on fumes into the next gas station just to find out that they wouldn't take my card. I got a couple pesos worth of gas and the guy sent me across town to top my tank at a better station. This place was actually pretty nice, so I enjoyed a couple cups of hot cocoa, had some breakfast, and recharged my mental batteries a little bit.

Around 5:00 a.m., I was once again headed toward home. It was so foggy that my rain gear was soaked and my vision was terrible. I creeped through it until the sun started coming up. As it started getting lighter, I noticed a sign that said I was coming up on another toll. My GPS showed the old highway just a few miles to the east, so I swerved off the road at my first chance.

Of course I wrecked. Then I couldn't get my bike push started. Finally, I got it going and made it over to the smaller town and got on the old highway headed toward Mazatlan. I was probably twenty yards out of town when my bike revved all the way up! *What the heck?* It was 6:00 in the morning. I looked back to see my chain laying on the ground. *Oh crap. Now what?*

So there I was—Sunday morning and probably two hours outside of Mazatlan, where I was supposed to meet Dave and Nian at church. It was maybe 6:00 or 7:00 in the morning. After a crazy night of riding though freezing mountains, building a new chain, evading toll booths, and praying that I wouldn't die, one of my greatest fears became a reality. Busted chain! I took a deep breath and got right to work fixing the piece of junk.

After a solid twenty-two hours of straight riding, I was getting a little frustrated. I wrapped my chain around the sprockets just assuming that I'd be able to hammer it back together again when, to my surprise, my whole master link was missing. So for the next forty minutes, I was crawling around on my hands and knees along some old Mexican highway. Finally I got mad and started trying to wire it back together the same way I had when I was a kid stranded west of Fillmore.

Some old drunk dude came out and started telling me that I was an idiot. He was right. My wire job didn't really work on such a big bike. So I hooked the two busted ends of the old chain together and rode back two or three miles to this tiny town that the old man had told me about. I started asking if anyone had motorcycle parts and just got funny looks. Turned out no stores liked to open on Sundays. Not only that, there weren't any parts stores in the whole town.

After checking two or three places, someone directed me down some long road in search of an old chop shop type parts guy. I went to where his place was and sure enough, chop shop. Nice bumpers, rims, and other car parts that were probably stolen off of cars. I knocked and yelled and started walking in his garage to see if I could find anyone.

Not more than two steps inside his garage, I found someone: his monster Doberman pinscher and rottweiler. They ran straight at me. I was ready to give up. I was just too tired for that. Just before they tore me apart—bam! They were both tied to long cables. Holy Crap!

Soon after escaping death by dog, a nice truck showed up and a bunch of guys piled out. They looked at me funny and asked if they could help me. I explained what was going on and most of them scattered, trying to find me a new master link. The ringleader of the bunch pulled up a chair and started asking me questions.

I thought it was funny that one of the first questions he asked me was, "So...you smoke weed?"

I told him no and explained why. Then I pointed to his Polaris 6X6 ATV and asked, "How did you get that thing down here?"

He proceeded to tell me that he had had it sent it from the States.

Puzzled, I asked what the heck he wanted a 6X6 down there for.

He explained how hard it was to get up to his marijuana farm, and how no police officer could get up there because they didn't have 6X6 ATVs. He then started bragging about how he had acres and acres of marijuana and how he pretty much ran the town because of it.

I think he expected me to be surprised or impressed at least, but I was so tired that I was like, "Oh, that's cool. So, you think you'll be able to fix my chain?"

He fed me some super good breakfast burritos, and we set out on the hunt for a new chain or master link. We went to five or six places and everyone was closed or didn't have anything of the sort. Finally, we went back to his shop and tried to fix it ourselves. We ended up taking apart another link, putting it through the busted link, and pounding the two together with a hammer. I push started my bike and it seemed to work fine, so I gave them $10 for their time and I was back on my way to meet Nian and Dave at church in Mazatlan.

It took me another two hours of solid riding to get to Mazatlan. By the time I got there, I had taken off all my gear, and I was back to shorts and a T-shirt and mad about how hot it was. I rolled into the south side of Mazatlan. I had been to Mazatlan before on a cruise. We had rented a Rhino and drove the whole city twice, so I knew right where I was. I drove right into town and headed toward the beach on the main road.

As soon as I headed toward the beach, I spotted the church! I had made it! I had finally met back up with Nian and Dave. The meetings were just getting over. I rushed into the church and asked everyone in there where the Americans were! No Americans here. Almost heartbroken, I washed up, walked out to my bike, push started it, and headed on down the road.

I rode up the beach for a while and decided to check my email. No word from Nian or Dave. I was pretty bummed out. I stopped at the north end of Mazatlan and enjoyed a bunch of Mexican carne asadas tacos and flirted with the waitress for a while. I decided to just keep going for a little bit while it was still light. I sent Dave and Nian an email saying that I was going to keep going and that if I made it to the state of Sonora, Mexico, I'd put a sign up for them on the Welcome to Sonora sign. I saddled up and rode on.

The next stretch going north from Mazatlan was brutally boring, not to mention the wicked headwind that kept my speed down to about fifty miles per hour. Not only did that suck but it killed my gas mileage as well. I rode north two or three hours until I was just so tired that I couldn't stand it anymore. I pulled off the freeway and got some gas. There was one hotel, but it was super expensive, so I kept on riding. I rode over to the ocean, expecting to see a nice beach.

When I got there, the water was brown, there was maybe a hundred yards of sand and a ton of rock and trash everywhere. There was one paved road that was maybe half a mile long, and both sides of it were lined with lowrider trucks. I got creeped out, so I hauled butt outta there. Once I left the disappointing beach, I felt better, so I turned my music on and jumped right back on the freeway headed north.

Right before dark, I started looking for places to camp or sleep. I was passing through huge farming towns and everyone seemed a lot more friendly. I found a nice place behind a truck stop where I could hang up my hammock but didn't feel good about it, so I just kept on a'riding, looking for a cheap place to stay. Before I knew it, it was 2:00 in the morning! I was starting to get delirious. I was willing to pay whatever at that point. Every little town was dark, and it looked like there weren't any motels.

Around 2:30 a.m., one of the scariest experiences of my life occurred. I woke up, and not in a motel room. Still sitting on my bike. Still moving. In the wrong lane. With a semi truck right in front of me! I instantly swerved into my own lane and escaped death by inches! Once again in my life, I knew that God had a purpose for me, because I should have died right there on that Mexican roadside!

I struggled to keep my eyes open for the next twenty minutes while I rode to the next exit. I was a mess! I got some gas, and a friendly gas station attendant told me where a "really nice place to stay" was. I rode down the street, and there it was. Motel Amor. Love motel. It was pretty much a whore house. I rode in and the lady asked me how many hours I needed. I told her all night. This place wasn't too bad, actually, because every room had its own garage so nobody would know who was there doing what with who. I put my bike in my garage, went in the room, rolled my tattered self up into my blanket, and passed out!

I had been riding for forty-two hours straight. I had ridden all the way across Mexico in one shift. I was a tired, tired boy. I had ridden almost 1500 miles without stopping to sleep. That has got to be some sort of record.

Jim Anderson

Day 90
Monday, April 26, 2010

I woke up in a cold sweat! Where was I? Why did I feel so beat up?

I realized I was wrapped up in my Paraguayan blanket, sleeping in a Mexican "motel" somewhere between Culiacan and Los Mochis, Mexico. I forced myself to get up. I took a well-deserved shower and changed my bandages that were now super dirty and probably doing more harm than good. I packed my bag, filled my bike with oil, loaded my bike, and by 10:00 a.m., I was back on the road toward home.

Finally, it was a really nice day. Pretty much ideal riding conditions. I had ridden some 200 kilometers when I realized that my bike wasn't running well at all. I wasn't getting any speed and it was sort of sputtering.

"Now what?" I muttered.

I pulled into a gas station and topped my tank. I unscrewed the oil filter cap and oil ran everywhere! I had put way too much in that morning. I stood back and thought about what to do. My first thought was that somehow gas was getting into the oil, because the oil looked much more runny than usual. The last thing I needed at that point was a blown motor! I dug into my pack for some tools to drain my oil, and then it occurred to me that I could just tip my bike sideways and dump the extra oil out. I did just that until my oil level was perfect. Once I got it to that point, I pushed started my bike, as always, and hit the northbound trail.

I stopped a couple times and checked the oil again. It was fine, but the thought of blowing up my motor made me nervous. I went maybe another 100 kilometers and came up on the city of Ciudad Obregón. I was sure there would be some sort of store where I could buy some oil, change it, and get back on the road. I was putting down the main road of Ciudad Obregón, when on my right—an answer to my prayers! AUTO ZONE!

I found my oil, the ultra bright headlight that was illegal in Brazil, and a few other little parts I needed to get my bike back up to good running order. In my broken Spanish, I tried asking the workers if any of them were mechanics or if they knew of any bike mechanics that could tell me why my oil was so runny. After talking to almost everyone in the store, a younger looking fellow walked in the door wearing an Auto Zone uniform.

One guy yelled, "Humberto!" and pointed at me.

Humberto spoke just a little bit of English. He asked, "Where are you from in the States?"

"Utah."

He looked at me and said, "So you know where Heber City is? I have been working construction there for the past four years."

After I told him that my grandmother and a good part of my extended family lived in Heber, we were best friends. He helped me check out and then let me follow him on one of his deliveries. He pulled over at his friend's bike shop and made sure they knew what was going on with my bike. He said they would take care of me. He rode off, and I pushed my bike into the shop.

The shop guys were busy, so I busted out all my own tools and got to work. I changed my oil really quick, hooked up a cigarette lighter plug on my battery so I could charge my phone as I was riding, and then I decided to see if I could fix my nonfunctional back brakes.

As I pulled my back tire off, little pieces of metal and dust went everywhere. My bearings were gone! Completely worn to dust and gone. The busted bearing had worn a good inch of my hub out and made it so the wheel was completely loose in the back—which probably had a lot to do with my sprockets and chains always wearing out so fast. Once we got it off, the guys told me that I needed a new back wheel. They called all over the city and nobody had one. I was ready to spend whatever to get up and going. After almost an hour of searching, I finally ended up putting my old tire back on and calling it good for then.

The guys let me use their internet. I sent Nian and Dave a

message and told them that I'd meet them at the border in Nogales if they hadn't already gone through. Once I realized that I had just written, *Meet me at the border*, it hit me just how close to home I really was. I bump started my beast, and I was full speed toward home! It was almost 3:00 p.m. when I started riding again. The next few hours of riding seemed to take years.

I rode through Hermosillo just before sundown. Right at dusk, the scenery around me reminded me of what I had always pictured Mexico would look like—cactus plants everywhere and just a dusty haze over the painted desert mountains. I was probably three hours from the border when it got completely dark.

The next three hours of riding were extremely strenuous. Most of the time I was standing up singing as loud as I could, trying to stay awake. I will admit I fell asleep at the handlebars again about an hour outside of Nogales.

About twenty miles from Nogales my heart began to race. I kept thinking, *I'm going to make it! I can't wait to see Dave and Nian here!* and many other things. I rolled through Nogales and didn't even slow down until I was at the border. I got to the border at 9:55 p.m. on Monday night. I looked around for Dave and Nian, but I figured if they were there, they would be waiting at the gate or office for sure.

I cut in line at the border crossing and rolled up to the border patrol agent. He rudely asked me for my documents. I took my helmet off, more excited to speak English than anything! I gave him a quick rundown of what my situation was and what the deal with the bike was. He was short with me and told me to stay put.

Twenty minutes later he came back with three other agents and told me that they were closed for the day and that I had to go back into Nogales, Mexico, to spend the night. I was heartbroken. How? He couldn't be serious.

I begged him to let me through. Finally, he said I could spend the night in the US, but I'd have to leave my bike in Mexico and walk into the US.

Yeah right, I thought.

Nogales was super dangerous. I argued with the guy for twenty minutes, and finally he just told me that I'd have to leave and come back the next day when they were open so I could fill out the proper paperwork to import my bike.

So I walked my bike back over to Mexico, push started it, and rode angrily back into town to look for a place to stay. I remembered seeing a Walmart and a mall on my way to the border, so I decided to stay there for a bit until I could get a plan. I went to a sports bar in the mall and got on Wi-Fi on Dave's iPhone. I checked my messages just to find out that Dave and Nian hadn't written to me. I stayed there until almost midnight. I left in search of my buddies and a safe place for me and my bike to sleep until the border opened at 7:00 a.m.

I went to a few different places just to find out they were either way too expensive or sold out or closed. I rode around the main business block toward the other side of town because it seemed a little safer. Riding around Nogales gave me the worst feeling ever. Almost every major intersection had a big police truck surrounded by guys with machine guns sitting in the middle of it. I couldn't quit thinking, *I gotta get outta here!*

As I coasted through the old part of town, I spotted a beautiful sight. A taco stand! I slammed on my working brake and ran over there. I ate like ten tacos while chatting up a storm with the old taco man. I had been telling him my story for maybe twenty minutes when he answered my prayers.

He said, "Well, why don't you just try to go in through the pedestrian entrance? They are open twenty-four hours a day."

I thanked the old fellow, smashed my last taco into my mouth, and hauled butt over to the pedestrian border crossing. Once again, I butted in front of a huge line at the border. I rolled up to the patrol agent. He was a huge black guy.

He gave me a huge smile and yelled, "Hey! You American?"

I yelled back, "Yes Sir! Been gone three months and it's darn good to be home!"

He asked for my passport. I showed it to him, he scanned it, gave it to me, and yelled, "GET OUT OF HERE!" while pointing toward the United States!

I jumped off my bike, pushed the heavy beast ten yards, popped the clutch, fired it up, and roared out of there! Once again, like I had done numberless times on the trip, I thanked the LORD for getting me out of a bad situation.

Once in the US, I went straight to the closest hotel and used their internet to let Dave and Nian know where I was and that I was on the road! I sent it, got gas, and hit the freeway! Words couldn't describe how good it felt to finally be back on American soil.

I was feeling great, so I rode on into the night toward Tucson. Somewhere around the area of Sahuarita, Arizona, it hit me. Or a better way to say it is *my helmet hit the handlebars.* I had fallen asleep while riding again! I couldn't believe it! I survived everything up until then, and I was going to die because I fell asleep! Forget that.

So I pulled off the freeway in search of good hammock trees. I found a great place just off to the side of an Ashley Furniture store. I stretched my hammock up, got in my sleeping bag (because it was actually super cold), and passed out! Few times in my life have I ever been that tired! If you Google 31.906679, -110.990574 and click satellite view, you can see the two trees I hung my hammock up in between.

Day 91
Tuesday, April 27, 2010

"Hey! Hey!"
Poke. Poke.
There I was, lying in my hammock. It was 3:30 in the morning. I was all tied up inside my sleeping bag which was taco'ed inside my hammock. I had only been asleep for an hour or two and, for some

reason, someone was rudely waking me up.

I peeped out of my sleep cocoon, and all I could see were bright lights. At this point, I was really confused. Did I die? Was I dreaming? Then I saw them—those old familiar red and blue lights. It took my eyes a while to focus, but when they did I realized that there was an officer standing about ten feet away from me with his hand on his gun. Then I realized that he was talking to me.

"Who are you and what are you doing?"

I reply, "I'm Jim, and I'm trying to sleep."

The officer then yelled, "Do you have any weapons?"

I replied in a super sleepy voice, "Yeah."

He asked me what it was, and I told him that I had a twenty-inch machete.

He continued asking me the same things for a minute or two, but I was extremely incoherent.

Finally, I just yelled, "What do you want?"

The officer then ordered me to leave my hammock. I slowly untied myself and fell out of my hammock.

"Where are you coming from," he asked me.

I sleepily replied, "Brazil."

"Don't mess with me!" he yelled.

The next twenty or so minutes were dedicated to me telling our story about how we made our voyage from Florianopolis, Brazil up until that point, where I was sleeping in podunk Arizona, in my hammock.

He, of course, didn't believe me.

I searched around and found my Brazilian documents and proved my case. I woke up a little bit more, and we talked for another good while. He had called two back up cars earlier. They showed up. So now I was standing there, surrounded by three cars with their lights flashing and six or so officers. I was just leaning on my bike smiling.

After talking our way out of trouble with the Venezuelan military police just a few weeks prior, a bunch of Arizona deputies were no big deal.

One of them got my information and went to his car. He came back a couple minutes later and whispered something to the other officer. He then came over to me and asked me if I had ever been in trouble with the state of Arizona.

I told him that I didn't think so.

He said, "The state of Arizona has a warrant out for your arrest. Are you aware of that?"

I laughed and said, "Yeah, right!"

"Did you get a ticket in Lake Powell in 2006?"

"Umm, yeah," I said.

He told me that he had to take me in.

I yelled, "YOU'RE KIDDING ME! I just rode a fetching dirt bike 16,000 miles through some of the most hostile countries in North and South America and you're going to lock me up in Podunk Arizona?!" I was so mad!

He calmed me down and after another twenty minutes of persuasion, he decided that he'd let me go back to sleep. I laid back down, and within minutes I was passed out again.

After another few hours of well-deserved sleep, I was up and back on the road. I rode fast and hard until I made it past Tucson. I stopped for gas right before I approached the outskirts of the Phoenix metro area. I remember smiling from ear to ear as I walked in to pay for my gas and chatted up a storm with the gas station guy. What a good feeling to be back in the US. Back home. Well, almost home.

I filled my bike and Gatorade bottle with gas and got ready to ride. As I tied my newly-filled Gatorade bottle by the other ones, I noticed that the Mexican gas was almost a brown color and the American gas was clear. All along people had told me how terrible Mexican gas was.

Back on the road, I rode all the way through to Phoenix. I stopped for more gas on the way out of Phoenix. A couple hours later, my bike started struggling as I was climbing in elevation and fighting a hard headwind. The climb up to Flagstaff was a long, cold one. I stopped at Maverick because it's adventure's first stop and I needed gas. I bought myself some delicious chocolate milk and doughnuts and hit the road.

The wind picked up even more as I got closer to the Grand Canyon. By this point, I was wearing all my clothes again with my rain gear on over that. It was pretty chilly. I stopped again at the Indian reservation gas station before Page. I topped my tank off and tightened my chain. It was in super bad shape. There were several rollers missing and it was extremely stretched. I got it just right, pushed started my bike and rolled onward.

I rode another hour or so and passed Page and Lake Powell. I just smiled as I crossed into Utah. Almost home! I had crossed Glen Canyon Dam and was about seventy miles from Kanab when my bike started shaking a little bit. I was right in the middle of the Indian reservation when I felt a pop. My bike's RPMs went all the way up, and I started slowing down. I looked down and…no chain.

I stopped at one of those little pull-offs where the Indians sell their souvenirs. I hopped off and walked back to where my chain dropped. I grabbed it and walked back over to my bike. One of the busted rollers had worn out the link, and it broke. *Now what? NOW what?*

I looked at my GPS and figured I was close enough to Kanab to hitch a ride into town, where I could hopefully find a chain or new link. I tried hitching a ride for almost half an hour. Nobody even blinked. I was standing up holding my chain, waving both my arms, and still people would just speed past. I thought, *Are you serious? What a bunch of loser people.*

After hitchhiking without any success, I walked over to my bike and sat down on the ground. As I looked at the chain and bike, I realized that all I needed was a new link clip. I propped my bike up and loosed the chain tensioners all the way up. Then I wrapped the broken chain around the sprockets and lined it up. It looked like I would be able to take out a whole link. I took the chain back off and went to work with a pair of vice grips and a big rock. Somehow I managed to break the chain link and get it apart. I wrapped the chain back on the bike and hooked the chain on. It just barely reached. Then I took the old busted part of the chain and smashed the link on over the chain rollers. I pounded it on tight and rolled my bike forward a bit to see if it would work.

Worked like a dream! I packed up my tools, put in my headphones, gave my bike a push, and I was off! A short hour later I was fighting a forty mile per hour headwind, my bike was struggling, and I was freezing! I fought through it and made it to Kanab.

I searched the whole town for bike parts and found nothing. I started getting ready to ride and then realized that it was freezing cold outside! I walked into the local Levi's store and bought every bit of warm clothes they had. I now had gloves, a beanie, a huge sweater, long underwear, thermal socks, and sweatpants to go along with all of the other clothes I was wearing and all covered up by my rain gear. I jumped on and rode hard as it was getting dark fast.

I pulled into Beaver at about 9:30 p.m. and got gas. The girl inside gave me a really funny look.

I looked at her, smiled, and said, "I'm riding my motorbike home from Brazil!"

I put my gloves on, got a good run, bumped my clutch and started my bike, and rode off into the foggy, windy night.

I spent the next hour and a half reminiscing about the past three months—just thinking about all the crazy nights, all the amazing rides, all the amazing people, all the answered prayers, and all the things I had seen. As I came down the last hill, coasting into my hometown of Fillmore, I caught a crazy tailwind and got my top speed of the entire three months I had been gone: 165 kilometers per hour!

As I pulled off the exit at Meadow, a crazy feeling came over me. Another mile later, and I could see my house off in the distance. It was about 11:00 p.m., so I was a little nervous that everyone would be sleeping already. Keep in mind that nobody knew I was coming home. The last time my family had heard from me had been almost three weeks earlier in Costa Rica when I had called home to have my shot card faxed to me. The last time I had seen my buddies was five days earlier in southern Mexico. My arrival at home was a complete surprise.

For all of the last three miles I could see that the lights were on at the house, and I smiled the whole way there. I pulled into the driveway, did a little circle on the front yard, and went straight up the eight steps to our front porch! As I got to the top, my chain came off and my bike tipped straight over! It made a huge crash as my cheap glasses shattered and my gear scattered everywhere.

I stood the bike up and looked in the kitchen window. There was my mother with the most confused/surprised look on her face, washing dishes right inside the window.

Another second later and she and my dad were on the porch with me. My mother instantly started to bawl. My dad laughed and then chewed me out for making them worry. It was pretty inconsiderate of me not to tell them what I was doing, but it made for a good story, and in the end, they were just glad I was home.

I hadn't been home more than ten minutes when my Dad said, "Get that stuff off and get in the bathtub! You're filthy."

I went and looked in the mirror, and he was right. I hadn't shaved in a couple weeks and hadn't taken a shower in days. I had been riding behind semi trucks to catch their tailwind, so my face was completely black with road grime. It took me a good thirty minutes of scrubbing to get all of it off.

I spent the next few hours telling stories and rejoicing with my family. I told them about buying dirt bikes on a whim and riding them home from Brazil with my buddies. I told them about traveling through thirteen countries in exactly three months, about meeting some of the most amazing people, and about seeing some of the most amazing sights in the whole world.

And I told them about the miracles I had experienced, about angels who had saved me when I put myself in dangerous situations. But some parts, I kept to myself—the parts where I came to know myself better, and most importantly, came to know God better.

ABOUT THE AUTHOR

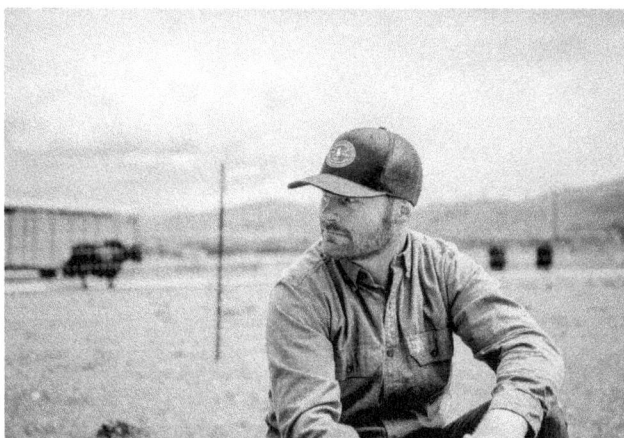

I'm Jim. I do what I want, whenever I feel like it. I enjoy getting out and experiencing the world. I don't enjoy video games. I love working, especially outside. I don't love liars. I say yes to almost anything. I say no to anything that conflicts with my morals or obligations. I cook a ME-ean steak. I don't cook good Mexican food. I am both an early bird and a night owl. The only thing that scares me more than skunks is hell. I love riding–dirtbikes, wheelers, my Rhino "The Patriot," snowmobiles, horses, snowboards, wakeboards, and much more. I got the swine flu. I got over the swine flu. My listening pleasures include everything from Johnny Cash to Jay-Z and everything in between. I strive every day to make everyone I encounter feel important and hopefully smile. I have terrible knees. I have great eyesight. I avoid confrontation of any kind at all cost. I love service and hate being yelled at. Join me on my journey. Never tell me you weren't invited!